DCPL0000070565

D1757855

941.95

R　　　　　　　　　　　　　　　**J**

Items should be returned on or before the last date shown below. Items not already requested by other borrowers may be renewed in person, in writing or by telephone. To renew, please quote the number on the barcode label. To renew online a PIN is required. This can be requested at your local library.
Renew online @ **www.dublincitypubliclibraries.ie**
Fines charged for overdue items will include postage incurred in recovery. Damage to or loss of items will be charged to the borrower.

Leabharlanna Poiblí Chathair Bhaile Átha Cliath
Dublin City Public Libraries

Dublin City
Baile Átha Cliath

Dolphin's Barn Library
Tel. 4540681
✳ KEEP ✳

Date Due	Date Due	Date Due
	0 9 JUL 2009	
	31-7 18.	

REPUBLICAN COBH

& THE EAST CORK VOLUNTEERS

SINCE 1913

KIERAN McCARTHY

NONSUCH

To Angela, for everything.

First published 2008

Nonsuch Publishing
73 Lower Leeson Street
Dublin 2
Ireland
www.nonsuchireland.com

© Kieran McCarthy, 2008

The right of Kieran McCarthy to be identified as the Author
of this work has been asserted in accordance with the
Copyrights, Designs and Patents Act 1988.

All rights reserved. No part of this book may be reprinted
or reproduced or utilised in any form or by any electronic,
mechanical or other means, now known or hereafter invented,
including photocopying and recording, or in any information
storage or retrieval system, without the permission in writing
from the Publishers.

British Library Cataloguing in Publication Data.
A catalogue record for this book is available from the British Library.

ISBN 978 1 84588 920 3

Typesetting and origination by Nonsuch Publishing
Printed and bound in Great Britain by Athenaeum Press Ltd.

CONTENTS

Foreword

In the 1980s when I first decided to explore and write about Cobh's role in the independence struggle, I did so for two principal reasons. The first was to satisfy my own obsession with history. The other was to challenge, head-on, the then bizarre climate of political censorship that existed in relation to the war in the north of our country. My aim was to tell the people of Cobh along with those further afield what took place in our town and in our name and that we had a great deal to be proud of through the heroic roles played by our forefathers in the Republican struggle. I also wanted to show through the recorded actions of those early Cobh volunteers, that war was far removed from being the romantic and glorious pastime that some believed it to be. I wanted to show that in war, mistakes are sometimes made leaving innocent bystanders dead or maimed. It was a reality which applied to all combatants in the Irish struggle but particularly to the civilian innocents who ended up in the wrong place at the wrong time, or to those who might have been wrongly fingered as informers and spies. The pain caused to families who never again saw their loved ones' bodies, an inevitable consequence of the espionage war as it was played out.

Through that story, I was above all hoping to expose the hypocritical manner in which official Ireland looked on its past and present; how it saw a past armed struggle as glorious, clean and just, while then viewing its later continuation as, thuggish, criminal and unjust, yet rarely being prepared to scrutinise and address the actual causes of the conflict. I wanted to question how the modern official term of 'The War of Independence' (1919-1921) is a grossly inaccurate and misleading description of Ireland's militant opposition to Britain's colonial rule. The War of Independence began long before 1916 and didn't end the day the Treaty was signed, nor with the order to dump arms at the end of the Civil War. The highly militarised period between 1919 and 1921 is more accurately and commonly referred to in Republican parlance as the 'Tan War'. Writing about and exposing these issues was how my contemporaries and I in the Republican Movement dealt with censorship in the 1980s.

This differed from the manner in which Republicans of another generation dealt with the issue however. Historical records, for instance, show that Michael Collins ordered or approved of the destruction of the printing presses of a number of newspapers that published anti-Republican editorials, the *Cork Examiner* and *Cork Constitution* among them. Between 1919 and 1923, three *Cork Examiner* reporters were shot for writing reports which were deemed to be anti-Republican. Some historians differ as to the actual reason why these men were killed, from them being mistaken as British agents leaving the Examiner offices, to a belief that some were actually shot by agents of the 'Anti-Sinn Féin Society' engaged in black propaganda. A more common practice at the time, however, was for reporters to be arrested (kidnapped) and forced to write retractions to their earlier reports at the point of a gun. Michael Collins was indeed a hero and a worthy one, but he became a hero in the eyes of the political establishment principally, because of the legacy he bequeathed to them. The irony however, was that if Michael Collins was born in South Armagh or West Belfast in 1960 instead of West Cork in 1890, he most likely would have been viewed and held with the same contempt that the southern political establishment reserved for that generation of Republicans.

Indeed, added to the ghostly and heroic names of Bobby Sands, Patsy O'Hara, Joe McDonnell and others, may well have been H-Block hunger striker Michael Collins in 1981. But that was then, and today so much has changed politically on this island that it is sometimes hard to imagine we are talking about the same place. Events over the last decade or so have shown that although they have sometimes been slow in coming, positive changes have been realised far quicker and with far less pain than any military action might have delivered them.

We have also learned that although armed struggle, while being just and honourable in its own time and place, should not be mistaken as a principled possession to be entered into for its own sake. There is, I believe, a genuine belief amongst many Irish people, particularly amongst those of the northern Nationalist/Republican community who were the principal victims of its imposition, that partition can and will in future be dismantled peacefully and naturally. It would be wrong and naive to say, however, that if the wrongs and injustices of the past were allowed to repeat themselves that popular support for armed revolt wouldn't surface once again. That is why it is of vital importance that those who make the history get it right by creating a society built on foundations of justice and equality for all on this island. When writing my original foreword in 1992, I expressed my firm belief then that armed struggle and that alone could overthrow partition and all the injustices that accompanied it.

Subsequent events have clearly shown that such a view no longer holds weight and my task with writing this updated account of Cobh's Republican past is to outline some local events involving Republicans over the past twenty years, while explaining how the Republican movement has arrived at its current position. I have mainly undertaken this rewrite though, because of subsequent new historical material relating to earlier Volunteer actions in Cobh which has only become available since the year 2000.

The size of this new material is so vast that it should greatly enhance the quality of this book. In relation to my own near thirty year involvement in the Republican movement, I intend where possible to give a frank account of particular events. But because many of the events of the last thirty years are very sensitive and fresh in the national mindset, it would neither be appropriate nor fair to write about them at this time. Perhaps in the not too distant future, when Ireland is fully grown up and at ease with itself and its past, those stories might be recorded and told by someone wishing to publish a later Republican history of Cobh. As a Republican, I naturally have my own take and view of our history. I do not however, have the power, the right nor the will to rewrite or distort that history. While I may have the power to write my own story, I do not have the power to write that of those that came before me. I can but report and record it as I find it.

My conclusions may differ somewhat from those of others, particularly from those who believe the 1916 Rising was a mistake, and the struggle for Independence unjustified, but as I wrote previously, it is the reader who will ultimately decide where we have come from and how we arrived here. For now though, I am confident readers of this book will enjoy exploring and learning about Cobh's proud past and its heroic contribution to the fight for Irish Freedom.

Kieran McCarthy, April 2008

Note on 2008 Edition

In 1960/61 a number of letters and historical documents were exchanged between two former Cobh members of the Irish Volunteers. One of those was Seamus Fitzgerald, then a Fianna Fáil senator who resided in Cork City. The other was Tim W. Cronin of Roches Row in Cobh. The communications were initiated by Tim Cronin after he sent a very impressive record of the Cobh Volunteers to Fitzgerald. Fitzgerald was indeed impressed by what he was given and when he returned it on 1 February 1961, he made the following comments to its owner,

> These documents will provide very valuable material for some local historian when we are all gone. Each document is more interesting than the next, particularly I think that Franklin's Almanac is most valuable and is worthy of a place in Cobh Museum. The young fellows today do not appear to have the same interest, but we can only hope.

I have no idea of what became of Tim Cronin's documents but I do know they never became part of the 'Seamus Fitzgerald Papers' which were opened to the public at the Cork City and County Archive Institute in 2000.

What Tim W. Cronin seemed to have achieved, though he may not have anticipated it at the time, was to awaken something inside Fitzgerald which told him it was time to start getting things down on paper before it was too late. The remaining eleven years of his life saw Fitzgerald make on and off attempts to compile information about himself and his former comrades, which he hoped would eventually be produced as a complete book on the Cobh Volunteers. Fitzgerald's own witness statement to the Bureau of Military History covering the years (1913-1921), is by far the most graphic and best written of all the statements by former Cobh Volunteer Officers. On 7 May 1969, Seamus Fitzgerald wrote to his former Commanding Officer Michael Leahy, about an agreed meeting they were to have at his home the following evening to discuss their joint recollections of the past struggle. He told Leahy that he had Jack O'Connell's witness statement which was made in the 1950s to the Bureau of Military History in his possession and that Mick Burke's widow had also agreed to lend him a copy of Mick's statement, and asked Leahy if he would bring his own one along also.

Ten months later, Fitzgerald wrote furiously to Leahy again, this time complaining about a very misleading article from Martin Corry which appeared in the *Cork Examiner* that day. When Corry wrote and tried to take credit for the 1921 capture of the British arms ship the *HMS Upnor* outside of Cork Harbour, Fitzgerald wrote, 'This is the last straw with respect to 'Corry's megalomania,' and that he was determined that credit for the *Upnor's* capture would rightfully go to Mick Burke. It was obvious that Fitzgerald had his mind set on writing a definitive and accurate account of the role he and his former comrades played in the Republican struggle. Alas, it would appear that the clock beat Seamus Fitzgerald and prevented him from fulfilling his dream, for he passed away soon afterwards in 1972. I was not yet a year old when Seamus Fitzgerald wrote the words to Tim W. Cronin in 1961, 'The young fellows today do not appear to have the same interest, but we can only hope.' I would like to think that I have proved to have sufficient interest in the subject to write about not only Seamus and his former comrades, but also about those who followed behind them, including some who suffered as much as he did as a young man, through incarceration, harassment and even death in pursuit of their Republican beliefs, and their struggle to address the nations unfinished business. Many of those have also since passed on, and as Seamus once said, their stories will one day prove to offer valuable material for some local historian. It is with a great sense of honour that I find myself the person to whom this task has fallen.

Kieran McCarthy

Acknowledgements

For all the assistance and help that I received with this project, there are many to whom I owe many thanks for making this book possible. The sources I used for gathering this information have been wide and varied. Undoubtedly, the broadest treasure of documentation which provided me with the most valuable information and gives an accurate insight into Cobh's Republican past, is held in the Cork City and County Archives, under the 'Seamus Fitzgerald Papers'- (PR/6). I would like to express a word of sincere thanks to the staff at the Archives at Blackpool, especially to Michael Higgins, to Peter, Tim and Brian. I know they must have been in dread of seeing me arrive in their doors, week after week; knowing they had many hours of tedious photocopying to follow. Their efforts are much appreciated. I must also say a big thank you to Curator Dan Breen of the County Museum at Fitzgerald's Park Cork, for his courteous assistance, while allowing me access, (including to photograph) the Michael Leahy papers. Thanks also to Mrs May MacGiolla for her assistance with Cobh Volunteer obituarys.

I am also indebted to Commandants Liam Campbell and Victor Laing of the Military Archives at Cathal Brugha Barrack Dublin, for assisting me with copies of the 'Witness Statements' of the Cobh Volunteer Officers. A word of thanks also to Kieran Burke and staff at the Cork City Library, for their kind assistance to me each time I called there to view the micro film records. There are countless individuals who assisted me with documents and photos, too many to mention here, but I must pay a special word of thanks to John Jefferies, who more than went out of his way to track down photos and information, both verbal and written for me. John's generous efforts ensured that I had access to information around the pre and post IRA split of the early 1970's, some of which would otherwise have remained untold. I must also pay a special word of thanks to fellow historian and author John Borgonovo, who selflessly provided me with much advice around the preparation of this book.

A Note on Cobh

Cobh is located approximately fifteen miles south-east of Cork City and is situated on the Southside of the Great Island, or An Oileánn Mor in Irish. Although Cobh town is only part of the Great Island, the inhabitants of the other villages and townlands to the east, west and north of the island generally regard themselves as Cobh-people. At the north-west, or back of the island, the area known as Belvelly is joined to the mainland by way of a heavy stone bridge, which is used as the only means of motor traffic to and from the mainland. It could thus technically be argued that Cobh, or the Great Island, is not really an island. At the other side of Belvelly Bridge is situated Fota Estate (and Fota Wildlife Park), and it runs parallel with the main Fota Road, which meets with the greater road to Cork or Waterford. Approximately two miles from Fota is the village of Carrigtwohill, whilst another five miles to the east is the town of Midleton.

To the south of Cobh in the harbour are situated three other islands; Spike Island, which is one mile out from Cobh near the harbour mouth, Haulbowline Island which lies to the west of Spike and a small island called Rocky is situated directly behind Haulbowline and cannot be seen from Cobh. Rocky was historically used by the British to store gunpowder in its underground magazines for its navy. Today a bridge runs straight from Haulbowline through Rocky and links up with the mainland at Ringaskiddy in the west of the harbour. Rocky Island is also home today to this state's only crematorium outside of Dublin. Apart from the many streets of Cobh that appear in this book, the following villages and townlands will also be mentioned:

Ballymore - North-east of the island
Carrigaloe - West of the island
Rushbrooke - South-west of the island
Cuskinny - South-east of the island
Belmont/Carrignafoy - North-east of Cobh
Belvelly - North of the island
East Ferry - Extreme east of the island
Newtown - North-west end of Cobh
Ballyleary/Ballinoe - North of Newtown
Tay Road - A road running parallel with the north of Cobh town from the east to west parts of the island.

1. The Origins of the Volunteers in Cobh

Following the fragmentation of the Irish Parliamentary Party at the end of the nineteenth century, a vacuum had been created on the Irish political scene. However, it was quickly filled with the emergence of several popular movements, which embodied the revival of a sense of nationality and Irishness. Emphasis was placed on Ireland's culture and Gaelic past, and organisations such as the GAA, the Gaelic League and Sinn Féin were set up.

Cobh, or Queenstown as it was known at the time, was a slightly different story. Although the town couldn't entirely escape the hot breath of the nationwide Gaelic revival, Cobh was still a Unionist stronghold at the turn of the century. This was mainly due to the presence of British troops in the town. Being an important harbour town which serviced the naval and military garrisons on Spike and Haulbowline Islands as well as Cobh itself from Belmont Hutments, and with the Admiralty buildings based at the Mount near Bond Street, the little town held the key to the maintenance of British coastal defences in the south of Ireland, known as the western approaches. Not surprisingly, it was effectively ruled by a pro-British merchant class who had every interest in retaining the link with Britain, the British troops being a valuable source of lucrative business for local traders.

The name of the town, which had been changed from Cobh to Queenstown in honour of Queen Victoria when she briefly stepped foot on the quay in 1849, rightly illustrated the attitude of the middle and upper classes. The pro-British atmosphere was further encouraged by the presence of the Royal Cork Yacht club, the oldest in the world and a meeting-place for the Unionists of the surrounding countryside.

It was against this background that James Connolly came to Cobh in early March 1911. He had been invited to speak by a few local socialists, of whom John Dowling was undoubtedly the best known. But they were soon to learn in a less pleasant manner just how firm the loyalty of certain people in Cobh was to the Crown.

Connolly had been invited to speak about the campaign for the introduction of government funding for free school meals for Ireland's children. As a young man he himself had joined the British Army to escape the slums of his native Edinburgh and he had served on Haulbowline. He

14

Leabharlanna Poiblí Chathair Bhaile Átha Cliath
Dublin City Public Libraries

now felt that it would be a good day's work to convert a few people to his mixture of Socialism and Republicanism, in what he called, 'That nest of parasites feeding upon parasites.'[1]

If he could appeal to some soldiers and sailors, many of whom were Irish and some of whom were living in Cobh, this would mean an undermining of the foundations of the Empire in one of its strongest outposts; but Connolly was in for a nasty surprise. The local Council Chairman, infamous for his exploitation of the local working people and encouraged by a mob, headed by a local priest, started a minor riot, forcing the socialists to beat a retreat out of town. Connolly returned a week later after one of his supporters had discreetly hired a room for a meeting at the Town Hall unbeknownst to the Council Chairman. On the night, a number of councillors who were leaving another meeting stayed behind to listen to Connolly speak. When this was later reported in the *Cork Examiner*, the Town Chairman Cllr Hennessy was furious and demanded to know under what guise the hall was rented out to the heathen Socialists. Because it soon became apparent that it was more of a dread of facing the wrath of the Catholic Church for daring to be in anyway associated with Connolly, some Councillors came near to apologising and wormed their way out of the fix by saying they were merely passing by from another room when Connolly was speaking. One councillor however, Cllr Bransfield, refused to back down and be bullied by the Chairman and said he wasn't a Socialist but the speech he had listened to was one of the best he had ever heard and he would definitely attend again if the speaker visited Cobh. Two years later, in 1913 when Connolly returned to help set up a branch of the Union, he found the atmosphere had thawed somewhat. This was also the year which saw the foundation of the Irish Volunteers.

This was in reaction to the creation of the UVF (Ulster Volunteer Force), a paramilitary force in the North. Though the forces of the 1916 Rising were mainly drawn from units of the Irish Volunteers, the organisation had no clearly defined policies at its birth, and was mainly seen to be in defence of Home Rule. At one of the initial meetings organised to set up the Irish Volunteers at Wynn's hotel in Dublin and prompted by the Irish Republican Brotherhood, there were a few not yet prominent names that would later hit the headlines and reserve their place in history. Casement, Pearse, Plunkett and MacDonagh were not yet members of the IRB. The inaugural meeting of the Volunteers for Cork City and County was held on Sunday 14 December 1913 in the City Hall, Cork. The hall was filled to capacity and many prominent speakers were present such as Liam de Róiste, Eoin McNeill, Roger Casement and Sean O'Hegarty (later to take over as O.C. of Cork 1st Brigade after the death of Mac Curtain). Although the crowd were enthusiastic enough, the media didn't know what to think

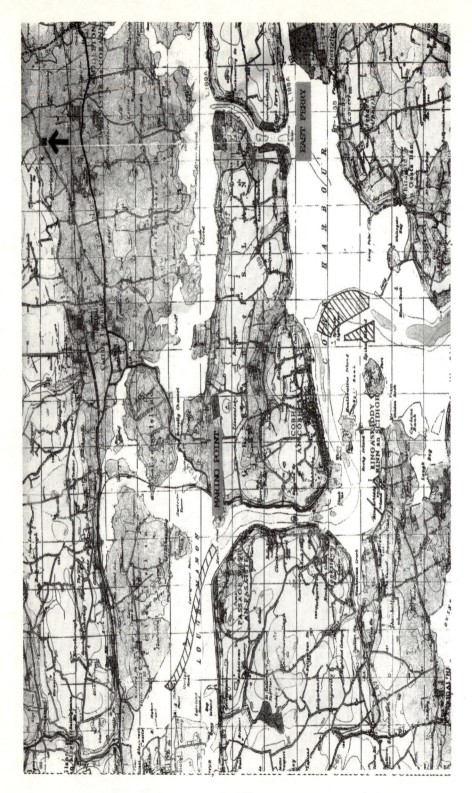

of the garrison on Spike Island, while Maurice Moore Place was named after a local Republican Volunteer who was executed after being captured at Clonmult in 1921.

Villa Park earned its name from connections to the English football club Aston Villa. It's very likely that it had been named while a Birmingham regiment was stationed at Cobh. In the years following the 1916 Rising, the interaction between the British forces and locals through football became less common, but in 1922 when Cobh Ramblers Football Club was founded, the British influence was to the fore once more. Ramblers first played their home games at Villa Park and their club colours were the same claret and blue used by their counterparts at Aston Villa. Ironically, British soldiers and Republicans were amongst the founders of Cobh Ramblers. This was possible, due to the British Army staying on at Spike Island as part of the Treaty settlement. While most local Republicans were involved with the organising and playing of Gaelic games, a few others had no problem togging out for Cobh Ramblers and leaving their politics off the field. Prior to the formation of the Volunteers, British army and naval bands regularly played recitals in the town during the summer months, and were widely welcomed by the local population.

One evening in early December 1913, Mick Leahy and others of a like mind stayed behind after Irish classes in the A.O.H. (Ancient Order of Hibernians) hall to begin the inaugural meeting of the Cobh Branch of the Irish Volunteers. The A.O.H hall was located at Rose Hill near St Colman's Cathedral and St Mary's Church of Ireland building. Those present at that first meeting were, Michael Leahy, Michael Hennessy, Michael O'Brien, Dan Cashman, Dan Collins, Maurice McCarthy, Michael Ware, Liam O'Doherty, Jimmy O'Connell, Paddy Whelan, Jim Ahern, Patrick Monahan, Liam O'Brien, Daithí O'Brien, Dick Hayes, Ned Butler, Jim Fitzgerald, Dave Fitzgerald, William Ralph, Donal Quaid, James Downey and Liam Murphy. Eoin McNeill's article 'The North Began' was read out.

Liam Murphy acted as secretary and the others agreed to sign up as members. Leahy later agreed to act as secretary for a period afterwards. Permission from the A.O.H. authorities was not sought for the meeting which might explain why there was so little publicity surrounding the event before and after it. When the meeting ended however, it was decided a deputation would stay behind to meet with A.O.H. personnel to seek the future use of the hall. The deputation met with Joseph Healy and Paddy O'Halloran who were committee officers of the A.O.H. Healy the chairman said he believed the Volunteers was a good thing but because Mr Redmond had made no pronouncement on the matter, and pending that, he could not allow them the use of the hall.

Of the twenty-two men who signed up as Volunteers that evening, at least seven would later join Leahy to play pivotal roles in the coming war with Britain and nearly all would take the Republican side in the bitter Civil War that would follow. One other person in the A.O.H. hall that night would also play no small part in the coming struggle. Joe Healy, or J.J. Healy, the name he used to operate his business under, was the local chairman of the A.O.H. and staunch supporter of John Redmond's Irish Party would in time, like so many other Irish people, change his political views and begin to support the Republican movement. Within six years of the Volunteers first meeting, Healy, a local building contractor based at the former national school across from Orelia Terrace, (the site of the present Town Community Centre) would provide the Volunteer Movement with much practical assistance, including offering his yard and work shop as a safe hiding place for wanted Volunteers. For now though, this small branch of the fledgling Volunteer army, needed somewhere from which to train and drill, and the A.O.H. hall was clearly out of bounds.

The Volunteers then applied to Cobh UDC and were given the use of a field on the outskirts of the town. An ex-Naval Warrant officer, James Downey, who was an enthusiastic Gaelic Leaguer, started drilling the men. About twenty five turned out at the first parade. A larger crowd of locals looked on and jeered them. Some Volunteers noted at this time that some individuals who looked down and sneered at them, used to run pass at the other side of the ditch with bowler hats held up on sticks, trying to give the impression they were policemen coming to raid the parades. Before long, another ex-serviceman Jerry McGrath agreed to drill the Volunteers along with John Garde, Bob Donaghy and Bill Hawes. The men hadn't a single firearm between them so they used wooden staves (replica rifles) and hurleys. Although confidence and morale gradually grew with the men's ability to adjust to military instruction, the numbers of those willing to join up remained static. That all changed in May 1914, after John Redmond decided to intervene and take control of the Volunteers nationally.

A sudden influx of Volunteers saw the local strength jump to nearly 500 in Cobh. Five Companies were then formed with a central committee overseeing and controlling their activities. The committee was led by Joe Healy as chairman, Tim O'Callaghan secretary and he was followed by John Riordan. There was no IRB representation whatsoever on the committee. A company was established at Belvelly and a section at Ballymore. Permission was sought and given for drilling to take place at the Baths Quay. This proved to be far more suitable for training and was more centrally situated for the bulk of the Volunteers who were based in the town. Micheal Leahy held onto a degree of control over at least some of the Volunteers as he remained in charge of drilling the Belvelly and Ballymore Volunteers. During this period, he regularly took the men on route marches to Carrigtwohill and Midleton and on one occasion to Mitchelstown's where they trained with local Volunteers from the area. A number of weapons also became available from various sources. In June, a route march of 480 men from Cobh to Carrigtwohill saw them attend a shooting competition there. Throughout the summer, money was collected for an arms fund, but it was withheld locally due to rumours that the Howth weapons were of an obsolete type. J.J. Walsh of the Volunteer Executive later attended Cobh and was satisfied with the local decision to withhold the money.

2. The First Split

When John Redmond made his impassioned speech at Woodenbridge in Co. Wicklow in September 1914, calling on the Volunteers to join with Britain and fight in the First World War, the consequences for building a truly revolutionary national liberation army was greatly hindered. A committee meeting was held at Cobh Town hall shortly afterwards, with Steve Moynihan in the chair and John Riordan as secretary. Tim O'Callaghan, Maurice McCarthy, Seamus Fitzgerald and Domhaill O'Ciosain were also in attendance. John Riordan then read out part of TJ Hannah's (secretary to Redmond) letter while refusing to finish it. He said, 'Gentlemen; nobody will oppose Mr Redmond's orders.' Moynihan and O'Callaghan agreed. When the others present disagreed, the Redmondites got very angry. Maurice McCarthy requested the matter would be put to a vote. O'Ciosain proposed a vote, McCarthy seconded and Fitzgerald supported, making it three for and three against. Moynihan then proposed the matter be deferred to a full committee meeting.

Seamus Fitzgerald opposed this saying that would be a foregone conclusion. Maurice McCarthy said that if the other committee members had any real interest in the Volunteers, they would have attended this meeting. The dissenters then called for a full general meeting to decide on the matter. The general meeting of the local Volunteers was called for the following Sunday at the Baths Hall, situated at the eastern end of the town front. The meeting saw a packed hall with Joe Healy presiding in the Chair. John Riordan proposed that the Cobh Volunteer Movement submit to Redmondite control. Healy seconded the motion and, in the course of a lengthy speech, reminded all that it was 'owing to the bravery and loyalty of Irishmen serving in his Majesty's navy and army that they were able to hold their meeting in peace and freedom that day. That they all knew where their duty lay and the destiny of Ireland was safe in Mr Redmond's keeping.[3] The meeting appeared to be unanimous in its support of this view. Then, prompted by Seamus Fitzgerald, Domhaill O'Ciosain made a counterproposal, that the Cobh Volunteers would remain loyal to their founder Eoin McNeill, but as O'Ciosain was not a great speaker and made his proposal under very noisy and hostile conditions, it appeared he was either not heard by the chair or didn't appear to receive a seconder.

Then Maurice McCarthy and Seamus Fitzgerald both held up a copy of Terence McSwiney's paper *Fianna Fáil* while O'Ciosain read an article from it dealing with Sinn Féin efforts to get the North German Lloyd Co. to send their lines to Cobh, while a British Government statement said that they would regard such calls to Cork Harbour as an intrusion. Maurice McCarthy then seconded the motion which was supported by Fitzgerald, amid cries of 'Get them out',[4] followed by boos and jeers. Then when Michael Leahy rose to speak, he too was booed by some of those around him and was actually struck by Charlie Finn who wasn't at all impressed by the dissenting voices.

The Chair, however, allowed Leahy a hearing, while facilitating him with a chair on which to stand while he addressed the meeting. It was clear from the hostility shown towards Leahy, O'Ciosain and the other Republicans by those around them and from the Chair at the top table that opposition to Redmond's call was well anticipated. It was also very clear, that those in control of the meeting were so sure of their position of strength that they felt comfortable allowing the Republicans to have their say. In the event, Leahy strongly objected to the recruiting of the Volunteers to prop up the British Empire, and said they had been established to fight for the freedom of Ireland. He then asked if any man present felt as he did, to follow him out of the hall. Of a hall of nearly 500 men, Leahy was joined by only eight others in the walk out. In doing so, they had to beat a hostile retreat from the place while being jeered and hissed and were very fortunate to escape without injury. The nine rebels then held a counter meeting outside of the hall and appointed Leahy as a delegate to go to Dublin and get in touch with the provisional committee. One of those, Paddy Whelan who later assumed the rank of Commandant and was Vice OC with the 4th Battalion of the East-Cork Flying Column, summed up the atmosphere of the meeting while making his witness statement to the Bureau of Military History in 1956.

I well remember a huge meeting in Cobh, attended by every 'man jack'[5] of the company, being addressed by speakers who were, in fact, nothing more or less than voluntary recruiting officers for the British army and navy. We were exhorted by one individual to join the British army and do what he intended to do, at the same time exposing a brawny blacksmith's arm which he proposed to steep in German blood in the cause of freedom. He seemed to be terribly sincere, but, strange to relate, he never did join the British army or, for that matter, any other army.

In a letter from Domhaill O'Ciosain to Seamus Fitzgerald recalling those events more than 40 years later, it was claimed Micheal Leahy had in fact instructed the Belvelly and Ballymore Volunteers to accept the Redmondite take over, and only changed his own mind at the last moment when some at the general meeting began to speak ill of the Gaelic League. Such an account however, doesn't fit squarely with Leahy's membership of the IRB, which was a total separatist movement that wouldn't countenance support for the British Military under any circumstances.

O'Ciosain, who later moved to Passage West as a school principal, had by his own admission been expelled from the Volunteers in 1916. The reason for his expulsion is not recorded, but it's very likely the person who oversaw that expulsion would have been Michael Leahy as his then commanding officer. Another man who didn't join the others in the walk out from the Baths Hall but left the Volunteers temporarily through disillusionment was Jack O'Connell. Jack, whose brother Jimmy was one of those present at the first A.O.H meeting, would himself also go on to play a major role in the armed struggle in East Cork with the Flying Column, and would later be one of the few Cobh Volunteers to oppose his former colleagues by supporting the Treaty.

Of the remaining hundreds of Volunteers who stayed behind in support of Redmond at the Baths hall meeting, only a handful would actually take up the challenge and go to fight for the British. They included the three drill instructors James Downey, Bob Donaghy and Jerry McGrath. Some of the fathers and relatives of Volunteers, who were themselves navy and army reservists, would be forced to join the British war effort. Others from Cobh who had no connection to either branch of the Volunteers would in time volunteer for the front with various British regiments. Some, like George and Freddy Clifford would never return from the front. Others, like Jack Damery and Frank Graham would return as very different men from the ones that volunteered, and would continue their fight for the freedom of the small nation of Ireland, through the alternative avenue of the IRA. Others still, would return to Cobh equally as bitter, and under the name of the British ex-servicemen's association would issue a proclamation condemning Britain's continued misrule of Ireland.

At the bottom of Ballard Hill at Belvelly, there was a large area of marshy land by a stream called the Potteries. Known for the high concentration of clay in its soil, some of the finest red bricks made anywhere were manufactured there. The name of the 'Belvelly Brick' was well known and exported wide and far. The British Embassy in India was one such building that was built with bricks from the Belvelly potteries. Many of the old streets and prominent buildings of Cobh, including the railway station and heritage centre were constructed with the use of the red Belvelly brick. The potteries which employed 120 were the main source of employment for the men of the locality, including many volunteers of the Belvelly Company. When Britain declared war on Germany in 1914, the owner of the potteries, Lord Barrymore of Fota estate, closed the place down. Barrymore was very aware that most of his employees were Volunteer members and were unlikely to find alternative employment. He therefore expected most if not all to volunteer for the front. As things transpired, however, no one from Belvelly volunteered for the front as part of Britain's war effort. Though initially offering their support to Redmond's National Volunteers, the Belvelly men would revert back to the Irish Volunteers in time, with one of their own, Ned Butler, (an ex-employee of the potteries) assuming command of the company. Of all the employees of the then vast Fota estate in 1914, only one man, a farm hand by the name of Coughlan, volunteered to fight for the British. He would never return from the front.

Following the split at the latter end of 1914, parade attendances of the Irish Volunteers in Cobh varied from between three to eleven from a strength of fifteen members on the Great Island. This was particularly disappointing after the men from Belvelly and Ballymore had sided with Redmond's National Volunteers. Although they were few, Mick Leahy, Seamus Fitzgerald and the others, kept themselves busy during this period by attending regular target practice after mass each Sunday at Lindsey's Quarry at the bottom of Ticknock. By the beginning of 1915, the Volunteers managed to purchase the occasional short arm from locally based soldiers who wanted easy cash for drink money. Leahy had also received a .22 Winchester rifle from Terence McSwiney in Cork, while Seamus Fitzgerald received a Lee-Enfield sporting rifle from Frank Healy BC.

Although the National Volunteers maintained a strong organisation locally, the Republican organisation won over the odd defector from time to time as it became clearer that few had any intention of heading to France to fight. It was around this time that Jack O'Connell came back into the fold. Others would come and go periodically and this meant that things had at least picked themselves up enough for the company to organise itself a steering committee. Leahy was by now the *de facto* leader and according to Paddy Whelan, it was around this time that Mick Leahy immersed himself in military manuals and charts to learn all there was to know about weapons and how to use them. It was clear from his behaviour

Seamus Fitzgerald: front-centre kneeling. Probably at Knockraha grenade factory around 1920-21.

that Leahy knew something the others didn't, and that the day for using their weapons might not be all that far away. Whether this was down to his membership of the IRB or just plain intuition, is not known, but he didn't spare any time in trying to prepare his men with what little resources they had for future battle. Evidence of how serious Leahy was about making these preparations, became available when he revealed to a colleague that he was putting a plan together to raid the National Volunteer hall to confiscate their rifles.

At first, this sounded like a good idea to his colleague who felt it was both viable and would provide the answer to all their problems. Then as they went about advancing their plans, they discovered from another Volunteer who had earlier defected from the Redmondites, that the latter's local leadership had handed in all their rifle bolts to the RIC following the split. In March 1915, the Cobh company attended the St Patrick's Day parade in Cork and later attended the Manchester Martyrs parade in the city. By now, the Cobh company were receiving attention from both the police and the Volunteer leadership in Cork City. Leahy claimed that Cobh, Carrigtwohill, Clonmult and Dungourney, were the only areas of East Cork that had any real Volunteer organisation during this period. There was much excitement amongst the company members when James Ahern arrived on parade one day with a beautiful Lee Enfield rifle that he had bought from a British soldier, the first of a few the company would acquire in that way.

In July, the manager of Queenstown Cooperative, Pat Curran and John Dowling, a fitter at Haulbowline, were served with exclusion orders by the RIC, ordering them to reside outside of County Cork. Both men left Cobh as did the towns Postmaster P.S. O'Hegarty when he was deliberately transferred to a post office in England the previous October, as was his brother Sean, but he resigned from the Post Office rather than submit to British pressure. On the 24 July, under Martial Law in Cork, General C. Hills issued the following exclusion order to Sean O'Hegarty, of 1 Wellington Place, Sunday's Well Cork:

> In exercise of the powers vested in me by the Defence of the Realm Regulations 1914, you are hereby ordered to leave and remain out of the following areas: the Borough of Cork, the Urban Districts of Middleton, Queenstown and Youghal. The Rural districts of Bandon, Cork, Kinsale, Midleton, Youghal No 1 and 2, within twenty-four hours of this order being served upon you., having first reported in writing your proposed place of residence to the Fortress Commander, Queenstown. In the event of you not complying with any of the terms of this order, you are liable to be tried by Courtmartial and sent to penal servitude for life or any lesser punishment.[6]

O'Hegarty's position as Postmaster in Cobh was filled by local man Paddy Kidney, the latter comfortably satisfying the security requirements of the local military and naval chiefs. The common thread between Curran, Dowling (the man who brought James Connolly to town in 1911) and O'Hegarty was their known connections to the IRB. One of the reasons given for P.S. O'Hegarty's expulsion was that he recently had been in communication with the German Ambassador.

O'Hegarty's brother Sean would go on to take over command of the 1st Cork Brigade after the death of Terence McSweeney six years later. The fact that Leahy, Fitzgerald and some of the others who were also employed as apprentices at the Naval Dockyard at Haulbowline had escaped censure, might have had something to do with their young ages and their not being considered a serious threat. In January 1916, Mick Leahy was selected from the Cobh Company to attend an officer's course at the Cork Volunteer hall at Sheare's Street. Following the completion of the course, he was formally appointed the Captain of the Cobh Company. After returning to Cobh, he immediately resumed training and preparing the men for the coming fight, and with the acquisition of much needed additional weapons. Seamus Fitzgerald was sent to Dublin with £11 and a note he had earlier been given by Paddy Curran to purchase rifles, which an advert in the Volunteer journal had carried. When he got to the Volunteer Headquarters at Dawson Street, he was met by Bulmer Hobson, who informed him the advert was incorrect and that there were no weapons. Fitzgerald's presence at the Dublin Volunteer Headquarters did not go unnoticed by the authorities; later this would play no small part in contributing towards his internment alongside Leahy..

Using their positions of employment, Leahy and other Volunteer apprentices at the naval dockyard at Haulbowline would drill with hurlies during their lunch breaks or at any other opportunity that presented itself. Leslie Pierce, the son of the harbour garrison adjutant, was a schoolboy on Haulbowline during this period and remembers the Volunteers drilling.

> I think more hurley sticks were cut out and manufactured in the dockyard's joiner shop than in any other commercial sports manufacturers in Ireland. During the midday break we used to go down into the dockyard and watch what seemed to be an innocent game of hurling and when apparently no 'cobs'(military police) were about, rifle drill was immediately proceeded with, the sticks taking the place of the rifle.[7]

3. The Call to Arms

One of the factors that contributed to the failure of the Easter Rising was the capture of the arms ship the *Aud*. During the preparations for the Rising, Roger Casement had gone to Germany to negotiate an arms shipment for the IRB, who at the time were pulling the strings of the Irish Volunteers. The arms were expected around Easter and were to be distributed amongst the country units in the south and west. Captain Michael Leahy and his second in command Seamus Fitzgerald met with Tomás MacCurtain at his Blackpool home on Holy Thursday and were given orders to report to the Volunteer hall at Sheare's Street, Cork on Saturday night with every available man, weapon, ammunition and piece of equipment. Before noon on Easter Saturday 1916, Leahy and Fitzgerald, with a couple of others left his mothers' house at Carrignafoy and proceeded down Ballywilliam hill towards the council reservoir on the Tay Road. There, they joined up with the other members of the company who were instructed to report there before 1.00pm. The men were then ordered to fall in, and after a roll call, it was established that among those present were: Mick Leahy, Seamus Fitzgerald, Paddy Whelan, Jack Stack, Joe Reid, Ernie Fowler, James O'Connell, William O'Regan, Danny Healy, William Ralph, Bunny Reid. The parade was also notified that Liam Ahern and Jack O'Connell would follow along later on bicycles.

Seamus Fitzgerald then proceeded to tally all weapons and ammunition. Present were 5 Lee Enfield rifles, 1 Martini rifle with 250 rounds of 303 ammunition, 15 revolvers of 32, 38 and 45 calibre with 180 rounds of

Mick Leahy.

corresponding ammunition and five Bayonets. There were no shotguns, pikes or explosives. No complete uniforms, but most present had breeches and leggings. All had haversacks, belts, bandoliers, groundsheets, water bottles, blankets, spare socks, and green Volunteer slouched hats. The small but disciplined local company then set off, on foot, on their journey to Cork City. Although Leahy and his men may not have been aware of it, and perhaps they wouldn't have been too bothered if they had, their movements that morning were being well scrutinised by the local RIC. Later when they were about 5 miles from the city, and as they passed Little Island, they were met by two mounted RIC men who followed behind. As Colonial Office records by Special Branch at Dublin Castle would later show, the Cobh Volunteers were observed marching off to meet up with other rebel forces in Cork City, and that Leahy and Fitzgerald were recognised as leading them.

Earlier that morning, Mick Leahy had been informed by local pilot, Michael Walsh, that a German ship had earlier been sunk or scuttled outside the harbour, near the Daunt Lightship. The local commander wasn't quite sure of the significance of this event but he considered it important enough to report it to Tomás MacCurtain as soon as they reached the Volunteer hall.

When they arrived, a guard was already in place around the hall. The Cobh Company were then told they would be on guard duty that night. In the mean time, they were detailed to bring supplies to the hall from

26

another part of the City. A driver was provided for the purpose and at one point a policeman attempted to stop the vehicle but later left it pass after Leahy pointed a revolver in his face. Paddy Whelan had earlier been posted as a lookout outside the hall to assist Leahy's crew who were collecting, amongst other things, petrol. As he tried to blend in and be as inconspicuous as possible, he found it a nerve-wracking experiencing as the street was taken up with swarms of policemen coming and going in all directions around the precincts of the Volunteer Hall. At one point he nervously stopped an RIC man and asked for a light for his cigarette, while all the time hoping Leahy and the others would bring the petrol by another route.

Later, all the men were advised to go to confession. MacCurtain and McSwiney slept in the hall that night, as did Maurice Ahern and other East Cork men under his command from around Dungourney and Clonmult. On Sunday morning the men were formed up outside the hall when word came by a messenger from Dublin. This led to a serious discussion amongst the senior officers and the general impression was that the parade was to be cancelled. Seamus Fitzgerald, John P. O'Connell, Willie Reagan and Jack O'Connell joined up with the cyclist company and proceeded on to Macroom, because he had already cycled to Cork and had had no sleep the previous night, Jack O'Connell soon became flagged and later turned back for the city.

The remainder of the Cobh Company marched with the rest of the city Volunteers to Capwell station and took a train to Crookstown. From there they marched on to Kilmurry where they joined the Ballinadee and other companies from West Cork under the command of Tom Hales.

Some of these local men were so poorly armed that all they carried were pikes. They then marched to Macroom before halting in the Square where they were dismissed. By now the weather had turned very wet and this was given to the men as a reason for the parades cancellation. With the exception of MacCurtain and MacSwiney, all then returned by train to Cork before marching back to the Hall in Sheare's Street where they were dismissed. The city men and most of the East Cork men returned to their homes but the Cobh men stayed on in the Hall. The next day at noon, Seamus Fitzgerald and some others were just about to buy some tickets for a show at the Opera House when a Volunteer rushed in and told them to report back to the Volunteer Hall immediately.

The men were told to take up action stations around the building. Sandbags were quickly filled and defensive positions were prepared at windows and loopholes and on the roof. By now a number of rumours were circulating about what might be going on elsewhere but nothing definitive. The Volunteers remained in their positions until 8.oopm.

Fitzgerald remembers Ernie Fowler braving it out on the roof despite having a bad attack of neuralgia. Later that night, Tomás MacCurtain and Terence MacSwiney arrived back in the Hall. There, some discussion took place among the officers which was clouded in confusion. Following this, all the Cobh men except Mick Leahy were sent home that night after leaving their rifles in the Hall with a guarantee they would be kept safe. Throughout the days which followed, with more and more news coming through of what was happening in Dublin, MacCurtain and MacSwiney realised they had been caught off guard by McNeill's countermanding order. The significances of the report of a sunken German ship outside Cork Harbour from Leahy on the Saturday, had by now become crystal clear, but only added to the confusion of what might have been, had different actions been taken. The Germans had earlier set about camouflaging a British ship they had captured in the war, changed the name of the ship to *Aud* and on 9 April the ship sailed out under the Norwegian flag.

Casement had travelled back to Ireland aboard a German submarine. The arms were to be landed in Tralee Bay. However, the British Admiralty in Cobh, under Admiral Bayly, were aware of Casement's visits to Germany, and knew that the possibility of German arms shipment coming to Ireland was something that could not be ignored. The British were thus keeping the southwest coast of Ireland under extra surveillance. Because the *Aud* had no wireless transmitter onboard, it was not aware of a change in the plans for landing the arms and when it landed in Tralee Bay its captain, Karl Spindler, could see no sign of Casement. When Spindler noticed the British ship *Bluebell* in the area, he quickly turned about and increased speed to make an escape. This naturally aroused the suspicion of the British sloop, and although the suspicious looking vessel sailed under a Norwegian flag and had the letters '*Aud / Norge*' painted on its sides, the *Bluebell* captain decided to follow the boat and intercept it. As Norway was a neutral country from the war, the captain felt reluctant to do anything that might compromise Norway's neutrality, so without firing a shot, the guns of the sloop were trained on the *Aud* while it was instructed to follow the *Bluebell* into Cork Harbour. However, before the two ships could reach the harbour, the crew of the *Bluebell* noticed that the supposedly motley-looking crew of which had previously been lounging the decks of the *Aud* had now changed into German naval uniforms. The Norwegian flag which had been flying from the mast head of the vessel had been replaced by the German naval ensign. And worst of all, the arms ship was now settling down in the water, having been scuttled by Captain Spindler, and with the crew taking to the lifeboats. The *Bluebell* had no choice but to pick up the survivors, and bring them back to Cobh, where they were duly placed in cells aboard the hulk *Colleen* which was moored alongside the jetty at Haulbowline.

The following day, Easter Saturday, the prisoners were placed in more secure custody on Spike Island. On Easter Monday they were taken aboard the aptly named *Adventure* and transferred to an interment camp in England. Meanwhile, back in the Volunteer Hall in Cork, Mick Leahy later said it was not clear to him if MacCurtain and MacSwiney were considering a surrender of arms but some form of consultations were going on in the Hall at that time.

Amongst all this tense confusion, this was the same period that MacSwiney would first be introduced to his future wife. While previously browsing in Liam Russell's book shop, Mick Leahy was approached by Miss Murphy who indicated a wish to be introduced to MacSwiney. Then one night during Easter week, she came to the Hall with some information about movements or intentions of British forces and asked to see Leahy. He in turn introduced her to MacSwiney who listened to what she had to say. For the next week, the Cobh men would report to work at the naval dockyard as if nothing happened. Liam O'Brien would visit Cork every evening hoping to bring back instructions for the local company, but no news was forthcoming. By now, and in addition to the captured *Aud* crew, a British sloop arrived in the harbour full of captured rebels from Galway.

The Haulbowline Volunteers also noticed at this time that an armoured railway car was under construction in the Dockyard boiler shop. This was to be used against rebel forces in the Dublin Rising but was not completed in time to see any action. The following Monday while at work, Leahy and fellow Volunteer Seamus Fitzgerald, were told to report to the Chief Engineer's office. From there, they were both placed under arrest by police and military and were questioned separately. Leahy was asked if he was the leader of the Sinn Féiners, to which he boldly replied, 'No I'm the leader of the Volunteers.'[8] The British military interrogator then retorted, 'Sinn Féiners is good enough for me.' The two Volunteers were then taken to Cobh RIC Barracks at Westview, where they discovered that IRB man Liam O'Brien had also been arrested. The three were then moved to the Detention Barracks (Victoria Barracks, now Collins Barracks) in Cork.

While in the Detention Barracks, the three men were again questioned separately several times, mainly for the purpose of establishing where the Cobh rifles were. One of the arguments used by their interrogators to get them to part with that information was the claim that the Cork City volunteers had handed in their arms and none of them had been arrested, so why should they now hold out? The men refused to give any information however, thus ensuring their continued detention and internment. On the day that Thomas Kent was executed in the Detention Barracks, the Cobh men were transferred by train with a large number of other prisoners to Richmond Barracks, Dublin. As they were leaving the Cork Barracks, Fitzgerald thought of a meeting they had had about five weeks earlier where Tom Kent made a suggestion in response to their lack of weapons, that they should manufacture their own pikes. The Cobh officer thought of poor Tom, and knew if they were ever to beat the British, pikes were out and they would have to match them with fire power.

Richmond Barracks was full with prisoners and the Cobh men were crowded into a room with 90 others. Leahy got lucky and managed to persuade a friendly sentry to post a letter home for him. This was the first news to reach Cobh of the men's whereabouts. The Cobh Urban Council sent the chairman, Grogan, and the Town Clerk, Campbell to visit the Cobh prisoners. While there, they also managed to get special permission to see Count Plunkett. A couple of days later, Mary and Annie MacSwiney and Miss Murphy got to visit Terrence. The men were soon separated, with Leahy, MacSwiney and MacCurtain being kept on at Richmond Barracks pending court-martial. This never happened however, and they were eventually moved to Wakefield Detention Barracks in Yorkshire. Later they were transferred to Frongoch in Wales where MacCurtain was Commandant of the South Camp for a while, then onto Wandsworth before they were eventually released by the end of the year.

In the meantime, while Leahy, MacCurtain, MacSwiney and others who participated in the Dublin Rising were enjoying political status at Frongoch Camp, Seamus Fitzgerald was communicating to the outside world reports of a far contrasting regime that was operating in Wakefield Camp. It would appear from messages he was having smuggled out, that the camp policy was at times harsh and brutal, much different to the Frongoch camp.

On 30 May he wrote to his mother claiming the prison authorities were releasing men daily in lots of twenty. He also said he had a visit from a nurse who was informed of his whereabouts from the Mother Superior in Cobh. By 1 June, he received his first letter from home. The brief letter from M. Cotter of 7 Albert Terrace Cobh, basically asked how he was and passed on best wishes from Lily Twomey and Dan Collins. The next day, he received a letter from his brother Paddy with a message from his mother saying a deputation from Dublin was to meet Asquith for their release. She also expressed hope that his friends would be sent to the same camp to keep him company. He wrote again to his mother on 5 June, thanking her for the food parcel but noted that the Bovril was confiscated. He was anxious about Patrick after being saved from the wreck of the *Black Prince* and relieved that father, a seaman was not involved. By the 6 June, his cousin William Fitzgerald in Durham wrote informing him that his letter had earlier escaped the censor and was passed on by the Mother Superior at Wakefield. 'It's impossible for me to try and console you after reading your letter. What wrong did you ever do that you should be made to suffer so much, and to think that I was compelled to join the British army and my countrymen being victimised like they are.'[9] The letter finished with William wishing he could trade places with his cousin the martyr.

On the 10 June, he wrote to his mother again and told her that 100 men had been transferred to Frongoch and didn't know if he would follow. He complained that there was no word of his appeal and feared the Queenstown police were blocking it. By 13 June, a jolly and humorous letter arrived from Ann Hannon, 'to show some of the Cailíní had not forgotten ye.'[10] 'Tell Mick Leahy we were asking about him and don't you boys get too fat in there. The Gaelic League branch has closed following ye'r arrest. PS, don't tell anyone that I wrote to you as I wouldn't like it to go around.' The same day, Fitzgerald wrote to his mother, stating that if it weren't for the food parcels that he was receiving from the outside, he would probably be dead by now. Two prisoners had already died in here, he wrote, 'Thank god for the Superior of the local convent who gives me a sandwich daily, how I long for bacon or ham.'

He continued by stating he couldn't understand why he has not been released and said he received word from Michael (Leahy) who said the conditions in Richmond were excellent. He also wrote that he had received a letter from Leo Ring who was still being held at Frongoch. The next day a short letter arrived from a fellow Volunteer back home Michael Hennessy, enquiring how he was and who could visit him. Hennessy, who would later share office with Fitzgerald on the Town Council, pressed his comrade to report all ill treatment happening at the camp, 'Your Countrymen at home will not have it.'

There is no recorded evidence of where the third Cobh man Liam O'Brien, was being held at this time. It's not known if he just faded away from the struggle after his release, or indeed if he survived internment at all. It is known however, that by 1920 the local Sinn Féin organisation was honouring him by naming its Cumann after him. It's also known that when Leahy and Fitzgerald were eventually released from Frongoch, they arrived back home together by train. The *Cork Examiner* reported:

A very large crowd gathered at the railway station for the arrival of the two naval dockyard workers Jim Fitzgerald and Michael Leahy who were interned following the outbreak of the Rising. Among those welcoming the men home were the Chairman and Town Clerk of the UDC. On Alighting from the train, the crowd broke over the barriers and lifted the two men shoulder high and

carried them through the town singing nationalist songs and cheering vocifer-
ously. At the request of the home comers, no band played. [11]

While Leahy and Fitzgerald arrived back home amid hero status, it is interesting to note how the political and security establishment were viewing
them before and after the Rising. What is known from Colonial Office
records is that District Inspector D.E. Armstrong of the Cobh RIC, had
made a written recommendation to the Admiralty on 13 April, a full week
and a half before the Rising, that five Haulbowline employees should be
discharged from employment there for being Volunteers and that such dis-
missals would have a good effect on the remaining employees. The memo
referred to Leahy, Fitzgerald and an Arthur Hurley of Friars Walk in Cork
by name. It said that the two Cobh men had been observed proceeding to Cork in Volunteer uniform on 17 March (St Patrick's Day) for a
parade. By 8 August, an irate District Inspector Armstrong reported to his
Special Branch superiors at Dublin Castle, informing them that Leahy and
Fitzgerald had been reinstated in their former positions as apprentices in
the Haulbowline Dockyard. The Admiral had informed him that the men
had not been found guilty of any offence and after being interviewed by
him they had been given directions that they were to be watched carefully.
On 24 August, the Vice-Admiral commanding, wrote to the local RIC
asking why Leahy and Fitzgerald were arrested and if they had cleared
themselves of all complicity in rebellious activities?

D.I. Armstrong wrote back stating that Fitzgerald was secretary of the
local branch of the Volunteers while Leahy was its Captain, and they were
in close touch with its Headquarters at Dawson Street, Dublin. It stated
that the Rebellion would have taken place in Cork only for:

(a) The capture of the *Aud* and its subsequent sinking.
(b) The arrest of Casement and
(c) The cancellation of parades by McNeill who is head of the Irish Volunteers.

D.I. Armstrong wrote, 'In the event of the Rising having taken place in
Cork these men would have been involved. I do not know the reason why
these men were released on the 4th. Leahy is still dangerous and shouldn't
be re-employed in His Majesty's Dockyard. I do not consider Fitzgerald so
dangerous now,' wrote the Inspector.

While Fitzgerald's experience at Wakefield may have left him somewhat
traumatised and not the best for wear after the treatment he endured there,
the RIC in Cobh must have suffered serious flaws in their intelligence if
they thought he was finished with the Volunteer Movement. In a follow
up progress report sent to the Crime Special Branch, Dublin Castle on 9

September, D.I. Armstrong reiterated the opinion that James Fitzgerald was not considered dangerous and that his term of internment had had a salutary effect on him. The report went on to state Fitzgerald's older brother Paddy had severed all links to the Irish Volunteers and Sinn Féin. It was perhaps this last comment that showed the weakness in the RIC's intelligence, since there is no record or mention of Paddy Fitzgerald ever having been a Volunteer or Sinn Féin member.

Seamus's younger brother Thomas was a member of the Fianna Éireann and another brother Michael, would soon follow and become a member. The latter would later fight in the Civil War and would personally become known to this author in later years. These were the only other Fitzgerald family members directly involved in the Republican struggle. By 11 December, D.I. Armstrong found himself backtracking a little on Seamus Fitzgerald when reporting to Dublin Castle. He stated that as far he was aware, there were no Sinn Féin activities in the district and that Queenstown hadn't any Sinn Féin clubs. There was however, a GAA club, 'The McDonagh Football Cub' and it was possible that Sinn Féiners met in the rooms. He added that this club had been established by Michael Leahy, James Fitzgerald and John Stack. The three were responsible for the payment of the rent of 15*d* a week. Two months later, Armstrong was back on to his superiors at the Castle, informing them that he was now satisfied the GAA club was a front for the Sinn Féiners who now numbered sixty-five, and that Leahy, Fitzgerald and Stack were pulling its strings.

4. The Awakening

On Easter Monday evening, a group of local young men were gathered at the railway station in Cobh. Most were members of Redmond's National Volunteers, though one was not a member of any organisation. As the men were chatting amongst themselves, a policeman on duty, Detective Burns came by and relayed the news from Dublin to them. On hearing the shocking account of the Rising in the capital, the Redmondites initial response was to express support for the British authorities in any way they could. The only dissenting voice in the group was that of a young grocer's apprentice named Michael Burke. Burke, who was born in Kilmallock in County Limerick, lived with his sister and her sailor husband at Donelan Terrace.

Within a year, the young apprentice would become a member of the Volunteers, and by 1920, would prove to be the most tenacious and successful IRA officer to ever hold command in Cobh. Burke's friends, who voiced opposition to the Rising at the railway station, though initially surprised by his opposing and radical views, would subsequently join him and become active members of the Cobh IRA too. Burke would receive his early Republican influence from IRB man Patrick Curran who gradually gave his apprentice a strong national outlook from their workplace at the Queenstown Cooperative. He would later recall that prior to 1916, being sent by Curran to meet with a carrier who was then drawing military stores to the Belmont depot at Cobh, and receiving a quantity of .303 ammunition to bring back to the IRB man. The execution of the leaders of the Rising had a profound effect on the young Burke. He was aware that Curran had been a personal friend of one, Sean MacDiarmada, and that his earlier errands collecting and moving weapons and ammunition were probably all connected to the national explosion that had taken place in Dublin.

The young, up and coming revolutionary moved to Fermanagh to work with Curran after the Rising, before returning to Cobh again in 1917. It was around this time that he joined up with the local Volunteers. One lesson that Patrick Curran had deeply instilled in his young apprentice which would serve him well in the coming years was to remain in the background and not to flaunt his membership of the Volunteers in public. Soon Michael Burke would meet up with a soldier home on leave from France. The soldier, named James Duggan of the Royal Horse Artillery, told Burke that he had a pistol in England and would send it on to him. The young Volunteer was pleasantly surprised when the parabellum revolver later arrived in a boot box with three magazines and about forty rounds of ammunition by train.

5. Raiding for Arms

One of the biggest lessons from the Easter Rising debacle for Volunteers outside of Dublin, was their utter failure as a credible fighting force due to their lack of weapons. Each Volunteer leader knew that acquiring weapons was something that ultimately would be the business of their own command areas to resolve. In time, Volunteer Headquarters would forbid the raiding of private houses for weapons. Florence O'Donoghue, Adjutant of the 1st Cork Brigade, once referred to this and admitted he had taken part in one of these raids for private weapons. It appears that Headquarters were opposed to this practice, because since most of the houses which possessed such weapons, were owned by Unionists and the Protestant landed gentry. They didn't want the struggle to be portrayed as sectarian. The reality however, is that if such raids had never taken place, the British would most likely still be in control of all of Ireland today.

By October 1917, Michael Leahy found himself arrested with Jack Stack for illegal drilling and were brought to Cork Gaol. They immediately joined a hunger strike there and were released again under the 'Cat and Mouse Act' before the week expired. One of the conditions of their release was that they had to regularly report to the local RIC Barracks. Leahy refused to do this and with Brigade instructions, went on the run and began organising other Volunteer companies throughout East Cork. He would later be appointed O.C. of the 4th Battalion (East-Cork IRA) in January 1918. Previously, in September 1917, he had completed his apprenticeship at the Naval Dockyard. When he was offered a job as an engineer on the British oil tanker *Olive Branch*, but refused it. The *Olive Branch* was subsequently torpedoed by a German submarine and sunk outside of Cork Harbour.

Meanwhile, Daithí O'Brien was selected as the new Commander of the Cobh Company. Later in the year, he would temporarily take over command of the battalion from Mick Leahy when the Commander was once again arrested. Command of the Cobh Company would in fact change hands many times over the next two and a half years as the British strenuously worked the system to remove and disrupt the chain of command. Leahy was very mindful of the British / RIC game plan and in turn had his own emergency plans in place for the whole battalion area. In the event of the British declaring all out open war against the Volunteers and in the absence of himself and other commanders, O'Brien was to take over command of the battalion. Seamus Fitzgerald would take over command of E Company at Knockraha, though this probably changed after he assumed the position of Chairman of Cobh Urban Council in January 1920. James Ahern would take over command of the Shanagarry Company, but again, as he was also elected to Cobh Urban Council and had almost immediately had to go on the run, that plan probably also had to be abandoned.

At the same time, O'Brien from Roches Row was a hands-on Commander who led from the front. He was quick to recognise his company's weaknesses and limitations, and soon set to work with plans to properly arm his men. One night in November 1917, with about twenty other Volunteers, O'Brien led a raid on a military lockup at Cobh railway station. Unfortunately, all they could find was a quantity of bandoliers, bayonets and some other small military items, but no weapons. O'Brien then turned his attention to the confiscation of weapons from private houses throughout the remainder of 1917.

By April 1918, the Volunteer leader hatched a bold plan where he focused on a local gunsmiths shop at Harbour Row. At the rear of

O'Keefe's gun-shop was situated the Volunteer Hall. On the night of the raid, O'Brien led nine others over a wall at the rear of the Volunteer Hall with the use of a ladder. Then lifting a window, the men entered the back of the shop and removed a quantity of lever action rifles, shot guns and a large assortment of ammunition. One of those who took part in the operation, Jack O'Connell, later said they went in and out of the building with the captured weapons, without arousing those who slept upstairs. The weapons were swiftly moved to an old empty vault at the Old Church cemetery before being moved on and buried in a large wooden box in a field near the Leahy family home at Ballywilliam. The local Company were compelled to vacate the Hall at the back of O'Keefe's gunsmiths at this point, but soon afterwards were allowed the use of the Ancient Order of Hibernians hall.

With the British threat of conscription now at its peak in Ireland, the strength of the local Volunteers had mushroomed to two companies. Around this time, Seamus Fitzgerald was delegated to go to Dublin to buy 1,000 rounds of small calibre ammunition from Michael Staines at Volunteer Headquarters.

A year later Fitzgerald would find himself in Dublin again, this time collecting rifle ammunition from Tom Cullen and Frank Harding. These discrete trips to the capital as well as local purchases from friendly soldiers, ensured that the Volunteers had at least enough firearms and ammunition to maintain a decent training programme. One day while engaged in target practice at Lindsay's Quarry, Jack Stack and Michael Burke were giving instruction to some Volunteer recruits when two RIC men arrived on the scene. With rifle in hand, Stack walked over and removed the target from its position and walked past the policemen as if they weren't there. One of them called after him and shouted 'Stop, Stack, I know you',[12] but Stack ignored the remark and carried on without being obstructed.

The watching recruits probably learned a far greater lesson in defiance, than how to fire a weapon that day. From their new base at the A.O.H. Hall, the volunteers experimented with cement bombs (castings of cement into which a stick of gelignite fitted), also canister bombs (ordinary gunpowder and fuse in a tin can). These crude bombs were tested but proved unsuccessful. The gelignite came to the Volunteers free from one of their own; John Moore of Ticknock who had a horse and cart and was on hire to the County Council to carry supplies of gelignite to quarries for blasting purposes. Moore would keep a few sticks of the gelignite from each trip and pass them on to the Company. In time, Moore's usefulness with explosives would prove to be of immense value to the Republican cause in East Cork.

Despite the new increase in Volunteer strength, Daithí O'Brien was

Mick Burke outside Mount Eaton in 1920.

careful however, not to use the new inexperienced men, while raiding for arms. One opportunity that presented itself on a plate for the local Commander was too good to ignore, but meant O'Brien had to enlist the help of a couple of young Fianna Éireann members to bring it to fruition. The IRA leader was made aware that a number of weapons on a Minesweeper moored at Cobh were visible from the quayside. The only problem was how to access the small arms cabin of the ship without arousing the attention of the crew. O'Brien eventually settled on the idea of allowing some young Fianna Éireann members to slip through the small porthole of the cabin to retrieve the weapons.

Daithí O'Brien and those with him planning the raid were amazed at the bravery and eagerness of the young Fianna members chosen to take part in the raid. On the night of the operation, everything seemed to go according to plan with the young Fianna boys easily slipping through the porthole and locating the weapons. Then as the boys started handing the rifles out through the porthole, one of them made a noise that alerted the crew. An alarm was sounded, leaving the boys to abort the operation and rush to escape. Unfortunately the two boys couldn't fit through the porthole at the same time and one, Tommy Hayes, was captured. Despite his young age, Tommy was subsequently tried and sentenced to five years imprisonment where he quickly found himself in Belfast Gaol. He immediately joined the hunger-strike in progress there and under the command of Austin Stack, took part in the campaign to smash up the prison furniture. The prison experience became too much for Tommy, and when he was finally released as a broken young man, he continued on active service

Volunteers training at Nuns Wood − Newtown 1918.

with the Volunteers throughout the war and remained on the Republican side during the Civil War. Having never fully recovered from his earlier ordeal, he was later admitted to a mental institution, where he died a number of years later.

During this time, in his continuing efforts to fully arm his men, Daithí O'Brien continued with the policy of raiding the big houses of the town for personal weapons. Near the end of October 1918, Dunlea House on the Lower Road, the residence of Captain George Usborne, deputy Harbour Master was targeted. A loud knock on the door brought a maid to answer it, where she was immediately brushed aside by three masked men who began taking down arms of various kinds including swords from the walls. However, Usborne, who had left the house a short time previously, returned unexpectedly and on seeing the three men engaged in removing his valuable collection of arms from the walls, decided to do his bit for King and motherland. The bold deputy harbour master seized one of the men and started struggling violently with him, trying to take the dagger the raider held in his hand from him. During this time Mrs Usborne and the maid, obliging as ever, had rushed upstairs and alerted a party of soldiers who were passing by in the street. Some of the soldiers consequently came to Usborne's assistance and helped him secure his prisoner, while O'Brien and his other colleague beat a retreat through the back door. The young prisoner was handed over to the RIC and was later identified as Robert Glanville, a native of Waterford who was employed at the Naval Dockyard at Haulbowline.

Daithí O'Brien wasn't at all fazed by the set back at Dunlea House and the capture of one of his men. He decided to put the unfortunate episode down to experience gained, and was determined to be better prepared the next time out. 1919 was but a couple of weeks old when O'Brien made his next move. This time his target was the small corrugated iron home of Mr and Mrs David Jones near Christchurch and the Rushbrooke Lawn Tennis and Croquet Club, then thirty-five years old and well established as a unionist country club. This time O'Brien had the perimeter of the house and access roads to it covered with scouts while he and two others went in. Jones and his wife were entertaining a visitor, Miss Tapp Stewart from Whitepoint, when the three gatecrashers burst in and demanded of Jones to hand over his guns. The former Navy man was at first reluctant, but upon seeing a revolver barrel pointed in his face, changed his mind and handed over his shotguns. The months of January and February were not good ones for the King's Liverpool Regiment, stationed at Belmont Hutments.

In January, someone unknown walked out of the place with a large quantity of bayonets. Despite investigations by the RIC and military police, no arrests followed. Then a few short weeks later in February, Daithí O'Brien decided to up the stakes by targeting the British Army itself for its weapons. O'Brien's boldness was probably influenced by the fact that a Republican Government was by now, elected and sitting at the Mansion House in Dublin and that the army to which he served, had given its allegiance to that government. He might also have been influenced by the shooting dead of two RIC men by Volunteers at Soloheadbeg in Tipperary on the same day the Dáil opened. Seamus Fitzgerald later said he remembered once discussing a plan with O'Brien to target the British armed guard that used to watch over the Admiralty reservoir at Spy Hill, but before he could give the matter further thought, O'Brien had gone away and carried it out. The reservoir overlooking the Burma Steps was important to the British as it supplied fresh water to the naval base at Haulbowline. The armed guard on watch at the facility varied from between four to six men. O'Brien had watched the patterns of the changing guards for a number of weeks and eventually decided on a location and time to best intercept the tired and weary guard returning back to their barracks at Belmont. At 3.00am one morning, O'Brien, Jack O'Connell and four other Volunteers, waited with revolvers in a gateway on the Carrignafoy back road for the military guard to arrive. When it did, an NCO and three other soldiers were jumped and caught completely off guard. Three of the soldiers instantly obeyed the order to raise their hands in the air. One was slow to respond however, and a single shot rang out past his ear. All were then tied up and left on the laneway.

The Volunteers then made off with the rifles, belts and ammunition. The weapons were moved to the vault at the Old Church Cemetery. Within hours, the military and RIC were scouring the countryside for the attackers and the weapons. One of the first Republican houses to be raided following the capture of the weapons was that of Michael Leahy's at Ballywilliam. Leahy's two younger brothers Paddy and Donal were arrested and taken away. Donal had in fact taken part in the raid while Paddy did not. Both men were later released without charge. The authorities continued to raid and search for those responsible and for the weapons. When they arrived at one house at Barrymore Avenue, belonging to another who participated in the attack, they didn't find the Volunteer, but did locate a revolver. The young Volunteers' father, who was a retired naval pensioner, took responsibility for the weapon and subsequently served a period in prison.

A week after the Carrignafoy raid and while the RIC were still trying to locate the missing rifles, two officers stumbled upon the hidden vault at the Old Church cemetery. Noticing that some of the ivy around the vault was dead, one of the officers became suspicious before opening it and locating the captured rifles. With the quickly changing climate sweeping the country, particularly in relation to the newly democratically elected government, morale was starting to wane amongst some in the military. About this time, a member of the Scots Cameron Highlanders came forward and told the Volunteers that he could get them in and out of the Belmont Camp to snatch 20 rifles with easy access. At the risk that this might be a plot to exact revenge for the earlier ambush at the Carrignafoy back road, Daithí O'Brien on the night, had twenty armed men posted at the eastern approaches to the Camp for almost the whole night, waiting for the promised opportunity, but nothing came of it. Some individual Volunteers also took measures and risks to locate arms for themselves. Mikey Kidney was one such Volunteer.

He worked on the French Estate at Cuskinny. This was a lovely sprawling Unionist estate which overlooked the bay on the eastern outskirts of the town. One night Mikey, who worked on the estate among the garden staff, secretly returned alone and smashed his way through the door of an isolated shed on the grounds. Once inside he gained possession of two shotguns before making good his escape. Leslie Pierce, the son of the harbour garrison adjutant, later relayed another experience which he witnessed as a boy. He recalled how the military launch *Wyndham* first called to Fort Camden at the outer harbour that day. Then it sailed to Fort Carlisle at the opposite side of the harbour. On the pier head at Carlisle was a stretcher party waiting for the vessel, consisting of two privates and a corporal. The patient on the stretcher was obviously in a sorry state, being well covered up with blankets. The corporal told the skipper of the

Wyndham that this was an 'urgent hospital case',[13] and the sympathetic skipper quickly unloaded all for Carlisle, after which the stretcher party brought the patient on board, reverently assisted by members of the crew and anyone standing around.

When the launch finally reached the Pier Head at Cobh there were plenty of hands to assist the unfortunate patient ashore. Naturally everyone assumed that he was en route to the military hospital at the Belmont huts, which was above the Holy Ground in Cobh. Maybe the prospect of nearing the 'Holy Ground' was a factor in the subsequent miraculous recovery of the patient, for no sooner had the party reached the top of the Pier Head than the stretcher straps were quickly released and the patient uncovered, jumped to his feet, exposing a collection of military rifles at his feet. Stretcher and blankets were thrown into the tide and the four men made across the pier, each carrying his own quota of rifles. They eventually disappeared from view and were all later posted as deserters. One must assume from the importance the four Munster Fusilier deserters had given to their smuggled rifles, that they were intent on selling them on to the IRA, if not joining up with the Republican Struggle themselves. In addition to the practice of some British soldiers actively giving up their weapons to the IRA, others unwittingly were making their weapons available to Republicans through purely complacent behaviour.

Michael Burke later recalled one such incident where a lapse of individual British security came face to face with local Republican vigilance. The incident happened in early 1919 when two local Volunteers noticed three British soldiers had left their rifles lying carelessly against a wall at the railway station, while they waited for a train. The Volunteers, who were also waiting for the same train, could see that the soldiers were preoccupied with the attentions of some young local women. Watching for the right opportunity, the Volunteers quickly seized the rifles, dropped them into a bread basket which was on the platform and calmly walked out of the station, carrying the basket and the rifles.

Around the latter part of 1917 after which he completed his apprenticeship at Haulbowline, Volunteer Paddy Whelan left Cobh with his family and moved to Belfast. His father had been transferred at the time to another lightship off the Co. Down coast. Michael Leahy had given Paddy permission to retain his .32 revolver and twenty-four rounds of ammunition, and also gave him a note of instruction to the Volunteer leaders in Belfast. Paddy immediately joined C Company in Belfast under the leadership of Roger McCorley, who at the time engrossed his men in tactical training at Cave Hill. During the 1918 general election, C Company acted as body guards for Sinn Féin election speakers. The speakers went by brake from meeting to meeting in the Falls division, and many of the meetings were rowdy. Paddy recalled how most opposition to the Republicans came not from Orange mobs but from mill workers who were staunch supporters of Joseph Devlin, the Nationalist M.P. for West Belfast. At one such meeting held in King Street, Belfast, Paddy was struck on the head by a brick and was rendered unconscious. Such was the level of competition that existed between nationalists and Republicans for the West Belfast seat. Paddy worked in Harland and Wolf shipyard at this time and recalled having many arguments with fellow workers over the then conscription debate that was sweeping the country. He also visited Michael Leahy and other Volunteers from Cobh who were held in Belfast Prison during different periods throughout 1918, and also bumped into a man there from Bandon named Diarmuid Hurley. Although he didn't yet know it, within a year he would meet again and serve under Hurley in the Midleton Company. Both men would in fact serve together in the future East Cork Flying Column.

Paddy Whelan returned to Cobh in the middle of 1919 with his .32 revolver. He tried for a job at his old workplace at Haulbowline, but the authorities there wouldn't have him. By now, Mick Leahy who had earlier been released from Belfast was O.C. of the 4th Battalion of East Cork, which comprised thirteen companies. Leahy was then employed at Pat Hallinan's motor engineering works at Midleton and got Whelan a job there also. Paddy immediately joined the Midleton Company under his friend Diarmuid Hurley who was then employed at the local distillery. In time, Jack O'Connell from Cobh would also join Leahy and Whelan working at Hallinan's Engineering Works and, within another two years, a number of other Cobh Volunteers would make their way into the ranks of the newly established Flying Column in East-Cork. Before then however, the Cobh Company was to suffer its first fatal casualty, though it would tragically occur by accident. It happened one morning in November 1918, while Volunteer Joe Reid of 43 Harbour Row was cleaning his revolver. Upon hearing a loud rush of feet coming up the stairs, Joe jumped off the chair believing it to be a British raiding party, and while scouring to hide the weapon, accidentally fired it. A single fatal shot entered the young man's stomach. What made the event all the more tragic was that the person who ran up the stairs and subsequently made the unfortunate discovery was merely his brother. Joe, aged eighteen, died two days later of his wound in hospital.

By mid-1919, 'A' or the Cobh Company as it was better known, had acquired such substantial quantities of weapons that Mick Leahy decided it was time to distribute them to other lesser armed companies in the battalion area. Leahy, who was working to a bigger plan with his colleagues on the Brigade staff, had arranged with Martin Corry and the

Knockraha Company to take possession of the weapons and store them before they could be distributed. Arrangements were made between the Cobh Volunteers and Corry's men to move the weapons by boat from the back of the Great Island to a point near Barry's Court at the south of Carrigtwohill. The idea was to avoid using the main roads which might draw the attention of British patrols around Belvelly Bridge and the Fota Road. This first large movement of weapons, proved successful and would be repeated a number of times again, as the Cobh volunteers continued to raid for additional supplies of weapons over the next two and a half years.

While normally a good deal of planning and reconnaissance work would take place before a raid was carried out for weapons, whether it would be on a private house or on a military patrol or installation, there were other occasions when Volunteers might have had to use their own initiative, and strike if they felt the opportunity presented itself and they felt equal to the task. The case of the two volunteers swiping the rifles from under the noses of the three British Squaddies at the railway station and making off with them in a bread basket was a perfect case in point. Now two months later, another opportunity presented itself when a number of volunteers who were passing by the 'Bench' near Harbour Row, noticed a couple of soldiers descending down East Hill from their Barracks at Belmont. The three Volunteers stayed chatting by the roadside trying to look as inconspicuous as possible. When the two soldiers, with their rifles slung over their shoulders, drew up in line with the Volunteers, they were immediately pounced upon and taken by complete surprise. The unfortunate victims wisely offered no resistance, allowing the Volunteers to scatter up through Harbour View hill with their bounty. The fact that the Volunteers were able to unleash a plan with such split-second timing, knowing which direction to flee and dump the captured weapons without them being found later, shows what support existed in the surrounding streets for the Republican cause at that time. The boldness of the snatch on a busy street in broad daylight, and the fact that Daithí O'Brien lived just a few hundred yards away from where it took place at Roches Row, might also give us a hint of his involvement in it.

On 4 July, Volunteers from Cobh and Midleton were brought together for a big operation involving senior Brigade officers. It was now becoming clear why the battalion O.C. was earlier keen to assist in the arming of other company areas outside of Cobh. The target was the British military Aerodrome at Ballyquirke near the village of Killeagh in East-Cork. Mick Leahy had more than thirty men mobilised and in place around the military installation before the proposed attack, with the intention of disarming the guard and taking all the weapons from the facility. He had earlier carried out a good deal of reconnaissance of the area and knew that a strong guard of the Wiltshire Regiment were quartered there. He had also received the backing from Brigade Headquarters for additional weapons and men to support the proposed raid. The Cobh and Midleton men had arrived by bike and on foot in pairs so as not to arouse suspicion, as had others from the City. These volunteers were all in their designated positions and waiting to move by nightfall but could not proceed until the Brigade personnel arrived by car. The car, it was proposed, would be used to ferry the captured weapons back to Cork. By midnight there was still no sign of the Brigade Staff car arriving and some hours later at the approach of daylight, Mick Leahy had to call the operation off.

The next day, he learned that the Cork men under the charge of Terrence McSwiney had taken a wrong turn on some by-road and ended up miles away from their intended target. Florrie O'Donoghue the then Brigade Adjutant, later wrote how he accompanied McSwiney and Jim Grey the driver with twelve rifles that night. He recalled how Grey had earlier borrowed the car which broke down more than once along the way. He also said Grey, who would come to live in Cobh some years later, insisted on driving without lights, which led to them getting lost in the by-roads and boreens of East Cork. MacSwiney was said to be gutted by the blunder, as it was later said it was the closest he would ever come to seeing direct military action against the British. Mick Leahy however, had not given up on mounting a raid on the Ballyquirke Aerodrome, and by 11 November, he had the complex surrounded with Volunteers from the Cobh and Midleton companies once more. The Cobh men had earlier left their homes in pairs on bicycles, some with extra rifles to supplement the Midleton volunteers who only had a couple of shot guns and revolv-

Portrait of a young Seamus Fitzgerald, probably while Chairman of Cobh UDC around 1920.

ers between them. When they arrived at Ballyquirke, they were met by a very dense fog, which caused some disorientation amongst those carrying the extra weapons. Apparently those who were waiting to be armed were lying in wait in one field while unbeknownst to them, those with the additional weapons under the charge of Daithí O'Brien, were in the next one, also waiting. Other battalion officers and men were strategically spread out and positioned in a four mile radius of the aerodrome. James Ahern was in charge of a section at Mogeely, while Seamus Fitzgerald was in charge at Killeagh bridge.

All the phone lines passing over the bridge were cut, thus isolating Killeagh, Youghal and everywhere east of Killeagh from Cork City and other towns to the west. This time the attack was timed for 9.00pm. An hour or so earlier, some of the Republican scouts near Killeagh under the charge of Seamus Fitzgerald, had intercepted and captured an unarmed soldier who was returning to Ballyquirke from Killeagh with the post for the camp. Fitzgerald, who was accompanied by Diarmud Hurley of Midleton and Maurice Moore and Paddy O'Sullivan of Cobh, ordered the prisoner to be taken to Mick Leahy, so he could be questioned about the layout of the garrison, and to show them through the maze of barbed wire at the camp entrance. Despite the threat of receiving personal harm for not helping, the soldier refused to co-operate.

Leahy then issued an order for the soldier to be taken back and held in custody while the attack proceeded. By 10.00pm, and despite the poor conditions, the commander had made his mind up to proceed with the attack, but before he or any of the others could make another move, the whole camp lit up. Floodlights flashed all over the barbed wire fence with the place been illuminated generally. Leahy immediately concluded that the British had either heard them, or seen something suspicious and knew there was something afoot, especially as their courier with the post was long overdue from Killeagh. He reluctantly had to abandon the operation once again.

One day, a month previously in October, while returning from a hurling match in Cork, Daithí O'Brien with four other Volunteers, noticed three armed soldiers boarding the train for Cobh. Those accompanying O'Brien were Jack O'Connell, Tom O'Shea, Jack Stack and Eddie Stack. Before boarding, O'Brien called his men together to formulate a quick plan of action to retrieve the soldier's rifles. The Republicans made a point of sitting in the same carriage as the three soldiers and soon struck up a friendly conversation with them. To give some credibility to the ruse, they even joined in the chorus of singing some popular army songs. Then just as the train slowed down before pulling into Carrigaloe station, the second last stop before Cobh, O'Brien gave a pre-arranged signal before all five volunteers pounced and took the rifles from the soldiers. After leaving the

Tommies a little bruised and stunned, the Republicans then left the train at Carrigaloe and boldly made their escape over the hill before making towards Newtown.

6. Serving Notice on the RIC

In the same month of October, a Brigade meeting heard a proposal to attack all RIC Barracks in the Brigade area simultaneously. In his later witness statement to the Bureau of Military History, Mick Leahy stated that he had first made the proposal and produced a clear plan to the Brigade of how it could be carried out. In any event, the Brigade staff was taken with the idea and agreed to develop plans to carry it out, pending approval from GHQ in Dublin. Tomas McCurtain, the Brigade O.C. travelled to Dublin to put the plan to the leadership, but in the meantime had changed it to include that every RIC barracks in the Country would be attacked on the same night. GHQ naturally dismissed the plan for a variety of reasons, but agreed that since the Cork 1st Brigade was the best organised in the country, it should proceed to further plans to attack all police barracks in its own area. By December, plans were well under way to attack three barracks in the Brigade area. Those selected were Ballygarvan, Kilmurry and Carrigtwohill Barracks, involving the 2nd, 4th and 7th Battalions.

The arms and men of the adjoining battalions were to be pooled together for the simultaneous operations. Then on the eve of the operations, word came through from GHQ in Dublin countermanding them. MacCurtain quickly learned that Mick Collins had vetoed the Cork attacks because he felt they would clash with a proposed plan to assassinate Lord French in the capital at the proposed time and would dilute that operations' propaganda value. The brigade was thus forced to put back the date of the operations and a new date of 3 January 1920 was set to carry them out. This delay did not suit every area, and by December 1919 there were signs that some RIC Barracks in the 4th Battalion area of East Cork were being fortified with protective steel shutters over their windows and doors. This led Mick Leahy to believe that someone might have been careless and engaged in loose talk.

In Ballygarvan, there was no active Volunteer organisation, but it was within six miles distance of the City, so the task of attacking it was given to the 2nd Battalion on the Southside. It was chosen as a suitable target because the police presence was felt to be less alert there. Two weeks before the date of the proposed attack however, the officer commanding the 2nd Battalion, Sean O'Sullivan, expressed doubts about the plan and said that after inspecting the area with his officers, they felt the barracks couldn't be taken with the arms available to them. The brigade sent its Adjutant Florrie O'Donoghue to investigate the problem. He found that O'Sullivan had lost his nerve for the fight and was overly concerned with possible casualties of his own men. O'Donoghue also found that O'Sullivan's junior officers had taken the least line of resistance in agreeing with him. O'Sullivan was allowed to resign. By then however, it was too late to make alternative arrangements, so the Ballygarvan attack had to be called off. The Kilmurry attack went ahead as planned, but the RIC defences there proved stronger than the Volunteers had anticipated, forcing them to eventually disengage without the capture of any weapons. Brigade staff learned a valuable lesson that night, leading them to play a more active role in future operations of this size.

Meanwhile, in the 4th Battalion area, Mick Leahy and his officers needed no such assistance or encouragement from the Brigade, as they carefully moved in to capture Irelands first RIC Barracks since Thomas Ashe took Ashbourne in 1916. In the weeks leading up to the attack, Mick Leahy called a meeting of the Cobh Company officers at his home at Ballywilliam. Those present were, Daithí O'Brien, Ned and Jack Stack, Tom O'Shea, Jack O'Connell and Mick Burke. Leahy gave them an idea of the general plan and informed each of what their respective responsibilities would be on the night. Daithí O'Brien was told to select forty of the most suitable men from the company for the pending operation but not to give them prior knowledge of what was planned. O'Brien sought the assistance of Mick Burke with this selection process. At least a dozen of those selected would be used in the felling of trees to block access roads between Cobh and Carrigtwohill on the night. Leahy had also instructed Diarmud Hurley of the Midleton Company to ready his men and to have the Midleton road to Carrigtwohill blocked also before the attack began. He also gave similar instructions to Martin Corry of the Knockraha Company to make plans ready for his side.

A wooden chest had earlier been dug up at a field near Leahy's home, and the lever action rifles that earlier had been taken in the O'Keeffe gunsmiths raid two years earlier, were taken to the home of Joe Collins on the Tay Road to be cleaned and stored over a trapdoor in the ceiling. On the evening of the attack, most of the Volunteers were instructed to make their way in pairs to their selected posts on bicycles. Jack Higgins was also selected as a dispatch rider for the operation. Earlier, Jack O'Connell had commandeered a van in Cobh. This was used to ferry himself, Mick Leahy, Tom O'Shea, James Ahern, Maurice and John Moore to the outskirts of Carrigtwohill. Earlier that day at noon, Daithí O'Brien called to the workplace of Mick Burke at the Kings Square Co-op. He informed

Burke that there was a hitch in connection with the van to transport the weapons. Neither man knew that O'Connell had separate plans to commandeer a van of his own. He said the only Volunteer in their group who could drive, refused to do so, as the van selected to be commandeered, was the property of a friend of his.

Burke knew another driver however, who although was not a Volunteer, was a sympathiser. The man agreed to do a job for Burke that evening, but was not told what it would entail. Later, the driver was taken to the safe house of Miss Hawes at Kings Square. The van to be commandeered was also parked in the same square. Daithí O'Brien was already waiting for Burke and his driver at the Hawes' home. He told the man what was expected of him that night, and found the driver was delighted to be chosen for such a task. The man was then given his tea and not allowed out of their sight until the designated time to move. After starting up the van, the three proceeded to Collins on the Tay Road, where they loaded up the rifles and equipment, before striking off for Carrigtwohill. On their way out along the Fota Road, they noticed some of their colleagues working discretely cutting trees. When they reached the rendezvous point for the Cobh Volunteers, on the outskirts of the village, all the weapons, grenades and ammunition was distributed before everyone got ready to take up their positions.

The Midleton Volunteers were by now assembled and waiting at the village schoolhouse under the command of Diarmud Hurley, while the Knockraha men were felling the last trees which were to complete the blocking off of the village. The telephone lines to the village were also cut, leaving the RIC barracks completely isolated. Mick Leahy, then instructed Mick Burke to select a man and go to the schoolhouse to collect two others of the Midleton Company armed with revolvers. All four men were to then go out onto the main street and, when the first firing of shots by the main firing party began, they were to shoot any RIC who might be on the street when the attack on the barracks opened. It appeared the RIC had become suspicious that something was afoot with the amount of strangers passing through on bicycles all evening. Despite this, it didn't appear to strike them however, that their own barracks would very shortly be the focus of everyone's attention. Some of the policemen were out on the street when Mick Burke and his companion were making their way up towards the schoolhouse. Suddenly they heard some noise and someone running down the street towards them. As they readied their revolvers, they were surprised to discover the fleeing man was one of their own colleagues, John Moore.

Moore, who would later prove crucial to the success of the pending operation, had naively made his way up to the police barracks to reconnoitre and judge the thickness of its walls. Before he could reach the barracks however, he was pounced upon and arrested by two RIC officers. The wiry and spirited Moore, who fortunately happened to be wearing an overcoat which was loose and oversized, managed to wriggle his way free, leaving it in the hands of two officers before fleeing. Burke immediately recognised the importance of Moore's escape and was more than relieved when he discovered the escapee had kept the necessary sticks of gelignite for the attack, in his jacket pockets which he still wore. Burke's other companion wanted to proceed after the RIC men to shoot them but Burke, realising the importance of maintaining the element of surprise, would have none of it and ordered the man to put his revolver away. Fortunately for everyone concerned, the RIC men retreated back to their barracks. When Burke and his colleague reached the Midleton men at the schoolhouse, they relayed Mick Leahy's instructions for them to proceed to the hayrick at the rear of the barracks. Leahy had earlier placed six men with rifles upstairs in Catherine Murphy's shop directly across the road from the front of the barracks. He himself took up a position with Tom O'Shea, Paddy O'Sullivan and six other rifle men with grenades in a hayshed at the rear of the barracks. Diarmuid Hurley, Joseph Ahern and a number of others from the Midleton Company joined up with Leahy's group with rifles and revolvers. Daithí O'Brien, Jack O'Connell, Maurice Moore and some others were positioned with rifles and shotguns behind a wall to the rear of the barracks also.

Paddy Whelan, who although still resided in Cobh on the weekends, was now a member of the Midleton Company. He had earlier been instructed by Hurley, to go with five others and detain every civilian on the street who tried to leave the village. As things would transpire, they would only have to detain three people on the night that willingly cooperated with their requests. Earlier however, before the attack commenced and before the RIC realised the seriousness of the situation, Whelan observed two RIC men pounce on the Cobh dispatch rider Jack Higgins as he passed through the street. As Higgins was being grabbed, he managed to bring his bike to the ground, thus allowing him the opportunity to escape from the clutches of the policemen and make off on foot. It was obvious that these were the same two officers who shortly afterwards would try to take John Moore prisoner. Shortly before midnight when everyone was in place, Leahy gave the order for the attack to commence. The RIC responded to the heavy and constant volleys of rifle fire by sending up Verey lights and returning fire on the Republican positions. Paddy Whelan later recalled the peace of that night being rudely disturbed by outbursts of rifle and revolver fire on the other side of the village. The attack was on, and he remembered for the first half hour feeling very on edge, 'There we were, listening to the continuous rifle fire, with no knowledge of how the attack was progressing. After the first half hour, I remember being satisfied that all was well; the firing was steady and continuous, and there was no sign of retreat. I began to feel happy and confident of success.'

Meanwhile, Mick Burke and the other three men with him felt there was no further point in waiting on the street as it was clear that all the RIC were in their barracks fighting it out. They decided to join their colleagues where the action was. They were then guided by a local man to an area near the rear of the barracks. Then as they tried to climb over an iron gate, they were fired on from the windows of the barracks. To make matters even worse, some of the Volunteers in the hayshed mistook them for escaping RIC and fired on them also. The men then managed to get to a safe position behind some pillars and slowly made it to the hayshed safely. By now, Daithí O'Brien, Jack O'Connell and their group behind the rear wall, were concentrating their fire on the loopholes in the steel shutters to try and prevent the occupants from sending up further verey lights. For some strange reason, the RIC never returned fire on Murphy's shop at the front of the barracks, possibly because they rightly concluded the main threat was coming from the rear. By 3.00am, it became clear to Mick Leahy that they couldn't penetrate the steel shutters and that the RIC would hold out for as long as it took. He decided there was no further point in wasting their much coveted ammunition against impregnable defences. The Republican leader then decided it was time to bring out the ace in his pack. Situated at the side of the barracks gable wall was a shed. Leahy instructed a select number of men to keep firing the occasional shot in the direction of the barracks to give covering fire to John Moore who would go into the shed and place an explosive charge in the gable.

Moore and a couple of other Volunteers dug out a number of carefully selected small holes, each big enough to take a stick of gelignite. After inserting the gelignite and setting the charge, the men then rejoined their comrades before they all took cover. After the explosion, the perfect breach was left in the gable, allowing two men at a time to enter into the barrack day-room. Leahy initially wanted to place some burning straw in the breach to smoke out the occupants, but later changed his mind because of the sergeant's wife and child in the building. A white flag of surrender was by now being waved from an upstairs window on the front of the barracks. Although the Volunteers over at Murphy's shop could see the flag of surrender and duly ceased firing, the others at the rear and the side of the barracks, had yet no idea of the intentions of those inside. These men continued with light fire on the building while it was decided Diarmuid Hurley, Joseph Ahern and Mick Leahy, would lead a small party through the breach and open up the front doors to allow the others through.

Before entering, Leahy instructed the others that they should cease firing once they heard him give the signal through a whistle blast. Once they were past the day-room, the men shouted an order up the stairs to surrender. When Leahy saw Mrs Casey on the top of the stairs with a baby in her arms and her husband Sergeant Casey close behind, he blew the whistle for the others to cease firing. He then told the woman to come down and that no harm would come to her and the baby. He ordered her husband to remain where he was with his hands in the air. The sergeant did as he was told. Mrs Casey and her baby were then escorted to the home of some friends in the village. Leahy then shouted for the other police officers to come out and join their sergeant. The front door of the barracks was by now opened up and other volunteers began piling through. When he had come through the hole in the breach, Jack O'Connell was faced with eight or nine RIC men descending the stairs with their hands in the air. Mick Burke, who came through the front door moments later, saw all the policemen lined up against the day-room wall with the hands in the air. Leahy then instructed Burke to go back to the outskirts of the village and collect the commandeered van and its driver.

When they arrived, the van was loaded up with all the police carbines, revolvers and a quantity of shotguns previously taken by the police in raids, plus grenades and ammunition. Joe Ahern and Tadhg Manley took the van and its contents to Manley's home at Tubbereenmire about four miles from Carrigtwohill. When he had earlier heard the explosion go off in the distance, Paddy Whelan knew by the silence which swiftly followed, that the attack must have ended in success. He ordered one of the men with him to take over as he was going to the barracks. The first two people he met when he entered the barracks, was Paddy O'Sullivan and Maurice Moore. He knew the lads well after going to St Joseph's boy's school with them some years earlier. All three would later join the 4th Battalion Flying Column. Whelan would also later see his two comrades lose their lives to British firing squads, after being captured at Clonmult. O'Sullivan had two half crowns in his hand and while showing them to Whelan, asked 'what would you do with them, Paddy?' To which Whelan replied, 'The same as you're going to do, Paddy'.[14]

After all the RIC were handcuffed and taken out onto the street, they were then marched to an area outside of the village and left there. When all the weapons, ammunition and documents were taken from the barracks, Mick Leahy lined up his men outside. He then congratulated them on a job well done, and after all sang a verse of the National Anthem, to which must have been a certain source of amusement to the local villagers, they were all dismissed. Before that, Mick Burke was again instructed to go to the end of the village to make sure all the outlying units had been given the order to stand down and disperse. When he arrived back to the area of the barracks, he found that all the others had already dispersed. He was now minus his previous mode of transport and so took an RIC bicycle from the barracks before peddling off for Cobh.

Michael Leahy and his battalion of Volunteers must have felt very proud men when they left Carrigtwohill village on the morning of 3 January. Perhaps they didn't yet realise it, but their military success was to set a new standard to follow for other Volunteer units throughout the country. Carrigtwohill would be the first of 492 RIC barracks to be abandoned by October 1920. The propaganda bonus from the capture was also immeasurably beneficial for the Republican Movement, with a *Cork Examiner* report in the days that followed, quoting the Barrack RIC Sergeant as saying hundreds of armed men swarmed the barracks, forcing them to surrender. In fact, the overall figure of those who participated in every facet of the operation was a little over fifty, while the actual number of men who physically fired on the barracks was no more than twenty-seven at any one time of the operation. For the British, the attack bore out their worst nightmare.

Since 1913, a radical element of the Irish Volunteers led by the secret IRB had been plotting an insurrection against the Crown. 1916 saw those outside of Dublin deprived of that opportunity by a series of blunders and uncontrollable circumstances. The British subsequently became aware that Cork was spoiling for the expected fight. They also knew that Michael Leahy of Cobh was one of those instigators, and was behind the development of the Volunteer Movement through out East Cork before and since his release from internment. Now, as they viewed over the damage to Carrigtwohill barracks, they must have been sick in the pits of their stomachs for knowing they had released Leahy from custody on at least four occasions since 1916. The effectiveness of how he and his men pulled off the capture of the barracks, must also have been very worrying, especially since it was almost noon of the next day before relieving forces arrived in Carrigtwohill. Ironically, most of the military had come from Belmont Military Camp in Cobh. These would be part of the same force that would participate in the round up of Republican suspects in Cobh in the days and weeks which followed the attack. Among many of the Volunteers that would be arrested and brought before an RIC identity parade at West View Barracks, would be Daithí O'Brien, Jack and Ned Stack, James Ahern and Michael Burke. There were of course, dozens of others arrested from the locality, but for some strange reason, the dispirited RIC officers from Carrigtwohill, refused to identify any of them as having participating in the attack. Although the vast majority were later released without charge, O'Brien and the Stack brothers were gaoled under the

DORA act.

The authorities also had their sights on Volunteer James Ahern, who was busy trying to get himself elected to the Town Council. The election was scheduled to take place on 15 January. Although he had no difficulty being elected, having topped the poll of candidates in his ward, Ahern was forced to go on the run almost immediately after his inaugural Council meeting. James Ahern was a seasoned Republican activist, having been around from the very beginning of the Volunteer movement in Cobh. The British were well aware of these facts and were probably sure he had played some role in the Carrigtwohill attack.

In the main, the authorities had a reasonable picture of who the main Republican players in the town were, and now that they were left with egg on their faces, were determined to make life as difficult as they could for the rebels.

7. Sinn Féin: The Politics of Revolution

Sinn Féin as a Party became involved in the political system almost by chance, with the participation of a few high profile individuals contesting Westminster by-elections in 1917-18. The successes which followed from these contests led many in the Volunteer movement to believe the power of the ballot box was as important to the struggle as the gun. The propaganda value from Republicans winning Westminster seats was also immeasurable in terms of influencing international opinion, particularly in Irish America. With the momentum now with them, and with the threat of conscription turning more and more people towards the politics of Sinn Féin, Republican leaders were laying the groundwork for the next General Election where they were hoping to win a majority of Westminster seats in Ireland. The plan was for all successful Republican candidates to boycott the Westminster parliament and instead sit in an alternative assembly in Dublin.

After the election was held in December 1918, Sinn Féin had won 73 of the 105 seats, and duly pledged to set up its own independent parliament in Dublin the following month. All successfully elected MPs, Republican, Nationalist, Unionist and others were invited along to attend the new Parliament at the Mansion House on 21 January. Only Sinn Féin members showed up however, to establish the new Dáil Éireann and only then, the twenty-seven members who were not in jail or on the run. The people of Cobh played their part in the election of the Republican candidate for their part of East Cork, through David Kent, brother of martyred Thomas, who was executed in 1916. Up to then, there was no sign of anyone of significance from the Cobh area displaying much aptitude for politics, with the local military men appearing content that theirs was the best organised company in the 4th Battalion area. But an earlier incident caused by careless behaviour on the part of Seamus Fitzgerald, meant that he inadvertently ended up on the election trail and found himself bitten by the political bug.

One day while at work at the Naval Dockyard, Fitzgerald was tipped off that the police had earlier found ammunition at his home during a raid. This led the Republican officer to flee the town and head to Dublin where he met up with Liam Cullen who put him up for a while. He immediately reported to Dick Mulcahy who put him in contact with James O'Mara the Sinn Féin Director of Elections. O'Mara sent the Cobh man north to Antrim and Down to assist in the election campaigns there. A year earlier, Fitzgerald had worked on the successful by-election of William T. Cosgrave in Kilkenny, and although De Valera had won a similar by-election in Clare a month earlier, it was the elections of December 1918 that really had an historic sense about it and grabbed the nation's imagination. Coincidentally, De Valera was in the frame again on this occasion as he's was the Sinn Féin name on the ballot paper for the West Belfast constituency while he waited in prison. West Belfast however, would be one of a few seats that would remain in the hands of Redmond's Nationalist Party in the guise of Joe Devlin. It would be 1983, before Sinn Féin would rest control of West Belfast, when the Party President Gerry Adams would take it from SDLP founder Gerry Fitt; Fitt would later be made a British Lord. Seamus Fitzgerald spent a week speaking at election meetings promoting the Republican candidates.

He was slowly coming around to discovering that he had a gift for oratory and was starting to like it. At one mixed indoor meeting in Ballycastle, he had to flee for his life before being assisted by Eamon Donnelly out of the town. He then finished up in Hollywood, County Down as election agent for Joe Robinson who was then in jail in Scotland. He wasn't at all fazed or deterred that Craigavon himself was the opposing candidate. While all this campaigning was in progress, Fitzgerald had successfully got word back to the Admiralty in Cobh, convincing them that he was away recuperating from an illness, and was granted sick leave from his job at Haulbowline.

Local election leaflet form 1920.

8. Taking the Queen Out of Cove

In the successful aftermath of the General Election, Seamus Fitzgerald saw the potential to develop Cobh politically. He was present at the opening session of Dáil Éireann on 21 January and was beginning to see the bigger long-term picture. Those in positions of leadership were already eyeing up the next elections which were less than a year away. In the meantime, the Volunteer Movement pledged allegiance to Dáil Éireann and the Volunteer Army from then forward became known as the Irish Republican Army (IRA). Mick Leahy, Seamus Fitzgerald and other officers spent most of the late summer travelling through out East Cork, swearing each and every Volunteer to make an oath of allegiance to the new Dáil. Instructions from the Brigade to all areas were for Volunteers to contest the Municipal and Urban Elections which were due to fall in January 1920.

In Cobh, the call was answered with five Sinn Féin and two Republican Labour candidates being elected. As only thirteen of fifteen seats to the Council were returned, the Republicans had clear control of Town Hall. Those carrying the Republican banner in Town Hall were; Seamus Fitzgerald, James Ahern, Michael Hennessy, Alexander Telfer, Charles Bailey, Maurice Downey and Dan Ronayne. Fitzgerald was immediately elected as the new Town Chairman. In his departing speech, outgoing chairman and Labour member Sean Moynihan expressed his hope to see Ireland a free and prosperous nation by the time Fitzgerald had finished his term. A month later, the two vacant seats on the Council were filled when John McCarthy of Sinn Féin and John Connolly of the Labour Party were co-opted, thus using the Sinn Féin /Labour alliance to its maximum benefit. Seamus Fitzgerald automatically became a member of the Harbour Board through his position as Chairman of the Council. He was also elected to the Cork Rural District Council and as the elected Chairman of that body was also elected to the County Council and was unable to fulfil his duties with the latter, he transferred the representation to Fitzgerald.

In an interview with the late Mrs Geraldine Norris (née Hawes) in 1988, she told this author that she was present at the Town Hall for the inaugural meeting of the Sinn Féin members in 1920. As a young girl with Cumann ná gCailiní, Geraldine went along to the meeting at the Town Hall with her older sister Lily who was a senior member of the local Cumann na mBan. The Town Hall chamber, overlooking Scott's Square(now Roger Casement Square) was full of observers and well-wishers hoping to get a glance of the Republicans in action. Geraldine recalled how the atmosphere of the chamber changed once Seamus Fitzgerald rose to speak. He had a natural gift with words and when he spoke, everyone listened, 'There was no need for microphones or modern speaker systems for Jim Fitz, he was a natural',[15] she said. Geraldine and her friends regularly attended Council meetings just to hear Seamus Fitzgerald and other Republican councillors speak.

For some, it was the only way they would see or hear official Ireland actually confront British rule in Ireland. For others, particularly Cumann na mBan members who assisted in getting their Sinn Féin colleagues elected, and having a stake in the new system, they went to the council meetings to support and encourage their political investments. But the strong political position that Sinn Féin now found itself, didn't happen by accident and a lot of hard work and toil was laid with the foundation that would help create that success. The British too would play their part in helping the growth of Sinn Féin with a series of political blunders. Throughout 1917 and 1918 several events contributed to the upsurge in the popularity of Sinn Féin.

There was the German Plot, the threat of partition, conscription, and probably most of all, the death of hunger striker Thomas Ashe in Mountjoy after a particular cruel attempt to force feed him. The tragic case of Volunteer Ashe, who had taken part in the Easter Rising, was only one among many, as Irish prisoners at this stage of the struggle were more often than not subjected to brutal treatment in British jails. Throughout this period Sinn Féin was hard at work organising public meetings to highlight the plight of the Republican prisoners in England and at home.

Their hard work was to pay off later in the elections that would follow.

The biggest gaffe the British Government made was no doubt the passing of the Conscription Act in April 1918. The predictable result was that the whole of Nationalist and Republican Ireland united against the measure, thus strengthening Sinn Féin - the only party that had taken a clear and unambiguous stance on the issue - even further. In an effort to undo the damage, the British Prime Minister Lloyd George really put his foot in it when he offered, as a sop to the Irish people, a Home Rule Bill based on the partition principle, thus adding insult to injury. Even the pre-Sinn Féin UDC in Cobh protested, though it is a matter of doubt whether the motion opposing conscription was really an expression of opposition to the Crown, or rather nurtured by a wish to stay out of the war. In any case the motion was carried, stating that,

the Queenstown Urban District Council protests in the strongest possible manner against any attempt on the part of the British government to impose compulsory military service upon the men of Ireland (…); that we warn the government and parliament for the disastrous consequences which assuredly will ensue if any effort is made to enforce it in the country.

With the whole of nationalist Ireland, and even the otherwise reactionary Catholic Church, united in the anti-conscription campaign, the British Government decided to try a different tactic. Using the pretext that Sinn Féin was conspiring with Germany, the British began making wholesale arrests, rounding up the leaders of the Volunteers, Sinn Féin and other nationalist organisations. Sinn Féin was declared illegal. But also the German Plot backfired on the British government, as the 'release the prisoners' cry, was certain to mobilise mass support especially in the political climate of the time.

When in November 1918, the war finally ended and a General Election was called for the following month, Sinn Féin was presented with an opportunity to translate its public support into political reality. Almost 2 million voters were on the register for the December election, all males over the age of twenty-one and for the first time also women over thirty years old. Sinn Féin stood on the policy of not attending the British House of Commons, to which Ireland had to elect 105 members, and instead an assembly was set up in January in Dublin, Dáil Éireann. On 22 December 1918 at 3p.m. a meeting was held in Scott's Square. It had been convened by the Chairman of the UDC, Stephen Moynihan, for the purpose of passing a resolution 'in common with the rest of the country', inviting President Wilson to Ireland.

The Peace Conference in the aftermath of the First World War was to begin in Paris in 1919, and the Irish hoped that their country would get an official recognition of its independent status there. Ireland was mainly counting on the support of the American President, who had stated that he was in favour of the rights of small nations. It was hoped that he would use his influence to get Britain to concede to Irish demands and recognise Irish independence. A big crowd had gathered in the square in front of the Town Hall on that day, and from the Town Hall itself a large American Flag was displayed. Several councillors were present, as was Seamus Fitzgerald the president of the local Sinn Féin party and Bishop Browne. In his speech, Browne extended an invitation to the America President, urging him not to overlook the Irish nation on the Paris Peace Conference when 'reviewing the oppressed condition of small subject nationalities.' [16] Another point made by the Bishop was that,

> If Mr Wilson succeeds in applying to Ireland at the Peace Conference the principles of government as enunciated in his 'Fourteen Points' and utterance, he will have done a greater service to the British Empire than generations of her own statesmen have done, for a contented, prosperous and peaceful Ireland will be a larger compensation to the British Empire for her vast expenditure of life and treasure in this hideous war than the seizure of the German fleet or the levy of hundreds of millions of money on the Central European states to replenish her much depleted treasury.

Stephen Moynihan, the UDC Chairman, also welcomed the American President to Ireland on behalf of Cobh and the Great Island, arguing that, 'strong nations shall not be free to wrong weak nations and make them subject to their purposes and interest.' The Chairman's resolution was passed amidst loud cheers for the President.

However, at the subsequent Peace Conference Wilson let Ireland down with a bang. Britain insisted that Ireland should only be considered an internal matter, and Wilson, despite pressure from the Irish community in America, had no intention of adding a major break with the British Government to his other international troubles in the aftermath of the war. Three weeks later another public meeting was held in Cobh, this time to protest at the imprisonment without trial of Irish political prisoners following the German Plot round-ups. In the event, the main speaker himself was arrested a few minutes prior to the meeting.

Sean O'Muirthile, the man who had played a key role in organising the IRB and after Frongoch was charged under the Defence of the Realm Act, which was very useful to the British when dealing with Irish unruliness. The *Cork Examiner* carried a report on the incident the following day, 6 January,

Considerable excitement was occasioned in Queenstown yesterday when a few minutes prior to the holding of the meeting Sean O'Muirthile, who was advertised as the principal speaker, was arrested by Head Constable O'Beirn and a force of half a dozen policemen. He was just in the centre of Scott's Square, where the meeting was announced to be held, and immediately taken to the police station which was a little up the hill in the same locality. Very quickly a large crowd collected and while Mr O'Muirthile was being escorted to the lock-up there were repeated shouts from those present and some stones were thrown, but no one was injured. For a time the situation looked ugly as the police drew batons, but on appeal from Mr O'Muirthile the crowd desisted from further stone-throwing. Meantime the Cove band had gone to the other end of the town and when they returned the meeting was proceeded with. It was very large and enthusiastic and included amongst the interested listeners were a good many American naval men … Mr James Fitzgerald, President of the Cove Sinn Féin club, who presided, said the best answer they could make to the unwarranted occurrence that had just taken place was that they proceed as quietly as possible with their meeting.

Several letters were read out at the meeting, one of them from Dr. Browne, the Bishop of Cloyne. In it he apologised for not being able to attend. The meeting was also attended by several other prominent speakers such as Barrister Healy and Michael Hennessy of Sinn Féin. Hennessy pointed out that the Irish had the same right to object to the British flag flying over Dublin as Lloyd George had to the German flag flying over London. Healy seconded the motion, adding that although his political ideas were not, 'on all fours', with those who had organised the meeting, he nonetheless had much pleasure in seconding the motion. The party to which he belonged has stepped aside to give the younger blood of the country a chance and according to the barrister, 'the real reason for the imprisonment of those men was that the government of all subject races, whether British or German, two methods were used, either the whip or the sop, and if you did not take the sop, the whip was used.'[17]

The meeting eventually ended with the singing of the aptly chosen 'The Felons of our Land.' Later that night O'Muirthile was removed from Cobh to the Bridewell in Cork, only to be conveyed to Dublin the next day where he was charged under the DORA. On the morning of the 5 January 1919, another successful meeting was held at Ballymore, just outside the town. Also here, Seamus Fitzgerald presided. On the proposal of Michael Hennessy a resolution demanding the release of Irish political prisoners was passed with acclamation. Both Fitzgerald and Hennessy were familiarising themselves with public speaking and were preparing for the opportunity to put their point across on the official political stage, when they would elected to the Urban District Council a year later.

On the 21 January 1919 Dáil Éireann held its first session in Dublin. All elected representatives of Irish constituencies were invited to attend the meeting in the Mansion House, but only Sinn Féin members turned up. There were also many observers present at the historic event, both domestic and foreign. Looking down on the proceeding from the Mansion House's balcony above the large oval room, Seamus Fitzgerald could feel an idea growing in his head. He began to ponder about the possibilities of building a real political base in his home town of Cobh. He was mindful of the local government elections being only a year away and was confident that if they got the right candidates in place, Sinn Féin could take control of the Town Council. There can be little doubt that in the back of his mind during this time, he was contemplating a personal mission that would oversee the change in status of his town in the eyes of his country and the world, by abolishing its unionist name.

For the greater part of 1919, Fitzgerald directed most of his energy into political building for Sinn Féin, while leaving others to dominate and take the initiative where Volunteer activities were concerned. While Fitzgerald was a little ahead of his time in terms of seeing the bigger picture and understanding the importance of having a political mandate to drive the overall struggle, few of his colleagues in the Volunteer movement in Cobh shared his enthusiasm for politics. Even his long-time friend and commanding officer Michael Leahy didn't understand all the fuss about politics. He had his own sense of right and wrong which was based on simple historical fact. The British had no right to rule Ireland full stop. He and his comrades didn't need a political mandate to confront them with force of arms in 1916, and they didn't need it now, although it was a comfortable moral bonus when it was there. While other Cobh officers like Daithí O'Brien, Mick Burke, the O'Connell brothers, the Stack brothers, the Ahern brothers and others believed politics was a distraction from the their main objective. None however, objected to the boost in popular support that the Sinn Féin electoral mandate brought to the overall struggle.

Although women were not encouraged to participate directly in elections by putting themselves forward as candidates, there was no shortage of female supporters stepping up to the mark to assist Fitzgerald and his comrades with the local election campaign. Sinn Féin's lot was made a lot easier with the issuing of instructions from the Brigade to its Volunteers to stand for election as Sinn Féin candidates. On 30 January, the new Republican members took their seats on the Town Council and with the two extra co-options a month later, including two Republican labour members; Sinn Féin took control of the town's local government. Perhaps it was down to clever vote management, but after the votes were counted, it emerged the most prominent face of Sinn Féin, Seamus Fitzgerald, had failed to top the poll in his ward. Of the two electoral wards in the town at the time, his colleague Charles Bailey, a publican from Scotts (Casement) Square, headed the poll in one ward, while James Ahern topped the other. Nevertheless, Fitzgerald was duly elected Chairman of the new council at its first meeting.

Among the papers of Seamus Fitzgerald at the City and County Archives, is a contract document dating to 1920 which indicates the Chairman and members of the Council were giving strong consideration to forming a Co-operative Society in the town, with a view to creating local employment. It is not clear if this was general Sinn Féin policy all over the country, or if it was initiated by Seamus Fitzgerald and his colleagues locally. However, it is clear that the co-operative never came into being, whether for a lack of support by a majority of councillors or because of some other reason. On 2 July Seamus Fitzgerald's finest hour arrived when a special council meeting was called to propose a change of name for the town. This was an occasion when the chairman found majority support for a very important resolution. The council itself, didn't debate in any great detail what options of names should replace the now despised one of Queenstown, nor did it feel it should even put it to the local people through a democratic plebiscite, and were probably very mindful that most of the local residents were deprived of expressing their views in 1849 when the name Queenstown was foisted upon them. Sinn Féin however, had debated the issue amongst themselves before it made the move through the local council. Two names the party had considered were 'Port Saint Colman' and 'Port Mannix'. The former, after the patron saint of the local diocese and whose name the local towering cathedral was named after; the latter, as a tribute to the patriot Archbishop of Melbourne of the time who was forbidden from revisiting Ireland to see his elderly mother, because of his outspoken criticisms of British rule in Ireland.

The Sinn Féiners, however, decided against naming the town after someone who was still living, and felt the time was not suitable for making a particular decision believing that in more settled times the citizens could decide on the best name for the future. So on 2 July 1920, when the Republican members of the council moved to have the name Queenstown removed at a special meeting, they proposed in its place the name of 'Cobh' as a temporary measure, or at least that was their intention. Fitzgerald himself had once described the name Cobh, 'as rather undignified' and not really meaning anything. When he moved the motion at the special council meeting that a discussion should follow on the desirability of taking immediate steps to change the name of our town from that gave to it by Queen Victoria of England in 1849, he was supported by Councillors Dan Ronayne and Maurice Downey. He then made the following speech. 'Mindful of the evils that were reined on Ireland during the Queen's occupancy of the English throne, it is considered she was of the biggest tyrants Ireland ever suffered under. The honour of the town that was supposed to have obtained by her landing here was nothing less than an insult and steps should be taken to wipe out that stain.'[18]

The Chairman then mentioned that the town used to be called 'Ard Nevin' but for many reasons thought for the present at least, the name 'Cove' should be adopted until things settled down under the Republican administration. Councillor O'Callaghan was less sure however, and felt people should be consulted before the name was changed. After a long discussion which followed, Councillor Ronayne proposed and Councillor Downey seconded that the name be changed to Cove. Then a resolution in the Chairman's name reading, 'that the name of our town be changed from Queenstown to Cove and respectfully praying our responsible Government to accede to our wishes', was passed with the record showing Cllr O'Callaghan having concerns about the people not being consulted.

Three weeks later at a meeting on the 23 July, the Town Clerk, presumably after taking legal advice, told the members that their action in changing the towns name was slightly irregular. This was of no real concern to the elected members however, who had already sent their approved resolution to the County Council for ratification, and then to the Republican Minister for Local Government, who gave sanction to it. Within a short couple of months the council had adopted a slightly Gaelic version of the new name which read 'Cobh'. On 11 October, the Town Hall received a letter from the LDA requesting a copy of the resolution adopted changing the town name from Queenstown to Cobh and asking for the Council to give authorisation to Mr Fawsitt, Irish Trade Commissioner, New York to publish at the Council's expense, notification of the change of name in shipping and other journals circulating in the USA.

Although it took the townspeople some time to get used to the new name, leaving some a little confused as to how it should be pronounced, for the vast majority it was merely a case of reverting back to the pre-1849 name of Cove in terms of pronunciation. For most though, who were living through some very heightened and hostile times, in terms of their relationship with their British rulers and their representatives, any name other than one that represented loyalty to the British Crown was to be welcomed. There were some dissenting voices however, and it's very likely that these went on public record representing a silent minority of local unionists. A report in the *Cork Examiner* following the Council's decision to change the town's name stated that the council move was criticised by a Mr Scott whose family was responsible for developing many of the fine buildings and streets of Victorian Cobh (Queenstown). Mr Scott was totally opposed to the change of name for reasons of family loyalty to the British Crown. The other person reported as opposing the name change was that of Barrister Healy. It is very likely however, that his opposition to the move stemmed mainly from its legal standing, and the lack of local consultation with the people. Barrister Healy was already on public record as speaking out against British misrule and had defended many high profile Republicans in the past, so it's very unlikely his opposition to the change of the town's name had anything to do with loyalty to Britain.

The New Year started badly for the British in 1920, with morale taking a particular bashing after the capture of Carrigtwohill Barracks by the Volunteers, and with the take over of Cobh Town Hall through the election of Sinn Féin members. Those events, which happened in January, should have served notice on the crown forces of what was yet to come. While Daithí O'Brien and Mick Leahy were each lying low after those events, and with Mick Burke, Jack Stack and Paddy O'Sullivan remaining in custody in Cork Gaol, command of the local company was temporarily in the hands of Eddie Stack, temporary in the sense that he too would soon be engaged in a cat and mouse game with the authorities. This would lead to him holding command of the company on three different (short) periods throughout the year. That began on 5 February when Stack was also picked up and held in custody until May. In his absence, command was handed over to Jack O'Connell. O'Connell was determined to build on the earlier successes and to keep his men active and alert. Local intelligence provided O'Connell with information that suggested a number of British rifles were there for the taking in the Rushbrooke area.

A regular British guard-party comprising of four men and a corporal moved between their camp at Belmont Hutments and Rushbrooke Dockyard where work was progressing on a building extension there. On 27 February, O'Connell and seven others were lying in wait for the return of the British Party for most of that Saturday morning near Bunker Hill, Rushbrooke. Among those with O'Connell were Jerome Collins, Maurice Moore, J. Grayley, Spud Murphy, John Verling, Pad Rafferty and John Higgins. Each was armed with a revolver that had earlier been removed from a dump at the home of Michael Burke at Donelan Terrace.

Jack O'Connell himself lived only around the corner from Burke at number 37 Barrymore Avenue. The new Commanding Officer cleverly predicted that since Burke was locked away in Cork Gaol, moving weapons from and to his home, which was really his sister's house, would attract little attention from the British. Before midday, O'Connell with his disguised and hidden men noticed five members of the Notts' and Derbyshire Regiment round the corner coming towards them. When the patrol got to within reaching distance of the Volunteers, they suddenly found themselves surrounded. With their blackened faces, O'Connell and his men immediately shouted orders to the troops to surrender while simultaneously shepherding them towards a nearby laneway. In the tense confused state they suddenly found themselves, the patrol leader surrendered his weapon to O'Connell. While three of the other nervous soldiers readily followed their Corporal and gave over their rifles, a fifth one panicked and tried to flee the scene. One of O'Connell's men swiftly followed behind, while shouting after him to halt. Upon receiving no positive response from the panic stricken soldier, the pursuing Volunteer fired a shot that immediately brought him to the ground. An overcoat was placed over the dying soldier to keep him warm, while his colleagues were tied up to allow their attackers time to make good their escape.

After gathering up the captured rifles, the Volunteers then made their escape towards Newtown where they were temporarily hidden. Unknown to O'Connell, Mick Burke had been released from Cork Gaol earlier that day, and it was he who later oversaw the collection of the captured rifles before they were properly dumped at Cuskinny that night. Meanwhile, shortly after he received the fatal shot to his throat, Private Newman was found on the side of the road by a passing cyclist who had just left work at the Dockyard. The local man named Griffin reported finding the soldier before he died and said the only words he uttered were that he had been shot. The cyclist immediately found help and got the soldier to hospital, but Private Newman later died that night.

Five days after the Rushbrooke ambush a large party of armed soldiers, accompanied by a number of RIC men and headed by a bugle band, marched from Belmont hutments to the dockyard and surrounded it to prevent escape. A stringent personal search of every worker in the dockyard was carried out, names were taken and the workers were marched individually before an identification parade said to contain at least one of the soldiers who had been disarmed outside the docks on the previous Saturday. However, nothing was found and after searching the workers and the precincts of Rushbrooke dockyard for some three hours, the soldiers had to return to their barracks empty handed. In a follow up statement, Bishop Browne used the words 'hideous', 'awful' and 'dreadful'[19] to describe the attack, and expressed his 'abhorrence' at the taking of the life of an unoffending young man by a gang of desperadoes who acted with the silly idea of possessing themselves of the arms carried by the soldiers.' Yet no matter how 'silly' the idea may have seemed, it had worked.

At a special meeting held on 19 April, the local council announced that the relatives of the deceased soldier, William Newman, would be compensated the sum of £2,000. This was obviously a testing time for Seamus Fitzgerald and his Sinn Féin colleagues on the council and there can be little doubt that they had consulted earlier with their party leadership over the issue of compensation for the soldiers' family. While no one was charged with the killing of Private Newman, the British were not going to sit back and wait for Republicans to launch their next attack. Instead they took the initiative and began a campaign of late night raids on the homes of many prominent Republicans around the town. These raids would set in train a cat and mouse game between the two opposing sides that would last up to the time of the Treaty. Over a period of time, Republicans would develop a system which allowed many of their wanted activists to flee their homes before the raiding parties could reach them. This system was based mainly on a simple flaw in the British strategy, namely their mode of transport. Unfortunately for them, when they decided to launch a late night raid when all others were asleep in their beds, they often did so by giving away the element of surprise by killing the night time silence with the sound of their Crossley Tenders (armoured car) engines.

From their base at Belmont Camp, practically every part of the eastern side of the town could be alerted to the sound of the Crossleys once their engines started. This in time meant for example that once the engines were heard starting up at around 2a.m., Daithí O'Brien would leave his house at Roche's Row which was in clear earshot of Belmont. His sister would also leave the house and knock on the windows of every Republican home along the way. She would then make her way up through Bond Street, still knocking on windows and warning those inside to get out and hide. She would continue into Bishop/Ferry Street and then turn up towards Orelia Terrace, where the last home she would knock up and alert would be that of James Ahern. Other Cumann na mBan girls would simultaneously be giving the same alert warnings from different locations in the town. In a short time these measures began to kick-in well and prevented the British from making headway with the arrest of senior Republican personnel. But not all of the British raids took place at night time, and if it were not for the part played by some sound contacts inside the British security system who regularly kept Republicans one step ahead, the local Volunteer machine would have been virtually neutered in a short space of time.

The volunteers had a number of people in Admiralty Buildings at the Mount which provided them with sometimes, vital intelligence. The two most noteworthy of these been Jack Kilty and Philip O'Neill who both worked as clerks in the Admiralty offices. An even greater asset to the Republican cause was that of Sergeant John Maher, a clerk in the R.I.C. District Inspector's office at Westview Barracks. Maher's regular tip offs were invaluable to the Volunteers, keeping many from seeing the inside of jail and worse. Complacency was to play a part in a set back for the Cobh Volunteers however, after some of its officers neglected to heed the warning which one tip off gave. On 15 March, Republican intelligence received a tip off that a general arrest of all Volunteer officers would be made the following day. Although each officer received personal notification of this, only Seamus Fitzgerald and one other bothered to take the necessary precautions to avoid arrest.

The next day, the British Army and RIC swooped all around the town of Cobh. Among those arrested was Daithí O'Brien the local company O.C., Councillor Michael Hennessy, John Verling of Newtown. J. Carney, Robert McDonnell, Andrew Fowler of the Tay Road, Richard Murphy, Jack O'Connell of Barrymore Avenue and David Quinlan of Dock Terrace in Rushbrooke. One of those lifted, Jack O'Connell later related the circumstances of his arrest. He told of how after the military and RIC swooped on his home, he and the others were brought to Cork Gaol where they were held for some weeks without trial before being served with an internment order and brought with sixty others by British destroyer to Belfast. After some weeks in Belfast gaol, some of the men were put on the cruiser *Dunedin* and brought to Fishguard. From there they were taken handcuffed in pairs to Wormwood Scrubs, outside London. Once there, O'Connell joined in a hunger strike of Republican prisoners that was already in progress. After twelve days into the protest however, he was removed to hospital in London.

A month later, he was released and returned to Cobh with Jack Stack, David Quinlan and Richard Murphy. Meanwhile in April a hunger strike was also in progress in Mountjoy Gaol with the protesting prisoners demanding their unconditional release. All over the country people showed their sympathy with the men by going on strike. Post-offices, banks, schools and railway stations remained closed in protest at the treatment of the Mountjoy prisoners. In Cobh twelve of the 1,000 or so Haulbowline workers decided to go to work anyway, much to the disapproval of the local people. On their return from the naval dockyard on 14 April, the men were awaited at the naval pier by a crowd of some 500 people who hissed and pelted them with stones. In Belfast, a similar hunger-strike led to the release of forty four prisoners from the south and west of the country, among them Cobhman John Verling from Newtown. Although Seamus Fitzgerald had managed to escape earlier raids and arrests, he was still regarded as the most senior public figure of the local Republican movement and one the British dearly wanted to make an example of.

In the early hours 20 March, the Lord Mayor of Cork, Tomás MacCurtain, Commandant of the 1st Cork Brigade, was assassinated at his home in Blackpool by Crown Forces. The following morning, Seamus Fitzgerald received a death notice through the post, threatening him with immediate assassination if any R.I.C. was shot in reprisal for MacCurtain.

Fitzgerald immediately passed the notice on to the Brigade before receiving an order back through the Battalion O.C. that he was to appear openly; that the Brigade intended to shoot a policeman and would offer him suitable protection. The Town Chairman obeyed the order and conducted his normal business in public. No policeman was shot however, not at least immediately, but Fitzgerald took some steps to improve his personal protection. He carried a small arm on his person at all times and continuously slept out. A few days later at noon, an attempt by Crown Forces was made to arrest him from his home at 19 East Beach. Though escaping by a matter of seconds, the elusive Republican officer and Town Chairman nearly killed himself after dropping sixteen feet from a back window to the Quay below. From that time on, he had to sleep at a safe house.

At a Council meeting held the previous day for the purpose of expressing a vote of sympathy with the wife and family of the murdered Lord Mayor, the following motion was passed. 'We extend our deepest sympathy to the wife, family and relatives of the late Lord Mayor of Cork and to the citizens of the city, and express our condemnation of the foul crime committed.' Speaking on the motion, Seamus Fitzgerald said he had known Tomás MacCurtain personally, having suffered incarceration with him in the Frongoch camp. During this time he had come to respect and admire the late Lord Mayor as a man worthy of Ireland and the high post he had filled as Cork's first citizen. The other councillors, in expressing their horror at the event, used such terms as, 'a most brutal and deliberate planned affair', 'a callous crime' and 'a glaring instance of oppression the country was groaning under.'[20] It was furthermore decided to place a wreath on the coffin and that the Council should attend the funeral.

On 28 April, a meeting was held at the Town Hall for the purpose of inaugurating a fund in support of the Tomás MacCurtain Memorial. The town clerk, Mr O'Reilly, who acted as secretary to the meeting, said he had been speaking to Revd Fr Kent (of Cobh), who apologised for his inability to attend the meeting and had given him a subscription towards the fund. The town clerk then read a letter from the Council Chairman, who wrote expressing his regret at his absence from the meeting held for the very commendable object of inaugurating a memorial fund in Cobh to the memory of his dead friend and gallant comrade, the murdered Lord Mayor of Cork, Ald. Thomas MacCurtain. Cork knew its mind exceedingly well when it selected him as its chief citizen to guide and watch over its destinies. Fitzgerald ended his letter with a strong appeal to the townspeople not to stint their subscription in the raising of the memorial to Alderman MacCurtain's memory. A letter from Barrister Healy was also read out at the meeting wishing it every success and intimating that he had previously subscribed to the fund. Republicans also expressed their presence in the town by less subtle means, by hoisting the Tricolour from the flagstaff at the Admiralty pier on several occasions. Thus in early April the following report appeared in the *Cork Examiner*, 'All day on 4 April a Sinn Féin flag, hoisted from the previous night, remained flying on the flagstaff at the Admiralty pier, Queenstown. After it had been got into position, the halyards were cut and the pole greased. A flotilla of destroyers, not previously based in Queenstown, arrived there about 8.00am. on the 4th. They left in the afternoon for Dublin.'

Similar incidents also took place in other parts of the country throughout 1920. The matter was eventually raised in the British House of Commons after Volunteers in Cobh had once again flown the objectionable flag, this time from Cork Harbour Commissioners flag pole at the beginning of July. The venue, the Pier Head, was well chosen as this was the pier from which military launches sailed to Spike and the other forts in the harbour. However, no measures were taken by the British government, probably because the RIC had by then more urgent matters to attend than the guarding of flagpoles in Irish ports.

9. The Capture of Cloyne RIC Barracks

On Saturday 8 May, Volunteers of the 4th Battalion were gathering near the village of Cloyne in advance of an attack on its R.I.C. Barracks. The Battalion C.O. Mick Leahy and Diarmuid Hurley had been carefully planning for the attack over the previous month. Although they had made every provision to meticulously execute their plan, they knew the Barrack garrison had been strengthened with manpower and steel shutters over its windows. They also predicted that the defenders would possibly be expecting a visit after the fall of Carrigtwohill and Castlemartyr Barracks in the previous four months. The latter fell after a crude, on-the-spot attempt when Hurley and a few of his Midleton men seized an opportunity to gain entry and snatch what weapons they could find.

As luck would have it, the men met with little resistance after finding the barracks Sergeant in bed sick. On this occasion however, Leahy and Hurley had no illusions about how difficult this one was going to be. Cloyne was a village situated about five miles south of Midleton and about sixteen miles from Cork. The nearest military garrisons were at Youghal, sixteen miles east, Fort Carlisle eight miles south, and Cork to the west. It was situated almost in the middle of the battalion area and ideally suited for attack. Mick Leahy decided that every available man of the battalion which then numbered about 450, would be utilised for the operation and given a sense they were directly involved in the independence struggle.

Thirty-five Volunteer officers and men from Cobh under the command of Bill Ahern were available and ready for action. Some were gathering on the Midleton side of Cloyne, while others were posted at the Midleton/ Cloyne side of East Ferry, to prevent British reinforcement from Cobh crossing by that route to Cloyne. Mick Burke of Cobh was put in charge of cutting the phone lines between the village and the outside. Trees were also felled to block all access roads to and from the village. Sentries were posted on all outlying Hamlets to ensure no one could leave and alert the outside world of what was about to go down. Men from Aghada blocked the roads leading to Cloyne from Carlisle Fort and the coastguard station at Roches Point. The Youghal-Cloyne, Ballycotton-Cloyne and Midleton –Cloyne roads were also blocked. Once that work was completed, Burke was then instructed to oversee that the civilian population, within fifty yards of the Barracks, were kept indoors.

Meanwhile, all the different firing parties were being issued with weapons, ammunition and explosives at the local school house in advance of taking up their positions. One of the more critical positions considered for the point of attack was located in a corn stores directly in front of the Barracks. That task was given to Paddy Whelan and Jack Ahern of the Midleton Company and Donal Leahy (brother of Mick) of the Cobh Company. While Whelan and Ahern were each armed with rifles, Leahy was armed with only a hatchet. The task of this three-man team was to keep up continuous fire on the windows of the Barracks whilst other parties were trying to gain entry from one or both houses flanking the barracks building. Mick Leahy had earlier decided after learning from the Carrigtwohill experience, that there was no point in employing a large number of riflemen who would pointlessly fire at steel shutters of the barracks and waste their ammunition. Instead, he would use two or three riflemen who would direct continuous fire on the building, thus providing cover for other volunteers who would move in close to the target to plant explosive devices.

These riflemen first had to undertake the nerve-wracking task of getting into the corn store without being observed from the Barracks across the street. The men casually walked down the village street to the stores, and found the entrance gate secured by a strong iron bar. Fortunately for them, Donal Leahy made short work of the bar, and they were inside in under a minute. The men immediately made their way upstairs where they took up positions by windows facing directly towards the barracks across the street. The men first removed the wire mesh from the windows to give them a clear view. Meanwhile, the bulk of Leahy's men with about 15 rifles and shot guns were taking up positions in houses on the main street close to the front of the police barracks. Another five or six riflemen were placed at the rear of the barracks to prevent a breakout. Then Just before 10p.m. Leahy sent two men into each of the adjacent public houses on either side of the barracks to hold the doors open for them when the pubs were due to shut at 10p.m.

Meanwhile, the main attacking party of about twenty men discretely made their way up the street towards the two pubs. Leahy found that the pub door on the Ballycotton (east) side of the barracks was closed. The pub door on the Midleton west side was held open, allowing some to enter. Others began smashing the other door on the east side with an axe but were still unable to gain entry. Mick Leahy then pulled an iron bar from the window shutters and use it to completely demolish the remaining shutters, before climbing through the bar window. He was immediately followed by eight others. While Leahy and his party were beating an entry through the pub at the east of the barracks, Diarmuid Hurley began the attack by firing a single revolver shot through one of the loopholes in the steel shutters of the barracks before dashing inside the pub on the west side with his party. The R.I.C. garrison responded by firing in all directions outside, and with sending up Verey lights and tossing out hand grenades. Meanwhile, Paddy Whelan and Jack Ahern were now hard at it directing fire at the barrack shutters at will. This undoubtedly had a devastating mental effect on those defending from the other side of the steel. While these two directed their fire from shutter to shutter, Donal Leahy sat on the floor between the two men with his axe in his hand looking down on the barracks and wishing he could play a more direct role in the proceedings.

Mick Leahy and his men ordered the occupants of the pub to immediately leave. They then set about dismantling bedsteads and mattresses before placing them up against the wall to protect those boring holes, setting fuses, and from grenades. Meanwhile, Leahy himself managed to get on to the roof and proceeded along with the intention of dropping a bomb down through the skylight of the barracks, but those on the other side of the street mistook him for one of the R.I.C. and fired on him. The commander had no choice but to beat a retreat back inside. Inside, he found that his men had successfully breached the wall with a blast, but it wasn't big enough for men to enter so they proceeded to set a second device. Hurley and his men on the other side of the barracks had a similar experience but instead of setting a second charge, opted to pour petrol through the breach and with straw, smoke the garrison out. After their second blast went off, Leahy and his men created a bigger breach from which to pass but by then, were forced back by the rising smoke and flames coming up the stairs from Hurley's fire. The garrison continued meanwhile with returning fire and throwing hand grenades onto the street outside, despite coming under new revolver fire from the breaches in the walls. Leahy then shouted an order for the garrison to surrender. He told them that the building was on fire, that there were no reinforcements coming and there was no dishonour in surrendering to avoid certain death by fire.

He waited but there was no sign of surrender coming. Then in the middle of intense firing, Paddy Whelan across the street at the corn store noticed a white pillow case being waved from a window of the barracks. He immediately stopped firing and ordered Ahern to do likewise. He could hear shouts of, 'we surrender, we surrender'[21] coming from across the way. Then he heard another shout 'cease fire'. The three men then dashed down the stairs and on to the street where the saw the garrison, a sergeant and nine constables march out with their hands in the air followed by Mick Leahy. The prisoners were then placed under armed guard. Leahy and some others then returned inside to collect what weapons they could find. The fire by then was starting to take hold, forcing Leahy to bring the sergeant back inside to show them where the weapons were kept. In the corner of one room, Leahy saw a box on fire, when he went to examine it, the sergeant shouted not to touch it as it held hand grenades. When all the guns and ammunition that could be rescued were taken back outside, Leahy called a casualty check. Diarmuid Hurley was wounded in his right arm from a ricochet and from a burn caused after starting the petrol fire. The garrison sergeant asked Leahy to give aid to one of his constables who also needed attention. Leahy recalled the man with a strong cockney accent suffering with a head wound. He instructed the two wounded men to be taken to Dr Power in the village, who duly gave them his attention.

Before they left the village that night, the wounded constable sent for Leahy and thanked him, saying, 'You are a true Christian; only for you I would have bled to death.'[22] He also told Leahy that he was going to resign from the force. The operation lasted three hours. Leahy later fell his men in on parade and congratulated them on an excellent performance. Everyone was then given their instructions to ensure they got home safely and that all the captured weapons and ammunition were dispersed. Those in all the outlying guard positions were alerted and stood down. Later while they were transporting the captured weapons to a prearranged hiding place with a horse and cart, Paddy Whelan and Jack Ahern came upon Mick Leahy outside the village, giving the RIC prisoners a lecture. The Republican commander warned them not to attempt to identify any of the volunteers they did battle with, and told them they should resign from the force and take up arms against the old enemy.

On 3 June British forces in Cobh once again came under attack when the local Volunteers decided to set the Naval Station alight. A communiqué was issued by the Admiralty, stating that an attack had been made on the Naval Station, resulting in the recreation buildings and their contents being burned to the ground, but the report was later denied by the Commander-in-Chief, who claimed that, 'no attacks were made on Queenstown naval base as stated. The only damage done to recreation ground buildings was that one hut was burned and two others damaged.' At a council meeting held on the following day, the chairman, Seamus Fitzgerald welcomed back Cllr James Ahern after an absence of four months. The council, 'were glad to see he was braving the gauntlet and that he had returned to his duties as a member of the council. Mr Ahern would be a valuable addition to the Council (hear hear).'[23] Ahern thanked the Council and said that he hoped to do 'all in his power' for the good of the town and the Council.

By now the campaign within the British Empire to save Ireland was beginning to move up a gear. The government of Britain had little interest in recognising political mandates, or people's right to self determination, even if it was asked by people of a small nation who had in no small way played its part in offering up its manhood in the recent Great War for the freedom of small nations. Instead, the government intended to show how it could rule with an iron fist where ever and when ever its writ was questioned. More and more troops poured into Ireland, many of them arriving through Cobh, and the 'Coercion Act' was announced, which gave increased powers to the military. Also during the summer, the Rob Roy Hotel in Cobh was raided by a party of soldiers. They held up everyone who happened to be in the hotel and during the raid, which lasted for an hour, prevented anyone entering the building. All rooms were invaded and clothing and luggage belonging to the guests were closely searched but nothing was found. This was the time of the Black and Tans' who had arrived in Ireland the previous month and it was also a time when another military regiment the 'Cameron's Highlanders' based at Belmont Camp, would leave its mark in the memory of the peoples of Cobh, Midleton and Carrigtwohill, for generations to come.

With raids and arrests increasing both by night and day by the Cameron as they were commonly known, no one was left feeling safe. People spoke of the noisy Crossley Tenders speeding onto a street before screeching to a halt outside someone's house, followed by lorry's full of Jocks who would jump off and head straight for a particular door before smashing it in. In a short space of time, the sight of swirling Scottish kilts jumping off the backs of lorries, became synonymous with smashed up homes and violence, and eventually with death.

When any given raiding party had a combination of Jocks and Black and Tans onboard, and if either party had earlier been drinking alcohol, then it was easy to see why many known Volunteers had gone on the run. Major General Douglas Wimberley, who served with the Cameron Highlanders at Belmont Hutments later, described the local community as a hostile one.

All around us those who were now called our enemies, the Sinn Féiners; all wore plain clothes, had their arms hidden, and spoke good English. It was very difficult for some weeks to teach the Jocks that we were now in what was largely a hostile country, and that maybe 75 per cent of all local inhabitants, both men and women, viewed us with enmity, active or passive; though these sentiments were largely hidden.

But many of these raids could never happen without initial police requests and supplied intelligence.

10. The Escape of Lord French

Through his open and public position as the elected Town Chairman, important intelligence often found its way to the Volunteer leadership in Cobh by first reaching Seamus Fitzgerald. If the forthcoming information was of a specifically important or sensitive nature, then Fitzgerald might often pass it on directly to the Brigade first. This is precisely what happened when it was brought to his notice in late July that Sir Hamar Greenwood, the British Secretary for Ireland, and Sir John French, Commander in Chief, were to land in Cobh from a destroyer on the following day. He was told that the two VIPs would be visiting the Admiral at his residence at the Mount near 'Top of the Hill', but didn't have precise details of the hour of the visit. Fitzgerald immediately took the information to brigade Headquarters in Cork and was given instructions that only French was to be shot. Returning immediately to Cobh, the Town Chairman relayed the instructions to the local Company Commander. Realising they had very little time to put a meaningful plan of action together and not having any real knowledge of which route French and his escort would take to get to the Admiralty Buildings, it was decided to mobilise enough men the next day (Saturday) to make up two attacking groups that would lay in wait for the target. One group would take up positions along the Bishop's Road and the other in a Stable at Sandymount.

It was felt the target would have to pass one of the routes on his way to the Admiral's house. Daithí O'Brien ordered that every available local rifle, revolver and hand grenade would be mustered in preparation for the operation. It was also agreed that Councillors Seamus Fitzgerald and James Ahern would publicly be seen about the town the next day so as to give the authorities the impression that local Republicans had no inkling of the imminent visit by the VIP's. The following evening, the two groups of Volunteers began to take up positions at the two selected locations, the larger group in the stables at Sandymount. When they arrived at the Admiralty pier on the town front, French and Greenwood were quickly whisked away by a speeding car and a heavily armed escort to the Admiralty. But Daithí O'Brien and his Volunteers were not yet properly prepared in their positions when the target passed at high speed. Undeterred, O'Brien resolved to get their man on his return to his ship.

From their positions at the stables, the Volunteers had a clear view of a scout Paddy O'Sullivan, who was positioned in a house about fifty yards up the hill from them. Standing near a top room window, O'Sullivan had a similarly perfect view of the Admiralty building which was less than two hundred yards to the east of him at the mount.

The hurriedly put together a plan, which, if it worked smoothly, would mean Paddy O'Sullivan receiving a signal from the Admiralty grounds. His brother, a wounded veteran from the First World War, and who now worked at the Admiralty, was to give the signal as soon as French was preparing to leave the grounds. Paddy in turn would shut the window of the room where he was positioned as a signal for those at the stables to get ready. As the hours went by, there was no sign of any activity from around the Admiralty or from the window at Paddy O'Sullivan's location. Then around 11.00pm. word came by O'Sullivan that French would be remaining the night at the Admiralty. O'Brien ordered all to disperse for the night and to return to the stable first thing the next morning.

Early the next morning, everyone resumed their positions, with those previously located at the Bishop's Road, now joining the others at the stable. After attending an early Sunday Mass, the Battalion C.O. Mick Leahy also joined the ambush party. The Volunteers by now were beginning to appreciate the magnitude and value of this operation and started to realise the propaganda it would generate if it were successful. The psychological blow such an assassination would have to Crown Forces morale in one of its strongest garrison outposts would surely be immense. Imagine the effort that such a blow would have on the mindsets of those directing British policy in Ireland from London? These were some of the thoughts that occupied the minds of some of those lying in wait at the stables.

Another one that weighed heavily on them and kept their adrenalin running high was the realisation that French and Greenwood would be heavily guarded by armed Cameron Highlanders and the Royal Marines upon their return, as they were when they arrived. If French was to be killed by either bullet or grenade, then surely Greenwood would more than likely fall too, and it must be expected that in the unavoidable skirmishes that would follow, the volunteers would take casualties also. O'Brien and his men surmised that this was probably why Mick Leahy had arrived on the scene and that he was sent along by the Brigade to ensure things would go to according plan and wouldn't turn messy. As the day moved on, there was no sign that the two VIPs were about to leave Admiralty buildings. By nightfall, word filtered through to the stables again that French would spend another night with the Admiral in Cobh. When they arrived back at the stables at Sandymount for the third time early on Monday morning, the Volunteers were in their positions for only a short time when word reached them that French and his escort had left by a totally unexpected route. Whether it was due to some piece of intelligence coming the way of the British about a proposed attack, or if it were a simple precautionary measure, a car had pulled up at the back of the Admiralty building out of sight of Paddy O'Sullivan's position. It quickly picked up the two VIPs before leaving the grounds and speeding down passed Bond Street before turning right towards Ferry Street.

At high speed, it then headed for Carrignafoy while passing close to Belmont Camp on its way. It then descended down Cuskinny hill to a waiting launch that was moored by a small pier in the bay. French and Greenwood were taken quickly back to the destroyer waiting for them in the harbour. Mick Leahy, Daithí O'Brien and the others were gutted by the manner in which French had escaped them. It was all the more galling for the Battalion Commander Leahy, when it was realised the target has passed the gates of his own Carrignafoy family home on his way to Cuskinny. It must also have been a galling sight for Volunteer Mikey Kidney, to witness all the military commotion on the French Estate as the Commander in Chief of British forces in Ireland, Lord French (no relation to his hosts) was being shepherded to his boat in the bay. In the absence of modern communication technology, like the mobile phone, Kidney was powerless to inform the volunteers back in town that their target was there on the estate. All he could do was to look on as the greatest target the IRA was ever likely to have in its sights, slipped away before his eyes.

11. The Shooting of District Inspector Mordaunt

The arrival of the Black and Tans in Cobh to offer support to the local RIC coincided with the arrival of the new District Inspector Mordaunt, who took up his new job with a strong degree of enthusiasm. Within a short number of weeks, local Republicans were in no doubt of who was running things at Westview Police Barracks and knew something would have to be done about it. Shortly after his release from Wormwood Scrubs in July, Daithí O'Brien was back in Cobh plotting as if he had never been away. On the morning of 1 August, he called to the work place of Mick Burke and asked him for a revolver which Burke willingly handed over. Shortly afterwards, he approached Seamus Fitzgerald outside of the local General Post Office for a loan of his personal revolver too. He said he needed it for a short while for a small job.

Known for his engagement in sometimes spur of the moment escapades without proper planning and forethought, O'Brien was fortunate that Fitzgerald reluctantly handed over his weapon. The Town Chairman didn't ask, but wondered what O'Brien was about to get involved in, especially as he was in the company of young James Glavin when he made the request. Glavin was in fact about to act as a look-out scout for what O'Brien and others were planning. Shortly before 1p.m. District Inspector Mordaunt left his Westview Barracks to go to his home for lunch at the Park near Laundry Hill. As he probably knew he was being watched, he didn't take the short route of about 150 yards up the hill to his home. Instead, he proceeded down the hill through Scotts Square, along Westbourne Place, then turned off up Spy Hill before heading along Bishops Road towards the Park near Top of the Hill.

Standing near the corner of Mansworth's Bar between Park Lane and Midleton Street, a young Volunteer, not yet sixteen years old, named James Glavin, was keeping a watchful eye over the Bishop's Road to see if their target was on his way. Forty yards up to the west by the entrance to the Park, Mrs Mordaunt and her young child were approaching from their house to meet their husband and father. With child in hand, the young woman didn't show the slightest suspicion or unease at the sight of three men working on what looked like a broken down van outside the gates.

In charge of the van was Donal Leahy who used to drive it for 'Delaney Grocers' in the town. Present with O'Brien and Leahy, were William

McCarthy of Carrignafoy and Jerome Grayley who lived over the road at Smalls Well. He would repeatedly glance towards the direction of Glavin for an expected prearranged signal. Despite the presence of his wife and child at the gates, O'Brien was determined to proceed as planned and leave the head policeman with a serious message. Then the moment arrived when Mordaunt came around the corner, and proceeded towards his wife and child.

It is not clear if O'Brien moved prematurely to avoid injuring his wife and child or if he ever intended killing him, but as soon as the first shots brought the policeman to the ground, his terrified wife intervened and used her own body to shield the attackers from finishing the task. One of the volunteers (probably O'Brien) struggled with Mrs Mordaunt and eventually at the point of his revolver, ordered her to give up her bravado and instead attend to her wounded husband. With three gunshot wounds to his thigh, the district inspector was soon rushed to Haulbowline Military Hospital where he was attended to.

As soon as word of the attack reached him, Seamus Fitzgerald was furious with Daithí O'Brien for not giving him proper warning. Although he was commander of the local company and didn't require outside sanction before proceeding with the ambush, O'Brien failed to take into account Fitzgerald's position as a marked man and that he also deprived him of a weapon to protect himself in the event of immediate retaliation, albeit temporarily. Mick Leahy, who had just arrived in town, was also unaware of what went down and was vulnerable to arrest too if he had been spotted by the authorities. O'Brien was duly reprimanded and told that officers must organise operations in a disciplined manner and keep themselves free from arrest and easy identification with such actions. All officers were instructed to 'direct' rather than exclusively 'operate'. His overzealous hands-on approach must have led to fears that some one might connect him (probably the policeman's wife) to the Mordaunt attack, as it was around this time that Daithí O'Brien left Cobh on the run, and was replaced by Mick Burke as the new Company Commander.

Immediately after Mordaunt's shooting, the 'top of the hill' area was flooded with police and military before they searched a number of premises in the area. The homes of Councillors James Ahern and Charles Bailey were among the first visited. Tenman's grocery shop and Monahan's guest house also came under the spotlight. A number of cars were also searched and people on their way to a funeral at Ballymore were stopped and searched. However, no one was arrested for the attack and some days later, Mrs Mordaunt's pride suffered a second blow when she was approached by three men while out shopping, one of whom asked her how her husband was recovering from the 'accidental shooting.'

The local Crown Forces were furious over the Mordaunt shooting, especially after the once promising District Inspector had thrown in the towel and resigned from the force. A week later on 8 August, a battalion of the Cameron Highlanders took complete charge of the streets of Cobh, which were packed with people awaiting the disembarkation of Archbishop Mannix from the liner *Baltic*. They placed machine-gun posts at both ends of the town, and armed patrols kept moving constantly along the main streets. The projected visit of Archbishop Mannix had received tremendous publicity, and bonfires had been arranged on the headlands and a great welcome had been assured him. As chairman of the local Council, Seamus Fitzgerald was on hand to present him with an address of welcome; special Dáil Éireann representatives had been delegated to welcome him.

When the ship reached five miles outside the port however, British agents went on board, placed the Archbishop under arrest, and transferred him to a destroyer which brought him to England, while the British Government forbade him to visit Ireland, Manchester or Liverpool. Tensions were so high in Cobh after it was learned of what happened to the Archbishop that Fitzgerald organised a large number of Republican stewards to patrol the streets that night. The situation was tense; wanted men walking side by side with Crown Forces. Everyone felt that any untoward incident might lead to serious trouble and disturbance.

The Republicans won the support and respect of the local people that night however, with everyone going home to their beds peacefully. Although the arrest and exclusion of the outspoken critic of British rule in Ireland had disappointed and angered many people, Seamus Fitzgerald nevertheless received the opportunity to deliver Archbishop Mannix his original welcoming address some years later. On 19 August, Mick Burke had his first taste of command when he oversaw an armed snatch of the mails leaving Cobh by train at Rushbrooke. As the train approached the platform, a large party of masked Volunteers split into different groups, thus ensuring that mail officials and crew were all covered. One group then entered the mail van and removed all the mail sacks, after which the train was allowed to proceed on its journey to Cork. Although the train was full of passengers, the raid was carried out with such speed and coolness that hardly anybody noticed what was going on. The mailbags were also taken in the direction of Cork, and most likely were passed on to the IRA brigade intelligence department there.

Republican intelligence had advanced to such a level by 1920 that the British were finding it ever more difficult to deal with the challenges facing them. These intelligence networks operated at various levels in society. IRA intelligence officers were being fed with information from sympathisers within the RIC and British army and navy. It was coming from people dealing with mails in the post offices and from individuals working on railway and shipping lines. More locally, it came from people working in shops, bars and hotels, and by ordinary people just going about their daily business with an ever increasing vigilant eye.

The IRA, some reports say, didn't have any scruples when it came to employing unusual methods to root out information and pressurising people to work for it. Also, the use of blackmail was never far from the picture. After taking over command of the local Company, one of the first things Mick Burke wanted to do was to have the upper hand in the intelligence war on the enemy. It was said, he was prompted in this direction by what he saw taking place at what was then known by Republicans as the 'Tommies' Playground' otherwise known as the 'Skating Rink' near the Lake Road. The Skating Rink was built by the American Marines who were based at Haulbowline and Whitepoint during the latter part of World War 1. It was built to entertain it's off duty members and was also used by the British and local loyalists. When the Americans left the Port of Cobh at the end of the World War 1, they handed the Skating Rink over to the care of the British military. From then on until the time they left Cobh after the Treaty, British soldiers and sailors continued to use the facility for entertainment and as a place for meeting local girls.

By 1919 however, when it was generally considered very suspect and dangerous for locals to be found conversing, let alone socialising with members of the Crown Forces, only ladies whose families were very loyal to the Crown dared to visit the Skating Rink. So if the report is true that some local girls from the Cumann na mBan, volunteered to work undercover at the rink, then they must have been very brave women indeed. Although the identities of these ladies are not recorded, we do know that some were treated with some hostility and suspicion by their own community and colleagues alike. Neither is there any record of whether any useful information was ever gained from these operations for the local Volunteer movement or if the cover of these young women was maintained with the British.

There is however, a record of a communication between Nita Murphy the local Cumann na mBan branch secretary and Leslie Bean De Barra (née Price) who was General Secretary of the Movement. Murphy reported in her letter of the fraternising by some local members with enemy forces and waited to be advised about what course of disciplinary action should be taken against the girls. On 16 September 1921 while the Truce was in operation, Murphy received a reply but it is not known if it was a direct response to her earlier request. There is some confusion here due to the accidental destruction of Cumann na mBan and (A) Company records which were left in her care.

It is believed that Mick Burke handed over all of the company's records to Nita Murphy for safe keeping when Free State forces landed in Cobh at the outset of the Civil War in August 1922. Murphy naively placed the documents in a number of shoe boxes before burying them in her back garden at number 21 Ferry Street, (now Bishop Street). However, when Burke returned to collect the documents some years later, he was horrified to find the boxes and contents had perished. The letter which Murphy received in September, referred to the three members whose punishment was sought and brought before the executive. For reasons of security, the three members were referred to as A, B, and C. The letter instructed that A and B were to be expelled and instructed that C should be suspended until her conduct improved. The director advised that the letter should be read out at the next branch meeting, and that it should be pointed out that the organisation would have to deal severely in future with girls associating with the enemy.

It was possible that Mick Burke might have carefully selected some young women volunteers for the espionage operation at the Rink. If so, it is also very likely that he may have deliberately kept his plans from their local leaders a secret, so that in the event of their cover being blown, the open hostility they would naturally receive from their own community would help them to further ingratiate themselves with the British. There is no mention however, in the later witness statement of Mick Burke or of those of his fellow local officers that any of the later successful military operations carried out in Cobh came about as a result of information received at the Rink. Neither is there any record of how long such an operation might have lasted. There is however, some evidence in the witness statement of another local Republican officer, which places some doubt over whether such an operation ever existed, and if Republicans would even countenance placing women operatives in such places of low moral standing. In his witness statement to the Bureau of Military History, Seamus Fitzgerald recorded that before the time he had to flee Cobh as chairman of the Town Council in late 1920, he was asked to a meeting at Cathedral House by Bishop Robert Browne. Browne, Fitzgerald noted, was a supporter of the constitutional nationalist position, though it was widely felt he was very pro-British in his views and expressed them in much the same way as his colleague, the Bishop of Cork, Bishop Cohalan. Browne assured Fitzgerald that his sympathies were very much with his people in defence of their liberties against the aggressive conduct of the Crown Forces. He intimated that his position was a difficult one however, as he had to keep on the best possible terms with the British and American Admirals who were based in Cobh.

While the Bishop was relatively silent about condemning the excesses of Crown Force activities, or at least in public or from the pulpit, he was prepared to be very vocal on wider moral issues. Fitzgerald says Bishop Browne made some very strong public protests about the conduct of American sailors, whose guilt was widely accepted, leaving them barred from going to Cork City. This behaviour, it is felt was related to public immoral acts through the widespread use of contraceptives (condoms). It was reported, that local people going to work on Monday mornings used to encounter enormous amounts of used condoms strewn around the quay sides of Cobh and Haulbowline, after the Americans. While Republicans might have differed greatly with their Bishop over the rights or wrongs of their military campaign against the crown, they and the townspeople to whom they represented were fully behind him on the question of American misconduct and morality.

It is for this reason that serious doubts must be placed over whether, Mick Burke, an officer who didn't tolerate bad language among his men, would have encouraged any young woman to engage with the enemy in such an environment. It must also be remembered that Burke and his officers had already in place a good intelligence network with spies working from within the admiralty and the local RIC barracks at West View, without having to expose young women to the moral and physical dan-

The funeral of John O'Connell passes Westbourne.

gers of the 'Tommies Playground'.

Meanwhile the battalion O.C. Mick Leahy had made better progress in the field of espionage in East Cork. It was just past 7.00pm on 5 June while on their way through East Cork to make preparations for a proposed attack on Ballycotton RIC barracks, Mick Leahy and Jack O'Connell had not long passed Carrigtwohill when they heard gunshots ahead of them coming from the Midleton direction. The two immediately picked up speed on their bikes and before long stumbled upon their colleagues from Midleton who had by then a cycle patrol of Cameron Highlanders surrounded and disarmed at a place called Mile Bush. The Cameron's, who had only taken up station in Midleton the previous day in a disused warehouse, were out on a cycle tour to learn the lay of the land. They were being shown around by an RIC guide by the name of Jerry O'Connor.

Earlier that afternoon Diarmuid Hurley and his volunteers spotted the 12 man cycle patrol leave the town. Hurley quickly got eight other armed Volunteers with revolvers together and headed out with the intention of ambushing the soldiers on their return at Mile Bush where they had set up a mock bowling match on the quiet stretch of road. When they arrived, the unsuspecting patrol of Cameron highlanders was completely caught off guard after one of the bowlers drew a gun and fired it into the air. Immediately surrounded and stripped of their rifles and equipment, the soldiers and their RIC guide were quickly ordered off the road and into a nearby laneway. A lone Cameron straggler who had stumbled upon the surrender of his colleagues, decided to dismount from his bike, took aim with his rifle and fired. When the volunteers returned fire however, the soldier ditched his rifle and ran. Hurley's men, who had separated O'Connor the RIC man, were anxious that he should be shot as he knew them all. He also knew Mick Leahy well, a factor that probably saved his life. O'Connor pleaded for his life and told Leahy that he would help the Volunteers in any way he could if they spared him. Leahy knew that the policeman worked as secretary in the Midleton District Inspectors office, and decided to take a chance with him. He warned the policeman that if he was ever taken prisoner while working in Midleton, he would have him shot immediately. O'Connor stuck to his side of the bargain. Every time the Camerons phoned the RIC barracks for a guide before launching a particular raid, the Republican mole usually took the message which he would quickly relay to Leahy.

Later, on the night of the Mile Bush ambush, the Camerons shot up the town of Midleton, smashing house and shop windows in reprisal for the loss of their rifles. The next morning, Leahy had the village of Ballycotton surrounded by volunteers from Cobh and Midleton. The men were armed with rifles, some of which were probably taken at Mile Bush the previous day. Leahy had already arranged with a local man by the name of Coleman to get them inside the barrack door. He was a regular caller to the barracks and it was felt wouldn't draw any suspicion. When they entered the village however, they discovered the Camerons had posted sentries around the area of the barracks. Leahy concluded that the authorities were expecting an attack and were probably led to believe this by the earlier Mile Bush ambush which they felt was the main purpose for the rifles being snatched. He called the attack off and ordered everyone to return to their homes.

12. Rifles Snatched at 'Top of the Hill' Quarry

Three weeks after the shooting of District Inspector Mordaunt at the Park, some vigilant members of the public brought Republican attention back to the locality once more. On the morning of Wednesday 25 August, Mick Burke was directed towards some interesting activity taking place at an old disused quarry off Ferry Street (Bishop Street) near 'top of the hill'. The area of the quarry then housed a forge belonging to an old blacksmith named John O'Connell. It was also used by its owner Mrs Coleman who kept pigs there. The forge bordered with a military fence, beyond which were a number of huts that were recently in use as a meeting place for British ex-servicemen, mainly veterans from the recent Great War. On the morning of the 25 August however, a party of Camerons were busy dismantling the huts. The area backed on to land near the Admiralty grounds at the Mount and was very close to where a number of Royal Marines used to be positioned on guard duty by the gate lodge of the Admiralty.

These were all factors that led to the Cameron's Highlanders and their corporal in particular to behave in a careless manner where their security was concerned on this particular Wednesday. The corporal had earlier instructed his men to stack their rifles in three piles while they worked. A sentry was posted guard over each stack of rifles. A staunch Republican herself, it is very likely that old Mrs Coleman was the first person to spot the stacked shiny Lee-Enfield rifles and concluded they were waiting to be snatched, before making contact with Mick Burke. When he arrived, Burke was careful not to arouse the suspicion of the Jocks as he endeavoured to learn the lay of the land. He first pretended to have some business with the blacksmith at the forge and in doing so, managed to get a fair picture of the British strengths and weaknesses from behind the fence and wicket-gate. He then left the quarry and went directly across the road to the Harrier Club building which was adjacent to the last house on the eastern part of Ferry Street and close to the entrance of the Presentation Brothers' College. From there, he had a partial view of the work that was taking place across the way. He then sent word through a Fianna Boy Scout member for other volunteers to report immediately to the harrier club with revolvers.

Before mid-day, those in the harrier club waiting to pounce with Mick Burke, numbered eight. But as things stood, the commander knew it would be virtually impossible to successfully snatch rifles from the Jocks while they had a sentry standing over each stack. He discretely paid another visit to the Blacksmith's forge in order to get another up-close look at the situation beyond the British fence. He was disappointed to find that things were much as he had found them earlier. After returning to the harrier club again, he instructed his men to disperse in ones and twos and to re-assemble back at the club again at 2.pm.

In the intervening period, Burke made arrangements with Donal Leahy to have his company van (Delaney's) waiting at St Colman's Square, to collect the expected haul of rifles and to get them quickly to a safe hiding place. At the designated time of their reassembly, Burke counted nine members who were armed with revolvers. Another six who had not been present earlier were armed with sticks and iron bars, two of whom were young Fianna boys, eager to get stuck into the task in hand. He then outlined his plan to the others. He and two others including one of the Fianna boys would take up positions at the forge. Three others would take up positions at the wicket gate opposite the forge and at a hand signal from him would hold up the sentry nearest to them. If no shots were fired, all the rifles were to be grabbed, the soldiers rounded up and their ammunition and equipment confiscated, but if any firing did take place, every man was to grab as many rifles as they could and run to the awaiting car before getting away as quickly as possible.

When they reached the forge Burke and his party noticed that only two sentries were now standing guard, leaving one stack of rifles unguarded. This prompted him to give an immediate hand signal to the others at the wicket gate to move. When ordered to raise his hands in the air and upon seeing three revolvers pointed in his direction, the utterly surprised sentry at the wicket gate offered no resistance. At the other end close to the forge however, the sentry was made of different stuff. When approached by Burke to put his hands up, he immediately resisted and while motioning to cock his rifle, Burke felt compelled to shoot him. In the confusion which followed, further shots were fired followed by a dash to snatch as many rifles as possible.

The attacking parties then left the quarry at speed before crossing the road and fleeing up through College Avenue. They then circled west through English's field before meeting up with the waiting van at St Colman's Square. After picking up his cargo, Donal Leahy and the van then left the Island at high speed before dropping off the captured rifles at a dump at Carrigtwohill. Every Volunteer and scout that took part in the raid, quickly dispersed to their homes. Shortly after he changed his clothes at his Donnellan Terrace home, Mick Burke took the bold decision to venture out and see what the community reaction was to the attack. Before long he came upon a military and police ring of steel around the Top of the Hill area. An RIC man, who knew Burke, refused to leave him pass through the cordon. Burke asked him why, before being told that a shooting and rifle snatch had taken place at the quarry. It was then that the Republican leader first learned that three soldiers had in fact been shot in the earlier melee. With a very convincing facial expression and posture, Burke told the policeman that it was a shame that such things could happen in Cobh. The policeman then replied 'on second thoughts, you can go through; I know you would have nothing to do it.' None of the Volunteers had worn masks and as children were leaving the nearby school around the time of the raid, and would have therefore recognised them, it was therefore with great credit that none had spoken out and fingered any of the raiders.

The quarry was left in total confusion and disarray following the raid. Twelve rifles in total were taken. Three soldiers were wounded, one, Private Young from Edinburgh would die soon after from his wounds. Some of the wounded soldier's colleagues were so badly shaken, that local people later reported seeing some of them running in a confused state in the opposite direction to their barracks. The Camerons didn't venture out from their camp at Belmont that night, or the next one. The Black and Tans on the other hand were intent on punishing the local people for supporting the lawless Sinn Féin murderers and gunmen as they saw them. The first port of call for the enraged drunken peelers was to the home of the Town Chairman Seamus Fitzgerald. The Tans continuously fired volleys through the windows of number 19 East Beach and repeatedly called on Fitzgerald to come out to face his would-be executioners. When they tried to set the building alight, they were distracted by the screaming appeals of local women begging them not to do so.

Eventually, the drunken lawmen burst their way into the house, smashing furniture and belongings along the way. Upon realising that the town's first citizen was not at home, they instead beat up his elderly father who was himself a retired British serviceman. Seamus was however in hiding in a nearby property about fifty feet away from his home. He knew the time for his remaining in Cobh was now over, however, and eagerly escaped the next morning by a small boat, while passing between several British destroyers on his way upriver to Cork City. Then on the night of 27 August, the Camerons decided it was their turn to let off some steam, and began an orgy of violence that was to last for nearly a week.

Led by the Battalion Sergeant Major Mackintosh, the Jocks smashed the windows and shot up many of the business premises right along the town front. Fitzgerald and the Town Council had earlier anticipated the backlash and warned people not to venture outdoors after 9.pm. Soon after leaving their camp at Belmont, the Jocks started wrecking houses, shops and pubs. Beginning at East Hill, windows were smashed; business fronts destroyed and furniture broken up. By the time the drunken Jocks reached Harbour Row, they were only getting into their stride, and it wasn't long before hand grenades and blast bombs were being tossed through shop windows. No place was safe in their path as Mackintosh and his men smashed their way along East and West Beach and didn't finish until they left their mark at the far end of Westbourne Place. They didn't show much favouritism either, as was shown towards the Swanton business at west Beach.

In an interview with the late Bill Swanton in the 1980s, he told me that his father was downstairs locking up his business when he heard the gunfire, explosions and shouting getting closer to his premises. Having a fair idea of what was going on outside, Mr Swanton who was a British appointed Peace Commissioner, mistakenly believed he and his business would be spared from attack. He soon discovered however, that the whole town was now regarded as the enemy as far as Sergeant Major Mackintosh and his rowdy gunmen were concerned. When his window came crashing in on top of him, the beleaguered Peace Commissioner was forced to take cover under a table, as a number of devices with lighted fuses followed into the premises. Fortunately for Swanton, none of the crudely made blast bombs ignited. Simultaneously, other members of the Camerons were also on the rampage in Midleton on the same night, while dragging two members of the Midleton Volunteer Company (the Buckley Brothers) from their beds before shooting them dead. Cobh Town Council made an open appeal to Admiral Tupper to use his influence to bring the Cameron terrorism under control.

After the first night of their rampages, the Council received thirty seven claims for damages to property totalling £3,728. The Jocks were not yet done however, and appeals to the Admiral proved pointless. The undeclared nightly curfews continued unabated in Cobh. Republican scouts patrolled the streets to keep people indoors while the Jocks continued on their drunken and violent orgies. By the night of 29 August the Camerons appeared completely out of control and decided to raise the punishment for the death of one of their members to a new level. George Walker was a thirty-six-year-old war veteran from Liverpool who was married in Cobh and lived below Cottrell's Row at the Holy Ground. On the same night while out on the street to bring in one of his children, he was shot by a party of Cameron Highlanders. Then while lying wounded on the ground, one of the attackers ran over and plunged his bayonet into his dying body. Walker was later taken the short distance to the nearby military hospital but died shortly afterwards.

The Scottish battalion were soon to learn of their mistake, for not only was George Walker an ex-service man, but he also worked on the Department of Defence launches that ferried military personnel to and from the harbour forts. The authorities in Cobh first tried to cover up the murder by stating that the Camerons had shouted a challenge to stop before opening fire, but that Walker had ignored the warning. To add to the plausibility of the story, they further claimed that the ex-soldier had been suffering from a hearing impairment inflicted during his time in the trenches of the Great War, and may not have heard the soldiers calling out. However, several testimonies given at the subsequent coroner's inquest contradicted this version of events.

John Hanlon, a labourer, told the inquest that on the night in question he had been on the steps leading down to the Mall, when he had heard two shots ring out, immediately followed by a slashing sound just yards away, where the deceased lay on the ground. The sound, Hanlon believed, had been that of bayonets. The labourer then explained that the Camerons had not been able to see him as he and his friends were hiding in the shade of the trees. He had heard one of the soldiers say to another, 'Hold my rifle till I pick him up.'[25] Both Hanlon and Walkers wife told the inquest that no soldier had called 'halt' or 'stop' at any time before firing their weapons. Another witness stated that she had heard the sound of shouting soldiers coming from Belmont hutments, followed shortly afterwards by the sound of shots ringing out.

A witness who had been visiting the Walker home just before the shooting and was a friend of the family, strongly criticised the British claims that George Walker had been drinking or had had a hearing ailment. Most likely, George Walker was more concerned with the safety of his children than of himself, which is what stopped him from running to safety when he spotted the Camerons coming in his direction. His death certificate was not released until 1949 (ironically the year when the Irish twenty-six-county state was proclaimed a Republic) and it stated that his death had been due to bullet and bayonet wounds 'feloniously inflicted by a patrol of the Cameron Highlanders'. No one was ever charged with Walker's murder or that of the Buckley brothers in Midleton and judging by the hands-on approach adopted by Sergeant Major Mackintosh, it would appear that the rowdy and murderous behaviour of the troops had been encouraged by those in command.

The fallout from the Quarry attack would have its long-term consequences too. Not only did Republican leaders in Cobh expect a backlash after the raid, but it was felt other victims would be sought out by the Jocks even after they had claimed the life of George Walker. The evening after Walker's murder, a large crowd had gathered in King's Square (now Pearse Square) to pray for the repose of the dead man's soul and for the release of Terence McSwiney (Lord Mayor of Cork), who was on hunger strike in Brixton Gaol. Suddenly a number of armed Jocks were spotted coming down the road. They were merely on their way to collect some equipment for their band at the railway station, but the crowd did not know this, and with the previous day's happenings still fresh in their minds, panicked. The people immediately dispersed, running for cover in all directions and falling over each other. There was a jam at the steps leading up to the Crescent, when many girls and women in the crowd tried to get up the steps. It was some time before calm was finally restored and people could actually believe that the Camerons had passed without firing.

Almost a year after the Quarry raid took place; the shame that that act inflicted upon the Cameron regiment was still raw amongst some of its officers. This unfortunate fact was to have terrible consequences for a totally innocent man who by no fault of his own played a small indirect part in that days events. John O'Connell, the blacksmith whose forge was used to launch the Quarry raid the previous year, was passing along Harbour Row on 29 May when a party of Camerons approached towards him. When the officer in charge of the patrol, Captain Gordon Duff, recognised the elderly blacksmith and ardent GAA supporter who was in his sixties, drew his revolver and shot him dead.

It was later reported (unconfirmed) that Duff was admitted to a mental institution. Major General Douglas Wimberley later wrote that one of his officers in Cobh was found to have regularly left his barracks at night time to exact his own revenge on Sinn Féin suspects from the Cobh and Carrigtwohill districts, and when this individual was later found out, he was admitted to an asylum. Wimberley didn't name the officer, but it might well have been Gordon Duff. Sergeant Major Mackintosh, who was later arrested by Mick Burke and Martin Corry during the truce, was court-martialled, found guilty and executed at Corry's home at Glounthaune for war crimes committed earlier at Carrigtwohill.

It is, I believe, worth looking at the events of the quarry raid from the British point of view. Not without a touch of arrogance, General Wimberley had already described the general population of Cobh as Sinn Féiners and said they dressed in plain clothes and spoke with good English.

His description of what took place at the Quarry on 25 August undoubtedly came from, reports that were taken back to Belmont Camp from those on the ground that day. He correctly concluded that the young officer in charge of the dismantling operation at the quarry unwisely ordered his men to pile their arms in stacks some thirty yards from where they were working with picks and shovels.

He described the first shots coming from the Sinn Féiners but makes no reference to any resistance to an order given to surrender by the rebels, or what was the then policy orders for sentries who were confronted with such orders by armed opponents. He thus gives the impression that a sentry guarding the rifles was shot at point blank without warning. This was immediately followed by Sinn Féiners jumping out of the ground floor windows with rifles and shotguns from the nearby houses at Ferry Street (Bishop Street) before a motor van pulled up and took away all the rifles, says Wimberley. It would appear from this account that those who reported the incident back to their superiors, either exaggerated the entire episode to save face, or that the local army command manufactured its own official version for reasons only it knew. None of the volunteers that day were armed with rifles or shot guns. Neither did any hide in houses other than the Harrier Club on the end of the street. No van pulled up to ferry away the rifles, as it was quietly secreted away at St Colman's Square waiting for the rifles to be dropped off.

Its driver, Donal Leahy was very mindful that both he and the company van might well be under suspicion for the attack on D.I. Mordaunt some weeks earlier and therefore wouldn't have taken the chance of pulling up in front of the troops with a company name painted on the side of the van. Only twelve rifles were captured that day, not every one that was stacked or held by the sentries, as indicated by General Wimberley's account. Far from it being a thoroughly well planned and ruthless operation, the quarry attack was a very quickly executed operation from a plan that was hastily hatched by Mick Burke after he saw an opportunity that was put to him only hours before, and with only a limited number of available hand guns for its participants.

Perhaps General Wimberley's account of how the Cameron's responded to the Quarry raid, offers a far more interesting insight into the mindset of the British military. 'The whole battalion felt very angry and ashamed that day. We, a famous regiment, had lost ten or twelve rifles to the rebels with but one casualty, the sentry; and without our having fired a shot. However, we were now learning our lesson, that we must be ever vigilant of all local Irish, and all were our enemy unless we knew them to be otherwise.'[26] 'It was however, most frustrating and unpleasant work for us all, and certainly we soldiers felt that we were not being given a free enough

hand by Parliament to deal with the situation with which we were faced.'
Wimberley then refers to the night his battalion broke loose on the town
of Cobh. He and other officers were dining in the mess at Belmont Camp
when word came through that a party of fifty NCOs and men under the
Regimental Sergeant Major were loose on the town. As the then assistant
Adjutant, he was sent out to investigate.

When he found them, they were armed with tools and wooden handles
and were systematically breaking windows of the shops that they passed.
'They were all quite sober, but felt they were not allowed to deal properly with their enemies, and they sensed, and rightly so, that many of the
inhabitants of Cobh were reporting their every movement to the local
Sinn Féin bands, and they decided they would retaliate.' At no point does
Wimberley indicate whether he reprimanded or charged anyone including Sergeant Mackintosh for their illegal actions that night. Nor does he
write if he even ordered them back to Barracks after he found them. His
near dismissive description of how he found his troops behaving is also
questionable. He refers to tools and wooden handles being used to smash
windows, but makes no reference to rifle fire or the use of hand grenades
and blast bombs, as was described by a number of witnesses including a
peace commissioner.

Wimberley especially refrains from making any reference to the murders
of George Walker two nights later, and the killing of John O'Connell the
blacksmith, or to the Buckley brothers in Midleton, or to the other clan-
destine killings of innocent people including children in Carrigtwohill
by members of his regiment stationed at Belmont Camp. One can only
conclude from his words that Wimberley endorsed, if not passively, the
lawlessness and murderous activities of those under his command. In the
following passage of his writings, he betrays such views clearly, 'However,
the Jocks had let off steam, and in point of fact their undisciplined actions
really did a lot of good, for the military authorities were forced to realise
that the troops were not prepared to stand, anymore, a policy of never
being supported, whatever politicians in London might be advocating.'[27]
Wimberley was at one with the Irish while describing the Black and Tans
in very poor terms; calling them 'no more or less than real thugs' for their
behaviour and the atrocities they carried out.

Without any irony however, he failed to express any fault towards his
own regiment when similar atrocities were committed, or when they
flaunted the law as a means of protest towards their own Government in
London. The General, nevertheless, gives a very helpful insight into how
things were done while he was stationed in Cobh. He refers very fondly
and in much detail of the great dinner party's that he and his fellow officers used to attend, courtesy of Admiral Tupper at Admiralty buildings.

'Here we could relax and enjoy ourselves, knowing the entire Admiralty Building was surrounded by an armed guard of Royal Marines.' [28] This close and friendly relationship with the Admiral might also in part explain why the Town Council appeals for him to use his influence to help bring the Cameron's to book for their illegal actions fell on deaf ears. Wimberley spoke of other parties that he and his colleagues used to be invited to amongst some of the other big houses throughout the town, and how these invitations dwindled to a few as the war intensified.

He referred to a case where the two daughters of a local Loyalist had their hair cropped as a punishment by the Sinn Féiners for having attended a Military Ball. He then goes on to speak with admiration for a local Catholic Bank Manager who braved it out by continuing to socialise and interact with the military, and whose daughters eventually married a couple of his colleagues. Seamus Fitzgerald, who was the Town Council Chairman at this time, later wrote defensively of Bishop Robert Browne who was regarded somewhat suspiciously by some of his flock for his close relationship with the Admiral. Nuala Killcullen, née Healy, the daughter of Barrister Healy, recalled as a young woman knowing Bishop Browne's niece and remembering well how she and her uncle would often attend dinners at the Admiralty and at Lord Barrymore's at Fota Estate.

Seamus Fitzgerald wrote how he had to flee Cobh in late 1920 after the Tans tried to kill him at his East Beach home, but shortly before that he had a meeting with the Bishop, who assured him that his loyalty was with his people, despite having an obligation to remain on good terms with the Admirals, the British one and previously with the American one, while his forces resided in the harbour. General Wimberley made no reference to the presence of a Catholic Bishop at the dinner parties held at Admiralty House, but it's possible the Admiral used different occasions to invite different guests to dinner at his residence. But perhaps Wimberley explains in a very telling way how his regiment totally flouted the law in Cobh, with a unique measure that was meant to keep British casualties to a minimum. Perhaps what they also unwittingly achieved, was to encourage quite a few of the local volunteers to go on the run.

About this time, we, as a battalion, started in Queenstown an unjust collective measure, which from our point of view, however, soon bore good results. One day, without warning, we rounding up and brought compulsorily into Camp at Belmont, which was surrounded with barbed wire, all the males whom we found anywhere in the streets of the town. They amounted to several hundred men. We made no exceptions whatever, and so those collected, much to their fury, were well known loyalists as well as suspected Sinn Féiners and included several retired officers of the British Army. Once safely shepherded inside our camp and our sentries, we paraded them all together, and took the names and addresses of every man, using Royal Irish Constabulary policemen, as necessary, to help identification when we thought any individual might be giving a false name. We then and there detailed them haphazardly, in small groups of five or six, as being 'on duty' for every night of the next month or two. We explained to them through a megaphone, as the present loudspeakers had not been invented then or at any rate were not yet in use, as to what being on duty entailed. It meant, we explained, that if a hostile incident occurred within the town boundaries of Queenstown, whereby any members of the Cameron's, or the police, were killed or wounded, we would at once arrest and hold and incarcerate in a cage of wire in our camp, all those half dozen civilians that we had detailed for duty for that twenty-four hours. Now this meant that those concerned had either to leave their homes and 'go on the run' as it was then called, in a hurry, or else wait in their homes till we collected them and then incarcerated them. By this arrangement, we calculated, that it was now probable that in the five or six men concerned, in any twenty-four hours, at least one of them would probably have some influence with the local town Sinn Féin leaders, and he would do his best to dissuade his friends from carrying out an incident against us during the period we had arbitrarily detailed for his duty and possible arrest. I may say this plan worked, so far as the town of Queenstown was concerned, surprisingly well.

Perhaps General Wimberley was a little economic with his facts however, especially where the gender of the arrested hostages were concerned. We know for example that women were also used as a weapon by the British to deter would-be Republican attackers, as in the case of the arrest of Cobh woman Lily Hawes. When Lily was arrested from her King's Square (Pearse Square) home and taken away to be interned at Waterford Prison by the Black and Tans, it was very likely that Wimberley's Cameron's were present at the initial raid. Passing on their way through every East Cork and Waterford town, the Tans had young Lily Hawes strapped up at the back of their lorry to deter would-be attackers. There were many, many Lily Hawes's out there however, and not all were Republican activists like she.

Nevertheless, the measures that Wimberley referred to, coupled with the fact that many of the local Republican officers that were now known to the RIC and Jocks, meant it was increasingly dangerous for them to stay around in Cobh. Despite such dangers, there were still some Volunteers willing to carry on raiding for arms in the locality. At the end of August a number of masked Volunteers carried out a night raid on Emmerson House at Rushbrooke, the home of Commodore C.S. Raikes. They found some small arms, but nothing of what they had hoped for. At the beginning of September the Volunteers struck again, this time raiding Olderburgh, on the Lower Road, the home of Mr Jim Galgey. Although the maid servants were assured that no harm would come to them, Galgey thought that this was an occasion that called for some good stern British resistance, even threatening to tear off the Volunteers masks. However, the self-made hero was told to stay put on the sofa while his house was being searched, and with very little other choice Galgey did just that. Again nothing was found to add significantly to the armoury.

In the weeks that followed the houses of Mssrs French, Hosie, Dillon, Hare and (Captain) Somerville were raided for arms, but no great quantity of arms was captured.

13. On The Run

By the summer of 1920, the local Company had already lost Jack O'Connell, James Ahern, Daithí O'Brien, his brother Henry, John and Maurice Moore, Charlie Reid and Seamus Fitzgerald, due to the pressure of them being known and hounded by the authorities. Unlike the others, Fitzgerald made his way up to the city to tie in with Brigade H.Q. The others hid out in different areas throughout East Cork, with nearly all sooner or later making their way to Knockraha to work with E company. E Company, under the command of Martin Corry, was a very busy outfit that operated locally with two specific purposes, at the behest of Brigade H.Q. The first was the manufacturing of hand grenades, at an underground bomb making factory at Blossomgrove.

Nearly every Cobh Volunteer that would leave Cobh on the run would have a direct role in the working and making of the hand grenades there at some stage or another. In fact the furnace used in that underground facility was taken from Rushbrooke Dockyard at the end of 1920 and discreetly moved into place at Blossomgrove, near Knockraha.

To begin with though, the furnace first had to be built, and one night under the command of Mick Burke, a party of twenty five Volunteers placed the watchman and a number of officials at the dockyard under armed guard. Armed sentries were then placed at vantage points around the yard. Many of the volunteers were competent tradesmen, i.e. ship-wrights and fitters trained in Haulbowline and Rushbrooke. After the machinery was started up, the men set to work making the furnace. Starting a 9.pm, they didn't stop until the job was completed around 2.am. It was then loaded up and transported off to its place of use at Blossomgrove. A short time later, the local Volunteers made another appearance at Rushbrooke dockyard where they raided the stores and took away a number of cross-cut saws and a quantity of electrical cable, the latter for the use in exploding land mines. This all happened in the month of October after Sean O'Hegarty O.C. of the brigade had visited Martin Corry with a plan to put in place a grenade making factory in his area. O'Hegarty already knew through Mick Leahy that two Cobh Volunteers, Daithí O'Brien and Charlie Reid were hiding out there on the run and that each was a moulder by trade with Fords in Cork. O'Hegarty had already decided that a long valley area in Knockraha between Kilquane and Butlerstown was ideal for what he was proposing. He was prepared to supply Corry's company with the finance and equipment to set up the operation, and told him he already had a four horsepower engine that would be ideal for melting the iron for the bombs.

After Corry had selected the site for the factory on McGrath's farm, a labour crew were selected from the Company and sent to work to dig out an area twenty feet long by eight feet wide by seven feet deep. The outer walls were constructed eight feet thick to absorb all the earth of the dugout. As a stream ran through the channel, a wooden floor had to be constructed over it to provide a dry floor to work upon. Next, sleepers from the railway line were procured to make a roof which was covered with earth and sally trees so that a person passing the field would not observe the factory. Into this was carried the motor and fan, with some heavy lifting required to install the Cobh made furnace. Four moulds for shaping the grenades were specially made by brigade members working in Henry Ford's in Cork and brought out to the dugout. The ingredients necessary for making the bombs were metal, some of which was brought by horse and cart from Cork, also iron gates, pots and material of this nature wherever it could be found. Sand and lime for making the cores had to be brought up from Passage West. This was brought to Little Island by boat and from there by horse and cart. Once up and running, the entire operation was supervised by Cobh officers including Daithí O'Brien, his brother Henry, Jack O'Connell, with Charlie Reid having overall charge. Seamus Fitzgerald would later join the others after he had to flee the City. A similar bomb making factory was later constructed at the east of Knockraha.

The other purpose for which the Brigade relied so heavily upon the Knockraha Company was their handling of prisoners and spies. E Company was chosen for this task because of the unique holding facility it possessed within its area for detaining prisoners waiting to be tried. The holding area was an old disused vault in the graveyard at Kilquane, Knockraha and with a secure steel gate and lock, was virtually escape proof. Because of the very sensitive brigade work that was underway in the area with the making of grenades, E Company had to be extra vigilant and always on its guard. This vigilance was to net the Company many undercover British operatives who undoubtedly were on spying missions in the locality.

These individuals, once captured and arrested would be first taken to Sing-Sing which became the nickname for the holding vault at Kilquane cemetery. Within a short time, the prisoners would be taken from there to face Court-martial. Very few walked away from a court-martial as it almost became a certain sentence of death for any unfortunate traveller or tramp that would unwittingly stray into E Company's area. If the unfortunate stray happened to have any past or family connections to the British services, then he had no hope whatsoever, and because of the constant state of emergency that the Volunteers found themselves operating under, it was the accused prisoner who was obliged to carry the burden of proving his innocence.

Corry and his Volunteers were steadfast in the manner in which they dealt with suspects, and as the British continued to send in their undercover operatives, and on occasions saturated the locality with large scale search parties, the Volunteers became more and more suspect of all outsiders who strayed onto their patch. Before long, the reputation of E Company and Sing-Sing became known throughout the whole battalion area, and this led to prisoners and suspects being transported from throughout East Cork to Sing-Sing for E Company's attention. Then by 1921, when the Black and Tan terror campaign and the espionage that fed into it was at its peak, Brigade HQ also became more reliant upon E Company to deal with suspected spies from its command areas. Some of the first burials of those executed from the Sing-Sing facility were around Carroll's Pond near Kearney's Cross. Others were later buried at an area called the Rea, and others still were reported to have been buried on Corry's own land at Sunville farm Glounthaune.

Corry himself was reported to have later estimated the number of executions from Sing-Sing as being thirty-five. His breakdown for the executed was seventeen members of the Cameron Highlanders, seven Black and Tans and eleven civilian spies. He didn't however, refer to those who didn't get to see the inside of Sing-Sing but for reasons of security were quickly Court-martialled at his own house and promptly executed and buried. One of the most infamous prisoners to face Court-martial in this way was Sergeant Major Mackintosh of the Cameron's who was based at Cobh. Of those who did visit Sing-Sing, two were Black and Tans who once had the misfortune of bumping into Daithí O'Brien at Carrigtwohill. O'Brien, who had the fiery reputation for impulsively shooting spies on the spot, got the drop on the two Tans and uncharacteristically disarmed them before taking them to Sing-Sing to face trial.

After safely reaching the city and making contact with brigade staff, Seamus Fitzgerald took up residence at No. 1 Motor Villas, Pope's Road, under the assumed name of Seán McGrath. More than two weeks had passed since Terence MacSwiney had been arrested on the 12 August and shipped off to prison at Brixton. Donal O'Callaghan, who was acting Lord Mayor in McSwiney's absence, sent for Fitzgerald and requested that he should take over Dáil Éireann publicity for Cork city and county and to act in conjunction with Cork Brigade Intelligence on a full time basis with such work. He was given a room to work from situated directly across from the Lord Mayor's office at City Hall, with a ready made staff of Miss Nancy Lehane who was an excellent short-hand typist with a fine knowledge of Irish.

Frank Buckley who worked as full time secretary to the Cork Sinn Féin executive, in close touch with Brigade Intelligence; Sean Moore who acted full time as registrar of Cork District Court; and Paud O'Donoghue who was in charge of the Belfast boycott campaign. Fitzgerald's work required the preparation of statistics dealing with raids, imprisonments, atrocities, etc., by Crown Forces which would be published in the famous *Irish Bulletin* controlled by Desmond Fitzgerald. His work took him around collecting sworn depositions covering every important phase of enemy activity and to prepare them for publication. He first studied very carefully the Blue Books and other books of Britain and other countries covering the late World War I period.

From them, he was able to glean how carefully he would have to work if his published statements were to be looked upon as authentic. He was also able to see from these publications how false the propaganda was of the World War belligerents and that there was no truth in such claims that the German Uhlans tossed young babies on their lances and cut off peoples wrists, and so on. The work was very dangerous for the now disguised and wanted Cobh Town Chairman, who did a fair deal of travelling to obtain immediate evidence of every shooting and outrage in Cork city and county. Much of his work was taken by Donal O'Callaghan to America, where he placed it before the American Commission of Inquiry and where it was subsequently published in the interim report of that body. Most of the depositions contained in the pamphlet 'Who burned Cork City' were obtained by Fitzgerald while the town was still burning.

Each night he would confer at length with its editor, Professor Alfred O'Rahilly, who prepared the foreword to same. Fitzgerald would later observe that every witness statement taken, had to be sworn, and none were refused, despite the danger attached to those making them. The pamphlet had to be prepared quickly and published before Hamar Greenwood would make his promised speech in the House of Commons absolving the

British Forces. They knew the pamphlet would obviously suffer if it were published under the aegis of Dáil Éireann or Sinn Féin, so it was therefore arranged to publish it under the name of the Irish Labour Party. The pamphlet was published and distributed a couple of days before Hamar Greenwood acted, and had a stupefying effect on the British Government and public opinion in general.

Fitzgerald's work also meant he was present at many post-mortem examinations with Denis Barry, O.C. of Cork Republican Police, into a number of murders carried out by Crown Forces in Cork City and County. These included among others, the shooting dead of Thomas Coleman a few doors from North Abbey Barracks in the city, the shooting and mutilation of six IRA Volunteers at Ballycannon, Clogheen, Cork and the murder of the Buckley brothers of Midleton. In order to obtain the most positive evidence, he engaged the services of Professor Moore, a Protestant and Professor of Pathology at University College, Cork, and Dr George Hegarty, who had served in the British army in the World War, to assist him arriving at a true verdict. Through these post mortems, they were able to establish accurate exit and entry gunshot wounds as well as mutilations caused by the use of bayonets.

In his reports, Fitzgerald had established that after they were taken from their Midleton home on 25 August, Sean and Batt Buckley were shot while in transit to Cork in a military lorry, and despite the Crown forces believing the two men were dead, Batt Buckley, although bullet riddled, lived long enough to tell his story. Fitzgerald also reported the rape of a middle-aged pregnant woman by Black and Tans in Blackpool, and a second attempt in the same locality where a woman successfully resisted her attackers. He submitted all his reports to the Brigade and to the Dáil Éireann Director of Publicity. On Wednesday morning, 8 December, while Fitzgerald was chatting with Brigadier General Thomson (Lord Thomson) of the Labour Commission in the Imperial Hotel, preparatory to their departure for Killarney, Thomson showed him a secret lengthy document showing the deposition of all the IRA brigades in Ireland, issued by the British Government. Fitzgerald immediately reported the document to Brigade H.Q. and was instructed to get his hands on it for at least three hours. He succeeded in borrowing it for the desired time period, and subsequently learned that the hotel was surrounded by Crown Forces in pursuit of him. By Christmas 1920, the Cobhman was beginning to feel he was surviving on borrowed time in Cork. He was regularly being stopped and searched and felt it was only a matter of time before he would be arrested. He had even been stopped by the famous Sergeant Chance, and had only escaped with tremendous luck.

The nature of his work meant that he was finding it increasingly difficult to escape being caught after curfew with important documents in his possession. After City Hall was burned, he and his staff located themselves in the judge's room of the Courthouse but had to vacate there after a few weeks to the Stewards House, Fitzgerald's Park. Shooting in that vicinity forced them to make a sudden departure, to locate the R.M.S.'s room in the Cork Mental Hospital, where Fitzgerald regularly slept in one of the Head Attendant's rooms.

Eventually the Mental Hospital was raided and Sean Hayes TD and others were arrested, but none of the records were found as they were carefully concealed under floor boards. After this, Fitzgerald and his team moved to a room at the School of Art but the British were hot on their heels, and one day while surrounding the building, captured all their records and equipment. The volunteers escaped however through a back way and into the Opera House. The loss of the records was a tremendous blow to Fitzgerald and his team. He was particularly worried for the safety of those who had made depositions against the British, as the original signed ones were among those captured.

14.
Death of a Second Lord Mayor

At 8:47am on Monday, 25 October 1920, a statement was released through Fleet Street, London which stated, 'Lord Mayor completed his sacrifice for Ireland at 5:40 this morning.' The one line statement was issued by Terence McSwiney's personal Chaplain Fr Dominic O'Connor. The event, as long as it had taken (seventy-four days of an agonising hunger strike) seemed to have caught the British Government off guard. The Government immediately released a captured letter dated from May addressed to the Lord Mayor in his capacity as Commandant of Cork No. 1 Brigade, seeking to tie him to the manufacturing of hand grenades (probably at Knockraha). The release of the letter on the same day as McSwiney died, however, only caused more criticism of the government, especially as McSwiney had at no time been charged with any offence implied by the communication to him. The next day, The *London Times* stated its objection to what it called 'attempts by the Government to saddle upon the Lord Mayor the crimes of which he never was convicted…Particularly odious is the publication on the day of death the letter referring to the manufacture of hand grenades…This action will only intensify Irish feeling.' At the inquest the next day Muriel McSwiney, his wife, appeared as the sole representative of the family. A battle of wills soon ensued when she refused to concur with the coroners repeated efforts to characterise Terence McSwiney's occupation as other that a 'Volunteer officer of the Irish Republican Army.' 'What was he?' the coroner asked. 'An Irish Volunteer,'[29] she answered several times until that title was finally accepted. On the morning of 28 October some 30,000 people, Irish and non-Irish alike, filed past the bier, draped in a green, white and orange tricolour at St George's Roman Catholic Cathedral in Southwark.

Among those who came to the cathedral was a young British Army officer named Clement Atlee who, some twenty-five years later, would succeed Winston Churchill as prime minister. Requiem Mass was celebrated by Dr Cotter, Bishop of Portsmouth, assisted by Dr Mannix, Archbishop of Melbourne, Australia. A large throng of lay people along with 400 members of clergy jammed the cathedral. Representatives of Dáil Éireann and members of Cork Harbour Board joined officials from British bodies, including the Lord Mayor of Southwark, the Mayor of Fulham and the Mayor of Battersea. After the service in the packed cathedral, the journey back to Ireland began with a 10,000-strong procession from the cathedral that included contingents from virtually every Irish society in London. The greatest source of concern for the British government appeared to relate to the British public who lined the streets in respectful silence. Upon their arrival in Holyhead, the mourning party accompanying the Lord Mayor's body found that British government had ordered that, rather than being allowed to go to Dublin, where a demonstration of public grief had been planned by Sinn Féin, and would be followed by a train trip across Ireland, the remains would instead be sent directly to Cork.

An ugly scene occurred at Holyhead as a result of this surprise announcement. The decision to re-route the Lord Mayor's body had come at the insistence of General Sir Henry Wilson. Wilson took a decision to go over the head of Hamar Greenwood, the Irish secretary. After making a protested fuss to Winston Churchill about the issue of the body going through Dublin, Churchill raced off to see the Prime Minister who overturned the decision. As a result of Wilson's intervention, the train to Holyhead was visited at 9:15pm. by a police inspector at Crewe station, who made his way to the chief mourner's carriage in search of Muriel McSwiney. On being informed that she was not on the train, he presented a letter to the Lord Mayor's brother Peter, who had journeyed from New York. Its contents caused consternation in McSwiney's family. It stated that it regretted to inform them that it could not allow the remains of the late Lord Mayor to be paraded through Dublin as it may lead to demonstrations of a political nature.

Therefore, the Irish Government cannot allow disembarkation of remains of the late Lord Mayor in any other part of Ireland except his native City of Cork. The inspector told the mourners that he was obliged to carry out his orders. The presence of 300 police officers on the train was a clear indication that the British Government was determined to carry out its demand. When it reached Holyhead, the doors of the train swung open, the police took on a menacing appearance as they formed up with a large party of Auxiliaries and Black and Tans that had arrived from Dublin on the morning boat. At 1:45 on the afternoon of Friday, 29 October, McSwiney's remains arrived in Cobh. There, the British Auxiliaries were met by a problem they had not expected. Of the hundreds of mourners that waited on the quayside, including the Town Chairman Seamus Fitzgerald and Bishop Browne, the Bishop of Cloyne, no one from the Republican movement or the Town Council came forward to claim the body, forcing the authorities to transfer the body themselves from the *Rathmore* to the British Admiralty tug, *Mary Tavy*. Later that afternoon, the *Mary Tavy*, with its blue ensign flying at half mast, arrived at Customs House Quay. After an absence of two and a half months, Terence McSwiney had finally returned home. The mourning party from Dublin arrived in Cork that evening, and the coffin was removed from the tug and placed upon the quay. At 9:30p.m., McSwiney's remains were carried into City Hall on the shoulders of an honour guard of Irish Volunteers, accompanied by acting president of the Irish Republic Arthur Griffith, Liam de Róiste and several other members of the Dáil.

After a Requiem Mass celebrated by the Bishop of Cork, assisted by four Irish bishops and two Australian Archbishops, the Lord Mayor was finally laid to rest. Shortly after her brother's burial, Mary MacSwiney received a letter of condolence from one of her former teachers at Cambridge University, from which she had received a teaching degree twenty-five years before.

It was only quite recently that I learnt that you are the same Miss McSwiney that was one of my students at Cambridge and I want therefore to send you a few words of warmest and deepest sympathy in your grief and trouble. I feel that it would not be so strange if you should dislike the idea of any communication just now with anyone English...I want you to believe that we hate and abhor what is being done in Ireland - that when we think of the death of your heroic brother and the suffering of the other Irishmen and women we are filled with bitter shame and sorrow, that we are not hoping and praying for an end to these horrors, but the moment we can stop them we will... The English people cannot long tolerate, when once they really know, the things that are being done in their name.[30]

While the above letter gives an idea of the goodwill that existed towards Ireland by some sections of the British public, the latter part of 1920 nevertheless saw an escalation of hostilities in Ireland. As IRA attacks on convoys of British Auxiliary troops and RIC increased drastically, the government introduced martial law in Cork and the south-western counties. The British policy of reprisals against military and civilian targets alike, reached a new height in December, when Black and Tans and troops burned the centre of Cork City. Not everyone on the Republican side was content with keeping the fight with the British confined to Irish soil. Persistent urgings by Cathal Brugha and others resulted in Michael Collins taking action to organise some spectacular military operations in Britain.

On the same night that Tom Barry and his West Cork column members were celebrating their earlier victory at Kilmichael, seventeen warehouses went up in flames in Liverpool. Under the direction of Rory O'Connor, other commercial targets were destroyed at various locations throughout Britain. Collins produced a list of the home addresses of Black and Tans and some of these were also attacked and destroyed. O'Connor attempted to expand his operations away and beyond the resources and men that were available to him. He drew-up unrealistic plans for incendiary attacks in London, Birmingham, Sheffield, Newcastle, Manchester and Liverpool, the destruction of railways, tube stations, reservoirs, the Ministry of Pensions and the homes of figures like General Tudor and Lord FitzAlan. Several key figures in the Collins network were picked up just before the November burnings, including Neil Kerr and Steve Lanigan in Liverpool and Paddy O'Donoghue in Manchester, and the Brugha/O'Connor offensive had a damaging effect on the arms smuggling routes Collins had built up.

By the following May he had repaired the damage to the extent that he was arranging for a ton of potassium chlorate per week to be sent from Liverpool under the guise of bread soda. In fact had a raid not driven Dick Mulcahy to escape across the rooftops of his hide out in Longwood Avenue, leaving his papers behind, seconds ahead of the Auxiliaries, very large scale operations would have taken place in Liverpool and Manchester during April 1921. These would have included the destruction of all British shipping in Liverpool and of Manchester's electricity supply. But the capture of the Mulcahy papers alerted the authorities and created a sensation in England when they were released to the press, not so much for the revelations about IRA strength and ruthlessness, as for the fact that included in the papers was a proposal made by an eccentric for infecting horses feed with glanders. This was taken up by the press as evidence of fiendishness on a far greater scale than merely blacking out a city and destroying a shipping fleet.

In January 1921, Seamus Fitzgerald decided to quit the city, and make contact with Daithí O'Brien who was holding up in Knockraha, working on the bomb factory there. Fitzgerald was welcomed back on board with the 4th Battalion and along with O'Brien and Charlie Reid, was looked upon as a specialist brigade unit, engaged in fulltime work, and was paid 30d a week for maintenance. Fitzgerald was happy with the set up and was satisfied with the security of the area, especially as the fox hounds of the United Hunt had passed through on a few occasions, and never detected their whereabouts in the field. Although E Company's commander Martin Corry, was under strict instructions from the brigade to not engage in any other military activity in the area, to avoid bringing Crown Force activity to the locality, it was apparent that Capt. Geary, with British Intelligence at Victoria (Collins) Barracks, had some knowledge of activity in the area, as the area was raided by Crown Forces on many occasions and had been surrounded by lorries and armoured cars. In fact five times during the fortnight preceding the Truce, the British raided and searched the surrounding fields. On one occasion, British troops actually fired in the general direction of the foundry, and although the men were armed with rifles, they didn't return fire, for fear of betraying their location and that of the foundry.

On 11 August 1920, the O.C. of the 4th Battalion, Mick Leahy, received a dispatch from Florrie O'Donoghue of Brigade Intelligence, instructing him to shoot a particular RIC Sergeant based in Cobh. Leahy travelled to Cobh to make the necessary enquiries, but found that the wanted Sergeant, from Cooraclare, Co. Clare did not reside there. The battalion commander decided to go to Cork the next day to see O'Donoghue, and get a description of the wanted man who might be in Cobh under another name. He first travelled across to Passage West, by boat and then by train into the City.

After making enquiries about the whereabouts of Florrie O'Donoghue, he was directed towards City Hall. When he got there, he found O'Donoghue in a meeting with the Lord Mayor, Terence McSwiney. O'Donoghue gave Mick Leahy the description of the wanted RIC man, but before he could depart again for Cobh, the Lord Mayor asked Leahy to stay on as there was a planned meeting of senior officers of the Cork brigades in the City Hall that evening, about 8.pm. Although Leahy only ranked as a battalion commandant at the time, McSwiney had enough trust and confidence in his abilities, to suggest that he'd attend such an important meeting. The meeting began at the appointed time, while a Republican Court was in progress in the main hall. The brigade meeting was not long in session when word came through that the military had surrounded the building and had begun searching. The meeting was instantly stopped, with the participant officers being ushered through a concealed exit to a hiding place somewhere between the ceiling and the roof. Before they could reach there, it was discovered that a key to this hideout was missing, leading McSwiney to send someone back to another room to locate the key. The soldiers were in the meantime getting closer, so it was decided to get out into the back yard and through the workshops at the rear of the building, in the hope of getting away in that direction. When Leahy attempted to climb a gate out of the yard, a bullet, fired by a soldier in the laneway outside, whizzed past his head. This forced him to jump back into the yard, leaving him and the others to realise that escape was impossible.

When they retreated into the carpenter's workshops, they we all arrested. Among the high profile officers captured in the raid were, the Lord Mayor and 1st Cork Brigade O.C. Terence McSwiney, Sean O'Hegarty Vice O.C., Florrie O'Donoghue Brigade I.O., Dom Sullivan, Brigade Adjutant; Liam Deasy, O.C. No. 3 Brigade; Dan 'Sandow' O'Donovan, O.C. City Battalion, and Mick Murphy, O.C. 2nd Battalion, Cork City.

The British officer in charge posted sentries at either end of the workshop with orders to shoot if anyone attempted to escape. Leahy found himself in an awkward predicament, as he had in his possession, the dispatch from Florrie O'Donoghue, instructing him to shoot the RIC man in Cobh. McSwiney too, had notes taken at the meeting. In an attempt to deal with this problem, the men collected in a group, allowing Leahy and McSwiney to tear up the papers into small pieces and throw them into the wood shavings on the floor of the workshop. One of the soldiers spotted the men and shouted not to destroy the papers. Leahy agreed with the soldier and threw some of the pieces towards him; they too, dropped into the shavings on the floor. The others then milled around making it impossible for anybody to put the pieces of notes together again.

When the British officer in charge arrived back, the sentry reported what he had seen regarding the destruction of papers. McSwiney and Leahy were each questioned about their actions. Leahy said he had torn up a letter from a girl friend. McSwiney adopted a different attitude, saying what had been destroyed were papers pertaining to his office as Lord Mayor. He also protested strongly of the insult to his office as chief citizen of the City. Shortly before midnight the men were marched under a strong military escort to Cork Barracks. On the way out of the yard of City Hall, Leahy managed to dump a razor (with his name on the case), extra socks and toothpaste behind a radiator. McSwiney and he also changed hats. The commandant of the detention barracks lined the men up and told them that, owing to the late hour, he didn't propose, then, to have each man searched; instead, they were each given a canvass bag with a number on it and told to put all their possessions into them. He assured the men, on his word of honour that that each bag returned intact to us the following morning when they would be opened and examined in their presence. As he was emptying his pockets, Leahy was surprised to discover, three .45 revolver bullets in the lining of one of his waistcoat pockets.

He quickly dumped them into his property bag and hoped for the best the next morning. The next morning they were brought into an office and told to turn out the contents of their property bags. When Leahy put his hand into his bag, he pulled a Rosary beads and the three bullets. Deflecting attention away from the bullets, he held up the beads and said, 'Surely I am entitled to keep this.'[31] The officer present agreed, allowing him the opportunity to discreetly slip the bullets back into his pocket with the beads. When he later returned to his cell, he hid the bullets high up the wall in a ventilator. With the exception of McSwiney who kept his captors reminded of his title of office, all gave false names. The men were kept in the detention barracks for a day, when they went on hunger-strike. Then they were transferred to the military barracks, where they were again interrogated by military intelligence officers. Needless to say, they denied having anything to do with the IRA or Sinn Féin. After five days in the barracks, they were astounded to learn that they were to be released; that is, all except Terence McSwiney. The men could not credit their good fortune on being released, and lost no time in getting out of the city. It was a miraculous turn of fate that they left when they did, because not two hours after they had left the barracks, a most intensive round up took place in the city. Thousands of soldiers were engaged searching every conceivable building. Leahy and the others became convinced by the sudden turn of events, that British military intelligence was so poor at that time that, with the exception of McSwiney, who was a well known public figure, they (the British) had no idea who they had held before releasing them, and for some reason, that they had in fact, made a most important capture which they had let slip through their fingers.

Indeed, it may not have been that British intelligence was so poor but that the IRA's was so effective. Leahy received a message from an RIC Inspector following his release stating 'There's not an RIC man in East Cork who will give him away.' Terence McSwiney was not as fortunate as had been his comrades, and was transferred to Brixton Prison in England where he died after a prolonged hunger strike on the 25 October. Following his release and the continued imprisonment of McSwiney, Mick Leahy was appointed Vice O.C. of the Cork No.1 Brigade. He was later officially appointed to that post on the day that McSwiney died. This appointment naturally meant that he was unable to spend much time in his old 4th Battalion area in East Cork. Diarmuid Hurley, captain of the Midleton Company, was appointed commandant of the 4th Battalion, in

Leahy's place, and Joseph Ahern, Midleton, was made Vice Commandant.

Following the abortive attempt to assassinate Lord French in Cobh in late July 1920, Captain Jack O'Connell left Cobh to work in Midleton with the same motor repair company which employed Mick Leahy and Paddy Whelan. When the Lord Mayor of Cork, Terence McSwiney, was arrested at City Hall a couple of weeks later, he had not been totally successful in destroying all the papers in his possession. One of the documents that the British managed to recover, was a letter written to him by Seamus Fitzgerald of Cobh, with a reference to O'Connell having been in charge of an ambush party that disarmed a party of soldiers (killing one) at Bunker Hill in Cobh some months earlier. The chaplain, who was attending Terence McSwiney in prison, got to hear of the captured letter, and sent word to the Cork Volunteers, who in turn passed it on to O'Connell. O'Connell cleared out of Midleton at once, and was now well and truly on the run. He headed straight for the city and with some help got himself a job with the Cork Harbour Commissioners. Councillor James Ahern of Cobh, who had already been on the run for nearly 10 months by that stage, soon joined him there.

In December, Mick Leahy was commissioned by Headquarters in Dublin to go to Italy to purchase arms, and it was arranged that O'Connell and Ahern would later follow on when they received word that the ship with the arms was ready to leave for Ireland; the two men were to act as engineers on the ship during its voyage from Italy. Leahy left Cork in December and as O'Connell and Ahern heard nothing from him by the end of January, they got fed up waiting and decided to leave the city. About two weeks before the famous Clonmult Ambush when the IRA faced the greatest loss in its history, Jack O'Connell and James Ahern bumped into Seamus Fitzgerald on the Lower Road, Cork.

The two men enquired about the 4th Battalion Flying Column they heard had been established by Diarmuid Hurley. The Column had in fact been in existence since October, and had been set up at Knockraha where Hurley was held upon the run. Fitzgerald knew the two men were on the run and wanted to keep themselves active and useful, but warned them of the dangers of becoming active members of the column. 'It would hardly be as dangerous as carrying those documents, that I did for you a couple of nights ago'[32] retorted Jim Ahern. Fitzgerald agreed to make the necessary enquiries and arrangements to get them into the column. He proceeded to Clonmult outside of Midleton where he knew the column was holding up. He was guided towards the farmhouse after making the necessary contacts along the way. When he arrived, he had expected to be challenged by their sentries, but was in the farmyard before he was recognised and brought inside to meet Paddy Whelan, Paddy O'Sullivan, Maurice Moore and young James Glavin, all from Cobh, together with some Midleton lads and others belonging to the column.

When Diarmuid Hurley arrived a short time later, he was very angry that Fitzgerald had come, probably because of the easy manner in which he had managed to approach without being challenged. The column commander was pleased to hear however, that O'Connell and Ahern were interested in joining them. It was agreed that the two men would join the others on the following Sunday. Fitzgerald left the Clonmult farmhouse that day with an uneasy and ominous feeling about the casual manner in which he had earlier being able to enter it.

Meanwhile back in Cobh, it appeared that Republicans were not the only ones on the run from the law. On the evening of 2 September 1920, three English policemen were seen approaching a captain of the Cameron Highlanders on East Hill, not far from his Camp. While pointing their revolvers at the officer, they attempted to place him under arrest, but the captain resisted and instead swiftly contacted his barracks at Belmont hutments. Shortly afterwards a patrol of officers arrived and ordered the policemen to surrender their weapons. Apparently one of the policemen was more than reluctant to do so, but being held at gunpoint by a Cameron Highlander, proved to be a convincing enough argument and he soon surrendered as well.

The three were placed under arrest and taken into custody at the barracks. Unfortunately there was no follow-up report on this incident or other acts of criminality by the military in the papers. But such matters were not about to impede on the military's planned campaign of raiding and arrests that by now were an everyday fact of life in Cobh. The Jocks and the Tans might not have been winning the war to drive all local Republicans on the run out of Cobh, but they were going to give it their best shot, and they were sure going to make life unpleasant for anyone who was found sheltering them. On the morning of 5 September a party of Cameron's raided the home of David Leahy and his family (no connection to Mick Leahy) at Barrymore Avenue (naval dwellings). After an extensive search of the house, a Volunteer uniform and a wooden gun were found. David Leahy Snr who had been a member of the volunteers when they were first formed, was placed under arrest and put in a military lorry, as were his two sons, Michael and David Jnr. By now a large crowd of spectators, on their way to Sunday Mass, had assembled, and the Jock soldiers kept their guns trained on them for a considerable time before eventually taking the three men away to Victoria Barracks in Cork. David and his son Michael both worked at the naval dockyard, Haulbowline, while David Jnr worked at Ballincollig Barracks.

At the subsequent trial on 20 September, Michael Leahy was charged with having in his possession a document detailing 'the construction of explosive substances' and with having been in possession of a certain suitcase found in Midleton at the end of July when the Cameron Highlanders had raided and searched a house. The suitcase had contained 'seditious literature', namely a copy of an *t-Óglach*, the official organ of the IRA, and had had a tie-on label with the name 'Leahy' on it; it had also contained a trade union card belonging to a Michael Leahy of Barrymore Avenue, but Leahy denied he had ever been in Midleton. Leahy may or may not have even been in Midleton, but it is very likely that the real owner of the Midleton suitcase was the former 4th Battalion O.C. who had not long before left Midleton to take up his new post as Vice O.C. with the brigade. He was also a former employee at Haulbowline dockyard and a union member. It was also not beyond the bounds of probability that the authorities were well aware of the true owner of the Midleton suitcase, but saw how the similarities in name could be used to penalise a second Republican family of the same name.

As things transpired, this Michael Leahy was acquitted owing to insufficient evidence. A few days later, the Cameron's once again carried out several raids in Cobh, searching houses in King's Square, and Harbour Row. No arrests were made on this occasion. However, while King's Square was being searched, a number of American tourists staying at the Rob Roy Hotel seemed very much taken by what was happening, and every window in the hotel that offered a worthwhile view of the raids was occupied for the duration of the search. On 12 October three arrests were made during military raids in the suburbs of the town. Those arrested were named as Leahy, Glanville and Maurice Moore. This would probably be the last time that Moore would be arrested before he would soon go on the run and join up with the East Cork Flying Column, however in less than five months, he would be killed by firing squad.

In early November a group of other Americans staying at the Rob Roy had a, 'wait till they hear this at home Honey', experience similar to that witnessed by their fellow countrymen a few weeks earlier. On Saturday evening several of the hotels guests gathered outside the Rob Roy to listen to a particular musician, who was singing national songs while accompanying himself on a banjo. The performance was greatly appreciated by the Americans who applauded and cheered the man. However, the musician had only left shortly when the military appeared on the scene, looking for the banjo-playing patriot. The hotel was searched, identification papers were checked, but the bird had flown. The search, having failed, the Cameron's then started firing shots in the streets and stopping passers-by for questioning.

Six arrests were made; one was that of Daithí O'Brien the former

Company O.C. who thought he would steal a quick visit home to Roche's Row, from being on the run. O'Brien was released shortly afterwards and like Maurice Moore, would soon skip town again, but unlike Moore, he would soon take up work on the Knockraha bomb factory. On 22 November, there were more raids, with some twenty to thirty arrests being made. Two lorries full of prisoners were taken to Belmont hutments by the Cameron Highlanders. The RIC also raided the Town Hall and examined documents but without results. They were probably hoping to discover and disrupt a Republican court which used to operate there regularly. The following day the troops carried out more arrests when they raided a lodging house in the town. Four people, who had arrived in Cobh only two days previously, and were due to depart on the liner *Celtic* to New York, were brought to Belmont hutments. They were a Miss Maloney, a native of Kerry, and Messrs Ryan, McNamara and McMahon. It is not know if these people were charged with any offence, but in any case they missed their passage back to the promised land.

Also in November the British Prime Minister announced that he 'had murder by the throat.' That this was far from the factual situation as was illustrated by his deeds, as it was from October onwards that the British really started pouring Black and Tans into Ireland in large numbers. From November 1920 to March 1921 some 1,000 freshly recruited Black and Tans arrived monthly on average. Likewise the Auxiliaries were reinforced. This was to prove the most critical period of the war, when the British would rely more on numerical strength, while the IRA reverted more and more to the use of highly effective flying columns. By the end of 1920 enemy intelligence had almost completely broken down, and large areas were under Republican control. Two weeks after Lloyd George had made his famous statement of having murder by the throat, Tom Barry and his West Cork flying column ambushed a convoy of Auxiliaries at Kilmichael, killing eighteen of them and capturing arms and ammunition. Three IRA Volunteers were also killed in the ambush. The Black and Tans, along with Auxiliaries, duly retaliated by burning and looting Cork City on 11 December. On the previous day, 10 December, martial law had been proclaimed in the south and west of the country by the Viceroy and it was to come into effect in Cork, Kerry, Limerick and Tipperary on 4 January 1921. It meant that henceforth the civil authority was placed in the hands of the military, the General O.C. of British troops in Ireland.

The measure made little difference to the Irish, against whom the enemy had for long employed every weapon in its arsenal. In the middle of December another round of extensive military searches were carried out by the Cameron's. As the last train out of Cobh was about to leave, a party of soldiers entered the railway station and, rushing up to the engine and ordered the driver at gunpoint to get off. All the men on the train, irrespective of age, were then ordered to get on to the platform and subjected to close scrutiny by the officers, who appeared to be looking for three specific individuals. Failing to find them, a number of Jocks entered the train, which was destined for Cork and considerably behind schedule. While some officers availed of the free ride to Cork, the remaining troops lined up the men still on the platform and conducted a rigorous personal search. Also on that night every man leaving town by the road towards Rushbrooke was stopped and searched. The British also raided the Dance Hall of the Queens (Commodore) Hotel, and arrested two young men, Danny Healy of Harbour Row, and a man by the name of Desmond from Passage West. It was also in December, just before Christmas that two members of the Camerons at Belmont decided to desert from their regiment. A few days before Christmas the soldiers were noticed in Kilmacsimon Quay, a hamlet halfway between Bandon and Kinsale.

They called to a house in the locality, which happened to be the family home of Liam Deasy (first adjutant West Cork Brigade at the time) for some food and cigarettes. Deasy's mother supplied them with both, but as soon as they left the house the two men were arrested by local Volunteers and questioned. They said that they were deserters from the Cameron Highlander regiment in Cobh and because they were cold and hungry they had asked for help. The two soldiers were Peter Monahan, a well educated and bright Scotsman, and Tommy Clarke, a man of lesser calibre than his friend, whose only ambition seemed to be to get away from the Army. The IRA was of course highly suspicious of the two men, and usually men such as Monahan and Clarke were court-martialled and executed as spies. Had these two men, for example wondered into the E company area of Knockraha, they would have almost certainly paid with their lives. However, on this occasion, the well-spoken Peter Monahan succeeded in convincing the West Cork Volunteers that their desertion had been genuine.

He explained how he and his companion were both disgusted with the trend of events in Ireland and had consequently decided to desert and offers their services to the IRA instead. They had left Ringaskiddy a few days before and had travelled across the country in an effort to locate the West Cork Volunteers. Monahan also told of how he had been a mining engineer in Scotland, and it was this part of his account that made the IRA decide to let the two men live. Their efforts to manufacture mines had met with little success so far and here was a man who could offer his knowledge and experience in this respect. Monahan thus joined the Volunteers, his mines proved less successful however. The first two mines fabricated by the Scotsman and used in an attack on Kilbrittain RIC barracks failed to explode, and in another attack, this time on Innishannon barracks, the mines again failed to explode. Monahan's mines were finally successful when one was detonated at the Drimoleague RIC barracks, causing a violent explosion, yet failing to blow the expected breach in the barracks wall and causing more damage to the surrounding houses than to the Volunteers target. Peter Monahan was also helpful in capturing an informer in early 1921 when together with two IRA officers he called at the house of the suspected 'Squealer'. The three IRA men posed as Auxiliaries and when the farmer in question heard Monahan's Scottish accent he exclaimed: 'Thank God, I thought you'd never come', then went on to give the names of many active Volunteers in the area. The farmer was court-martialled and executed later that night.

Volunteer Peter Monahan was to lose his life during the Crossbarry ambush in March 1921, but not before one of his mines had effectively saved the lives of other Volunteers. A few hours into the ambush, the section of Volunteers to which Monahan belonged found itself almost completely surrounded by enemy forces and it was decided by the group commander Lordan that they should try to break out from their position before it was too late. The planned escape came too late for Monahan however, who had already been mortally wounded. Rolling in agony, he accidentally wound the wires of one of the mines around his body; it was to save the lives of the other volunteers. Just before making a run for it, Lordan thought of detaching the electric wires from the exploder of the mine and bringing the latter with him. However, in moving Monahans body, his arm accidentally made contact with the plunger and detonated the mine. A terrific explosion followed, sending a huge cloud of earth and dust into the air.

In the surprise and confusion that followed, Lordan succeeded in getting his men out of their entrapped position and into safety. Not all Camerons were so sympathetic towards the Irish people and its demand for freedom however. In fact those of the calibre of Peter Monahan were far and few between. The Cameron Highlanders were a most loyal British regiment, with most of its officers coming from the Loyalist/Protestant tradition of Scotland. Sectarian attitudes were rarely far from the mindsets of some of those in charge of raiding parties and while many parts of Ireland were suffering under the lethal excesses of the Black and Tans and Auxiliaries, the people of Cobh, Carrigtwohill and Midleton in comparison, were more concerned with the behaviour of the Scottish.

In time, this behaviour would develop into a clear pattern of horror, with many attacks. The village of Carrigtwohill would suffer the brunt of these attacks, with most of the victims coming from the civilian population. Meanwhile in Cobh, the town continued to suffer both daily and night time raids by the Scottish throughout the remainder of 1920 and 1921. While Republican intelligence had reliable lines of communication with secret sources in the local RIC barracks and Admiralty buildings, allowing for regular forewarnings of pending raids, it had no such luck when the source of the raids were coming from Jock H.Q. at Belmont. For this reason, the Republican community had to develop its own early warning system of alerting each other when it would learn that a raid was coming. This was never going to be a foolproof system however and the Scottish would from time to time get through and locate their target. On one occasion when this happened, it demonstrated beyond doubt that the Scots had come with murder on their minds.

This was when they made an unexpected late night/early morning raid to the home of the Moore family at Ticknock, on the outskirts of the town. The raiding party arrived unexpectedly in the weeks following the execution of family member Maurice, who had been captured after the Clonmult ambush. On this occasion it was Maurice's younger brother Michael they had come looking for. Moore, aged twenty, was ordered by an officer to get dressed, while others were busy out the back breaking bottles around the yard of the labourers cottage. When they were ready, they ordered the barefooted prisoner, dressed in just his trousers and shirt outside to the yard. Moore received a severe beating with a number of heavy blows to his head, stomach and ribs from rifle butts, and was under no illusions of exactly what was going on.

He knew they were going to shoot him whether he ran or not and therefore was determined not to allow the broken glass to deter him from escaping. Although the area of the back yard was poorly lit, Moore had the advantage of knowing exactly where the perimeter fence was high or low. He first caught the Scottish squadron off guard by capsizing the two nearest to him while simultaneously taking off for freedom. Rifle fire immediately cracked all around him but the Republican had already made it over the fence and escaped down the fields towards the neighbouring Ballyvaloon Farm of John Joe Burns, whose ditches he hid in for the remainder of the night. Although his shredded feet and upper body were not the best for wear after his experience, Michael Moore had managed to survive the night.

The Jocks on the other hand were not about to give up so easily and would make a return visit to the Moore household a few nights later. The local company commander Mick Burke, as well as the general population of Cobh, was now faced with a very real possibility that the Jocks were giving up all pretence of respecting law and order, and were openly reverting to murder. If Burke had had any doubts about this, they were soon dispelled when the Jocks returned to the home of the Moore's a few nights later. This time Michael was not at home but his elder Volunteer brother John and his father were asleep when the Scots quietly crept up to the bedroom window of the cottage.

While one of the death squad slowly lifted up the window, another tossed in a bomb. Miraculously, the bomb rolled under the foot of one of the beds before exploding. This allowed the occupants to escape without serious injury but left the bedroom destroyed. Michael Moore later succumbed to the internal injuries that he had received from the Jocks almost two years earlier and died. He was the family's second son lost to the war with British forces. A fourth brother, Andy, was also targeted by Crown Forces and was taken prisoner by the Jocks at Belmont. Andy Moore was effectively a hostage and was openly used by the Jocks while they tied him up on the back of their lorries while they went on raiding parties throughout East Cork. The only Moore brother to escape the wrath of the British was the eldest son John. Ironically, it was John who caused most heart ache for the enemy, while being the man who supplied the gelignite and blasted the breach in the gable of Ireland's first ever captured RIC barracks at Carrigtwohill. John also played a major part in helping to set up the brigade bomb making factory at Knockraha. He would later take the anti-Treaty side in the Civil War, and like so many others, including his close friend Daithí O'Brien, would later be forced to emigrate to the U.S., after the Civil War.

While on the one hand it might have looked like the Camerons were making inroads into the smashing of the local IRA Company, the reality was in fact very different. The pattern of raids and arrests all pointed in one direction, that Scottish intelligence was very old. Every Republican who had been forced on the run or whose home were recently raided had been a 1916 Volunteer, or had even been there from the beginning in 1913. RIC intelligence on the current Volunteer membership had either dried up, or local police officers were less than willing to participate in the dirty war. The new breed of Volunteer under the command of Mick Burke, was a different entity altogether. Burke, who didn't join up himself until 1917, was never one to parade around in Volunteer uniform or flaunt his membership of the movement publicly. This was why he could confidently walk up to a British checkpoint immediately after a Republican operation had taken place and engage the police in normal conversation without fear of being arrested. Burke, expected those under his command, to think, behave and operate as he did. He knew that while the raids on the homes of well known Republican families like the Moore's, the Ahern's and Leahy's would be unavoidable from time to time, there were others living in the Ticknock locality that were also providing a great service to the Republican cause, and who were never likely to come under suspicion by the authorities.

One, a neighbour of the Moore's, Philip O'Neill worked in the Admiralty as a writer. O'Neill's membership of the IRA was a closely guarded secret, a fact which proved very beneficial to the Republican cause. Not too far away from the O'Neill's and Moore's was the farm belonging to John Joe Burns, mentioned earlier. John Joe, who slaughtered his own cattle and had a butchers shop in town, was a Republican sympathiser, and regularly co-operated with local Volunteers.

One day while John Joe had a number of rifles hidden in hayricks in a field, he received a warning that the Jocks were in the locality. Along with a couple of Volunteers, John Joe quickly removed the rifles and got them off the land. When the Jocks arrived, they made straight for the hayricks to search them. Upon finding nothing there, they departed again but returned the next day to search the fields again. It was clear the Cameron Highlanders were acting upon some tip they had received locally. Another cottage at Ticknock belonged to a young couple, the Walsh's. The man of the house worked as a gardener at the Admiralty. He had no interest whatsoever in political affairs and successfully got on with his job and life oblivious to the war that was being played out around him. This man's wife was very different however, and harboured very strong Republican views. In another two years, the couple would bring their second son Sean, into the world. Mrs Walsh and her two sons would later play a prominent part in the Republican struggle over a period spanning decades. Her youngest boy Sean would later work as a grocer's messenger boy to Mick Burke, and would receive a similar grooming from Burke, as he had earlier received from his IRB mentor Patrick Curran. The relatively new murder Squad at Belmont, might have been using the Moore's and their peaceful surroundings at Ticknock to practice and perfect their trade, before moving on to other areas of East Cork and while their presence might have come as an initial shock to Mick Burke, ironically, Burke would be one of those who would later bring one of the Murder Squads prime movers to justice.

A sharp intensification of the war was witnessed in 1921. It was also the year that reorganisation took place within the IRA, and brigades were organised into divisions. The three Cork brigades became part of the First Southern Division under the command of Liam Lynch (this brigade also comprised the West Limerick Brigade). By this time Mick Leahy had been promoted to the position of Vice O.C. of Cork No. 1 Brigade with Diarmuid Hurley taking over as O.C. of the 4th Battalion. The listed strength of the First Southern Division was some 33,000 men, or a quarter of the entire IRA. (However, it must be pointed out that these weren't necessarily active Volunteers, but also included those who were available but did not actually take part in the action). February was to prove a particular bad month for the Cork Volunteers. Several IRA men were captured and executed, the single greatest loss occurring at Clonmult, where practically the entire East Cork flying column was wiped out. Five men were killed in action, seven were shot having surrendered and a further two were later executed.

15. The Flying Column

The Cork 1st Brigade leaders had been considering for some time how to best utilise those on the run, while at the same time offering the enemy more effective military opposition. By the month of September 1920, the number of Volunteers who had been forced to flee their own company areas in the 4th Battalion had reached such a level, that brigade leaders saw a big security problem developing further down the road if they didn't respond now. The idea to start a flying column was thus considered after it was felt its advantages would far outweigh the disadvantages. After the Brigade had taken its decision, Mick Leahy immediately made contact with Diarmuid Hurley who, like himself, was also on the run. As Hurley was now in Command of the 4th Battalion and was a marked and wanted man in that area of command, it made perfect sense that those whom he commanded and operated with, would keep on the move with him.

Leahy and Hurley devised a plan where the column would be a full-time efficient unit that would not exceed a certain size. It would train hard and move from area to area to carry out military operations in the 4th Battalion area of command. Its members would be put up, fed, sheltered and looked after by carefully selected supporters in those areas. Its strength would be regularly supplemented by other members of the different companies who found themselves on the run, while existing members who needed a break, would rest off before rejoining again later.

Not all its members would be those that were on the run however and some would be selected for their already proven experience. On 1 October, Cobh man Paddy Whelan was paid a visit at Hallinan's Engineering Works at Midleton by Mick Leahy. The Brigade Vice-O.C. who himself had to flee from the same workplace not long before, told Whelan that he had been selected for the column and instructed him to report to Diarmuid Hurley at Knockraha. He also explained that because only a week or so before, Jack O'Connell had to flee from the same work-place, it would only be a matter of time before he too would be fingered for arrest. Whelan willingly accepted the invitation and joined the column. Initially six Volunteers including Whelan, reported from Midleton's 'B' Company to Hurley at Knockraha. This number quickly mushroomed to sixteen, with five others from Cobh joining up, as well four from Ballymacoda, Aghada and Killeagh. One of the reasons why Hurley and Leahy wanted to limit the size of the 4th Battalion column was because of its mainly flat terrain in its command area, which was well serviced by roads.

Enemy garrisons were positioned at Cobh, Midleton, Youghal, Fermoy, Carlisle and Cork, and as such were positioned to overrun the area in quick time if it had to. The location of the column depended on information received as to the movements and activities of the enemy. When it was learned that the military were paying particular attention to any district, the column was moved to that district, with a view to attacking it. Starting out from Knockraha, the column moved to Shanagarry, then to Ballymacoda, Ladysbridge and on to Aghada, but with no appearance from the military. The column was very disappointed at Aghada as they had earlier received very good intelligence of a daily patrol from Fort Carlisle. This fort was situated at the mouth of Cork Harbour, on its eastern side, while its counterpart, Fort Camden, and was on the western side of the harbour. Fort Carlisle was near to the Aghada/Cloyne area. Although the column waited without luck in their ambush positions in the freezing cold for most of 11 December for the appearance of the expected British patrol, they were quite glad when darkness fell so they could withdraw.

From there, they withdrew to the village of Cloyne and took up billets in the house of the local company captain, Bertie Walsh. Bertie had been on the run himself, and the military had only raided his house on the Sunday prior to the column's arrival. Diarmuid Hurley was acting on the premise that lightning never strikes the same place twice. His plan was to billet there for the night, and for the next day before returning to Aghada on the night of the 12 December. All was well until the next morning at 9.am. which was a Sunday. Paddy Whelan and Jack Ahern were up and about when they heard the drone of military lorries entering the village. Whelan rushed upstairs to warn Hurley and the others but they were already up and dressed. As Whelan was shouting the warning, he could hear the Camerons banging on the hall door with the butts of their rifles. Two Volunteers who were covering a window with their rifles saw a Jock soldier take up a position behind a wall about fifty yards away. Paddy Whelan also saw this soldier and knew the house was totally surrounded. Moving down the stairs, he took up a position on the first floor landing. He had just arrived there when two of soldiers had succeeded in smashing in the hall door. He immediately opened up with his revolver from his position, forcing the soldiers to make hasty retreat. Hurley then ordered everyone to get out the back way, but upon learning of the other soldiers were positioned around the back, he re-evaluated the situation.

At the side of the house on the main street was a large gate which led into the yard at the back. This gate was wide open, as was another one at the opposite side of the street. Whelan volunteered to explore this as a possible route of escape. He first got into the yard around the side of the house, and being familiar with the lay-out of the village, looked towards the cross roads, about sixty yards on his right. He could see no sign of the enemy, but felt convinced that some should be in the vicinity of the cross. He decided to place his cap on the muzzle of his rifle and raise it up above the wall to draw their fire. The ruse was successful, with two shots in quick succession being fired at the cap. He again looked towards the cross, and was just in time to see a soldier take cover behind a street corner. He immediately took up aim and succeeded in keeping the British soldier pinned down there with his own fire, while signalling to Hurley and the others to advance towards the gates across the way.

The Column then came out in pairs and dashed across the street while Whelan kept up rapid fire on the enemy position. When the last man had passed, he made a quick dash for the gate himself before closing it behind them as they headed for Aghada. Whelan would later recall a remarkable incident that happened when he was initially in the yard of the Walsh's house before he crossed it and opened fire. A British Mills grenade was tossed over the wall and landed about two feet in front of him. It burst with a dull sound, and remained where it fell in two equal parts, an omen that all would be well for that day. Also while in the yard, he was some-what bemused by a game of soldiers that was being played out between Jack Ahern and a Jock soldier on the other side of the wall. Jack would shout, 'My turn now Jock', before raising himself over the wall to fire. The Cameron Highlander on the other side of the wall, would duly reply with, 'My turn now Paddy' [33] before returning fire.

After the column had escaped from Cloyne by about a half of a mile, they heard the sound of intense rifle and Lewis machine gun fire which they were sure was directed on Bertie Walsh's house. Hurley and his men, although pleased for making a very lucky escape, were disappointed with the Cloyne company who had acted very poorly as sentries, and allowed them no advance warning that the British were coming. The Cloyne men did however get word to Midleton quickly that the column was sur-rounded, and although help was quickly dispatched to rescue the column in Cloyne, word soon got through that they had in fact escaped.

Following the Cloyne incident, Hurley decided that the Aghada area was too dangerous for the column, so they moved to an unoccupied farmhouse at Kilmantain, a few miles north-east of Midleton. While there, Hurley received word that a joint RIC/Black and Tan patrol was operating in Midleton each night. The column commander was determined to attack this patrol if the conditions were right, so he first sent Paddy Whelan and Jack Ahern into town to note and report the strength and disposition of the patrol. The entire column moved into Midleton on 27 December, under cover of darkness, and assembled at a sawmill in Charles Street. Ahern and Whelan continued on towards the main street. It was arranged that Whelan would take up a position at the corner of Charles Street which was situated about midway in the main street, and at right-angels to it. Ahern posted himself further down the street, near the Midleton Arms Hotel.

Both were armed with .45 Webley revolvers and wore trench coats and caps. Whelan was only about five minutes at his post when he saw a patrol of Black and Tans, marching slowly towards him. They were moving in pairs, about six paces apart and on both sides of the street, four pairs on his side and two pairs on the opposite side, together with an old RIC man named Mullins. All were armed with rifles and revolvers, with the rifles slung over their shoulders. Present in the last pair on Whelan's side was a Constable Gordon with whom he was well acquainted before he joined the column. When passing, Gordon noticed Whelan and, evidently surprised at seeing him for he shouted, 'Hello Paddy.' Whelan replied, 'Hello Gordie', [34] his usual way of addressing him. He feared for a moment that the friendly peeler was going to break ranks and come over to chat to him, but fortunately he carried on with the patrol. The men waited for the patrol to pass further down the street before they exited the main street and reported back to Hurley with their findings. Hurley was satisfied that his sixteen men were up for the task in hand, as they all knew and had intimate knowledge of the layout of the street, knowing every doorway and shop front. He issued the men with their orders. Ten of the Volunteers took up positions in doorways between Charles Street and along about forty yards of the main street up to the Midleton Arms Hotel. The remainder did likewise on the opposite side of the street. Paddy Whelan was at the corner of Charles Street and Main Street while Hurley was at the Midleton Arms Hotel end of the street, on the same side. It was decided that when the patrol was between both their positions on their return journey, Hurley would open fire, and this would be the signal for the others to open up with their revolvers.

The men were barely in their positions five minutes when the patrol re-appeared on its return journey, in the same formation as before. When he acted, Hurley judged his shot to perfection, and at once all of his men opened fire upon the enemy. The Tans were taken completely by surprise and, in a short time, the attack was over. Some of the Tans did return fire, leaving a couple of Volunteers with narrow escapes. Dan Cashman of Midleton was very lucky to be carrying a cigarette case in his vest pocket.

It was badly dented by a bullet and probably saved his life. Jim McCarthy of Midleton, although not a member of the column, took part in the attack, and was wounded in the wrist. On the enemy side, Constable Mullins was shot dead with six of the Tans badly wounded, some of whom died later from their wounds. Some of the patrol threw their rifles onto the street and ran away. Whelan's friend 'Gordie' survived the ordeal uninjured, leaving the Republican somewhat relieved, as he was not considered to be an evil natured policeman. Two Tans were lying on the footpath near Whelan and were bleeding profusely. Sergeant Maloney of the Midleton RIC had been sent earlier to the house of a British ex-officer, to collect the man's uniform.

The sergeant was returning to the barracks with the uniform when the shooting broke out, leading him to come under fire also. He was shot in the foot and dropped the uniform only yards from Whelan and the two fallen Tans. Whelan later knelt beside one of the wounded Tans and spoke to him. He gave Whelan his name and said he was from Liverpool and promised to resign from the forced if he lived. He also offered Whelan his wallet but the Republican took it from his hand and placed it back inside his tunic breast pocket. He then got the uniform which Sergeant Maloney had dropped, folded it and placed it under the Tan's head. The man had lost a lot of blood, leaving Whelan feeling that he was probably one of those later reported as having died. He picked up an extra revolver and rifle from the capture, as did most of column who participated in the attack. The attack lasted less than twenty minutes and took place a few hundred yards from the RIC barracks and about five hundred yards from the military post. The column withdrew by the same route they had earlier arrived. All the men were in great form, except Paddy Whelan who was having mixed feelings due to the intimate contact he had had with the two wounded Black and Tans. Those mixed feelings were shattered the next day however, when the Black and Tans along with the Cameron highlanders launched official reprisals on the homes of Edward Carey and John O'Shea in the town.

In early January 1921, Diarmuid Hurley received information that a niece of Sergeant King of the Midleton RIC was suspected of sending information to the local District Inspector. It was suggested that she possessed a typewriter for the purpose. The suspect lived with her uncle the sergeant and his wife at the Cork Road, Midleton, a few hundred yards from the RIC barracks. Diarmuid Hurley decided to search the sergeant's house for the typewriter and asked Paddy Whelan to accompany him. The men arrived at the house about 8.pm. while each was armed with a .45 revolver. When Mrs King opened the door, Hurley proceeded inside and asked to see her niece and ordered her to follow.

Hurley and Whelan both entered the sitting room where they found the sergeant and his niece seated before a blazing fire. The sergeant remained seated and perfectly cool, not showing the slightest sign of fear when confronted by the two men carrying revolvers. Hurley told him their business, but the sergeant said he was not aware of any typewriter being in the house, nor did his niece pass on any information to either the District Inspector or the military. Hurley said he would search the house, and requested the niece to accompany him, leaving Whelan to look after Sergeant King and his wife. The sergeant didn't waste any time in letting Whelan know that he knew him, saying he remembered him from working in Hallinan's Engineering Works, which had been burned down soon after he had left the place. The sergeant assured Whelan that the RIC had nothing to do with the burning. Everyone knew that Mr Hallinan was a well-known Loyalist, and that his brother, Major Hallinan had fought with the British during the First World War. The RIC and the District Inspector were well acquainted with these facts. While Whelan was prepared to take such arguments on board, he also knew that whoever burned the engineering premises, also knew that four wanted Republicans had been employed there at different times over a the previous three years. Having thoroughly searched the house without finding any evidence to incriminate anybody, Hurley returned to the sitting room and informed Sergeant King accordingly. He expressed the hope that he had not alarmed Mrs King unduly. While leaving, he ordered the sergeant not to report the incident to the barracks for at least half an hour. The sergeant's niece accompanied the men to the door and chatted for a few minutes. Hurley jokingly suggested cutting off the girl's hair. Whelan in turn said it would be a pity to destroy such a lovely head, before they both left.

Shortly afterwards, it became commonly known throughout the town that Hurley and Whelan had visited the Sergeant and his niece, with the comment made about the latter's hair, now having turned into one of a serious threat. In fact the niece had since been telling her friends that Paddy Whelan had made the suggestion, and were it not for Hurley, the threat might have been carried out. Some days later again, Diarmuid Hurley, Joe Ahern, Jack O'Connell and Paddy Whelan were passing near the Midleton locality when they decided to call to the home of two elderly Loyalist ladies for food. The four pretended to be undercover British officers and were warmly welcomed in for a hearty meal. During the conversation which followed between the hosts and their guests, the ladies said they were sorry to be unable to report of the whereabouts and habits of the IRA, but said that two of them, Hurley and Whelan, had the audacity to raid Sergeant Kings house in the town a short time previously, and that only for Hurley, Whelan would have cut off the hair of the sergeant's niece.

16. The Gun Runner

A decision was taken by G.H.Q. near the end of 1920 to purchase a shipment of arms in Italy. A plan was put together between Michael Collins, Liam Deasy and Florrie O'Donoghue on 16 December; though it's believed Collins had been quietly working on the plan for some months before that. The plan was to involve some careful manoeuvring by whoever piloted the ship towards the shallow landing point in West Cork. O'Donoghue then stated that he had the right man for job; the vice O.C. of the Cork 1st Brigade Mick Leahy had served his time as an apprentice marine fitter and had plenty of experience with ships. Sean O'Hegarty later briefed Leahy and instructed him to go to Dublin and report to Michael Collins for his passport and papers for Italy.

Leahy went to Dublin on 2 January and made contact with Gearoid O'Sullivan the Adjutant General, at his office over the 'Reliable Tailors' on the North Quays. O'Sullivan took Leahy to Devlin's public house in Parnell Place. When they entered, Leahy was surprised to find nearly all the G.H.Q. staff assembled and a merry party in progress. Michael Collins, who seemed to be master of the revels, was not at all impressed when Leahy opted for lemonade while everyone else was happily engaging with a plentiful supply of whiskey. No one in the room showed the slightest interest in why Leahy was present in Dublin. The party was a prelude to the wedding next day of Tom Cullen, the Quartermaster General.

The next morning after the wedding breakfast, Leahy finally got to discuss the Italian business with Collins, O'Sullivan and Sean Ó Muirthile,. It was decided that he should proceed to Italy via London and Paris and that while in London, he should make contact with Art O'Brien who would arrange for the provision of a passport for him. When he got to Paris, he was to make contact with Sean T. O'Kelly who would advise him of the preliminary stages of the project. Arriving in London, Leahy made contact with Art O'Brien and Sean McGrath. The two men coached Leahy in how best to present himself before the Foreign Office for his passport. Collecting and filling out the necessary forms was to be the easy part, but finding someone reputable to witness his bona fides was another matter. The Cobh man was to pass himself off as a clerical student by the name of John C. Lane. The two local I.R.B. men suggested that he should seek the help of a priest to act as his witness, but Leahy couldn't see how a priest could undertake such a task, after cross examining him about his upbringing and education etc., without seeing him for the impostor he was. He instead located a priest himself whom he knew had sympathies to the movement and eventually secured the passport.

When he reached Paris, he made contact with Sean T. Kelly and his staff. They carefully coached him as to his part in the project and those he should meet once he reached Genoa. On 28 March, he finally made it into Italy after crossing at the Swiss border at Modena. When he reached Genoa, he met Donal Hales. Hales taught in the University there and was married to an Italian. He in fact had spent most of his childhood in Italy and blended in perfectly. Hales explained to Leahy that D'Annunzio who, with a private army, had recently seized Fiume in the face of the Allies, had likened his force to the IRA and his aspirations for Italy were like that of Ireland's to be free. Hales introduced Leahy to three of D'Annunzio's officers in the Fiume coup. With the Cobh man's smattering of Italian, he was able to communicate with them and understand their sympathy towards the Irish fight for freedom. England was apparently the arch enemy in connection with their endeavour to secure Fiume as Italian territory and one of them indeed, Captain Frugonie, had fought for the Boers against Britain. The other two Captains Bardi and Lungie were equally enthusiastic for the Irish cause, but Frugonie wanted to accompany Leahy back to Ireland in the arms ship and take a hand in the fight.

The ship selected was called the *Stella Maris*, a four masted barque with an auxiliary engine, and was one of five ships owned by the Federaciona della Mare, the powerful Seaman's Union. These ships normally sailed out of Genoa in ballast to England for cargoes of coal from Newcastle. This time, the *Stella Maris* instead of travelling light was going to carry rifles, machine guns, revolvers and proportionate ammunition to Ireland, unload at the pre-arranged landing place and then go on to Newcastle for coal. In his later witness statement to the bureau of military history, Mick Leahy insists that once the ship reached its landing point, it was not to be beached like some historians have since written. He claimed that the plan was for a number of smaller boats to bring the arms ashore from the ship. Provision for this had already been made by the brigade with West Cork Volunteers.

The site for the landing was picked because it was screened from the sea. It was in the channel inside Rabbit Island, about 400 yards off Myross Strand, a place close to where Collins had grown up. The Vice O.C. of the Skibbereen Brigade, Patrick O'Driscoll was put in charge of the landing operations, after plans for the overall landing operations had been agreed by Liam Lynch, Sean O'Hegarty and Florrie O'Donoghue. Temporary units were put together for the construction of dumps. A number of small boats were put on standby with specially fitted boxes for carrying the arms and getting them ashore. The roads and laneways leading to the landing beaches were to be guarded by large numbers of Volunteers when the time arrived for the landing. Time passed and soon began to drag, which was a source of worry for Leahy. The arms were available in plenty but there was no sign of money coming from Ireland, in fact there was no dispatch of any kind about the plan, neither reference to money, landing place, arrangements for receiving the arms or anything about the project at all. Donal Hales' sister Madge went out to visit him on holidays but she had no information to offer them either. Leahy's own expenses for living were fast dwindling. He had earlier been instructed to stay at the Bristol Hotel, the most expensive in Genoa. Luckily for him, he declined and took up residence in a more modest hotel, for he would have otherwise been broke by now. Soon he had to dip into his own money. The ship was in the port and the owners were constantly asking when the venture was coming to a head. Eventually there was nothing for Leahy to do but to go to Paris to see Sean T. Kelly and discover what the problem was.

He arrived in Paris on Easter Sunday only to discover that Sean T. was in Brussels. None of his staff were in a position to enlighten him about the purchase money for the arms. He was now down to his last £10 Bank of Ireland note which he shouldn't have been able to change. It was his own money, to be used only as a last resort. Fortunately, Sean T. O'Kelly arrived back in Paris that night. But unfortunately he was unable to offer Leahy any news about the project, and advised him to go to London where Art O'Brien would have closer contact with G.H.Q. in Dublin. Leahy then left that night by the midnight express and reached London the next afternoon. He made contact with Art O'Brien once more but O'Brien too was unable to get any word as to arms shipment. He eventually informed Leahy that he should return to Ireland.

When he returned to Dublin, he was attached to the Purchase Branch under Liam Mellows, but he never received an explanation from Collins or anyone else as to why the Italian purchase never went ahead. There has been much written as to what actually went wrong with the Italian arms project, or the 'Italian cabinets' as they were referred to in dispatches, but when one considers that Leahy had only returned to Cork two weeks before the Truce came in to being, one must ask why the venture began from a very enthusiastic background by all the participant parties, but suddenly was left fade into obscurity. Fours days before the Truce came into effect in July, Collins wrote to Donal Hales, sending him a cheque for his expenses. In an accompanying letter, he implied that they in Dublin were not very satisfied with their messenger in the latter stages of the proceedings. It has been speculated that Collins was hinting that Leahy may have been identified by British Intelligence when he returned to Paris to see Sean T. Kelly. But surely such an explanation doesn't really stand up. Leahy was forced to return to Paris only after he was starved of money and instructions from Collins.

Secondly, if Leahy's presence in Paris with Sean T. O'Kelly was deemed to be a security risk, why was he instructed by Collins people to visit O'Kelly in Paris to receive his earlier instructions to begin with? Depending on which Civil War view people came down on, its been suggested by some people that De Velera was not in favour of the arms shipment coming in while moves towards the truce were in the offing. Others more cynically suggest that Collins, who equally was aware of the pending truce, also favoured the scrapping of the Italian project, for it would have undermined his later argument that the Volunteers were not in a position to resume the war with the British if the terms of the Treaty were not favourable. Mick Leahy, the man at the centre of the affair, offered his own view on this in his later witness statement to the Bureau of Military History:

> One of the main arguments used by those in favour of acceptance of the articles of the agreement for the Treaty was the shortage of arms and ammunition. As Collins and some of those closely associated with him were continually engaged in overtures with 'peace' representatives of the British Government from the autumn of 1920 up to the Truce of 11 July, 1921, it is possible that he [Collins] was simply playing for time so that with people tired of war and the IRA unable to procure any arms and ammunition from Headquarters, the way would then be clear to settle with Britain for something much less than a Republic.[35]

17. Slaughter at Clonmult

The column moved to a about a mile from Clonmult village around mid-January 1921. The house was in an isolated position, and could be reached from the main road by a long narrow winding boreen. It was about 600 yards (as the crow flies) from the road, and was between the villages of Lisgould and Clonmult. The farmhouse was invisible from the road until one reached Clonmult, as it was situated on a slope running from the main road to about half a mile below the house. Between the house and the road, the land was covered with heather and some trees scattered around the vicinity. The house itself was a one-storey building with a thatched roof. There were three small disused farmhouse rooms and one large living room and kitchen. There was one small window in the back and three in the front of the building.

The location was considered a safe place, particularly as it was in a very friendly area, practically to all the young men of the volunteers. As was customary whenever the column moved into a district, the local IRA

Company was instructed to be always on the alert, to report movements of enemy troops who might happen to come into the area. In addition the column would also post its own sentries at crucial look-out positions, and would have volunteers detailed to patrol the roads around the immediate neighbourhood during the night. It was never intended to defend the house if it came under attack, so it was not prepared for defence. If enemy troops were to arrive, it was anticipated that their presence would have become known well in advance. It was always Hurley's intention that in such a scenario, the building would immediately be evacuated and the column would do battle with the enemy from outside on its own terms. When a combination of unfortunate circumstances came into play on Sunday 20 February 1921 most of the column was led to the slaughter at Clonmult that day, and is remembered as the worst military defeat suffered by the IRA in its history.

The day before on Saturday 19 February, Diarmuid Hurley received a dispatch from brigade headquarters, informing him that a military convoy would be carrying a cargo of explosives by rail on Tuesday, or Wednesday from Cobh to Cork. The column commander was instructed to attack the convoy, but if he felt the job was beyond him and his men, he was to report to headquarters accordingly so the brigade could make alternative arrangements. Hurley showed the dispatch to Paddy Whelan who expressed similar discomfort and insult by its tone. Both men along with Joe Ahern felt that they and the column had proved themselves many times before, and always without the help or direction of the brigade.

Hurley decided to take Joe Ahern with him to look over the Cobh Junction area the next day to select an ambush site. Paddy Whelan was to then take over command of the column in the absence of the two most senior officers. The column had at this time a Ford car at its disposal with Joe Ahern as its driver. At the very last moment however, Hurley decided that he needed someone from the Cobh area with him who was familiar with the Cobh to Cork railway line, and so asked Paddy Whelan to join them. Hurley in fact had a choice of six Cobh column members whom he could have taken to Cobh Junction with him that day. When he made the uncharacteristic decision to not leave Whelan in charge and instead take another Cobh Volunteer with him, it was undoubtedly one of the fateful factors that would later lead to disaster that day. Hurley then consulted Whelan and Ahern for their opinion as to who should take over command in their absence. Both men suggested Jack O'Connell as their natural choice. Jack had not only previously held command positions with a number of operations in the Cobh Company area, but he also worked in Midleton and took part in military operations with B Company there.

Unlike the other three officers however, O'Connell was never tested under enemy fire, like that of being on the other end of an ambush, as the others had been in the Cloyne situation. Neither did he previously have the responsibility of command over so many men in a static position. He had only been with the column for just over a week, and while he was a well seasoned and dedicated Volunteer officer, and although he was familiar with and well known to all the Midleton and Cobh men, he may not have been as familiar with the basic routines of column security. In his brilliantly researched book *The Battle of Clonmult*, Tom O'Neill's thorough re-examination of what happened that day raises the possibility of ill-feeling between Paddy Higgins and Jack O'Connell due to the latter receiving the position of command that day, as being a contributing factor in how the men responded when confronted by the crisis. While Captain Higgins may have been the next most senior officer after Whelan, in terms of how long he was a member of the column, and while he may have resented Captain O'Connell for receiving that command, it is hard to see how this could have been a serious factor in how things would later develop. In his own witness statement, O'Connell makes the point that he and his men started packing up and preparing to move out to their new appointed destination at Leamlara, shortly after having a meal, and not long after Hurley and the others departed for Cobh Junction. He stated that he and his men were all but ready and were waiting for their guides to arrive and show them the way, when the British appeared out of nowhere.

The casual nature of his men around the place including that of the two sentries filling water bottles at the well, does not give the impression that there was any ill-feeling in the camp up to that point. In fact it was this casual behaviour which ultimately made the column pay such a heavy price that day. O'Connell seemed to have made a fatal mistake when he had earlier ordered the sentries to withdraw and prepare their kits for the move-out. He should not have done so until the guides had first arrived safely, or at the very least, until he had replaced the sentries with others who were already packed and ready to leave. O'Connell insists that he did not order the sentries to withdraw that day. If he didn't, who did? And if they withdrew of their own accord, why were they not re-posted? This mistake was undoubtedly the biggest contributing factor in what would transpire later. Another of course, was the fact that the column had been in place at the same location for about five weeks, leaving it vulnerable to detection by spies and informers. Like those of the Cloyne Company who had earlier failed to provide the column with an early warning system, the local Clonmult men would also be found wanting that day.

The bitter reality was that while Hurley and the others were now enroute to Cobh Junction, an enemy convoy was on its way from Victoria Barracks in Cork, to Clonmult to capture or kill him and his column.

While the two sentries at the well left their rifles back in the house, they had their revolvers with them. The others had about fifteen rifles, three shotguns and about fourteen revolvers, six grenades and a good supply of ammunition back in the house, when the first shot were fired. Just before that, Diarmuid (Sonny) O'Leary, while glancing out one of the windows spotted some British soldiers crawling past the gateway at the far side of boreen. The two men at the well, Michael Desmond and John Joe Joyce encountered enemy fire almost immediately and returned fire with their revolvers. They were greatly outnumbered and out-gunned however. Desmond died at the well. Joyce, though mortally wounded managed to crawl back to near the house and shouted to warn the others inside, of the perilous situation as seen from outside.

The house had by now come under fire from all sides. There was only one exit from the house and it was now under constant fire. The men never trained or prepared for such a situation. It was never meant to be like this. Jack O'Connell was probably as much at a loss for answers as the others. After probably realising the mistake of withdrawing the sentries, he still knew it was up to him to find a way out for his men. In his witness statement, O'Connell says it was around this point that he held a council of war meeting with three others. He favoured a breakout sortie from their perilous position as the best and possibly only way of leaving the place alive. Presumably, Capt. Paddy Higgins was one of those he consulted with. In *The Battle of Clonmult* Tom O'Neill refers again to the conflict between Higgins and O'Connell at this point, leading Higgins to refuse to favour a breakout. The conflict between these two men, we are told, was over O'Connell being given command over Higgins, and that Hurley and Joe Ahern were less inclined to favour Higgins because of his less than positive aptitude for action during the ambush of the Black and Tan patrol in Midleton the previous December.

As O'Connell had absolutely no part or control over Higgins' action, or lack of, during that earlier ambush, or over who Hurley chose to offer command to, it is probably far more likely that Higgins just didn't have the stomach to face the ugly reality of war outside, and preferred instead to remain behind the relative safety of the cottage walls, in hope of reinforcements soon arriving. O'Connell was under no illusions as to how dangerous it would be to attempt the breakout but saw no other way, and knew that it was up to him to show leadership. After distributing the reserve ammunition and grenades, O'Connell led the breakout with four others following close behind.

The others, who remained on in the cottage, intensified their fire to offer cover for their escaping colleagues as they began singing the 'The Soldiers Song' in defiance of their closing enemy. With a bayonet fixed to his rifle, O'Connell dashed through a hail of enemy bullets across the yard to a gateway. He then turned up to the right, and was fired on by two soldiers from the corner of a field bordering the west of the haggard. Returning fire, he wounded one and forced the other to run back. It was then that he looked back for his companions but discovered that he was alone. He proceeded back down the boreen as a far as a disused shed. From there he couldn't see the doorway of the cottage, but judging from the intensive rifle fire; he judged it would be madness to attempt to rejoin his comrades inside. He decided the best thing to do would be to break through the military cordon and get some help locally. O'Connell was not aware that three of those who were following had already been shot, and the fourth man had escaped back into the house.

The first to follow O'Connell was Michael Hallihan. He was shot immediately outside the door. O'Connell's close friend, Capt. James Ahern from Cobh, was next out. He managed to make it for two hundreds yards before being shot climbing a ditch. Capt. Dick Hegarty was next out but only made it to the fence in front of the house before being shot. The last man out was Capt. Sonny O'Leary. O'Leary managed to make it close to the haggard where O'Connell had earlier shot one of the enemy, but on seeing the others fall, decided it was no use, and manoeuvred his way under fire back into the house. From the small shed, O'Connell circled the house and went down a blind boreen. Near the end of it, he was fired on by an officer. Returning fire, he managed to halt the British fire for long enough to allow him to leave the boreen and proceed up a hill along some high ground overlooking the house. From there, he fired on two soldiers he saw running towards a cross roads. He also saw a party of five soldiers converging on the house from the north-west. He went to two farm houses at the boreen in the hope of finding a bicycle but had no luck. He then continued down the boreen until he came to a road junction where he met two young men. He soon learned that they were local Volunteers. O'Connell questioned the men to establish how many arms were possessed by their company. The men said they had seven or eight shotguns that were kept in a farmhouse near the local graveyard. O'Connell instructed one man to go off and find help and whatever weapons they could and bring them to that point. The other man he asked to come back towards the house with him, to see what was happening. The man was very reluctant, however, and finally refused to go, but went off with his companion to collect the arms. O'Connell made back towards the house but was fired upon by the military as he was going down the boreen. He turned again to get out of danger but was followed by two soldiers who fired on him continuously. They had obviously been detailed to get him.

Back inside the house, Paddy Higgins was still holding out in the belief that help was going to come from somewhere, possibly from the local Company. He and his men continued to return fire on the British as much as they could from their vulnerable positions. An attempt was made to make a breach in a back wall. Bayonets, knives and forks were used to remove stones and clay. Eventually a hole big enough for a man to crawl through was made. Sonny O'Leary volunteered to try the breach first but as soon as he put his head outside, he received a shot to the head, and had to be pulled back inside by his comrades. He soon lapsed into unconsciousness because of his wound. Meanwhile, Jack O'Connell had made it back to the relative safety of where he had earlier met the two local Volunteers. This time he met another man who arrived on a push bike, and who turned out to be the captain of the local company. The man told him that the nearest active service unit of the neighbouring North East Cork battalion was located near Ballyroe, six mile to the north. He told O'Connell he was going off to seek help from that source. The North East column did arrive later that evening, but after travelling on foot, were too late as the engagement was over. On a number of occasions throughout the battle, officers from the Royal Hampshire Regiment had called on the Volunteers in the house to surrender. The Volunteers however, were not about to give up yet and face certain execution under the terms of the recently enforced martial law in county Cork. They were determined to hold out as long as they could in the hope of being rescued. By 5.30pm things took a turn for the worst when the Auxiliaries and Tans arrived on the scene, as they were carrying petrol amongst their deadly arsenal. They had positioned themselves at the western end of the house. When the fumes from the burning thatch started choking the Volunteers inside, they knew the game was up. Word was passed on and agreement was reached with a British officer that the lives of the remainder of the column would be spared if they surrendered. Capt. Paddy Higgins ordered his men to throw their weapons in to the fire before they surrendered. Seventeen-year old John Harty was first to venture out of the house. He was one of the lucky ones, and had the good fortune of receiving a blow to the head by a rifle butt as soon as he appeared. It was after Harty went down unconscious that the killing started. The others were lined up against a wall of the haggard with their hands up.

The Auxillaries quickly leapt into action, moving down the line and shooting every man as they went. Christopher O'Sullivan, David Desmond, Jeremiah Ahern, and his cousin Liam Ahern, Donal Denehy, Joseph Morrissey and young James Glavin were shot dead. Capt. Paddy Higgins recalled a Tan putting a gun in his mouth and squeezing the trigger. He later said he felt he was falling through a bottomless pit. Then he thought he heard a voice saying 'this fella is not dead, we will finish him off.' He said only for the regular military coming along at that point, he too would have been finished off. The arrival of an army officer ended the killing spree. Fortunately for the others who were delayed coming out of the house with the semi-conscious Sonny O'Leary, their appearance at the front door was timed with a British officer having gained control from the Auxiliaries and Tans. These were Maurice Moore and Paddy O'Sullivan who carried O'Leary out. They were followed by Robert Walsh, Edmund Terry and William Garde. They were immediately ordered into the haggard where they were detained and searched. The battle was now over.

Twelve IRA Volunteers were dead, eight wounded and only one had escaped. The fallout from Clonmult would continue for some time after however, as the killings were not yet over, in fact they and the threat of further punishments relating to that day would not cease until the Truce later in the year. Cobh had already lost two sons at Clonmult and it would soon lose two more to the firing squad.

Jack O'Connell had waited as long as he could for help to arrive. There was no sign of the local Volunteers coming back with the promised weapons, nor was there any sign of the North Eastern column arriving to offer his surrounded men some respite and chance of escape. By the time O'Connell saw the thatch of the cottage go up in flames, he knew it was already too late. He then left the area and headed for Knockraha. Meanwhile, Diarmuid Hurley and the others were finishing up their business at Cobh Junction when they heard the droning of military lorries approaching. They were still on the railway line, so hid down out of sight of the occupants of the nine or ten vehicles that were passing on their way to Cork. The three Republican officers had no idea that their captured comrades were on the lorries. After the convoy had passed, they proceeded to their car with the intention of meeting up with the rest of the column at Leamlara.

When they reached Killacloyne Bridge, a couple of miles west of Carrigtwohill, they were stopped by the Captain of the Cobh Company Mick Burke. He broke the terrible news to them that the column had been wiped out but for one man. He had no further details to offer them. The three men were staggered by the news, with Hurley being particularly frantic. He asked the others where they thought the survivors would go. Paddy Whelan suggested Canavan's house at Knockraha. The men then headed straight for Knockraha. On the way, they ran into Daithí O'Brien and Seamus Fitzgerald who were returning from David Cotter's house with the bad news. They discussed a possible counter attack but decided it was too late. When they reached Canavan's, they found a devastated and lost Jack O'Connell waiting there. He told the men all he knew about what had happened before he joined Hurley, Whelan and Ahern and headed

A Company Vols attend Old–Church cememtery to commemorate their comrades 1922.

back to examine the scene of the slaughter. On arriving there, the men crossed the field to the ill-fated house which was still burning. There they found the bodies of their comrades laid side by side in a field adjoining the house, and with a long canvass sheet covering their faces. Some local people had arrived after the British had left, collected the bodies and laid them out. Paddy Whelan undertook the heartbreaking task of uncovering their faces and identifying them, calling out each name consecutively. The task was a slowly accomplished one, and was only managed in-between sobs. There were two distinct pauses as he went along the row; he had extreme difficulty in naming Liam Ahern (Joe's brother) and Jerry Ahern (Joe's first cousin). The mental anguish that Hurley was under was palpable.

All four men, Diarmuid, Joe, Jacko and Paddy sobbed with a terrible grief and sense of loss at the fate that had befallen their beloved comrades, some four or five whom had bullet holes in the face, just below their eyes. There was nothing the men could do but cover up the faces of their dead comrades and make their sad departure to Leamlara. That night, Jack O'Connell and Paddy Whelan shared a bed together. Whelan put his arm around O'Connell to console him, and reassured him that he had done all that was humanly possible to save the column. From his hide-out at Knockraha, Seamus Fitzgerald must have also been hurting and feeling guilty for facilitating Ahern and O'Connell into the column. Earlier, their surviving comrades had been taken to Midleton for identification before being shipped off to Victoria military barracks in Cork. It was clear earlier on, that the British weren't very sure of who exactly they had killed and who they had in custody. For a brief time, they thought Diarmuid Hurley was among the dead, but even when it became clear that he was alive and free; it still didn't disguise the magnitude of the British victory or its impact on Irish morale.

The people of Midleton and Cobh were devastated by the news but united in grief. It was the first time since their formation in 1913 that the Volunteers had faced such a military setback and challenge. It was Cork's 1916. For the first couple of days after the attack, people were left speculating as to who exactly was killed and who had been taken prisoner. The families of those whose sons and brothers were on the run, were not sure if they had been with the column or if they were hiding out in other places. This wasn't cleared up for some time until those working in Knockraha and elsewhere got word home to their families that they were safe and well. Even Mick Burke, the O.C. of the Cobh Company was now entering new ground and had to work closely with the families of the two dead volunteers and those of their two captive comrades.

It is not clear if Burke had sent Lily Hawes of the local Cumann na mBan to Cork to identify the remains of James Ahern and James Glavin on behalf of the families, or if she took it upon herself to do so. Hawes, who was reportedly close to Ahern before he had to leave Cobh on the run, was led to a corrugated iron shed where the bodies were laid out in Victoria Barracks. When she first set her eyes on the state of his bullet riddled body she lashed out at the British sentry left guarding the bodies. It was reported the young soldier broke down himself and apologised for the state of the bodies but insisted that that was how they were brought in. The role that Hawes had played that day at Victoria Barracks did not go unnoticed and within a few short weeks would lead to her internment at Waterford Gaol. On the Tuesday after the Clonmult battle, Cobh UDC held a special meeting where it offered a vote of condolence to the families of the fallen Volunteers. The Town Council in turn received letters from the families of Ahern and Glavin. The latter's father wrote: 'It is a source of consolation to us to realise that our son gave his life, in the company with his gallant and brave companions, many of whom were natives of Cobh, for our dear country.'[36] A little more than one year earlier, Volunteer Capt James Ahern was elected to Cobh Urban District Council, having topped the poll in his ward. Almost immediately after attending his first meeting, he was forced to go on the run due to harassment by the military authorities. It was always very likely that he was going to end up a member of the flying column.

Volunteer James Glavin was the youngest member of the column. Only

Volunteer Paddy O'Sullivan.

seven months before his death, James Glavin was the fifteen-year-old scout who kept lookout for Daithí O'Brien and others on top of the hill before they shot District Inspector Mordaunt. The young eager Fianna Volunteer was obviously talent-spotted by O'Brien, and although he didn't refer to him by name, it is very likely that Glavin was the brave Fianna Éireann member that Mick Burke referred to in relation to the Quarry attack in August 1920. It is not clear how Glavin came to be a member of the column, but he would have had to come highly recommended by some senior officer before Hurley would have taken him onboard. On Wednesday 23 February, the people of Cobh turned out in their thousands to pay their respects to their fallen sons. From Saint Colman's Cathedral, they followed the funeral cortege to the new Republican plot at the Old Church Cemetery below Ticknock on the northern outskirts of the town. But the Republican mourners were not the only ones to offer a show of strength that day.

Overlooking proceedings from high on 'Cnoc' hill, the heavily armed Cameron Highlanders had spread themselves across the entire western slope, to offer the maximum reminder to all who saw them that they were still calling the shots. Geraldine Norris, née Hawes, the younger sister of Lily, vividly recalled that day for this writer in 1988. As a young member of Cumann na gCailíní, she remembered marching along with the thousands of other mourners down Ticknock Hill. As she looked up towards 'Cnoc', she was completely taken by the sight of so many Camerons with their rifles trained down upon them. She estimated that every member of the Belmont-based battalion must have been up on the hill that day, with many others probably drafted in from outside of Cobh. After the two local Volunteers were laid to rest in the Republican plot, the mourners left the old church cemetery and started making their way back to town again. Very few would have passed the cottages on the right of Ticknock Hill

Volunteer Maurice Moore.

without having a sympathetic thought for the occupiers of one house. The pain and anguish of the Moore family was only beginning, as was also that of the family of Paddy O'Sullivan who were each awaiting court-martial. The court-martials began on 8 March at Victoria Barracks, after which Maurice Moore and Paddy O'Sullivan desperately tried to use each other as alibi witnesses. O'Sullivan said that he was in fact held as a prisoner of the IRA at the Clonmult house. He said he fell out with the IRA after the military raided a Republican court in Cobh, of which he was its secretary (clerk), shortly before.

Following Republican suspicions that he had talked and betrayed his comrades to the military, he had to go on the run. Maurice Moore backed up O'Sullivan's claim and said that he had earlier received a message from James Ahern to the effect that they had O'Sullivan held prisoner at Clonmult and needed him there to identify the prisoner. The story failed miserably to make an impact on the British who duly found Moore, O'Sullivan and O'Leary guilty. After a number of failed appeal attempts, where public petitions were set up in Cobh, Midleton and Killeagh, the two Cobh men were finally executed on 28 April.

Twenty-four year-old Maurice Moore came from a respected Republican family which produced four fighting sons to the IRA. He was educated at the Presentation Brothers School Cobh and later worked as a plumber's mate at the Naval Dockyard at Haulbowline. He joined the Volunteers in 1916 and became one of the most trusted members of the Cobh Company. He took part in all the early operations undertaken by the 4th Battalion in East Cork including the capture of Carrigtwohill RIC Barracks in 1920. Moore was also one of the first volunteers to join up with the Flying Column when it was formed and took part in almost every operation undertaken by the Column up until the time of his death.

Paddy O'Sullivan was one of three Republican brothers and was born at Carrignafoy in Cobh in 1899. He was educated at the Presentation Brothers' Schools in Cobh and subsequently worked as an overseer at the Haulbowline Dockyard. Along with his close friend Maurice Moore, O'Sullivan joined the Volunteers in 1916. Like Moore, Paddy O'Sullivan took part in many of the IRA engagements around East Cork with the 4th Battalion. He joined the Flying column with Moore, and as many of their comrades later observed, the two Cobh lads were inseparable and could be seen fighting side by side during every engagement the company or column were involved in. Prior to joining the Column, Paddy O'Sullivan also acted as Clerk to the Parish Republican Court in Cobh.

He was described as a talented hurler of great promise. He played in the senior ranks for Cobh GAA and later for the Collegians at UCC. O'Leary's death sentence was commuted to penal servitude for life. Later that morning at 11.am., a Solemn Requiem Mass was said for the souls of O'Sullivan and Moore at St Colman's Cathedral by Revd D. O'Keefe. The earlier morning mass at Rushbrooke Convent Chapel was also celebrated by Revd P. Fouhy for the same intentions. Revd Fouhy, who himself suffered with shell-shock from his time as Chaplain to the military during the 1914-18 war, was particularly moved by the men's sacrifice. It was another black day for the people of the locality. All the shops in the town remained closed for the day. After the executions, Republicans went out for revenge, and not always in a properly organised way. Anyone who had previously given the IRA the slightest reason to be suspicious of them was now vulnerable. Two nights after Ahern and Glavin were executed; the IRA struck in the village of Carrigtwohill. An ex-soldier by the name of Michael O'Keeffe was snatched off the street. His body was discovered the next morning with a label attached declaring him a spy.

Contrary to other published accounts of the O'Keeffe killing, Mick Leahy could not have ordered the arrest or otherwise of the suspected spy. By his own account in his later witness statement, Leahy was in fact attached to Liam Mellows Department of Purchase in Dublin at the time, and didn't return back to Cork until July. Secondly, as Vice O.C. of the Cork 1st Brigade, Leahy was no longer O.C. of the 4th Battalion. That post was now the function of Diarmuid Hurley, and had been for the previous six and a half months. Leahy therefore couldn't have ordered Daithí O'Brien to bring O'Keefe in for questioning. It is far more likely that O'Brien being the impulsive operator that he was, and with revenge on his mind for the lives of his Cobh comrades, took it upon himself (possibly with others from Knockraha where he then operated) to arrest, try and execute the ex-soldier.

In the space of a week, the British responded in kind. From their Belmont headquarters, a group of Camerons operating in plain clothes attempted to instil terror into the population of Carrigtwohill. Coming so soon after the killing of Micheal O'Keeffe, it became apparent that Daithí O'Brien and the IRA probably had got the right man, or at least one of them. On the 8 May, a six man squad of Camerons entered the village, kicking down doors and firing in the street indiscriminately. One of the Jocks stood out more than the others because of his huge physique. In time, the regular appearance of this big man among what would become known as the murder squad, would lead to his identification as Sergeant Major Mackintosh. This in time would inevitably lead to the Sergeant Major receiving his own rough justice. On the night of 8 May, Mackintosh and his men had rounded up three local Republicans named William Bransfield, Jack Hayes and Dick Masterson. The men were taken to the end of the town. Bransfield a railway worker was shot dead but his two colleagues managed to escape. Masterson cleared a ditch and hid out in the middle of a field for the night, expecting the murder squad to search for him in the ditches rather than the middle of the field. The IRA in Midleton were not sitting back either. On Saturday, the 14 May, about 3.pm., RIC Sergeant Joseph Coleman was having a drink in Buckley's public house and grocer's premises on the Main Street, when he was shot dead by a local Volunteer.

When four policemen arrived on the scene, two of them were sent to get a doctor and a priest to minister to the dying sergeant. They were ambushed at the southern end of the town and the two Black and Tans, Thomas Cornyn from Cavan and Harold Thompson, an Australian, were killed. The IRA then attacked a second party of police who were sent to the scene and during this engagement a constable McDonald was wounded. Volunteers placed a note on the dead body of Constable Thompson which read simply, 'revenge for Clonmult etc.' Volunteers from the Midleton area were convinced that Thompson was present at Clonmult. That same day, two unarmed gunners from the Royal Marines Artillery stationed in the Coastguard Station at East Ferry were drinking in a public house in Ballinacurra outside of Midleton. That evening, while walking back to their station, they were snatched from the townland of Loughcarrig. The two Marines had grass stuffed into their mouths before being shot dead. Their bodies were then dumped in a local quarry.

Meanwhile, Mackintosh and his growing Death Squad at Belmont were not at all put off by the Republican challenge. On the night of Saturday 15 May, they were back in the Carrigtwohill and Midleton areas once more. This time local people estimated the Jocks to number as many as twenty. There would be no random killings this time, but specifically selected targets. They first raided the home of John Ahern of the Midleton Company at Ballyrichard. When he was not at home, they took his brother Michael. Next they went for Richard Barry, of Knockgrifin, Midleton and then for

Michael Ryan of Woodstock, Carrigtwohill. Ryan was also missing so they took his brother John. When they arrived in Carrigtwohill village, they began firing indiscriminately in the streets, while banging on doors, to terrorise the local people. They eventually came to the door of an elderly man named Richard Flynn. When Flynn saw them coming, he tried to get away out through the back door. He had only got a few yards however when the murder gang opened up, killing him instantly. They then went inside his house and brought out his son who was deaf and mute and put him in the back of the lorry with the others. They then took their prisoners to the western end of village near the first cross road that branched off for Cobh. The prisoners were then interrogated by torture. Timothy Flynn who could not speak almost had his hand severed from the prodding of the bayonets. The death squad were not succeeding in gaining any information from the prisoners however, so they began to line them up for execution. John Ryan was the first to be shot dead. His head was left facing into a gully with his legs out on the road. When Ahern and Flynn (the mute) saw what happened to Ryan, they decided to make a run for it. They frantically made up the road towards Carrigtwohill village again. On the way, they came to a stile on the left hand side which was near the entrance to a bog. As they both went over the stile, the Jocks opened fire upon them. Michael Ahern fell down dead on the spot, but Timothy Flynn managed to escape his attackers. Luckily for him, Macintosh and his battalion decided they had done enough for the night, and withdrew back to their barracks at Belmont in Cobh.

The next morning, the relatives of the dead were aided by others of the village in the collecting of the bodies. When the saw that Timothy Flynn was missing, a full-scale search was organised around the fields, drains, and ditches of the locality. Eventually, the missing lad was found huddled up in the corner of piggery near Tullagrein by Cobh Cross. He was immediately taken to a local doctor who examined the severe torture damage that was inflicted upon him by the Death Squad. The British appeared to have an inflated picture of the strength of the Carrigtwohill IRA, and this might have explained in part why the village was singled out for special punishment. It was probably also true that it was considered a soft target by Macintosh and his gang. In spite of the number of spies that were eliminated by Republicans, the death squad at Belmont always seemed to know when to strike at Carrigtwohill. After the first four victims were killed by Mackintosh's gang, the Knockraha Volunteer Company agreed that it would patrol Carrigtwohill at night time and post men in selected vantage points in wait for the death squad.

Corry's men continued to do this for about six nights a week for some time, but the Jocks would never show when the Republicans were in the vicinity. It soon became clear, that someone in the village was still in communication with Belmont. A unit of Cobh Republicans arrived in Carrigtwohill one evening to arrest another suspected spy. The man was working near Barryscourt on the outskirts of the village. When the Volunteers moved in to arrest him, his reaction confirmed what they had already suspected. Once in custody, the prisoner was taken down to the local curate Fr Fouhy to administer the last rights of the Church before he was executed. The priest pleaded with the Republicans to spare the man's life, but he was told the decision was irrevocable. After his confession, and while the prisoner was being taken from the curate's house, he decided to make a dash for freedom. The IRA however, had both sides of the street lined with men, and when the suspected spy got about forty yards from the curate's gate, he was shot down.

Early the next morning, the mail coach to Midleton was held up when its horses refused to pass the dead body on the roadway. Furious that another of their spies was found out and eliminated in Carrigtwohill, the British responded by inflicting more punishment upon the village. But as fewer people were now willing to talk to them, their intelligence on the local population soon began to crumble. One evening when a house near the bottom of Minister's Hill was raided, the Camerons found four bicycles in the shed. These they believed were owned by the IRA, and so burned the house to the ground as punishment. The four bicycles were in fact owned by the four sons of the house who were employed at the Naval Dockyard at Haulbowline.

Weekends in Carrigtwohill eventually became synonymous with terror and this led to the men leaving the village for a couple of days at a time, while women went to the local church or convent. But while the Belmont-based Jocks were engaged in their own private war with the people of Carrigtwohill, and a tit-for-tat espionage war with the local IRA, on a different level, the IRA had made serious progress in locating the Clonmult informer. In the same month of May, Volunteer members of the 1st Battalion, Cork No. 2 Brigade arrested a suspected spy in the Watergrasshill/Glenville area. The ex-soldier by the name of David Walsh told his captors that he was from Shanagarry in East Cork and was in the locality looking for work. Walsh was initially questioned by the Company Captain but without much success. He was then taken to a freshly dug grave where was told he would be shot if he didn't confess. He was also told that if he did confess, he would be exiled to Australia. Believing that a full confession was the only way to save himself, Walsh eventually confessed to all. He told his captors that he had seen the 4th Battalion men at Clonmult, and of meeting a military party on his way to Cork later. He informed a military officer of what he had seen, and personally led them back to the site at Clonmult. For this he was paid a lump sum and was taken on as a permanent paid spy at £1 per week and the promise of a lump sum for any good catch made on his information. Walsh also gave the names of other paid informers. The informer was subsequently tried by court-martial for espionage and found guilty and sentenced to be shot. After the sentence was carried out, the Adjutant of the Cork No. 2 Brigade sent a letter to the O.C. of the 4th Battalion, Diarmuid Hurley, outlining its findings.

In little more than a week, Hurley himself would be shot down by the British. However, there appeared to be some evidence that not all Republicans were satisfied that the death of the informer Walsh had provided the Republican community in East Cork with proper retribution, and on 12 July, the day after the Truce came in to being, Major G.B. O'Connor, an esteemed member of Cork's Chamber of Commerce, was shot and killed outside his home in Douglas. A prominent Protestant unionist who was openly vocal against Republicanism, O'Connor's real crime was that he earlier had testified against IRA prisoners captured at Clonmult.

After the tragic events at Clonmult in February, the 4th Battalion column had become all but defunct. Diarmuid Hurley had decided to split the remainder of the column into small groups that would strike in different areas. Paddy Whelan, Jack O'Connell, Joe Ahern and himself stuck together and made up one such group. For some time prior, members of the 4th Battalion had been experimenting with explosives for the making of landmines. This had come about when one Ballinacurra Volunteer, Tom Hyde discovered that fishing smacks in his area were using disused coastal artillery shells from the British harbour forts as ballast. Prior to 20 February Tom Hyde had sent another Volunteer, Paddy O'Reilly with one of the artillery shells to show Diarmuid Hurley at Clonmult. Hurley was impressed with what he saw and instructed Paddy Whelan to pack the shell with explosives and show O'Reilly how to use an attached exploder (detonator). O'Reilly and Hyde had already decided on a suitable target to try out their new weapon. They concealed the device under a pathway regularly used by a party of Cameron Highlanders between their barracks in Youghal and the local firing range. There were two routes that the battalion used to get to and from the range. Eventually when the Camerons' party used the right one, Hyde and O'Reilly were near by with about 150 yards of a detonating lead between them. When it exploded, the device had gone off slightly sooner that was expected but still managed to kill a number of the Jocks including some of the regimental band, and allowed the attackers time to escape in the confusion that followed. Hurley's column had never got the chance to use the mines themselves. On the morning of 10 April that would change when Hurley and his unit moved in to place one of the mines on a roadway between Youghal and Midleton at Ballyedekin in the neighbourhood of Churchtown. The Volunteers had earlier received word that a convoy of British troops were en route from Youghal to Cork via Midleton.

The unit leader recruited another local Volunteer named Mick Kearney for the job as he was very familiar with the local area. The Volunteers had concealed the mine under a load of stones on the road and were separated by about 100 yards of lead which was under the control of Joe Ahern who was positioned down a narrow by-road. Hurley was close to Ahern and was to signal when to detonate the device. Jack O'Connell and Paddy Whelan were concealed on the same side of the road but about 150 yards from the others. Their job was to open fire on the convoy when the explosion took place, in order to help the others to escape. There was to be no straight stand-up fight with the British who would vastly outnumber the Volunteers. The main purpose of the attack was to test the effectiveness of the land mine. About 4p.m., Mick Kearney, who was concealed on high ground, but visible to the others, signalled the approach of the convoy. As expected, it was a large convoy of four Leyland lorries and five Crossley tenders full of military. After receiving the signal via Hurley, Joe Ahern pressed the plunger. The deafening roar of the mine sent a cloud of dirt and stones hurling into the air. Kearney the scout had misjudged the signal, leading the device to be set off too early. This resulted in the lead lorry being halted by the explosion, but causing no harm to the others behind. Jack O'Connell and Paddy Whelan immediately began firing on the stationary vehicles. The occupants quickly jumped out and returned fire upon their attackers. Ahern joined O'Connell and Whelan, who quickly ran to the nearby by-road after coming under severe and superior fire. The three men started to run crouched along a furze covered ditch where they continued to come under fire from the quickly advancing troops. Soon the tops of the furze bushes were being cut from over the heads of the men, particularly O'Connell and Ahern, who were both six footers, by machine gun fire. The men could soon see over the fence in the adjoining field that a party of about thirty troops were closing in on them in extended formation. Fire from these troops was getting heavier all the time before it suddenly eased as quickly as it began. Then they realised that the British had redirected their fire after Diarmuid Hurley who they could see running openly across a nearby field.

It was then they realised that the Lewis machine-gun fire had all the time been coming from the scene of the explosion. This allowed the three men some respite, as they crawled through fences and over ditches before eventually escaping. They soon made their way to the cover of some trees where they could see the military searching the fields a few hundred yards below. They were very concerned for the fate of Diarmuid Hurley, however, who they were sure must have been shot or captured. Mick Kearney the scout had by then made well his escape. The men made their way to the safety of Murnane's farm house a few miles away at Coppingerstown. To their amazement and delight, they found Diarmuid Hurley was there waiting for them. All four men remarked at the speed with which the British military managed to get themselves into action and launch a counter attack, following the initial shock of the explosion. They also realised that if they were ever to use the mines to their maximum potential and avoid the type of close escape they just had, they would need to overcome the problem of signal and detonation. Although they didn't receive any later reports of British casualties, they were convinced that some in the convoys lead lorry that day must have been casualties.

The next two mines to be used on the enemy were organised and detonated by their founder, Tom Hyde. The first was placed against the courthouse in Midleton in early May. This was a particularly brave and daring act as the courthouse adjoined the RIC barracks, and the mine shells when filled weighed 100 pounds. When it exploded, the mine didn't cause the expected damage, but managed to rattle the nerves of the garrison inside, who responded by firing indiscriminately out on the street. In the space of a week, Hyde and others of the Midleton Company exploded another mine under a lorry-load of troops at Carrigahane about a mile outside Midleton, towards Castlemartyr. On that occasion, Hurley, Whelan, O'Connell and Ahern had not long moved out of Murnane's of Coppingerstown which was a few hundred yards from the scene. Fortunately for them, they were unaware of Hyde's plans and had moved out in the opposing direction of the target.

18. Death of a Leader

In early May, Diarmuid Hurley and his unit were contacted by Con Leddy, O.C., of the North-East column. Con invited them to join his column in a proposed attack on a convoy of military in West Waterford. Hurley and the others proceeded to Con Leddy's headquarters at Conna, about six miles west of Tallow, Co. Waterford, where they met Con and his officers in O'Keeffe's house. After some discussion, it was decided that Con would select the ambush site, and that all would meet again on 28 May to make the final arrangements. The night before the prearranged meeting, Hurley and his men slept in the townland of Bloomfield on the Carrigtwohill side of Midleton. The morning of 28 May Hurley had learned that a cycle patrol from Cobh had raided several houses in the Carrigtwohill area, and were permitted to return to Cobh freely.

The battalion O.C. was particularly annoyed that his earlier instructions to all company commanders to have Volunteers on duty at all hours and to take any steps in their power to harass the enemy; even if only, in this instance, the roads had been sprinkles with broken glass, to puncture the bikes of the military. Hurley considered this matter more important for him to go in to Carrigtwohill and enquire into the matter rather than keep his appointment with Con Leddy. He instructed Tom Buckley of Midleton and Paddy Whelan to go to the meeting at Conna, and he would go himself to Carrigtwohill. When Hurley reached a junction in the road about a mile from Carrigtwohill, there was one road leading to Carrigtwohill and another to Lisgould. Just as he was about to take the road to Carrigtwohill, he stumbled upon a foot patrol of RIC and Black and Tans from Midleton. The Republican leader was instantly recognised by some of the patrol and was ordered to halt. Hurley however, knew the game was up and didn't intend going without a fight. He immediately threw his mills grenade and opened up with his revolver, while making a dash for cover along a low fence. He had little chance of making an escape however, as his numerically superior enemy opened up on him. Before he could make it to the corner of the fence, Hurley was hit and died where he fell. For some unknown reason, the patrol left Hurley's body where he fell and returned to their barracks. Perhaps they might have felt his comrades were also in the locality and didn't want a showdown with them.

Meanwhile, when they arrived at Conna, Paddy Whelan and Tom Buckley waited for hours before learning that Con Leddy would not be able to keep his appointment with them. They then decided to return back to meet Diarmuid Hurley and the others. It would ironically be in the village of Clonmult where they would learn of the sad news of their leader's death and his remains being brought to Gurteen. Joe Ahern, Paddy Whelan and Jack O'Connell, then made arrangements to have the body taken to Dr. John Walsh in Midleton where it was embalmed. It was then moved with the help of John Kelleher to Churchtown where it was temporarily interned in a vault in the local cemetery. After the Truce in July, Hurley's body was re-interred, with full military honours, in the Republican plot in Midleton cemetery with his earlier fallen comrades.

An unfortunate development which happened after the Hurley killing was to have long-term and devastating consequences for the unity of the 4th Battalion, and as at least one historian has already recorded, leading to some taking opposite sides in the later Civil War. It is somewhat difficult to form a totally accurate picture of what took place around the succession of Battalion Commander to Diarmuid Hurley, as there are two contrary accounts given in the witness statements of Volunteer officers Paddy Whelan and Seamus Fitzgerald. What is well established however, is that both men took opposite sides in the Civil War, and while the terrible mishandling of the selection of Hurley's successor may have in part given rise to a Cobh – Midleton split, it should be remembered that Paddy Whelan and Jack O'Connell, who took the side of the Midleton (Free State) Company, were themselves from Cobh. So what could have led to this unfortunate turn of events?

Paddy Whelan's account is as follows:

Early in June 1921, the company commanders of the 4th Battalion assembled at Dungourney to elect a Battalion O.C.. The meeting was held in the open, and was attended by about twelve officers, including Joe Ahern, Jack O'Connell, Daithí O'Brien (Cobh), Martin Corry (Knockraha) and myself. I explained the purpose of the meeting, and said that no matter who was elected, we could never be fortunate enough to have a commander as good as the late Diarmuid Hurley. All were agreed on this, and I then proposed Joe Ahern as O.C.. Martin Corry seconded the proposal which was passed unanimously. Joe Ahern then suggested that a Vice Commandant should be elected. To my surprise, I was proposed by Daithí O'Brien and seconded by Martin Corry. This was also passed unanimously. Joe and I held these ranks until the Truce of July 1921, and on the formation of the National (Free State) Army, we joined up and held the same ranks in the then 42nd Infantry Brigade.

Seamus Fitzgerald however, gives a somewhat different account of whom and how Diarmuid Hurley's replacement came into being,

Michael Leahy, the Brigade Vice O.C., was now back from Italy, where he had been some time working with Hales to secure a large quantity of arms, a mission which, unfortunately, proved unsuccessful. Leahy visited us at 'E' Company in Knockraha and discussed with me who the best successor as Commandant for the battalion would be. The remnants of the column consisted only of Joe Ahern, Vice O.C., Paddy Whelan, and Jack O'Connell. Joe Ahern was quietly assuming authority, but Leahy was adamant that he was unsuitable for command, and I agreed. The only choice was to restore Daithí O'Brien to his old command, and this was done in a rather nebulous way. Leahy had had to demote O'Brien for hasty action in the past, and he also did not wish to have any difficulties with Ahern, who also lost a brother at Clonmult and was bursting for command. [37]

It is clear for anyone who reads both accounts, to conclude that each cannot be consistent with the other. Both accounts also leave unanswered questions. If Fitzgerald's account is correct, then it must have taken place very late, possibly in the weeks leading up to the Truce when Leahy was back in Cork. So why was Leahy so determined to prevent Ahern from having command, and why did he and Fitzgerald believe the man was unsuitable for the position? Surely if he was good enough for the position of Vice O.C., he was good enough for the top position. He had taken part in virtually every military operation with Hurley and the others of the column and had given a good account of himself. Perhaps, the most important factor in his suitability for the position, however, was his having the confidence and respect of those who worked and operated closest to him. If Fitzgerald's account is correct, then it begs the question, what exactly was their problem with Ahern, and why was Leahy in particular prepared to risk the unity of the East-Cork IRA by taking such a drastic and unnecessary measure. After all the years of hard work that he had personally put in to building up the 4th Battalion from scratch when few others were around to do it, why was he now prepared to blow it all away because of some personality clash? Furthermore, why would Leahy replace Ahern with O'Brien, an officer he was forced to demote previously, and why did he chose to consult Fitzgerald who although was a well respected officer among the Brigade staff, held no position of command himself?

On the other hand, if Whelan's account is correct, why is there no record of Daithí O'Brien or Martin Corry ever making a case to defend their earlier support for Ahern and Whelan at the Dungourney meeting? In his written account of that meeting, Whelan placed in brackets, 'Cobh' and 'Knockraha' after the names of O'Brien and Corry respectfully, but not in relation to the other officers who supposedly attended that meeting, why? Was he merely emphasizing those men's names and company address's because they later took the opposing side to him in the Civil War, or was he hinting that Mick Leahy had later made a solo run in undermining Ahern's position? But maybe there is a third position here which holds the answer, and perhaps Fitzgerald and Whelan had both given us factual accounts, with the real answer being in one line of Fitzgerald's statement, 'The only answer was to restore Daithí O'Brien to his old command, and this was done in a rather nebulous way.'[38]

Perhaps Ahern and O'Brien both held the position of battalion commander, depending on which Company area Volunteers were aligned to. But if Mick Leahy felt he had solved a problem through such a cop-out, he was greatly mistaken, and this one action would later come back to haunt him and the future of Republican Cork.

There is another unfortunate link to this story however, which in part sheds some light on why Mick Leahy acted as he did and probably why

Fitzgerald supported him. Some time after Leahy had returned to his old position in command as Vice O.C. of the 1st Cork Brigade, he was said to have received some disturbing reports about the behaviour in the Midleton area of officers under the command of Joe Ahern. This alleged unbecoming behaviour was happening during the height of the Truce and was said to have involved, heavy drinking, intimidation and even the occasional armed robbery. These were allegations that couldn't be ignored, leading Mick Leahy to launch an immediate local inquiry. He unfortunately found there was some foundation to these allegations. His response was to remove Ahern from his position of command. He was also very mindful of the possibility of alienating others in the Midleton Company by taking further action against other officers. In hindsight he possibly would have brought about a far more positive outcome had he disciplined the other guilty officers and let it be known why they were being reprimanded.

As it transpired from Leahy's discrete action, the guilty and disgruntled officers were able to portray Joe Ahern as a hard-done victim by the interfering Leahy who had pulled rank against their company, which he always made sure played second fiddle to Cobh. With the clouds of Civil War looming large on the horizon, the leaders of the Midleton Company took the first possible opportunity to align themselves against Leahy and their former colleagues by being the only company in Munster to turn Free State *en-masse*. It was also reported at the time that the reason why Leahy had earlier gone to Knockraha to seek the opinion of Seamus Fitzgerald about the suitability of Joe Ahern for command, was that when he (Leahy) arrived back from Italy via Dublin, he began to make his own enquiries about what had happened at Clonmult in February. Although this is now the subject of speculation, there were some unsubstantiated rumours that Leahy had discovered there had been a lot of drinking and socialising by the Volunteers, in the village of Clonmult in the time leading up to the ambush. This, some believe is why Fitzgerald agreed with Leahy that Ahern was unsuitable for command. The subsequent lines of division which came about as a result of Leahy's disciplinary action against Ahern saw a bitter closing of ranks among the Midleton officers, particularly by those of the column that had survived Clonmult. It is worth noting here that Jack O'Connell and Paddy Whelan; each from Cobh, also remained loyal to the Midleton Company which later went Free State. It is clear that their experiences of Clonmult had created a bond of loyalty that no disciplinary action (rightly or wrongly) could undo. Because Daithí O'Brien decided to emigrate to the US immediately after the Civil War, he never got to make a witness statement to the Bureau of Military History. Martin Corry, although becoming a TD soon afterwards, and spending more than the next fifty years in public life, for some strange reason also failed to make a witness statement.

For these reasons, we may never really know what took place between Mick Leahy and Joe Ahern, and how the decision to fill the position left vacant by Diarmuid Hurley's death was taken. I believe we can safely conclude however, that something drastic took place which led the Midleton Company to decide to turn against the rest of their former battalion colleagues by putting themselves at the disposal of the Free State army.

19.Cobh gets its own TD

In late April 1921, while working at the Knockraha bomb factory, Seamus Fitzgerald was told that his name was being considered as a third Sinn Féin candidate with the existing members of Tom Hunter and David Kent on the ticket for the forthcoming General Election, but only if Liam Lynch didn't express an interest in the position. There was a commission established by Sinn Féin to select its candidates for Cork North East. Liam Lynch was selected as the third candidate in his absence providing his acceptance could be got. David Kent then proposed Fitzgerald as a substitute candidate in the event of Lynch not accepting the nomination. Kent also agreed to make contact with Lynch to establish the outcome one way or the other.

With no word forthcoming from Lynch over the following weeks, Fitzgerald received the nomination and was duly elected a TD after polling day. The fact that he was a virtual absentee candidate, having been forced on the run for nearly six months, only added to his support among the voters of Cobh and other East Cork towns. It could be said that Fitzgerald became a TD by default however, because it later emerged during the Treaty debates, while he was in conversation with Liam Lynch, that David Kent, had never relayed the message to Lynch informing him of his nomination. Lynch did however inform the Cobh man that he was quite satisfied he had been elected.

20. Republican Courts

Under Dáil authority, each parish had a court which functioned with certain jurisdiction, with Parish Justices and Republican Police. In Cobh, Seamus Fitzgerald sat as Chairman of the Parish Court regularly, particularly before he was forced to go on the run. Paddy O'Sullivan who was later executed after being captured at Clonmult, was the Clerk of the Parish Court. Maurice Downey later took over from O'Sullivan. The Courts were held openly, very often in the Town Hall. Crown Forces who often made surprise raids on the Courts, would be shown signed forms which the litigants would have signed agreeing to have their differences arbitrated upon. As such was legal under British law, the Crown Forces were unable to do much to hinder the courts. In addition to his many Republican roles, as Councillor, TD, soldier and bomb-maker, Parish Judge, Dáil Publicist, Fitzgerald was also President of the East Cork District Court, to which appeals from the Parish Courts would go for hearing and which had higher jurisdiction.

Jerry Murphy, a solicitor's clerk in Midleton, was the District Court Clerk. Most of the District Courts were held secretly, though in broad daylight, in some farmer's house some safe distance from any town. Often fifty or sixty people attended such courts, with their accompanying array of legal men, solicitors and barristers, and the proceedings lasted for hours. Decisions were well received, and the legal men were loud in their praises of the work of the courts. Land cases were difficult ones for the District Courts, as some persons trying to take advantage of the state of war felt that they could push forward land claims which would be hard to justify under normal circumstances. The Courts however, would more often than not arrive at fair and just decisions. A typical sitting of the Cobh Parish /District Court can be demonstrated by the following listed cases before the court for hearing on 25 January 1922.

In a particular local case that required arbitration, between Capt. Stewart French of Marina Cobh, and the Cobh Branch of the Irish Transport & General Workers Union, Seamus Fitzgerald TD, for some unknown reason declined to act as Arbitrator and instead consulted with the Minister for Agriculture, Patrick Hogan. On 3 March 1922, the Minister replied, notifying Fitzgerald of the appointment of Mr B. McAuliffe as the new Arbitrator for the case.

CIVIL CLAIMS

No. REG	PILAINTIFF	DEFENDANT	CAUSE OF ACTION
20	Frank Dolan	Daniel Meade	Arrears of Rent
32	Daniel Kelleher	William Walsh	Price of Cow
33	John Healy	William Murphy	Rates Due
19	Margaret Frahill	Ml & Mgt Murphy	Possession of House And Fix Fair Rent
17	John McCarthy	Daniel & Mrs Cronin	Possession of Shop & Rooms and Claim Arrears of Rent- £30

ADJOURNED CIVIL CLAIMS

29	J J O' Sullivan	Prudential Assurance Coy	Monies Due
13	Prudential Ass Coy	J J O'Sullivan	
31	Eugene Riordan	Daniel & Mrs Mary O'Regan	
30	Ed O'Brien	Mrs Mary O'Reilly	Mrs Mary O'Reilly

APPEAL CASES

36	Major Watt	John Carroll	Possession of House
10	Mrs Kate Power	Maurice Power	Order for Maintenance

21.Escape from Spike

Fishermen working in the Cork Harbour area proved helpful to the Republican movement in more ways than one. Not only did they provide the material for creating landmines from empty artillery shells, but some of them were always on hand to provide boats and equipment to Republicans at short notice. One such occasion of this help was demonstrated in April 1921 when three high profile prisoners were spirited away from under the noses of the authorities on Spike Island. Spike had a long history as a place of detention. It had been used by Cromwellian and Williamites as a place for convicts awaiting deportation to the different convict settlements such as the West Indies and later Australia.

The brutality and horrors suffered by the transported prisoners finally called an end to the penalty of transportation to some convict colony, and convict prisons were established in Ireland. Spike Island was chosen as the site for one of these prisons and was opened in 1847, remaining in existence until 1883. During the period 1919-1921, the British again chose Spike as a location for locking up unruly elements. It was, in reality an internment camp for holding Republican suspects. In late April, the local Volunteer commander Mick Burke was visited by a Brigade Staff member Denis Barry, with an urgent request for him to report to Brigade HQ in Cork. Burke duly set off and met with some staff officers at Master's Restaurant at Marlboro Street. He was told of a very serious situation that was developing on Spike Island.

Among the hundreds of Republican internees being held there were some senior, high-profile officers whose true identity they feared the British could discover any day, and possibly send them forward for court martial and execution under the terms of the new emergency legislation. There were three prisoners in particular that the Brigade staff wanted rescued as soon as possible. They were Sean McSwiney from Cork (brother of Terence, the martyred Lord Mayor), Tomás O Máoiléoin, alias Sean Forde of East Limerick and Sean Twomey of Cork City. The internees on the island were cramped into rundown huts, some without windows and doors. The food was so bad that many prisoners refused to eat it and relied on food parcels from outside to survive. A hunger strike would break out in May over these conditions but for now, brigade staff were particularly worried that the British would make an example of McSwiney were they to learn he was the brother of the late Lord Mayor. The true identity of the much wanted Ó Máoiléoin was also made known to the authorities on Spike by a rogue prisoner who recognised him. Before they could send him forward for Court-martial though, they first needed someone to come forward to identify him. The man they chose for this task however was executed by the IRA before he could reach the island. It is believed that Liam Lynch, fearing for Ó Máoiléoin's wellbeing, inspired the brigade to launch the escape bid. The situation was soon recognised to be of the utmost urgency, with time not being on the side of the prisoners. Staff officers discussed the situation with Burke, and told him of what role he was to play in the rescue of the three men.

Within days Burke and the brigade had set up communication with the prisoners through Fr Fitzgerald, the Prison Chaplain. Saturday 29 April at 11a.m. was set as the date and time of the rescue. The three prisoners had earlier managed to get themselves on a work detail with the construction of a golf course on the north-eastern side of the island. This it was felt was how they would happen to be outside of the fort at the designated time. In the meantime, Mick Burke had to get hold of an appropriately sized boat for the job. He quickly accomplished that task through the reliable assistance of local mariner Ned O'Regan who provided his aptly named launch *The Raider*. Burke's next task was to crew the launch with three reliable Volunteers. For this he picked George O'Reilly, Andrew Butterly and Frank Barry. Burke didn't inform his men of the arranged date and time of the planned escape, but did tell them that he wanted to take the boat on a dummy run on Saturday morning. When they set out from Cobh that morning at 9.30a.m., the *Raider* broke with tradition by flying a small Union Jack flag from its rear. Burke was not very familiar with the workings of the launch and while making a brave attempt to steer the vessel out the harbour towards Spike, he collided with an incoming launch from Spike that was laden with soldiers. The language which the very annoyed military used towards Burke was not very pleasant, but was probably not as bad as they used some hours later when they realised who had hit them.

When they reached their *rendez-vous* at the appointed time, Burke and his team could see the three prisoners at work rolling the golf links, under an instructor and an armed soldier as guard. Less than a mile away, a British destroyer was anchored, and didn't seem too interested in the activities of the launch flying the Union Jack. The course sloped down to the sea at the north-eastern corner of the island, and on the course, near the water was a hollow where the prisoners used to have a break for a smoke. They were often joined there by the guard, but on this particular morning the armed guard didn't join Ó Máoiléoin, McSwiney and Twomey for a smoke; instead he stayed up on the slope, well visible from the barracks fort. Also keeping an eye on the three men on this particular day was a soldier, armed with a revolver, separate from the one with the rifle.

Meanwhile, down on the tide and moored a small way off shore, Burke and his crew were doing their best impression of fishermen at work. The Republican commander was all the time becoming more anxious as he couldn't understand why the prisoners were not making a break for freedom. He knew they couldn't wait around for too long without drawing attention to themselves, and felt that something must have happened to prevent the three prisoners from making a run for it. Eventually, he decided there was no use hanging around as the prisoners must have been prevented from escaping on this occasion. He ordered the others to haul in the gear as they were going to return back to Cobh. But just as Burke had made the decision to quit, he and his men noticed the prisoner's spring into action. They could see from their boat near the shore, Ó Máoiléoin, half creeping and half running, made up the slope to the sentry, but the sentry, not knowing whether this was some kind of game, hesitated on what to do. By the time he had made up his mind it was too late; when Ó Máoiléoin got too close for comfort, the sentry discovered that he had no round up the breech when he attempted to pull the bolt. He paid the full price for his negligence, for Ó Máoiléoin struck him a blow on the head with a hammer he had earlier been using on the axle of the lawn-mower. The sentry went down without a sound, but to make sure that he would be out for a long count, Ó Máoiléoin struck him a second blow. The supervisor and other armed soldier had already been overpowered by Twomey and McSwiney, and offered no resistance when they were tied up with ropes brought ashore by Burke, and gagged with towels. Burke also offered a rope to tie up the sentry that Ó Máoiléoin had felled up on the hill, but they insisted he was going nowhere and didn't need tying. Ó Máoiléoin did take the sentry's rifle though. As soon as he got the three men into the boat, Burke set off at speed towards Paddy's Blocks near Ringaskiddy about three quarter of a mile away. The Raider had not long got out of sight of the golf course when it started to give trouble. Burke had discovered that while they were alongside close to the shore at Spike, some seaweed had got into the water pump, stopping the circulation of the engine.

Looking back towards Spike, one of the men noticed the sentry that they neglected to tie up, had regained consciousness and was hurrying towards the fort. Burke hurried to free the pump of the seaweed while the launch spluttered its way towards Ringaskiddy. When it reached about 50 yards short of Paddy's Blocks, the overheated engine seized up. The men could see the military swarming out of the fort on Spike down towards the golf links. Burke was careful to ensure that all but two crew members were by then lying flat on the boat. The remaining two were steadily pad-dling close to shore with oars. Once they had waded ashore, the escapees and crew were careful to get out of view of those on Spike, who were probably misled by the Union Jack which still flew from the launch.

Once back on dry land, Burke and the others made to meet up with the pre-arranged transport that had been arranged by the brigade. There were seven in all in his party, and to his horror, he discovered that their transport consisted of a pony-and-trap driven by Sean Hyde, a brigade officer and another, making it a party of nine, all of whom could not pos-sibly be accommodated in the trap. The successful escape of the prisoners being Burke's main concern, he instructed that they make a hasty escape in the trap with Hyde, where they and the captured rifle were taken to a safe hiding place. Burke and the other Cobh men were now in a predica-ment as to how they would get back to Cobh without being detected. Looking around, he spotted a young lad in a small boat off shore. He called him ashore and told him that they urgently needed to get up river. The four men then pulled as hard and as quickly as they could until they reached Monkstown about two miles away. They then sent the young lad back with his boat to Ringaskiddy. Unfortunately for the young innocent lad, he was arrested upon his return and was later interned, probably on Spike Island. Once in Monkstown, the four Cobhmen decided to split forces. Frank Barry and George O'Reilly took the ferry straight across the river to Cobh, while Burke and Andy Butterly boarded a train for Cork. The train hadn't travelled far when at Glenbrook Station it was boarded by military and police.

The two men were searched and questioned, but their explanations were accepted. When they reached Blackrock, they left the train and walked the remaining distance into the city where Burke reported the success of the operation to brigade staff at Miss Wallace's in St Augustine Street. He and Butterly then walked the eight mile journey to Knockraha where they also reported the success of escape to the 4th Battalion O.C. Diarmuid Hurley. All four Volunteers made it back to Cobh safely, where for days, the topic of conversation on everyone lips was the great escape from Spike. Once again, it was with great credit to the people of Cobh, some of whom must of have witnessed the strange sight of four local Republicans head off that morning in a launch that flew the detested Union Jack flag, that they remained silent and didn't report it. By then, the British had discovered how they had been conned by the Union flag. They still had no idea of the identities of those who masterminded or carried out the rescue, but they did have possession of the launch and knew the identity of its owner. Both Ned O'Regan and his launch's skipper Duster Walsh were ready for the questions. Each stuck to their story that the launch was missing when they reported for work that morning, and didn't report it for fear of been implicated in some nasty crime. Strangely enough, whether it was for a lack of evidence or not, both men were released. The authorities impounded the launch however, and didn't return it to O'Regan until after the Truce, and only then minus its engine. Ned O'Regan later presented the *Raider* to Mick Burke as a souvenir to mark memorable deeds and times.

22. The Sinking of British Sloops

Three weeks after Burke led a bold escape from Spike Island, he and his men were engaged in nautical manoeuvres again, but this time they were intent on sinking vessels rather that using one to escape. It was brought to Burke's attention that three British sloops and three trawlers were moored at Carrigaloe, about a mile west of the town of Cobh. It was established that there was a watchman on each vessel at night time, and a naval patrol launch visited them at regular intervals day and night. Burke and his officers put a plan together to sink the vessels. On the night of the attack, Thursday 18 May, Burke with eight others, and armed with revolvers, boarded the ships and removed the watchmen from each. They then opened the sea cocks before breaking them. The watertight doors were then smashed with sledge-hammers. The watchmen then released as Burke and his Volunteers made good their escape. Early the next morning, Burke returned to Carrigaloe with another officer, and from a safe distance, observed that all that was visible of the ships were their masts and funnels, the remainder were well under water. This operation came as a terrible blow to British morale and later on the night of Friday 20 May a party of off-duty Royal Marines went on a drunken rampage in the town.

Starting at 9.20p.m. they started shooting in the main street indiscriminately. Before long they were hurling blast bombs through the windows of several houses in East and West Beach, while the windows of other houses were shattered. The whole incident lasted for three quarters of an hour before finally a number of Cameron Highlanders succeeded in restoring order (ironically it was the Marines who had to restrain the Camerons during their rampage the previous August). Strangely enough, although the culprits had been captured and the marauding marines were marched away to the naval pier under Cameron escort, his Majesty's Highlanders then spent the rest of the evening stopping and searching Cobh civilians. Once again it was an ex-serviceman by the name of Quaine who bore the brunt of the earlier attack when he sustained serious chest injuries. Another man, who worked as a wireless operator at the Admiralty, was also severely wounded and had to be removed to the military hospital at Haulbowline. A few of the British equally sustained injuries at the hands of their naval countrymen, though none of them seriously. In fact a heroic Cameron was seen displaying his wounds to some very interested colleagues.

The damage done to several business premises throughout the town was extensive. Mrs Fitzgerald of the Rob Roy Hotel had an unnerving experience when, standing at the door of the bar, she saw three Marines at the corner of the square who shouted to her to 'get in out of it.' [39] She quickly moved inside but scarcely done so when a bomb was thrown into the barroom and exploded, shattering glass windows and doors, blowing a hole in the floor and creating the dream of every teetotaller by smashing all the liquor bottles in the room. Miraculously Mrs Fitzgerald escaped injury, although her blouse didn't come out of the attack looking any better. Mrs Coleman, a publican at West Beach, had a similar narrow escape when a Mills bomb hurled through the window of the pub exploded inside the counter, with customers diving for cover. Once again windows and bottles were blown to atoms. The drapery shop of Mr Swanton, only a few doors away from the pub at No. 13, was also bombed by the Marines, as was O'Hara's barber shop at Harbour Row. The windows of a local tobacconist and several civilian houses were also shattered.

Jasper Wilson was a child at the time and was with his father, who owned a chemist shop at West Beach. Jasper later told his son of how he was ordered to get behind the counter when the first explosions were heard in the area. The occupants of another nearby premises were absorbed in a game of chess when the bombing started, and the subsequent explosions knocked all the chess pieces over. An identification parade was later held at the Admiralty, but it was more of a face-saving exercise than anything else, as the culprits had already been identified, having been disarmed and escorted back to their barracks by the Camerons after their rampage. But if the British thought the sinking of their sloops and trawlers at Carrigaloe was a one-off easy and opportunist attack by Republicans, they were soon to learn that the local IRA was becoming more and more bold and innovative.

Some time earlier, Mick Burke had received fourteen pounds of gelignite from the Battalion Quartermaster to blow up Belvelly Bridge, the only land communication between Cobh and the mainland. Burke wanted to make life as difficult as possible for the Jocks who used their headquarters at Belmont in Cobh to launch raids throughout the East Cork region. Even the Death Squad had to pass over Belvelly Bridge to get to their victims off the island, and without this way of passage, their task would be infinitely harder to achieve. On the night of the operation to blow up the bridge, Burke with a number of other Volunteers, were unable to dislodge the keystone in the short time they had in the hours of darkness. They did however manage to place three pounds of gelignite in the water traps at each side of the bridge and fired them, badly damaging the bridge and destroying the water main.

Burke was still left with eight pounds of buckshee gelignite and soon set about looking for an appropriate target to use it on. He had for some time being toying with the idea of striking a blow in the heart of the Lion's Den at Haulbowline. He considered using some Volunteers who worked at naval dockyard, to bring off some spectacular operation there under the noses of the enemy. Through the local RIC, and its own intelligence sources, the Admiralty had for some time tried to be more security conscious and alert when recruiting and hiring personnel at the Haulbowline dockyard. Big lessons had been learned since the time when Mick Leahy and Seamus Fitzgerald had been interned in 1916 while serving as apprentices at the dockyard. But for all the Admiralty's vetting and security measures, Republicans still had Haulbowline well penetrated, with a large portion of its company members employed at the dockyard. Burke decided to be very daring in how he would use the remaining eight pounds of gelignite, and decided to give the British a lesson in how to destroy a Destroyer.

He selected two Volunteer workers at the yard, whom he felt wouldn't be lacking in nerve, and would be up for the task. The two men, Donal Collins and Jack Clarke, were briefed by Burke about the particular Destroyer that was selected as the target. It was the same ship that both men were then working on (HMS *Trenchant*), leaving them in an ideal position to carry off the operation successfully. For security reasons, all repair workers had to be off the ship each evening by 4.30p.m. Burke briefed the two Volunteers in the use of the explosives and explained that they would have to lay and prime the explosives just before everyone was due to leave the ship on the designated evening. They were told to ignite the fuse through a large lighted candle, which when burned down, would set it off about two hours after everyone had left the ship. Wednesday 1 June was set as the date to plant and activate the bomb. Just before 4.30p.m., when everyone else was preparing to call it a day, Collins and Clarke discreetly went about their task oblivious to their fellow workers. They then calmly left the ship in the dry dock with all the other workers. Exactly three hours later at 7.30p.m., a thunderous explosion was heard echoing around the harbour. Prisoners on the nearby Spike Island were no doubt smiling in the knowledge that their colleagues from Cobh's 'A' Company had been hard at work with some defiant effort. The bottom plates of the 'Trenchant' were severely damaged in the explosion, forcing the ship from going back into service for a number of extra months. The dockyard itself, also had to be shut down for three days, but not before it was visited by the Admiral from Cobh the next day (Thursday 2 June). The Admiral had expressed a wish to examine the damage personally, and from the fifteen hundred employees at the yard, the man he chose to show him around the ship was one of its destroyers, Donal Collins. Not only did this demonstrate the desperately poor state of the navy's system of intelligence and security, but it must have also left Collins with the incredible task of trying to keep a straight face while showing the Admiral around the ships damage. A couple of weeks later, John Verling was arrested at his home in Newtown and taken into custody.

A Rushbrooke dockyard worker by the name of James Jones was also arrested at the golf links just outside Newtown. Both men were taken to Belmont for interrogation. In the same month, after receiving instructions from Brigade H.Q. to seize the passports and tickets from all men of military age leaving Cobh for the USA. Mick Burke undertook the task with a good degree of enthusiasm. This was to happen on the night before a ship was due to sail from Cobh. The idea was to discourage such men from leaving the country at a time when the Republican government considered they should remain and help in the fight. In one night alone, after mustering the whole company together, and splitting up in to groups of twos and threes, every hotel and guesthouse in the town was searched, with more than eighty passports and tickets being confiscated. Earlier, the Town Council had passed a motion calling upon the young men of Ireland to stay at home and work for the new Republic, and expressed a wish that it wouldn't become necessary for drastic steps to be taken to enforce the measure. Mick Burke later expressed the view that his company's action in passport confiscations went a long way towards having the desired effect.

By the month of May 1921, even Mick Burke had become known to the authorities as a prominent Republican. One day he was arrested from his place of work at the Co-op in King's Square by a party of British, who took him back to their camp at Belmont. While there, he was interrogated at least twice a day, leaving him with the awkward task of trying to remember what lies he had told at the previous sessions. On two occasions the soldiers on guard gave him every opportunity and encouragement to escape. Burke instantly saw through this ruse, and knew they were waiting to put a bullet in his back. It also told him that the authorities must have known how senior his rank was in the local Volunteer organisation. The Camerons even resorted to putting their own intelligence officer in the same cell as him, hoping to pass him off as a prisoner in the hope that Burke might talk and reveal something of interest. The exercise was a disaster though, as Burke knew exactly who his cellmate was and nearly bored the man to death. During one interrogation session, another intelligence officer, Captain Morrison brought Burke over to a door, where a list of names was posted. Morrison pointed to the names which had a red pencil mark crossed through them, telling him those people were dead.

He then pointed to other names on the list that had a black mark through them, as belonging to those who were currently in custody. He then asked Burke to explain why his name was fifth on that list. Burke replied by saying it had to be a mistake as he belonged to no anti-British organisation. Although he wasn't on hunger strike, Burke refused to eat the food that was given to him while in custody. When asked why, he said he was under doctor's care and the food he was given was unsuitable. He was then taken to the military hospital below Cottrells Row, before Dr Tarrant, who treated him rather abruptly at first. When the Republican leader told the doctor who he was, the man's manner changed immediately. Tarrant asked Burke what food he had been given in his cell; Burke told him bully-beef and beans. Tarrant replied that such food would kill a horse. He ordered that the prisoner be put on a diet of rice and milk puddings. On his way back to his cell again, Burke was brought in for more interrogation by Detective Copperthorn of Westview barracks, as well as two military officers.

After a number of hours, the military officers left to retire, leaving Copperthorn alone in the cell with Burke. The seasoned detective knew he was making no progress with his prize prisoner and at the conclusion of the interrogation, turned to Burke and remarked 'Burke you are known far and wide'. The prisoner was then put back in his cell, and to his great surprise, was released within the hour. Once outside the gates of the camp, the bewildered Republican made his way to his home at Donelan Terrace, where his relieved sister began to prepare him a proper meal. Before Burke could manage to take a bite of food however, he was alerted to the noise of lorries pulling up outside the house. He quickly darted out the back and over the wall and into a neighbouring house. The military surrounded the house back and front while searching for the illusive Burke, but he had flown the coop just before them. He knew the time for sleeping at home would now be a thing of the past and from then forward, slept at Cobh Hospital. Along with other Company members who were in a similar predicament, Burke was looked after by the doctor, matron and nurses who always kept a bed for them.

It was around this time (still in May), that Mick Burke received an intelligence report that the Cameron Highlanders at Belmont, had formed a specially selected number of its members into a murder gang that was operating in the 4th Battalion area of East Cork. He had suspected as much, after the recent visits to the Moore family at Ticknock. This was another reason why he had left his sisters house at Donelan Terrace, as he didn't want her and her family there visited by the same gang. Burke was also now concerned on a personal level that some of the Jocks knew what he looked like, since his recent incarceration at Belmont. How well Burke's face was known to the Jock 'Death Squad' however, would soon be tested when he and a number of other company members ran into the Death Squad at Belvelly.

It happened one night after the Belvelly section commander, Ned Butler reported to Burke that he suspected that an underground passage existed between the old castle near Belvelly Bridge and the big stately house on Fota estate. Butler felt the passageway might prove very useful for members of the company who were forced on the run. Burke arranged to visit the castle one night with Butler to explore its possibilities. On the particular night in question, he was accompanied by his first Lieutenant John Moore. As they each cycled along to the meeting, they heard the noise of a lorry coming from behind them. Each put on speed, with Moore turning into the nearest farmyard they came to. He was soon captured and arrested. Burke carried on for a bit further before stopping and throwing his bike over a ditch. He then fled through some fields to safety. Moore was very fortunate that he was only taken back to Belmont for questioning that night. He probably survived the event, by giving a false name, for had the Jocks known that he was one of the Moore family, a family they had been trying to kill for weeks, they would have hardly passed up the opportunity to execute him, especially in the circumstances they had caught up with him. Burke, for his part was not put off by the experience, believing that it was just an unfortunate piece of bad luck that they happened to run into the Jocks on that particular night. A few nights later, he and seven other Volunteers were back in Belvelly again, and on this occasion got to explore for the tunnel with Ned Butler. Unfortunately, they couldn't find any sign of an underground passageway. Their bad luck wasn't to end there however.

On their return back into Cobh, they ran straight into a British death squad again and the officers took their eight prisoners to a nearby farm house for questioning. Burke was sure that this meant they were going to be executed, since the questioning was not going to happen at Belmont. Fortunately, Burke was singled out by an officer to be questioned first. It also became clear to him that none of the squad seemed to recognise who he was. The officer in charge accused Burke of belonging to a secret organisation because of a badge he wore on his coat with a half moon on it. Burke denied the charge, saying the badge was one worn by members of the Primrose League, a Loyalist society. The officer then ordered Burke to stand aside. The other Volunteers were then searched and ordered to strip naked. Nothing incriminating was found, and to their utter surprise and relief, they were released.

Only two months remained before a Truce would come into being between British and Republican forces, but the state of play in the war between the two before then, could best be described as the storm before the calm. The terror inflicted by the Cameron Highlanders around east Cork, was in full swing.

In Cobh, few Republicans slept in their own beds anymore, with many fleeing the town completely. Others held out locally for as long as they could. Some like Mick Burke, slept at Cobh Hospital, others were put up in beds at houses belonging to Catholic and Protestant clergy members, while others still, were looked after by good and decent neighbours. One Volunteer officer, Tom O'Shea privately hid out with his sister and brother-in-law Jack Damery at their rented home Villa House, on the Newtown Road. Damery, who returned badly injured from the First World War, was also an IRA Volunteer, but as he worked as a civilian worker on Spike Island for a period following his return, he was not suspected by the enemy.

Despite this, the authorities raided the Damery home on a number of occasions looking for Tom O'Shea. Fortunately for him, his brother-in-law, who was a gifted joiner by trade, had constructed a secret panelled room, where he would quickly retire to, every time the engines of the enemy were heard approaching. By the time June came around, Mick Burke would realise that he was stretching his luck by hanging around in the open in Cobh. He would carry out one last military operation before he would leave. He decided to launch an attack on an RIC patrol at the Park, the same location where Daithí O'Brien tried to kill D.I. Mordant more than a year before. With three other Volunteers, each armed with hand grenades from the Knockraha factory, Burke waited for the patrol to pass. As the patrol passed, the volunteers tossed the grenades before making good their escape. The Top of the Hill area was rocked by the sound of explosions, but the RIC officers received only minor injuries, and suffered mainly from shock. Shortly afterwards, Burke decided to quit the town. He reported to the battalion leadership in Midleton and was posted to the Ballycotton area.

23. The Truce

The election that had taken place in May following the Government of Ireland Act had proven a resounding victory for Sinn Féin. All 124 Sinn Féin candidates were returned unopposed, the only non-Republican candidates being the four Senate members for Trinity College who were also unopposed. The former UDC Chairman of Cobh, Seamus Fitzgerald, was elected TD for East Cork. Lloyd George now had two options: he could either pour more troops into Ireland in the hope of defeating the IRA, something he had not been able to achieve during the previous years despite saturating the country with tens of thousands military and police, or he could agree to calling a truce and sit down with the Republicans at the negotiating table. There is some evidence that Republican leaders, particularly on the part of Eamonn DeValera, were giving out some public hints that Republicans were prepared to talk. It had been suspected that the British were privately treating with Arthur Griffith who was then in jail, but there is now evidence that Michael Collins had also been in secret talks with a senior member of the British secret service.

The trick for De Valera was to show that such overtures were being made from a position of strength, not weakness, but there was no doubt that by mid 1921, the British wanted to talk more than Republicans. About six weeks before the Truce was agreed, David Kent TD (Castlelyons) sent a message to Seamus Fitzgerald TD at Knockraha, that he wanted to see him. Kent informed Fitzgerald that he had shortly before then, been taken by armed escort from Spike Island interment camp by special launch to Cork and on to Victoria Barracks. There, he was interviewed by General Strickland and an Intelligence Officer named Kelly. They told him that he was released because they believed that he was the strongest-minded Republican in the South, and they wished him to establish contact for them with De Valera. They asked him to bring a message to De Valera. They certainly did not understand Kent's strength of mind and character though. He firmly refused to establish contact for them, believing it to be a trick to capture De Valera. He also refused to be the bearer of any message to the Republican leader, and advised that the correct and only way would be for their leaders to get in touch with De Valera by direct means. Kent also refused to answer any questions as to what settlement would be agreed to, and when departing he demanded a guarantee that he was under no obligation to them. Kent asked Fitzgerald to arrange a meeting with the brigade staff so he could brief them on the British meeting. Fitzgerald immediately arranged such a meeting with, Joe O'Connor, Florrie O'Donoghue and Dan Sandow O'Donovan in the City, where Kent relayed to them the full account of the Strickland meeting.

By the end of June, Lloyd George sent a letter directly to De Valera requesting him to attend a peace conference in London. After some weeks of negotiation, both sides of the conflict eventually agreed to an unconditional truce while the negotiations were taking place, and on 11 July the truce came into force. The curfew in Cobh was finally suspended and negotiations could get under way. The country expressed a collective sign of relief. Republicans who spent a year and more on the run were able to return to their homes without fear of arrest or molestation. Bonfires and street parties were held in Cobh, and just like in the aftermath of 1916, Republicans were treated to hero status. Mick Burke returned from Ballycotton to resume command of his local company. Seamus Fitzgerald, Daithí O'Brien and the other Cobhmen working on the grenade factory at Knockraha, also came home to join in the celebrations. The decision to declare a truce may not have been all that difficult for the British Prime Minister.

By June the Northern government was already functioning and Lloyd George could rest assured that at least the richest and most industrialised part of Ireland would remain in British hands. He also needed peace more than the IRA did: the cost of trying to defeat Republicans was increasing by the day, money was sorely needed in his own country where there was an economic recession. Furthermore, the British troops were needed elsewhere as another colony, India, was getting worryingly restless. For the ordinary rank-and-file Republican soldier, the first weeks of the truce offered nothing but a great sense of euphoric achievement. Most were of the opinion that they had beat the British to the negotiating table, and their leaders would therefore be negotiating from a position of strength. But not everyone believed they were home and dry to the Republic yet. Seamus Fitzgerald later wrote that he and his comrades, who operated at the brigade bomb factory, spent a week at home celebrating in Cobh, before returning to work the next week making hand grenades again. It wasn't long before Fitzgerald and his team were ordered by the Brigade to leave Knockraha and set up similar units in Youghal (10th Battalion area), and Gurteenfluck, Ballingeary (8th Battalion area) and this kept him busy up until December. Fitzgerald had been assisted in this work by Tommy Power of Youghal who was later killed in Kilmallock during the Civil War, Jim O'Connell of Cobh, Frank O'Donoghue of Cork, with Nick Kelly as pattern-maker. Henry O'Brien of Cobh (brother of Daithí) was put in charge of another new factory in the 7th Battalion area, so the Brigade had four factories, exclusive of the Knockraha operations. It was evident that many at leadership level felt a return to war was a strong a possibility. Mick Leahy and Florrie O'Donoghue had been touring all the brigade areas of the first Southern Division in the weeks leading up to the Truce and happened to be in Mallow when the Truce was announced. Both men were of the firm opinion that the army was in a very good position of strength, it was better armed than ever before and was well manned with the best of experienced officers, should it have to return to war again.

On the home front in Cobh, just like in every town and city in Ireland, the ranks of the local company were flooded with new recruits looking to jump on the popular bandwagon. Mick Burke later wrote that during the height of the war before the truce was called, he had a solid company of men numbering 120 that he could rely on at any given time, and that excluded those who were on the run or in gaol. People like Mick Leahy, Seamus Fitzgerald and others, saw the situation just like 1914 all over again, when John Redmond gave his stamp of approval to the Volunteers, and its ranks in Cobh swelled to many hundreds. The new recruits this time were called 'Trucers' and were frowned upon by their older colleagues and seen mainly as opportunists. The title was given to the recruits, to distinguish them from the genuine Republican fighters who had risked life and limb over the previous years for the Republican cause.

None of the Trucers had ever suffered for their beliefs, and very few would in future. Many would fade away again as soon things soured and they watched the country divide itself over the Treaty. Many more would opt for a wage and a new career by joining the new Free State (National Army). Only a minority would remain on and fight with the IRA in the forthcoming Civil War. As the summer passed and the negotiations dragged on, many people began to realise that nothing was as straight forward as they had earlier thought. Many watched as the Northern Parliament had been functioning on its own for a number of months, and had in place its own security forces. Republican prisoners were still just that – prisoners, despite the truce. While the Republican leadership was seen talking with the British, things were less quiet in Cobh and more specifically on Spike Island, where the truce had changed nothing for the men that had been interned there during the course of the war. It became obvious that the British were using the prisoners as one of a number of bargaining chips throughout the negotiations with the Republican leadership.

Conditions for the internees on the island were worse than ever, with the authorities provoking and pushing the men as far as they could. Then on 28 August a hunger strike of some 450 men broke out. The question of a hunger strike for unconditional release had earlier been put to a vote of the camp internees, and out of 473 men, 450 decided that they would be willing to embark on a strike (the remaining twenty-three included hospital cases and a few others had been declared medically unfit for such a venture). As a result of the vote, the following demand was forwarded to the Governor of Spike:

Take notice that we, on behalf of the internees here, demand immediate and unconditional release on the grounds that the English government has neither legal nor moral right to hold us by force. If the internees here are not released by Tuesday 30th inst. at 6 pm. we will refuse and continue to refuse to partake any food until our just demand is complied with, and thus bring the opinion of the civilised world to bear on the inhuman manner in which the British people and their hired government are treating one of the small nations from which the late war is alleged to have been fought. [40]

The notice was signed by the officer in command of the internees, Henry O'Mahoney (in 1938 O'Mahoney became the Chairman of the Cork County Board of the GAA), His second in command was Tom Quirke (later elected a Senator). Tom Barry, the leader of the West Cork Flying Column, who had given the British military a bloodied nose on more than one occasion, volunteered to go to Cobh in an attempt to visit Spike and try to defuse the situation. However, he was refused permission to enter the camp and was informed that such permission, for the purpose of 'discussing matter'[41] with the prisoners, could not be granted to him. Barry was also told that the large-scale strike had already begun that evening (30 August). It had become very obvious that the tension on Spike Island suited the British and if there was to be a resolution of the problems there, they would only come about as part of the overall negotiations with the Republican leadership (leading to a favourable treaty for the British) and would not be brought about locally by an upstart like Tom Barry. It also seemed likely that through contentious issues like the Spike hunger strike, the British were trying to lower the expectations of the Irish people in advance of the treaty negotiations. Considerable anxiety was caused in the city when this news became known; especially as the general feeling had been that Barry would succeed in coming to some sort of agreement.

After returning from Cobh, Barry made the following statement:

> The action of the GOC 6th Division in refusing me an opportunity to arrange matters is evidently one calculated to prevent a settlement without the drastic step of a hunger strike by the internees. It is also apparent that he has followed the precedents set up by him at the beginning of the truce of placing difficulties in the way of the smooth working of the conditions agreed to between the Irish Republican Army and the British Army. [42]

That all was not quiet in Cork during the supposed truce is shown by a report issued by Barry around the same time: Summary of complaints. The following are the numbers of more serious breaches of the truce terms within the 'martial law' area by the British forces:

1. Wanton brutality to the people, 20
2. Provocative conduct, 22
3. Carrying of arms, 59
4. Interning of prisoners whose terms of sentence have expired, 19
5. Systematic interference with the people (including taking of motor cars and parts thereof, bans on fairs and markets, meetings, creameries, etc, 33. Total: 153.

Reports seem to indicate that the hunger strike on Spike was called off after a few days, but that another broke out later in the autumn. According to a former internee, who was present when the harbour forts were handed over to the Irish in July 1938, the massive strike broke out in October:

> That strike, 'was the most hectic thing in which I ever took part. It had been preceded by a short hunger strike in May, just after one of our companions named White, from Meelick, had been shot by a sentry. We used to play hurling every day in the barrack square, and one day the ball went into the barbed wire. We were forbidden to touch the wire, but White went after the ball and while retrieving it a sentry fired and wounded him. Next day he died. The big strike, however, did not start until October, when we decided that we would get out of the place by bringing our grievances into the public arena. We barricaded up all our doors and windows and said we wouldn't come out.
> Outside we could hear the military breaking their way through, and eventu-

ally we could see them through the cracks in the barricades. We built up the barricades again, but the military forced their way in and immediately we started a most tremendous scrap. The soldiers came at us with their trench tools [long batons]; lengths of rubber tubing with lead at the end, and other implements suited to hand-to-hand fighting. We grabbed anything near our hands, some of us used our bare fists and our feet, and for over an hour we fought them hand-to-hand in the quarters. I shall never forget it. Men fought with their nails and on all sides you could see bunches of soldiers and internees locked in embrace. As they fell, others fell over them and at times there was as many as forty men sprawled on the floor with the tide of battle raging over their bodies.

Of course we had no chance against the well armed soldiers and in the end we had to give in under the strain. Many of us were badly hurt and had to get hospital treatment afterwards and the leaders were put in cells for the night. We were left in our quarters, wrecked as they were that night, and the next night we were turned out into the moat and threw down loaves of bread as if we were Polar bears in a pit, but we caught the loaves and threw them back as they landed on the ground. This was the most peculiar hunger-strike that ever took place. That afternoon, the prisoners were brought up from the moat and given excellent food – better than we ever got on the island before.[43]

The protest had been called off after concessions were promised to the prisoners. One result of the strike was that representatives of the Prisoners Inspection Board (set up by the Irish and British during the time of the truce) came to visit the camp. It was as a result of this inspection that a month later all those who hadn't been released by then, were transferred to other prisons in the south. Another former internee present on the festive day in 1938 when the forts were handed over continued the story:

In the meantime, however, life was made worth living on Spike. We had a very busy time engineering an escape. The visit to the moat had set some of the leaders planning an escape and from A–Block we started tunnelling to the moat. We used our hands, sticks which were available in plenty since the time of breaking up our quarters. At inspection time, we covered the hole with debris and eventually there came the day when we actually struck the moat and saw the sky above us. We all waited that night with expectation. Seven of our number were selected to make the escape, Henry O'Mahony, Bill Quirke, Tom Crofts, (later O.C. of Cork No.1), Maurice Twomey, Dick Barrett (quartermaster of the prisoners), a man named Leddy from Ardmore in Waterford, and a man named Buckley from Mitchelstown. Earlier that day, one of our men, Bill Quirke, who was in command of the prisoners in Block B, got into a friendly conversation with the British officer who came to make a daily inspection of the block.

While they were both standing in from a rain shower under an archway before taking parade, Captain Gabb turned to Quirke and out of the blue asked 'Don't you think this is the one safe prison there is?' Quirke agreed, but little did Gabb and the rest of his garrison realise what was afoot, and that Quirke and six others would not be around the next day. When darkness fell the seven went out through the hole and we covered it within as they left so that no trace of how they made their exit was left. They were not missed that night because when the soldiers came around on inspection some of us slipped through from Block A to Block B when the inspection of Block A was completed. Thus, when the counting of heads took place in Block B, apparently everybody was present and correct.

Henry O'Mahoney, one of the escapees and at the time O.C. of the Spike internees, tells:

When we left the moat we went up a ladder which we had manufactured from pieces of wood. Haulbowline, another island – close at hand and also occupied – looked like an immense stage with the floodlights ablaze. Cobh in the distance seemed like the New York skyline on New Year's night, and to add to the illuminations the big searchlights came into play completing anything but a favourable setting for a bunch of prisoners just launched into a new world. Then we got over the eighteen foot high outer wall and rolled down the bank on the Currabinny side. We made our way in the darkness along the shore to where some boats were beached, but they were un-seaworthy for some reason or other, so we had to go inland and hide in a cowshed until quiet fell on the fort. We were quietly discussing our next move when to our astonishment a soldier and his sweetheart (later to become Captain and Mrs. Kennedy) came to the door of the outhouse. Our hearts thumped for about an hour before the soldier and his girlfriend took their departure. About midnight we went towards the pier where a sentry was on guard. Three other sentries were off duty, probably in the pier-hut playing cards. The sentry's beat was from the pier to what was known as the clubhouse, and when he turned to go to the clubhouse, we went behind his back to the pier. We saw a few boats tied up some distance out from the pier and Leddy swam out and brought one back. Off we started, rowing towards Cobh, Henry O'Mahony, from Passage West further up river, acted as our guide across the harbour. It was a very bad night with rain falling and high seas running. This it was that saved us. There were four searchlights from the island and two searchlights from cruisers in the harbour always sweeping the harbour, but our small boat was often lost in the trough of waves that we evidently escaped notice. At all events we landed on the Holy Ground Quay below the Belmont garrison of Cameron Highlanders. We had no idea at first of what part of Cobh we were in. We left the boat behind on the strand with a note beneath the oars thanking the British for the kind loan of their boat. We then headed up the nearest hill which to our horror brought us to a location just below Belmont Camp where the Camerons were station. We quickly turned back and found a narrow side road (Glasson's Avenue) which led us to freedom. From there we made our way west to Newtown to the Stack family where we dined. After that we made our way by devious routes to Cork. This was on 16 November [44]

By that time things had quietened down on Spike, the *Cork Examiner* noting on 20 October that,

> From external appearances, things have simmered down somewhat at Spike Island. No bursts of cheering by the prisoners have been heard over at Cobh since Tuesday morning, and this is taken to indicate that for the time being the worst of the proceedings are over. Parcels for the untried prisoners leave Cobh as usual, but there is reason for believing that they have not been given to them for the past few days but are being dumped instead. Tents for occupation by armed guards have been pitched on the grassy slopes of the island, which is now guarded with vigilance by night and by day there is no possibility of circumventing. A destroyer, relieved daily is moored immediately between it and the mouth of the harbour, and its searchlights, supplemented by those at the harbour entrance, constantly play on the island during the night while searchlights in position on the ramparts of the fortress which surmounts the island are deflected at an angle which enables the operators to sweep the very blades of grass with rays of blinding brilliancy.

However, although they might have been able to see every inch of grass according to the poetic *Examiner* journalist, the guards were not capable of spotting seven men rolling down the slopes on their way to freedom. A Spike Island internee wrote to his father following the protest (dated 26 October):

> All I have left in the way of clothes is just what I am wearing. I am across in Block A for the last few days in hospital, but am nearly alright now and I am getting up this evening (I am presently in bed with my head bandaged up). We had a fairly nice time here for the last 12-14 days. We had Alderman Staines and the Commission here yesterday, and both sides agree that this place was uninhabitable, so it looks like a shift for us soon, or else release. The latter, I hope. I would like to let you know all that occurred here, but it will make better telling than writing. There are a lot of hospital patients here, so there is plenty of work for the medical men attending us. [45]

The conditions in the internment camp on Bere Island, which was situated in another Cork 'treaty port' (Castletownbere), were not much better than those on Spike, and like Spike camp, it was also visited by Alderman Staines TD (Chief Liaison Officer IRA) and a British military officer. The Prisoners Inspection Board advised that both camps should be closed, and from the beginning of November small batches of internees started being released from both Spike and Bere. Those not released were transferred to Kilkenny Jail and Maryborough (now Portlaoise). The prisoners were brought to Cobh aboard the two garrison launches in the harbour (the *Cambridge* and the *Wyndham*) and amidst cheering and singing of the 'The Soldiers Song', then put on a train taking them to their new lodgings.

Also in November, small numbers of prisoners were released from other prisons in the country, especially from Rath and Ballykinlar (near Newry). Thus on 11 November Paddy O'Sullivan, who had been interned in Ballykinlar camp in the north for the previous twelve months, returned to his home in Ballyleary, and shortly afterwards another local internee P. Rafferty was released from there and returned to Cobh. Eight days later on 19 November, the internment camp on Spike Island closed. For one man though the releases came too late. Alderman Tadhg Barry of Cork was shot dead by a British soldier at Ballykinlar camp on 15 November. Whereas the British authorities claimed he had been shot dead while attempting to escape, this was denied by many eyewitnesses who said that Barry was killed while waving at some internees who were leaving the camp as they had been released. Tadhg Barry was one of the officers who had attended the training course in the Volunteer Hall, Cork, in early 1916, at which Cobhmen Mick Leahy and Jack O'Connell had also been present. Alderman Barry received a very impressive funeral, with in the procession, members of Republican organisations (the IRA, Sinn Féin, TD's, the Gaelic League etc), and his coffin was shouldered by Volunteers of the IRA Company to which he belonged. Several other organisations were also represented at the funeral, such as the fire brigade, the Harbour Board, and even organisations such as the Confectionery and Pastry Cooks Trade Association, literary societies and the Cork Brushmakers. Present also were the members of Cobh UDC. Several messages of sympathy arrived from the internees that were still on Bere.

From 9 December onwards most internees were released from Maryborough, Waterford Jail, Ballykinlar camp, Arbour Hill, the Curragh, and other camps and jails. On the 19 December, Dick Kelleher arrived home in Cobh, having spent a year in Ballykinlar, as did Lily Hawes who was serving a sentence in Waterford Jail. A few days later saw Richard Murphy returned to his home at Whitepoint's railway cottages from Ballykinlar. While negotiations for a peace treaty were under way in London, the townspeople of Cobh had to do a bit of their own negotiating when in September 1921 an incident arose involving the Royal Navy and local traders. In that month a deputation of some sixty people approached the Town Council to highlight their grievances; these were the traders who used to travel out to the passenger liners at the mouth of the harbour to sell fruit and souvenirs such as blackthorn sticks. On behalf of the deputation Mrs Donovan and Mr Thomas McGrath told the councillors that their livelihood was to go to the liners in their own boats and sell their wares. (Cllr Saunders at this point interjected to say that this had been going on for the past thirty or forty years), but that the Admiralty had stopped the practice recently, and the traders now wanted the Council to intercede on their behalf with the Admiralty. Cllr Telfer (SF) backed up the story: he had seen a Navy launch driving the people away a few days previously and had been told that this was done because the vendors were suspected of gun-running with their baskets. The Council chamber erupted in laughter at this remark. Cllr Saunders then proposed that if the traders were not allowed out in their own boats, the shipping agents should be asked to give them permits to travel out in the tenders, and the Councillor asked why they could not get passes from the Admiralty.

However, the traders said they would prefer to have a permit to travel out to the liners in their own boats rather than the tender. The British, however, were not that far off the mark in focusing on the traders in relation to gunrunning. Small quantities of firearms had been smuggled into Ireland from America over the previous three and a half years, many through the port of Cobh on transatlantic liners. The British government and the Admiralty were under no illusions that the IRA was training and preparing for a second round of fighting if the need arose, and were fairly certain that the importation of arms would be an essential part of that process. But while the Admiralty was expending its energies by focusing on small time souvenir traders, in a short few months it would itself become the unwitting provider of a huge arsenal of weapons to the IRA.

Dolphin's Barn Library
Tel. 4540681

24. The Execution of Sergeant Major Mackintosh

One day, when the Truce was not long in operation and at a time when some British forces were acting very provocatively and mistreating the prisoners on Spike Island, Martin Corry was in Cobh, discussing the situation with his battalion colleague Mick Burke. Burke expressed the view that it wouldn't be long before the British would start pulling out of the area. Corry asked him if he was going to allow Mackintosh go with them, given that he was a senior member of the Death Squad that had carried out a lot of murders in the Carrigtwohill area and had shot three children. Burke explained that it wouldn't be easy, as not a single member of the Cobh Company could identify Mackintosh. He was also mindful of the dangers of undertaking a bid to capture the murderer, while the truce was in operation. The two men concluded that they could take a chance and wait to see if the truce collapses before dealing with Mackintosh, or they could use the truce to outfox him and deal with him now. They both agreed that if he didn't deal with him now, he would most likely return to Britain a free man for the war crimes he had committed here. Corry reminded Burke that the British had some months before found his hat and coat in Corry's house in Glounthaune and that this property was probably being held at Belmont Camp. He said there was no good reason why they both couldn't use the hat and coat as a reason to visit the camp and with any luck; they might discover what the Jock Sergeant Major looked like. When they entered the camp at Belmont, the two men asked to see Captain Morrison, who was the only person there that they knew, after they both had been interrogated by him previously. Corry also knew a civilian worker there by the name of Johnny Grandon.

Grandon was from Corry's area in Knockraha and worked in the camp canteen. A veteran of First World War, Grandon often supplied Corry with information he had picked up at the camp, and this was why Corry could not now ask for him by name. Mackey's Bar on Harbour Row was the pick-up and drop-off point for Grandon and his brigade contacts. He would call into Mrs Mackey each day for his regular packet of fags. If a message from Corry or other brigade source was waiting for him, he would later find them in the particular packet of cigarettes that Mrs Mackey had kept for him. If he had a return message he wanted delivered back, he would leave it on Mrs Mackey's counter in an empty fag box.

Some time later, someone would call to the bar, purporting to collect a packet of cigarettes on Grandon's behalf. One piece of information Corry had learned from Grandon was that Mackintosh was physically a very big man. The two Republicans smiled at the British captain as he came out to meet them. They explained that they had come to collect Burke's hat and coat which had earlier been taken in a raid. Morrison was equally pleased to see the two men and was clearly happy that regardless of the context and reason he had for dealing with them in the past, it was now well behind them. The Captain's initial response to the men's request for the hat and coat was that the clothing items had been used by his men while on raids previously and were no longer in existence. Then through a broad smile, he told the two men that he would give them all the hats and coats that money can buy, if they would return all the rifles they had taken from his soldiers over the previous years. Morrison was genuinely disappointed that he was not in a position to return the hat and coat, but chirped, 'anyway, come over and see the Colonel. He will be delighted to meet you now that all is over.' [46] As they passed through the camp on their way to the Colonels office, Burke and Corry's eyes were sweeping from left to right in search of the infamous Mackintosh.

When Morrison knocked on the colonel's door, an orderly answered. 'Colonel Cameron then?', he asked. They asked where he was and asked to bring him out to them. When the Colonel arrived out, Captain Morrison said, 'I would like to introduce you, Colonel Cameron to Martin Corry and Michael Burke. I am sure now that all the fighting is over you will be glad to meet them.' [47] Cameron gave the two men a bitter glance before replying, 'I would have a lot more welcome for Burke and Corry here if you brought them six months ago.' [48] With that he banged the door in their faces. Morrison was clearly disappointed and embarrassed by the Colonel's attitude. It wasn't lost on him either what the Colonel had just said about bringing them to him six months earlier, given that Morrison had Burke in custody at that time, but were released in error.

Then in a gesture to cheer himself up and put a pleasant face on the situation, the Captain suggested they should go down to the canteen and have a drink. The two men agreed, while all the time looking out for the illusive Mackintosh. Then all of a sudden a very big man appeared at the door. 'Oh' said the Captain, 'Sergeant Major Mackintosh, come over here till I introduce you to Captain Burke and Martin Corry.' [49] The Sergeant Major agreed to join the three men at the canteen for a drink. When the four men arrived at the canteen together, Johnny Grandon nearly fell over with fright. The two British officers were disappointed when the Republicans only drank lemonade and wine. They all chatted away for a while before the Republicans made their excuses for having to leave. They were now both satisfied that they had Mackintosh identified. Burke quickly put a team of five sturdy Volunteers together to capture the Sergeant Major at the earliest opportunity. He also placed a number of scouts around the precincts of Belmont camp to watch for Mackintosh leaving the facility. Then on the Wednesday evening following Burke's and Corry's visit to the camp, a car pulled up along side the off-duty Sergeant Major as he was walking down East Hill on his way to socialise in the town. Five Volunteers sprung from the vehicle and attempted to bungle the prisoner into the car. The Volunteers were under strict instructions not to display any fire-arms in public. The big sturdy 6ft 4inch Mackintosh was not going easily though, and injured a few of his attackers in the melee. He was eventually overpowered by the Republicans, and forced into the car, before he was taken away at speed to Martin Corry's house at Glounthaune. When they arrived, the prisoner was taken from the car and brought into the house where he was court-martialed before Captains' Corry, Burke and second lieutenant Con Cremin of 'E' Company. Mackintosh must have looked on in horror as two of three men seated in front of him, were only days before drinking with him in his barrack canteen. Now they were before him in their roles as judges and his likely executioners. He must have wondered how he could have ended there facing certain and imminent death, while a truce was supposed to be in operation.

In his opening address as President to the court-martial, Corry informed Mackintosh that he was not being tried for any of his duties as a soldier, but rather for the murder of three children. In his reply to the charge, Mackintosh desperately opted to use a line of defence that would prove to be very controversial in another major war crimes tribunal in Nuremburg, Germany more than two decades later. 'Anything I done, I did it as a soldier being under orders'.[50] After the consideration by the court-martial, the prisoner was sentenced to death. He was then given a period to make his peace with his maker, after which he was taken out at the back of Corry's house and executed. It wouldn't have taken a great stretch of the imagination for the British back in Belmont Camp to figure who had got their Sergeant Major, or what they would have done with him. Some of his own regiment who were looking to the future and the prospect of going home, may have even felt he had met with natural justice. In any event, there was no great fuss made of the whereabouts of Mackintosh. Maintaining the truce appeared to be a far more important objective for the Cameron leadership.

However, an incident which took place a short time later demonstrated that at least some Jocks were put out by what might have became of their Sergeant Major. One day while a convoy of the Jocks were travelling from Cobh to Victoria Barracks in Cork, they encountered a man running suspiciously towards a ditch close to Killacloyne Bridge near Glounthaune. Despite the truce being in place, one of soldiers opened up with a Lewis machine gun and sprayed the ditch with gunfire. What he had actually seen was two railway workers running towards the Bridge for shelter after it began to rain. One of the men; Colman Savage was struck by the fire and fell dead into a drain. Although the officer who had fired his weapon could not have known that Savage was a local IRA Volunteer, he probably had a fair idea that they were in Corry country and that his Sergeant Major's body was probably around there too.

It has been generally accepted by those in the know, as well as by those of Corry's company who dug the graves, that Mackintosh was one of a number of executed prisoners that were buried on Corry's own land. Those bodies, it is believed, were the result of some hastily convened trials and executions carried out in unusual circumstances. Those burials were reported to be in addition to the many others carried out by 'E' Company at Carroll's Pond in the Knockraha region.

As time went on, some myths and legends grew around who exactly was buried at Corry's, but there can be little doubt that some were, and that Sergeant Major Mackintosh was one of them. About five years after Mackintosh's death, this writers' grandparents came to live in the locality of Glounthaune. The young couple, Jim and Ellen McCarthy and their four children had left their native Macroom in West Cork, and moved in to the old lodge house at the entrance to Corry's farm at Sunville. My grandparents could best be described as a typical couple of the time. Jim McCarthy had lost two brothers Cornelius and William to the 1914-18 War with the Munster Fusiliers, while his wife's mother; Bina McSwiney was a cousin to Terence, the martyred Lord Mayor. Martin Corry at that time was a young and active TD with the new Republican Party-Fianna Fáil, which shortly after found itself in government. As fortune would soon have it for both Corry and my grandparents, they would be the successful beneficiaries of a new government scheme where the County Council would set about building cottages on small agricultural holdings. This involved Corry selling an acre of land to my grandparents to farm, while the County Council approved to fund the construction of a cottage on the site. As a young boy of seven years of age, my father remembered the day the building contractors for the council arrived to mark out the site for the cottage. The contractors, Brownes of Carrigtwohill, in turn hired the Hogan brothers of Cobh to carry out the block work. My father vividly recalled hovering around that day as the grown-ups discussed the business of where every thing should go. At one stage he became curious when his parents broke away to one side from the others and began what seemed to be a serious conversation. The fact that they were soon whispering made him more curious, so being a nosy child, he moved a little closer to find out what was going on. From what he could make out, his mother was insisting that she didn't want the chicken shed located down near the cottage as it would be dirty, would smell and attract vermin. She wanted it to be built further up the back of the acre. It was then that my father heard something he never understood until years later. He heard his father whisper in a forceful voice to his mother, that they couldn't put the chicken-pen up there in case the hens would expose the bodies by continuously scratching the soil for worms and insects. As the years passed, local people, including at least one of my father's immediate family, had claimed to have seen strange unexplained activities take place in an area on the far side of the ditch of the family acre.

Those who claimed to have witnessed the mysterious sightings, which always took place at night and in the dark, said they could see from a distance what looked like a circle of lighted lanterns hovering around a particular spot beyond the acre, or the high field as it was better known. Most people of the locality, including those who had had the eerie experience of seeing the unexplained apparitions, and those who were old enough to have remembered the sound of shots in the late hours of the night, were of the opinion and quietly accepted that they were related to earlier war activities. We probably will never know for certain how many prisoners were executed at Corry's farm or the identity of all those buried on his land, since all who were involved have long since passed on. We do know however, that Corry and his men of 'E' Company, had the unenviable task of having to imprison, interrogate and very often try, execute and bury prisoners sent onto them from other 1st Cork Brigade areas. The Brigade leadership had earlier chosen 'E' Company for this task because of its relatively quiet and secluded surroundings, and its close proximity to the City and to East Cork. We know for example, that Sergeant Major Mackintosh was not the only member of the Belmont based Cameron Highlanders in Cobh to be captured and executed by Corry's 'E' Company.

Corry himself had estimated that from at least thirty-five prisoners that his men had executed and buried in the area, most were members of the Cameron Highlander Regiment, numbering seventeen. However, because there is no apparent verifiable record of the number and identity of all those that were handed over to 'E' Company for trial, and because Corry went on record some years later as saying he was working from mere estimates of the executed, he unfortunately left the door open for others to later distort the facts in an attempt to rewrite history. For some strange and unexplained reason, Martin Corry was one of a few surviving IRA Volunteers of officer rank, not to have made a Witness Statement to the Bureau of Military History in the 1950s. This is all the more strange, given that Corry, a TD, was never shy of publicity and would often recount his war exploits to the press, leading others to some times claim that, he took credit for operations that were carried out by others. On 1 July 2007, a strange article appeared in the *Sunday Mirror* newspaper, relating to a supposed and brutal execution of a former RIC man that allegedly had taken place in Corry's house.

In the article, written by Andrew Bushe, it was alleged the former policeman, Michael Williams was fingered by Republicans for his part in the murder of Cork's Lord Mayor Tomás MacCurtain, and was taken prisoner by five men on 15 June 1922, as he left mass. The *Sunday Mirror* story was based on recently released secret files that had been handed over to the National Archives office by former Justice Minister Michael McDowell. The report was based entirely on a 1924 Garda file which relied on the word of an alleged informant as well as an anonymous letter sent to the former policeman's mother and signed by a 'sympathetic mother.' In September 1924, Williams's family solicitor sent a letter to the Department of Justice saying, 'By all accounts this farm (Corry's) is a veritable cemetery.' The solicitor, Horace Turpin referred to the anonymous letter that Mrs Williams had received, and was clearly accepting it as credible information. The letter told in great detail what had happened to her son when he was supposedly taken to Corry's house. It alleged that Mrs MacCurtain, the Lord Mayor's widow was present as a witness to the court and that Sean O'Hegarty (1st Cork Brigade) acted as President of the court. The anonymous letter told in very colourful and emotive language, how Williams and another unnamed prisoner had ropes put around their necks after having the death penalty passed on them. How, the ropes were thrown over a beam and pulled and pulled for hours, while the unfortunate victims struggled in their desperate agony. 'Oh God, what a death.' The executioner Corry, and his accomplices having enjoyed the inhuman sport for some hours, retired for a rest and a drink, and left the unfortunate and unhappy victims struggling in their half-strangled condition. 'When the executioners returned, their victims were riddled with bullets, and then buried on Corry's farm, where many other victims of his (Corry's) lie buried.' This writer however, has a problem with the veracity of the above story. A number of things about it don't fit with what we already know.

For one, it is very unlikely that Corry was at large and free at the time to be involved in such a case. Mick Leahy claimed that virtually every officer and man of the 4th Battalion was interned by the end of the Civil War. It was alleged to have taken place three days after the truce was called between Free State and Republican forces at the end of the Civil War. Are we to believe that who ever took Williams prisoner in June 1922, held him in captivity for the duration of the Civil War, until Corry was released and ready to deal with him?

Secondly, Martin Corry didn't drink, leaving the anonymous account of the execution, totally at odds with what we know about the man. Neither is there any record of Corry, ever having previously executed a condemned prisoner by hanging. It also appears incredible that Republicans would have had present at such a court, the dead Lord Mayor's widow, and probably more incredible that she would want to be present at such an event. But what is most incredible about this story, is the ludicrous claim that Sean O'Hegarty was present and acted as chairman of the court-martial. Sean O'Hegarty had resigned his position as O.C. of the 1st Cork Brigade and the IRA at the outset of the Civil War, having spent months as a member of the neutral IRA trying to broker a peace between the opposing factions of the army. Cobh man Mick Leahy was appointed O'Hegarty's successor on the day the Four Courts was attacked. It is therefore incredible to claim that O'Hegarty would have had the authority, let alone the frame of mind to be involved in such a venture.

The recently released file refers to a memo from Garda Chief Supt P. Fahy in Cork, dated October 1924. Fahy had received information from his own sources that also pointed towards Williams being buried on Corry's land. The Garda Superintendent refers to such sources being of word of mouth. Perhaps that is why he never sent officers along to investigate or dig up the Corry land for Williams's body. It is far more likely in this writer's opinion, that the claims made against Corry and the anonymous letter, were the result of Civil War bitterness by people from the locality who already knew of the pre-Civil War bodies that were buried on the Corry land, and were hoping that such common knowledge would help make their claims sound credible.

25. The Treaty

The initial hype and sense of victory that surrounded the declaration of the truce had subsided some what on the ground over the intervening five months, up to when the Treaty was signed. Local leaders like Mick Burke and Martin Corry had correctly sensed that had they not dealt with some local loose ends, like the Mackintosh matter before a final agreement was secured with the British; they would never have been able to bring closure to them. Republican delegates signed the treaty in the early hours of 6 December 1921 in London. Several of the Irish delegates had been rather hesitant about the contents of the treaty, especially regarding the measure of 'independence' that was to be granted to Ireland, and the partition of the country (when in actual fact Ireland had already been partitioned in April), but Lloyd George's threat of 'immediate and terrible war' convinced the last two hesitating delegates to sign: they weren't prepared to carry the responsibility of war on their shoulders (although most likely the British Prime Minister was only bluffing) and chose the easy way out.

However, what was the easy way out for the delegates, was to prove the hard way for Ireland. The treaty was based on the partition proposals contained in the Government of Ireland Act. There had been elections in May, in which the Six Counties had elected its own regional parliament within the United Kingdom. A rigged border and rigged constituencies gave the Unionists a safe majority, whereas in the South, Sinn Féin had been unopposed except for four Trinity College seats.

In the treaty, the twenty-six counties, or 'Free State' as the southern state became known from then on, was offered Dominion status with power to control its own finances and taxation system. The Free State was allowed to raise its own army, but had to recognise the King of England as its head of state, and it also had to acknowledge the Crown's representative in Ireland, the Governor General. (To prove this allegiance an oath had to be taken by all members of the Dáil).

Furthermore the treaty provided for permanent port facilities for the British navy and military forces in thee Irish Ports, one of them Cobh. The text of articles concerning Cobh read as follows:

> The government of the Irish Free State shall afford to His Majesty's Imperial Forces: (a) in time of peace such harbours and other facilities as are indicated in the annexe hereto (…) Annexe I. The following are the specific facilities required: Queenstown (b) Harbour defences to remain in charge of British care and maintenance parties. Certain mooring buoys to be retained for use of his Majesty's ships.

Throughout December the second Dáil debated the Treaty, as did other governing bodies in all parts of the country. On Friday 30 December 1921, there was a special meeting of Cobh UDC for this purpose. Seamus Fitzgerald, who later opposed ratification of the treaty, was joined by other Sinn Féin councillors. On the recommendation of the Chairman Daniel Ronayne of Labour, who had been elected in January following Fitzgerald's departure, the members first met in private for an hour. Cllr. Tim McCarthy (Commercial) said that as the member responsible for getting the requisition signed which had summoned the Councillors to the meeting, he proposed that the Council should approve of the ratification of the treaty with Britain and call upon their representatives in the Dáil to support it. Councillor Downey (Labour) then proposed an amendment:

That we the members of the Cobh Urban District Council, take this opportunity of reaffirming our allegiance to Dáil Éireann and express our confidence
that as a united government it will bring the national cause to a successful
conclusion; that we are of the opinion that unity within the Dáil under any
circumstances is essential for Ireland's future and peace, and trust that the Dáil
members will do all that is humanly possible to achieve that unity; that we urge
the members of the Dáil to do everything in their power to bring about an
honourable settlement of this present crisis; that we furthermore trust the people of Cobh will continue as theretofore to stand firm and calm in the support
of Dáil Éireann and do nothing that may tend to divide the country. [51]

Councillor Hennessy (Sinn Féin) seconded, and both the proposer and
seconder pleaded for sides not to be taken and emphasised the need for
unity. Because there was a proposal and an amendment, and since neither
of the two withdrew in favour of the other, the issue had to go to a vote.
For Cllr McCarthy's motion, five councillors voted in favour, including
one from Sinn Féin (Michael Fitzharris).

For Cllr Downey's amendment, seven Councillors voted in favour,
they were: Bailey, Telfer, John McCarthy, Hennessy, (all Sinn Féin), and
Ronayne and Downey of Labour. Seamus Fitzgerald, who was also the sitting TD for the area, abstained from voting. The amendment was carried.
It's not clear if Seamus Fitzgerald felt he could best serve the interests of
national and local unity by abstaining from the Council vote, or if he was
just trying to be clever, and wait to see how things panned out. However,
when it came to the time for the Dáil to debate and vote on the terms of
the treaty, Fitzgerald was anything but neutral. He later took a very strong
anti-Treaty position, inside and outside of the Dáil. It is also unclear if the
people of Cobh thought any less of Fitzgerald for the position he took, but
what is clear is that his Dáil seat would soon be taken from him by his pro-
Treaty opponent and former colleague Michael Hennessy.

In January 1922 the solution was finally ratified in the Dáil by sixty-
four votes to fifty-seven votes. When Seamus Fitzgerald, Tom Hunter and
David Kent voted against the Treaty, they gave East Cork the distinction of
being the only constituency in all Ireland to vote unanimously against the
treaty. A report in the *Irish Independent* newspaper the next day, 5 January,
referred to one particular speech by a young Deputy from Cork:

James Fitzgerald of Cork, in opposing the Treaty, declared that those who bore
the brunt of the fighting were almost unanimous against the Treaty – war or no
war. The people longed for peace, rather than for the Treaty. He spoke slowly,

and rather hesitatingly, but somehow he made one listen to him with more attention than other orators whose opposition was couched in passionate vein. It was the first speech on the opposition side that sought clearly to answer the arguments of the Treaty on practical, as apart from an emotional, basis.

Fitzgerald later said that when he had seen Harry Boland off on a liner from Cobh to the US before the Treaty was signed, he recalled Boland remarking that the key to the country's future, 'would hinge on whether the British demanded allegiance to the Crown.' The treaty was not only to split the second Dáil, but also Sinn Féin and the IRA, and it was responsible for the outbreak of Civil War. De Valera, who had played his cards cleverly by not attending the London negotiations and sending Collins instead, lead the anti-Treaty side and when the treaty was accepted he resigned as President. De Valera's opposition to the treaty was related to technicalities such as the oath to the British King and the Governor-General. The fact that the division of Ireland was contained in the treaty did not disturb him greatly, (in fact he had said in a speech to the Dáil in August 1921 that if the Republic were recognised, he would be 'in favour of giving each county power to vote itself out of the Republic if it so wished').[52] De Valera's speech at that time was obviously designed and intended for British ears in advance of the truce negotiations.

We can now safely assume that Lloyd George had studied Dev's speech word for word and took on board its obvious message that the green light would be given to a partitionist settlement. After he resigned, Arthur Griffith took over from De Valera as President. A new election date was set for June, and until then a provisional government was formed to accommodate Britain's refusal to recognise the first and second Dáil's. Britain was insisting that it technically had closed a treaty with a non-existent government, so to solve this anomaly; a provisional government had to be created. The British, in fact, were well aware that in the existing divisive climate in the country, especially in light of De Valera's resignation, the setting up of a Provisional Government was sure to divide further and bring forth a Civil War. It was of this provisional government that Liam Mellows of the (IRA Army Council) said that it was acting not from the 'will of the people, but fear of the people.'[53]

He was correct: above all, the people of Ireland wanted peace, not war. However, many people did not understand the issues involved or what the Treaty really stood for. To them it meant a cessation of hostilities, and the Provisional Government used the general confusion of the public to its advantage. First of all it made a calculated promise of a Constitution with Republican aspirations. It was not explained how the government intended to make up a Republican constitution without violating the terms of the treaty and when the constitution was finally published, on the morning of the June election, it was too late for the public to pass judgment on it before voting, and more important: it was too late for Republicans to derive any advantage from its terms by pointing out to the public that they had been tricked (there was nothing whatsoever Republican about the constitution).

The ignorance and confusion among the Irish people was also used by the Catholic Church to its advantage. The Church supported the treaty as it had not been happy at all about the way the IRA has succeeded in uniting the working and farming people of Ireland during the Tan War, and was now eager to regain what power and influence it had lost to the IRA. Although the pro-Treaty faction of Sinn Féin wasn't exactly the horse it wanted to be seen betting on, Griffith and the other leaders of the party were still bourgeois (as opposed to the rank and file) and they were thus felt to be a safer bet by the Church than the uncertainty of a continued war, with the possibility of a victory for the far less bourgeois IRA.

To many ordinary people, the fact that Michael Collins supported the Treaty (albeit only as a 'stepping-stone') was another reason to come out in favour of it. It is rather ironic that Collins, one of the treaty's signatories and the creator of the gradual 'stepping-stone' theory, had in May 1919 written: 'We have too many of the bargaining type already, it seems to me that Sinn Féin is inclined to be less militant and more political, it is rather pitiful.'[54] Throughout January the British and Provisional governments began releasing prisoners to gain the goodwill of the people. The British government granted a general amnesty for all political offences committed in Ireland prior to the truce (the term 'political offence' was not applied to those who had been convicted, some 1,000 Irishmen).

The IRA also split over the treaty. No one liked the treaty, but many of the pro-Treaty IRA believed, or were led to believe, that the Irish Free State was merely a stepping stone to the Republic, and that partition of the country would only be temporary. These people didn't see any contradiction in calling themselves Republican and supporting the treaty, and when subsequently the Free State Army was formed there were some very Republican-aspired people within its ranks. Jack O'Connell and Paddy Whelan, both veterans of the 4th Battalion Flying Column and O'Connell a Clonmult survivor, were undoubtedly the most senior from Cobh to have taken the side of the treaty. Their allegiance however, was more than likely to those other survivors of the column, in the Midleton leadership who adopted a pro-Treaty position because of a personality clash with Mick Leahy.

Others within the IRA did not share Mick Collins's taste for half measures; they were mainly the rank-and-file and field commanders, particularly in the south of the country, who had felt certain that the IRA was winning the war, and would complete the job if it were to go to another round. None of the commanders on the ground, particularly in the Munster region, were impressed with Collins assertion that the Volunteers didn't have the weapons and ammunition to go another round with the British. Brigade and divisional commanders knew such a claim to be a complete falsehood. They also knew that up to the time of the truce, they were beating the British hands down in the Intelligence War. More than anything else though, they knew that they had forced the British Government to concede on the moral issue of Ireland's right to self determination before the world, and it was there that Lloyd Georges bluff should have been called on his threat to launch an 'immediate and terrible war'.

On 16 January, Ernie O'Malley of the 2nd Southern Division, repudiated the Authority of the GHQ. A month later on February 18, Tomás O'Maoileoin (alias Sean Forde) who escaped so dramatically from Spike Island eight months earlier, issued a communiqué in Limerick, stating that: 'We no longer recognise the authority of the present head of the army, and renew our allegiance to the existing republic.'[55] In March, Dan Breen and Sean Hogan were smuggled back to Ireland through Cobh, after spending the duration of the truce in the US, and after receiving a telegram from the leader of the 1st Southern Division, Liam Lynch warning that the army was in dire trouble, and they were needed at home. In April, Republicans took over the Four Courts in Dublin. Then on 1 May, five leaders from both sides of the army met to try to find a way out of conflict. They included Dan Breen and Florrie O'Donoghue, on the Republican side and Mick Collins and Richard Mulcahy on the pro-Treaty side. They later issued a statement saying that war seemed all the time inevitable and that such a war would be a calamity which would leave Ireland broken for generations to come: Sean O'Hegarty also negotiated separately with Mulcahy.

All were eager to maintain army unity, but the problem with the joint statement was that is was based on acceptance of the treaty. While O'Hegarty, Breen and O'Donoghue were acting independently of the IRA rank and file, the Dáil agreed to meet the signatories of the joint army document. O'Hegarty spoke for the anti-Treaty signatories of the statement but it amounted to little. While the joint statement was broadly welcomed by the Dáil and by people like De Valera who were all the time working to secure unity, a simultaneous development that was taking place in Kilkenny as O'Hegarty was addressing the Dáil showed that not everyone was for unity. As O'Hegarty was desperately trying to save the peace, someone of authority on the part of the Provisional Government had sent troops down to Kilkenny to dislodge Republicans from a local barracks that had earlier been vacated by the British. For local commanders like Mick Burke in Cobh, a deep distrust of politicians had grown on him. He could see how their political leaders had sold them out. Whether it had been through weakness or treachery didn't really matter now, the Treaty was a disaster, and nobody at leadership level on the pro-Treaty side had the courage to admit that a big mistake had been made, or that national unity should be more important than forcing a treaty which nobody believed in, upon the people. But the day of people like Mick Burke were far from over.

26. The Capture of the *Upnor*

In early March, while attending a parade to commemorate the late Tomás MacCurtain in Cork, Mick Burke was approached by the Brigade O.C. Sean O'Hegarty. He invited Burke along to a Brigade Staff meeting after the parade. There, he was told about a British War Department vessel, named the *Upnor* that was loading warlike stores at Haulbowline for delivery at Woolwich Arsenal, and that he was to make arrangements to capture her at sea. After her capture she was to be taken to Ballycotton where she would be unloaded. The brigade would arrange for the unloading and transport of the cargo. Burke was also given a contact name of a Cork Volunteer 'Delourey' working at Haulbowline, who would let him know when the 'Upnor' was putting to sea. Delourey was the person who had brought the arms move to the attention of the Brigade. Burke was then to phone the All-for-Ireland club, at Emmet Place, Cork, where the brigade staff were standing by.

When he returned to Cobh, Burke detailed a man to make contact with their representative on Haulbowline and inform him that he was to notify Burke once he learned the *Upnor* was ready to leave. Burke also organised a crew which was to man the vessel that he selected to proceed to sea after the *Upnor*. Several of those he recruited for the job were not IRA members, so he didn't inform them of what the job entailed. A week or so elapsed when Burke received word from his contact at Haulbowline, that the *Upnor* was scheduled to set sail at 11a.m. that day, 29 March. Her cargo included hundreds of rifles, machine guns and hundreds of boxes of ammunition, Verey lights and other military stores.

Burke immediately made contact with the Brigade H.Q. and soon a car from Cork with about fifteen Cork IRA men, amongst who were Mick Murphy, Tom Crofts and Sandow O'Donovan, all brigade officers, arrived in Cobh. The men were armed with revolvers. Mick Murphy carried a

Lewis machine gun. Also with the Cork men was a sea captain named Collins, who was to take over the captaincy of the *Upnor* once she was captured. Collins was not an IRA member. Arrangements previously made by Burke to commandeer a particular boat to follow the *Upnor* to sea did not materialise, but luckily, the tugboat *Warrior* had berthed at the Deepwater Quay in Cobh that day, about noon. Burke and his men boarded her with the intention of taking her over and making to sea but found the captain had gone ashore.

With his own crew onboard, Burke and some others went ashore in search of the *Warrior's* captain. They knew they couldn't put to sea, for if the captain returned to the quay and found his boat missing, he would report it to the admiralty and the alarm would have been given. Burke and the others searched the hotels and shipping offices in the town and eventually found him in the very last office on their list. They took the captain prisoner and placed him under armed guard in the Rob Roy Hotel. Lloyd's shipping agent, Horne, was with the captain when they found him. Horne was a Protestant and a Unionist and saw Burkes and his men take the captain prisoner. Mick Murphy asked Burke what they should do with the fellow. Burke told Horne that if he gave his word of honour not to discuss with anyone what he had seen he would be at liberty to go. Horne shook hands with the others and gave his word and was let go. The time was 2.pm. and the *Upnor* had a two-hour head start on the Republicans. They boarded the *Warrior,* with Captain Collins in charge of her and made for the open sea.

The Republican crew worked so hard to build up steam, that the original crew feared the boilers would burst and offered to do the job themselves. Burke agreed to the offer. As they left the outer harbour, Burke told Captain Collins to set a course for Waterford. Collins had no idea what was afoot and did as he was told. When they left the harbour and faced the open sea, there was no sign of the *Upnor,* so Burke asked the captain to alter course for Portsmouth. The Captain did this and the *Warrior* sailed on for Portsmouth for several hours and, just as dusk was falling, the crew sighted the *Upnor* and her escort of two armed trawlers. Fortunately for the hunters on the *Warrior,* the escorting trawlers were moving steadily ahead of the *Upnor* by about two miles. The *Upnor* was making slow speed as she was towing a barge. The *Warrior* quickly closed in on her before one of its crew shouted to its captain to stop, saying he had an important message for the captain, as the same time waving an official looking envelope. Falling for the ruse, the *Upnor* slowed before coming to a stop. A small boat was lowered from the *Warrior* which Burke and a few others used to go alongside and board the naval ship. Once on board, the Republicans produced guns and held up the captain and any crew that were in sight.

Mick Murphy ordered the captain, at the point of a Lewis machine gun, to leave the bridge. The man was thunderstruck, and said, 'This is piracy on the high seas, do you realise what this means?' Murphy replied, 'We are taking over now'[56] and ordered the skipper below decks. Realising that the Republicans meant business, the captain quietly complied.

Meanwhile, the *Warrior* had pulled alongside the *Upnor* and a further party of Republicans joined the others onboard the munitions carrying ship. Burke then put a new crew in charge of the ship, with John Duhig of Cobh as its new skipper. Duhig, a member of the Cobh Company was a seaman of long standing. He happened to be in Russia in 1917 and was greatly influenced by the Bolshevik revolution there. Captain Collins on the *Warrior* was instructed to set a course for Ballycotton. The *Upnor* with John Duhig in charge, followed. Darkness had by now fallen and both vessels were nearly forty miles off the Irish coast. The British escort trawlers had gone ahead, oblivious of the fact that the 'Upnor', with its precious cargo, had changed hands.

The journey to Ballycotton was uneventful and the *Upnor* pulled up alongside the pier at Ballycotton around 4 am. on the morning of 30 March, where the task of unloading the vessel commenced immediately. Upwards of a hundred lorries of all kinds, with over 200 men, all under brigade charge, were waiting to collect the cargo. It was not until 6.pm. that the last lorry left the pier. The cargo comprised of 1,500 rifles, 55 Lewis and 6 Maxim machine guns and spare parts, 3 Vickers machine guns, 3,000 hand grenades and rifle grenade throwers, guncotton and 500,000 of .303 ammunition, 1,000 revolvers and one thousand .455 automatic pistols with a comparable amount of ammunition. The quantity may be judged by the time it had taken to unload and the transport required to remove the cargo. As Mick Burke boarded the last lorry to leave Ballycotton, a grey shape loomed up at sea. A British man-of-war searching for the missing *Upnor* was prowling and retracing the last journey of the missing ship. Her escort ships tried to make contact with her, and after failing to do so, informed the British naval authorities that something was amiss. When he returned to Cobh, Burke went to bed for a few hours.

Some time later, he was told the Admiral wished to speak to the officer in command of the IRA in Cobh. Burke spoke with the Admiral by phone at first, and was told he wished to see him in person. With Volunteer Denis Duggan, Burke called to Admiralty Buildings for the meeting. The Admiral told Burke of the captured *Upnor* and asked if he had any knowledge of the incident. Burke replied saying he knew nothing of the matter, but promised to raise it immediately with headquarters. The Admiral seemed pleased with the interview, demonstrating once more, the appalling state of British Intelligence. Burke and the brigade had always been ahead of the Admiral however, with their own agents working inside the Admiralty building. Among the most valuable of these during Mick Burke's term as leader of the Cobh Company was John Kilty, a clerk on the inside.

Burke later stated that Kilty regularly obtained information from confidential documents which was passed on to the brigade. In particular, Burke sung the praises of Kilty for supplying the letters of the naval code, a few letters of which were changed weekly by the British and which, after a few weeks, would give the complete code. This was transmitted by Burke and his team to the Brigade H.Q. in Cork. It is also very likely that Kilty was the IRA's Brigade contact which tipped them off with telegraph transcripts that exposed a Naval Intelligence network operating in Irish ports. The typed transcripts even offered the name of the spymaster (Captain Reginald Hall) who was director of the spy-ring. It is not very clear if the Cork 1st Brigade was operating under its own steam in the capture of the *Upnor* and its cargo, given the apparent divisions in the army at that point over the treaty. Martin Corry later claimed that he and his men of 'E' Company were responsible for transporting the captured cargo to a location at Macroom, where it was later distributed throughout Munster.

One telling aspect of the entire operation, from start to finish, is the absence in available records of anyone from the Midleton Company having taken part in the operation. This was possibly due to the fact that divisions between the mainly pro-Treaty Midleton Company and the anti-Treaty Brigade had already surfaced before then. One must also wonder how a hundred and more lorries could have passed by Midleton, both ways, in a twelve hour period without arousing the attention of the local forces. What the Midleton leaders did with such information, if anything, is also unclear. We do know however, that Michael Collins was livid when he learned of the *Upnor's* capture, not least for realising such quantities of weapons had fallen into Republican hands. At first, Collins accused the British of masterminding the whole affair, and or colluding with his opponents, the IRA. The First Lord of the Admiralty, Churchill denied this, but Collins didn't believe a word of it, nor did he accept Churchill's estimates of the amount of arms captured in the raid. Collins's suspicions were certainly understandable: prior to the *Upnor* seizure, there had been speculation in certain London clubs, which had been mentioned in the House of Commons, that guns were to be made available to the IRA. Collins must have thought that Churchill was out to destabilise his regime, thus facilitating a British return. In any case, he worded his suspicions diplomatically when sending the British Prime Minister a telegram:

We do not charge collusion from high responsible authorities, but we are convinced that there has been collusion from subordinates. It is absurd to believe that a vessel containing such quantities of arms and ammunition be left open to seizure in an area where it is notorious our opponents are well armed.

One can only guess what the Admiralty sources must have thought of all this. Certainly Churchill was lying about one aspect of the case. The British War Office officially estimated that 381 rifles and 700 revolvers were captured in the raid. If indeed that was all the weapons the *Upnor* had been transporting when she was captured, one of her lifeboats might as well have carried them, and why was the ship towing a large barge behind her. One of the brigade staff officers in charge that day; Dan 'Sandow' O'Donovan later put the record straight when he revealed a full inventory of the captured arms. The British War Office also told Collins that Tom Barry and the Harbour Master, Cork Harbour Board, were responsible for the 'Upnor business', but again Collins wasn't prepared to accept this as the sole explanation. In the House of Commons, Churchill shortly afterwards outlined his version of events, among them that on arrival at Ballycotton the *Heather* had found the local population engaged in looting the vessel.

According to Churchill the incident constituted 'a grave and dishonourable breach of the truce'. The fact that such an elaborate conspiracy could be set on foot in Cork without the Provisional Government having any early information of it, showed that their control over this district was 'practically non-existent.' It would appear that Churchill was attempting to gloss over his own governments embarrassment by placing the spotlight on Collins weaknesses. Newspaper reports of the *Upnor's* capture were also interesting. On 31 March the *Cork Examiner* first carried a report on the incident. It stated that while the Captain of an English tugboat had been engaged ashore on business matters with a local shipping agent, he was amazed to see his vessel, which he had left lying in the harbour with the crew onboard proceeding to sea at speed.

Mystified by her unexpected movements, the captain signalled her to return, but no notice was taken of his order. While for the time being he is unable to offer any definite explanation of the tugs' mysterious departure, the captain is convinced that the crew did not sail of their own free will.

Telegraphic and telephonic communication between Cobh and Cork and other places was suspended this morning, owing to wires having been cut, and vehicular traffic on the main road leading to Cork was blocked at various points owing to felled trees. A destroyer left Cobh this morning under secret orders and it was reported later that a second destroyer was hurriedly preparing to leave port. Later it was reported that wires in East Cork direction were out of order, but no definite explanation of the cause was given.

Another report on the same day mentions that several roads to Cork had been blocked by felled trees, among them the main road from Youghal to Cork. By Monday the press had started to put the pieces of the *Upnor* mystery together. It was by then clear what the cargo of the vessel had consisted of, and who was responsible for the change in ownership. It was reported that prior to the mysterious departure of the *Warrior*, lorries with men had arrived in Cobh, and on the same day a large number of lorries with many men had passed through the village of Carrigtwohill (which lies on the direct route between Cork and Ballycotton).

More than one hundred lorries had been seen going eastward in the Midleton -Youghal road. The lorries had been returned to their mystified owners in Cork on the following day. That it had taken the British and Provisional authorities so long to establish what had happened to the *Upnor* shows how ambitious and bold the 1ˢᵗ Cork Brigade operation had been. The fact that so many men and resources could be secretly mustered and utilised at such short notice, and complete their task with such clockwork precision, shows how dominant the Republican brigades' writ ran in Cork at that point. This in the main was due to the daring and professionalism of its commander Sean O'Hegarty and would act as a warning to Collins and his government of what might lie ahead.

27. The Take-Over

Despite the spectacular capture of the *Upnor* from under the noses of the British navy, and the embarrassment it created for the Provisional Government, Republican leaders were still having a difficult time keeping up the morale of their men. Throughout the Tan War, Republican volunteers had experienced hard enough times, but stuck it out due to the goodwill and support they received from the general public. Now that the war appeared to be over, they had nothing to show for it only hunger and unemployment.

The once biggest employer in the region; the naval dockyard, was no longer an option for the young men who did all in their power to destroy and banish its managers from their country. But now there was a new employer on the scene who was offering the attractive wage of 24d (£1.20) per week, plus regular meals, a gun and a nice uniform. To try to counter this, local Republican leaders, first through Sinn Féin, wrote to the Town Council. On the 10 February, the Council received the following letter from Robert MacDomhnail of the Liam O'Brien Sinn Féin Cumann,

A Chara, would you kindly place the following before the next meeting of your Council: We, the above, respectfully demand that in all cases of work being offered in the district, twenty-five percent (25%) preferential consideration be given to those who fought and suffered in the cause of Irish freedom. A list of these men could be forwarded to you if desired. [57]

Less than a week later a similar letter was sent to the Council from the O.C., Óglaigh na h-Éireann, Michael Burke:

A Chara, Please bring to the notice of your Council the following resolution: 'that the M.C. of 'A' Company IRA desire to bring to the notice of the Council the fact that many of our men have for months been unemployed and have consequently suffered extreme privations. We therefore request that in any new work undertaken by Cobh UDC, or any department over which it may have control or influence, these men should get first preference. We do not think it unreasonable to ask that the IRA men should constitute at least 25% of such employees.' Is mise, M. De Burca.

Two weeks earlier on the 6 February, the 2nd Battalion of the Queen's Own Cameron Highlanders marched out of Belmont hutments for the last time. As they made their way through the town, the local people listened to the singing of 'The March of the Cameron Men' before the joyful Jocks boarded the SS Bandon at the Deepwater Quay. The Staffordshire Regiment moved in to Belmont for a short time after, but vacated to Mick Burke's men on 1 July. Burke had already taken over the Admiralty Buildings on 16 May and Westview RIC barracks as early as 8 March. On 20 February, the town united to commemorate the first anniversary of the Clonmult massacre, in which two local men died and two others were later executed after their capture. It would probably be the last occasion where those on either side of the Treaty divide would congregate together before the outbreak of Civil War.

From early morning on the 20 February, no work was done in the town and surrounding districts and this general abstention of labour as a mark of respect to the Clonmult dead was upheld throughout the whole day. At 10a.m. a requiem mass was held in St Colman's Cathedral (or as the Cork Examiner put it: 'that sacred edifice in which many dead IRA men worshipped during all their young lives'). In fact the Cathedral was not able to hold all those who wanted to join the service and many people had to stay outside. When the Mass was over, a large number of IRA volunteers formed up outside of the cathedral. Headed by members of the Belvelly Pipe Band, and followed by hundreds of local people, a parade was led to the Old Church Cemetery where a commemoration was held at the

Republican Plot.

When in March the Provisional Cabinet prohibited an IRA Army Convention, the division between the Free State government and the IRA was acknowledged formally. At first Richard Mulcahy, who had replaced Cathal Brugha as Minister for Defence, had fully been supportive of the General Army Convention, but when following local IRA conventions throughout the country, it had become clear that 80% of Volunteers opposed the treaty, Mulcahy and the pro-Treaty Cabinet banned the convention. The convention went ahead anyway at the Mansion House, Dublin. It was something of an anti-climax after the dramatic build-up to it. Mick Leahy later recalled that his men from the 1st Cork Brigade went to the convention 'in battle formation with full equipment and an armoured car.'[58] The strength of the IRA was estimated at 112,650 at the meeting. However, this was the listed strength of the brigades, not the actual number of men in the battlefield. Henceforth there were to be two armies in the country: A Free State one and the IRA. On 7 April, with Civil War clouds gathering over Ireland, the Cobh Urban Council received a letter from the local Sinn Féin Cumann:

A Chara, I am directed by the above to submit the following resolution for the consideration of your Council at its next meeting: resolved that we request the leaders of the different national political groups in the country to call together a representative National Conference to see if any means can be devised whereby the unity of our country can be required and the threatened political chaos averted, to construct a definite National Programme so that a common basis of agreement can be created and the national, social and economic functions of the nation can be continued in the peaceful and orderly way. We further request that directions be given from the Conference to the people of Ireland, and to the public press of this country, to suspend all political activities until the findings of the Conference be known.' Is Mise J. Keating, Secretary. [59]

The call for a national conference probably came too late: on 13 April Rory O'Connor, together with other Republican leaders, seized the Four Courts in Dublin and established the IRA headquarters there. In itself this could be seen as the anti-treatyites seizing buildings vacated by the British, but the Four Courts were more than just another building, being situated in the middle of Dublin, which was otherwise the centre of the pro-treatyites. Michael Collins was initially reluctant to attack the Four Courts and rid it of the Republicans. The shooting of Sir Henry Wilson soon changed the situation. In the North sectarianism had flared up following the conclusion of the treaty, and Nationalists were shot, assaulted and burned out of their homes on an almost daily basis. The Army and police turned a blind eye, sometimes even lending a hand in the anti-Catholic pogroms. One man who was considered to be partly responsible for these atrocities was Sir Henry Wilson, who was an active military adviser to the Stormont regime, and known for his sectarian outlook. When in June two Irishmen who had served with the British Army in WWI subsequently shot Wilson dead in London, the anti-Treaty IRA was blamed, although it was Michael Collins himself who had given the orders for the shooting.

The IRA Executive sent various Cork IRA men over to England to investigate escape possibilities for the two Irishmen, Dunne and O'Sullivan (as did indeed Collins) and several plots and schemes were hatched to free the Volunteers, but none was ever carried out. British troops that were still in Ireland were ordered to recapture the Four Courts and stop the IRA once and for all from parading openly through the streets of the capital. However, General Macready, Commander-in-Chief of the British Army in Ireland, advised otherwise: though he was certainly as bitter an enemy of the IRA as anybody, he feared that an attack by the British on any faction of the Irish in the Free State would only have the effect of reuniting them against the British. Churchill consequently issued an ultimatum to the Provisional Government: unless the occupation of the Four Courts was ended immediately, Britain would resume the war. Collins did not want to be seen to be bowing to British pressure, but on the other hand the last thing that he wanted was the British returning in force to reoccupy the country, and thus on 29 June, with British-supplied artillery, the Free State Army fired the opening shots of the Civil War by blasting the Four Courts. That Collins had not once but twice buckled to British threats of war, had probably lost him what little credibility and respect he had left with his former comrades. When in difficult circumstances Collins had to make the big decision, he was faced with the possibility of war no matter which way he turned.

He chose to go to war with his own people, and ignored the advice and pleas of his former comrades, who insisted that united; they would beat the British through either moral argument or by war if needed be. Republican leaders had accurately judged it, like General Macready that a united and determined IRA was the last thing the British needed. While the attack on the Four Courts has been described as the opening salvos of the Civil War, it can be argued that a state of virtual war had already existed for some time. The IRA had been raiding barracks for arms and ammunition, there had been the *Upnor* arms haul, and various post-offices and banks had been convinced at gunpoint to hand over their funds.

During the first half of 1922, Cobh mainly made it to the newspapers because of several hold-ups and raids in the town. The Cobh Volunteers seem to have been particularly active when it came to fundraising in this manner, and even the rate-collector of the town, Mr O'Sullivan, had a hard time trying to keep rates collected out of Republican hands. The local IRA, not impressed favourably by the rate-collector's guts, sent him an anonymous threatening letter, but the threat was never carried out and it is likely that some of the Sinn Féin councillors may have had something to do with this. In the meantime O'Sullivan had his young daughter lodge the money in the bank each Friday to draw attention away from himself.

Prior to the General Election which was due to take place on 16 June, Michael Collins, of the pro-Treaty side, and Eamonn De Valera, leading the anti-Treaty faction, had agreed to have some constituencies, in proportion to their respective strength in the Second Dáil, uncontested (Sinn Féin was to stand for election as one party on a single panel, and candidates were to be distributed on the panel between the two sides in the proportion of sixty-four pro-Treaty and fifty-seven anti-Treaty).

In Cobh an election meeting was held on 7 June. It was a public meeting in support of the three panel candidates for East and North East Cork. Various speakers expressed the hopes they were putting in the Election Pact, feeling confident that it would effectively undo the treaty split and reunite the country. This belief that the split had been a foolish mistake and that all was now, thanks to the pact, back to the good old days (albeit without the British), may seem a bit naïve looking back, but it was certainly the general feeling at the time that Civil War could still be avoided and that a Collins/De Valera pact would prevent the Free State from falling into turmoil and more bloodshed. Present at the meeting were several councillors and of course the three panel candidates, all of them anti-Treaty. Seamus Fitzgerald was one of the candidates. His address from the windows of Town Hall started off by reading out a telegram from Sean Hales, a TD who had been invited to speak on behalf of the pro-Treaty faction that evening, but had been prevented from doing so owing to 'unforeseen circumstances.'[60] After having read the telegram of apology, Seamus Fitzgerald continued his address, saying that it had been several years since he last addressed the people of Cobh from that window, and that on that occasion he had asked them to stand by Michael Collins, De Valera and Arthur Griffith. Now he stood there for the same purpose: he wanted them to stand by Collins, De Valera and Griffith. Fitzgerald told the crowd that he did not know whether they were pleased with the selection they had made on the former occasion, 'when military and Black and Tans ruled the roost in East Cork,' but that at the time there had been very few individuals willing to go forward to represent the Republican interests. The TD stood when the English soldiers and police tried to ravage East Cork with fire and with bullets; the situation at the present was much different, and it was easy to fight elections now. Fitzgerald told his audience that he had volunteered to stand down as a candidate if Mr Hennessy was willing to take his place on the Coalition National Panel, but his offer had been refused by Hennessy during a meeting of Cork representatives the previous week.

Fitzgerald was apparently annoyed that his former Sinn Féin colleague, who was now standing as an independent, was acting opportunistically and would split the anti-Treaty vote. As to the treaty itself, Seamus Fitzgerald pointed out that people wanted unity more than they wanted the treaty, and that this realisation had been one of the reasons for establishing the election pact by pro-and anti-Treaty followers. The treaty alone did not bring unity to the people, according to the TD, and he knew a large section of the civil population would be against it. He knew that men who had been out on the hillside, who had seen men shot down on all sides, and who did not know what it was it was to sleep in a bed, would feel sore over it if people accepted less than those men thought they were entitled to.

The treaty had been accepted under duress and fear, and Fitzgerald asserted that Michael Collins would agree with him. It was not a question of individual fear, but the fear that a more powerful nation could impose her will on them. He said that he had done his best to have the treaty rejected by the Dáil at the time, because he believed that they could get more out of England. Clearly referring once again to the Independent election candidates, Fitzgerald said that individuals who spurned their efforts to unite in the interest of the country would be directly responsible for any bloodshed that may possibly ensue in the constituency (not knowing that one of the men he now spoke favourably of, Michael Collins, would only a week later reject the election pact and thus, in Fitzgerald's words, 'be responsible for any bloodshed that may ensue').[61] He also warned his audience that there was the possibility that those candidates who had refused to stand down may be out to break the pact and bring back the British.

Each one of the three panel candidates present had, 'gone out, for the twelve months preceding the truce, with the fighting men on many occasions with muskets on their shoulders, men to whom sleeping in a house was unknown for many months' and, 'it was the individuals who never did these things who are supporting a candidate who saw it fit to remain some 170 miles away from the country' (a reference to Hennessy).[62] A similar meeting was held again a few days later, and it was presided over by Michael O'Brien (President of the Gaelic League). This time the addresses were delivered from one of the windows of the Rob Roy Hotel. Seamus Fitzgerald was one of those present, but the most eminent speaker was Eamonn De Valera, who had come to Cobh to recommend the panel candidates and the pact he had entered into with Collins. Again the argument was forwarded (by P. O'Keeffe TD) that the election pact was the best way to secure a stable government. De Valera in his speech repeated the same thing in more words. He wanted the members of the second Dáil to be returned because he felt that they 'would be better able to bring about ordered conditions in the country than any substitutes they could find for them.'[63]

All the panel candidates, said De Valera, agreed on the necessity of having ordered government, whatever other differences might be. In the present Dáil, every class and section of Irish society was represented, they even had women (a remark that met with laughter from the crowd) and they had 'the distinction of being the first government in the world, with the exception of Russia, of having a lady member of the Cabinet'[64] (applause now being added to the laughter). Seamus Fitzgerald then addressed the audience, once again stressing the importance of unity, then adding an argument that was bound to raise support among the Cobh people, namely that he was looking forward to the day when Ireland would be given definite control over her own coast and Irish ships would be the only defenders of their security from foreign aggressors. Two days before the General Election Michael Collins suddenly changed his mind and dropped out of the pact, when he urged those gathered at a public meeting in Cork to vote for anyone they fancied, not necessarily the (Sinn Féin) panel candidates.

When the votes were counted, the pro-Treaty side had won the election, but did not achieve an overall majority. However, they were supported by Labour, Farmers, Independents and Unionists and therefore had the backing of 94 out of 128 members of the new Dáil. Seamus Fitzgerald's earlier concerns about non-party independent candidates splitting the vote, turned out to be well founded. John Dineen, who put himself forward as a Farmer Candidate on the ballot paper, topped the poll after receiving 6,989 votes. David Kent of Sinn Féin came in second place with 5,198 votes, while Michael Hennessy, the former Sinn Féin member and now independent Cobh Councillor, took the third and final seat with 5,029 votes. Thomas Hunter and Seamus Fitzgerald, the remaining two Sinn Féin candidates, lost their seats after winning 3,409 and 3,189 votes respectively. It appeared those voters of East Cork who favoured the Treaty were left with no alternative but to vote for Dineen and Hennessy as opposed to the three anti-Treaty candidates. Hennessy in particular, who up until shortly before the election, was a sitting Sinn Féin Councillor, would have had the added bonus of being seen by many voters as a compromise candidate between the pro-and anti-Treaty factions. Not only was Hennessy's candidature seen by Fitzgerald and others as the height of opportunism, but to add salt to the Republican wounds, he then entered the Dáil and offered his support to the pro-Treaty government. The third Dáil election result (June 1922) for the Cork East and North East constituency did however, produce some interesting figures. The total Sinn Féin/anti-Treaty vote was 11,796 while the joint non/Sinn Féin vote of the other two candidates was 12,018; though some of the latter vote was certainly intended go to a neutral candidate.

The new constitution was published on the morning of the election, too late for the public to pass judgement on it before casting their votes. There was hardly anything Republican about it, despite promises by the pro-treatyites that this would be the case. The King was still the head of the Irish government and his representative in Ireland, the Governor General, had to sign every bill passed by the Dáil before it could become law. The British Privy Council became the most superior court in Ireland and an oath of allegiance to the Crown was made mandatory for every member of the Dáil. For months, many high ranking Republicans worked tirelessly to make peace and bring about army unity. Some like Sean O'Hegarty and Florrie O'Donoghue of the Cork 1st Brigade worked under the name of the 'Neutral IRA' to avert Civil War, and when war did eventually break out; they resigned their positions from the IRA.

Others like Dan Breen and Tom Barry came close to opting out also, but were pushed to take sides by what they saw as the intransigence of some Free State leaders. As things would turn out, the loss of Sean O'Hegarty's leadership to the First Cork Brigade and its first class Intelligence Officer; Florrie O'Donoghue, would later prove a major factor in the easy fall of Cork.

After the attack on the Republican Four Courts, sporadic fighting had began to spread through various parts of the country and on 12 July the third Dáil appointed a Council of War. In the south, where counties Kerry and Cork had remained staunchly Republican, IRA Volunteers were rallying to arms. From the 10 July to 4 August, the IRA ran three columns of war news and propaganda each day in the Cork Examiner newspaper, after they had taken its offices over. But although the IRA had the military advantage in the south, with many of the best IRA Brigades in arms and with a large proportion of the barracks vacated by the British under its control (in early July the only remaining pro-Treaty post in Cork had been taken at Skibbereen), it was inevitably only a matter of time before the superior resources of the Free State Army began to tell. Large consignments of arms and ammunition were regularly supplied to the Free State by the British, who took a comfortable back-seat in the war. Between 31 January and 26 June 1922, the British had supplied 11,900 rifles, 79 Lewis machineguns, 4,200 revolvers and, 504 grenades.

By the middle of August they had further parted with eight eighteen pounder artillery pieces and by September some 27, 4000 rifles, 6,606 revolvers, 246 Lewis guns and five Vickers guns had been delivered to the Free State government. It is very clear from the initial and relatively small amount of weapons handed over by the British, that they didn't fully trust all of the Free State leadership. They could probably never be fully sure that their weapons wouldn't be turned back on them at some later stage. It is a small coincidence, that just around the time that Michael Collins had fallen in Cork; the British began to substantially increase the flow of weapons to the Free State Government. It's also worth noting that one of the principal reasons why the hero of West Cork's Flying Column; Tom Barry, had given for his earlier reluctance to oppose the Treaty was because he had received a promise from Michael Collins that once the situation had stabilised, a united effort using all the British supplied weapons would be used to recapture the six counties.

Barry's initial faith in Collins was short-lived however, and with the Provisional Government's continued contacts with the British up to June, Barry threw his lot in with the Republican HQ at the Dublin Four Courts. From there, he and other Republican leaders, made some serious attempts to bring about army unity. They discussed turning their weapons on the British army in the north. This they felt should be the real focus of the Republican army; to reclaim the partitioned six counties, but more than anything else, it was believed that it would re-unite the Irish army once more. In the Four Courts, Tom Barry, Rory O'Connor, Ernie O'Malley, Dick Barrett and others discussed the need to import more arms. They had learned that the Provisional Government, under the command of its army, was training a new police force in a camp at Kildare. The Four Courts executive discovered that two lorries containing men, arms and ammunition would be travelling towards Dublin on a certain night. These were to be waylaid. A Crossley tender, an armoured car and other vehicles commandeered by the Four Courts men set out at intervals for Kildare, then stopped outside the Curragh so that all the cars would travel in convoy. Tom Barry, Rory O'Connor and Ernie O'Malley halted a lorry, explaining that they wanted to have another go at the British. Many of the men on the lorry agreed and handed over their arms without question. Most of the convoy, which was led by Barry and O'Connor, proceeded towards the police camp in Kildare while Ernie O'Malley with a few men remained to cut the telegraph wires. The lights of the cars were seen in the darkness. Barry and O'Connor went ahead and succeeded in getting all the rifles and ammunition. They were even assisted by those on guard duty at the camp who provided them with tenders to remove the stuff. Some of those on guard even turned and went back to the Four Courts with the Republicans. Tom Barry's claim about Michael Collins earlier promise was no isolated one.

Two years later, an attempted mutiny within the Free State Army was put down before it had a chance to take off. It coincided with a machine gun attack on a launch full of British soldiers as they were coming ashore at Cobh from Spike Island. The attackers, although IRA, were wearing Free State uniforms and launched their bid to kill as many British soldiers as possible from a Rolls Royce car at the end of the Admiralty (Kennedy) pier. It would appear that it was not only IRA Republicans who had problems living with the Treaty, and the British military presence in any part of the Ireland was an affront to their beliefs and principles. Around the same time, a number of high ranking Free State officers issued a public statement expressing great disappointment with the political direction their government was taking, particularly the manner it which in had given up on the goals and aspirations of their late Commander in Chief, Michael Collins. It had been generally accepted that the latter part of the statement was a reference to Collins goal of moving to take back the North. It has already been written that up until the time of his death, Collins had been secretly supplying weapons over the border to northern IRA units who were effectively the only people offering protection to the nationalist community from Loyalist and State Pogroms.

In July 1922, from his headquarters at Belmont Camp in Cobh, Seamus Fitzgerald had taken on the role of Battalion Quartermaster. Through various shops and business in the town which were sympathetic to the Republican cause, Fitzgerald would make numerous daily requisitions for goods and materials to supply his scattered battalion. One particular item which seemed to be in demand more than any other, and were sometimes requisitioned a few at a time, and almost daily, were bicycles for the Fianna dispatch riders. A typical requisition note dated July 1922, was handwritten on a plain piece of note paper with the heading 'Na Fianna Éireann Cobh', 'Sir, I would be much obliged if you would supply two bicycles for official business, for the period of one hour. Signed, W. Glanville – Commandant.[65] Quartermaster Fitzgerald, whose family, also operated a Newsagents, Stationers and Tobacconists at 16 East Beach Cobh, also requisitioned goods from that business. A company invoice dated 22 June 1922, was made out to the O.C. of 'A' Coy IRA at Belmont Hutments Cobh. It included billing for '8 O. S. maps of Cork & district … scout whistles.' A second invoice was made out on the same date for the same source for twelve packs of Lambkins cigarettes costing 6d and was signed for by M O' Brien. Another requisition was made to Fitzgerald Brothers for five cartons of 200 cigarettes at a cost of £2.10 on 29 June, for the Military Hospital Cobh and was signed for by Charles J. Grayley.

It is not very clear if Mick Burke and other battalion officers had a plan against the growing Free State threat. He had men in occupation in Belmont, at the Admiralty and at Westview police barracks. Martin Corry's E Company had by now taken over Fota House as Battalion Headquarters. The Belvelly section under the command of Ned Butler had a permanent armed guard in place at Belvelly Bridge. It would appear that Burke and Corry had made basic security arrangements against the possibility of a takeover of the Island. What the two company commanders were not prepared for however, nor was Burke in particular ready for, was the possibility of the free-staters arriving by sea. Republicans did have some crudely made mines placed around the inner harbour, but they were mainly a token gesture and were there to give the remaining British presence in the harbour, the impression that it was part of a far more elaborate mine network. Burke was right when he guessed that Admiral Somerville would tip off the free-staters about the harbour being extensively mined. But he had greatly misjudged the situation by believing that that alone would be enough of a deterrent, and that the real threat would come by land, at the Fota/Belvelly approaches.

Many of the newly-recruited Free State soldiers were inexperienced, but that had been more than compensated for by a strong government machinery behind them. The press was totally hostile to the IRA; the Church excommunicated all Republicans, in fact every section of the middle-class establishment threw their power behind the Free State to crush the so-called 'Irregulars' (IRA). During the first two months of the war there were many direct confrontations, but as the Republican defence line (running from Waterford in the east to Limerick in the west) increasingly strained, and several Republican strongholds were lost, the IRA reverted to guerrilla tactics that had proven so successful during the Tan War. Many of the old and more experienced members of the 4th Battalion decided to move north to help their comrades defend against the closing Free State net around Munster.

On the home front around the Great Island, Burke, Corry and Fitzgerald were preparing and making defences but with what were now mainly inexperienced recruits who never had seen action before. For ten months one of the more shameful episodes of Irelands history dragged on, with almost 800 killed and some 3,000 wounded in a struggle between Irish men and women. By 29 July the Free State Army had taken control of Limerick and Waterford. The pressure became too much for Arthur Griffith, who would have been happy with a dual monarchy when he first founded Sinn Féin; all he wanted was an assembly to administer Irish affairs, but with England and Ireland sharing the same monarch (in other words, a return to the situation as before the Act of Union). Griffith died of a heart-attack, and Michael Collins was shot shortly afterwards, both deaths occurring in August 1922.

Also in August Cork, the only large town occupied by the IRA, fell into Free State hands. At this time the Republicans controlled the inner harbour, whereas British-manned forts and warships held Cobh harbour. Collins had earlier pressed the British government to hand over the forts held by them under the terms of the treaty, but when this was refused it was decided to make a coastal landing close to Passage West. The main reason for choosing Passage West instead of Cobh for the landing was that Free State forces were convinced that there was an extensive minefield in Cobh harbour; Naval Intelligence had thus advised against a landing here as it was not known where exactly the supposed minefield was. On 7 August three ships sailed for Cork, the *Arvonia* which was destined for Passage West and with it Gen. Emmet Dalton who was in charge. The *Arvonia* carried 450 troops, eighteen pounder artillery pieces and an armoured car. Many of the new recruits on board never handled a weapon before. They were instructed in the use of machine gun training while on their journey south by Col Lawlor. The Captain of the *Arvonia* was very apprehensive about the mission and was convinced his vessel would be lost to mines in Cork Harbour the next day.

The remaining two free state ships were destined for Youghal and Union Hall. The commander of British naval forces in Cork Harbour, Admiral Somerville later admitted that he had assisted the Passage landing by informing Dalton of where the mines were, but Dalton was taking nothing for granted and when the *Arvonia* entered the harbour, he took on board a Pilot with Republican sympathies. The Pilot, Joey O'Halloran refused at first to cooperate with Dalton, but when a revolver was put to his head, he piloted the ship safely up the harbour towards Passage West. When she first appeared outside of Cobh, the Volunteers couldn't identify the *Arvonia*. Mick Burke then sent a boat out to identify her. However, it was unable to make contact with her. Burke consequently ordered out the 'patrols', three cars with machine guns mounted on them, and they followed the ship on the road running parallel to the river to Rushbrooke. A warning shot was fired, but still there was no reply and the *Arvonia* nosed silently on with the three cars dogging it along the bank, Lewis guns trained on her. Finally the ship anchored at Carrigaloe, opposite Passage West because she met a path of sunken vessels which were blocking her way. Dalton wasn't taking any chances though and didn't want to rush into any booby traps. Burke ordered one of the Volunteers to fire a burst across her bows, but Dalton had already ordered all his men below decks before they first entered the harbour.

The ship remained mysteriously silent while its leaders figured out their next move to get safely to Passage. Burke nervously made for the nearest telephone at Fota, to report the presence of the ship to Brigade HQ in

Cork. He told Michael Murphy what had happened and that he may have fired on a civilian ship, but he was told he did not: the enemy had landed in Cork. Burke must have kicked himself that he underestimated the free-staters resolve to arrive by sea, and that he didn't seriously consider mining the harbour. There was little opposition as the Free State forces landed: they came under fire from the coastguard station and the schoolhouse (with a few casualties in the subsequent exchanges of fire), and several buildings were set alight by the IRA, but apart from that Cobh changed hands relatively quickly. In a subsequent newspaper report the situation in the town on Tuesday 8 August was described as follows:

About 9.00am, smoke was seen ascending from the military hospital buildings, situated over the waters' edge at the eastern end of the town. Its appearance was quickly followed by a dense volume of smoke rising from behind the belt of trees which top the hill side to the rear of the military hospital. A second volume not far distant in the same locality then began to ascend and it was at once guessed by onlookers that the Belmont hutments were also on fire. Looking along the crest of the hill, a little westward, it was now discovered that the magnificent buildings know as the Admiralty House were rapidly burning; also Springfield House, lying higher up on the hillside to the north-east. This discovery had scarcely been made before it was seen that the Admiralty signal station, immediately east of St. Colman's Cathedral, was a mass of lurid flames, in fact looking at the ring of burning buildings on the hillside, it was at the Signal Station the red gleam of fire was manifest to observers at sea-level, which included the navy men on board the light cruiser *Carysfort*, who lined the shore-side of their ship while interestedly watching the conflagration. About this time it began to be generally known amongst the people that during the night-hours National troops had passed by the town on their way up the harbour to Passage, and that Irregulars had made an attempt to blow up the iron railway bridge near Fota, which accounted for the absence of newspapers [in Cobh] on that day.[66]

A general warning was issued to all shipping by the British Admiralty not to use Cork Harbour because of cross-river firing (the Volunteers were firing at the landing Free State troops from across the river at Carrigaloe). For three days, Republican Volunteers managed to disrupt and make impossible the discharging of munitions and supplies by Free State forces at Passage West. A number of Free State soldiers were killed and wounded by the constant fire directed at them from the top of Carrigaloe hill across the river. On Thursday 10 August Cork City was evacuated by the IRA, and local IRA officers were ordered to send their men to their own unit areas and await instructions.

The Great Island was shelled when more Free State reinforcements arrived onboard the SS *Lady Wicklow* on the 10 and Fota House, where Burke and his men had retreated after adding the old RIC barracks at Westview to their list of destroyed buildings, was now also destroyed. On the 13, three units of the 4th Battalion regrouped amounting to 120 men under the leadership of Mick Burke, Martin Corry and Seamus Fitzgerald. Although the odds were stacked against them, and knowing there was little left to recapture after burning their posts before evacuating them earlier, Mick Burke led his unit in a guerrilla attack on the Free State Headquarters in Cobh. Although the attack was largely ineffective and was merely a gesture operation to let the new occupiers know they can expect more of the same resistance, the following men joined Burke in the assault, Denis Duggan, Tay Road, Cobh. Tom Lehane, Tay Road Cobh. John Moore, Ticknock. Patrick O'Keeffe, Bishop Street. J. O'Keefe Clonmel, Co. Tipperary. William Kelly, Castlemartyr. Jack Higgins, the Mall, Cobh. Peter O'Shea, Kings Street, Cobh. Danny O'Halloran, Ballinoe, Cobh. William Ahern. Andy Butterly, Tay Road, Cobh. Thomas Hayes. Maurice Twomey, Cloyne Terrace, Cobh.

On 14 August the *Cork Examiner* was back in circulation and the following article appeared on its front page, written by one of its journalist, who had been selected for the 'honour' of accompanying the SS *Lady Wicklow* when it sailed from Cork to Cobh on the Saturday.

> There was quite a hearty greeting at Passage and Monkstown, but this paled into insignificance when compared to the enthusiastic reception at Cove. Hundreds of children, many of whom were fishing with very long rods for mackerel along the Deepwater Quay, were the first to realise what was about to happen, as the *Lady Wicklow* and her deck crowded with Ireland's soldiers, slowed down and shaped a course for the tenders moored to the quay. Those with the long fishing rods looked like a Lilliputian guard of honour. Before the disembarkation actually took place all the available standing room near the railway station was occupied. The cheers of this big gathering were loud and prolonged, being repeated again and again. One sarcastic old salt remarking that the 'black gaiters, trench coats and green collars were not fashionable now.' So dense was the throng of delighted inhabitants that a way had to be cleared for the troops before they could form up.[67]

The *Cork Examiner*, which had only six months earlier been lamenting the death of IRA Volunteers (as illustrated by the account of the Clonmult commemoration in Cobh), had clearly not appreciated being hijacked by the IRA, and was overjoyed to be back under bourgeois influence. After leaving Fota House in flames, the retreating Republicans had nowhere left to retreat to. Cork and Fermoy had fallen into Free State hands with Cobh.

Most of the defending Republicans were captured as they attempted to escape or were soon rounded up. Some of those who had operated with the scattered 4th Battalion before being captured were as follows; Michael Cotter of Carrigtwohill, Tom Lehane Tay Rd. Cobh, Liam O'Doherty French's Ave Cobh, Frank Deasy Killacloyne, Carrigtwohill, Frank Barry, Harbour Row, Cobh, Dan Murphy, Rushbrooke, Cobh, William Barry, Midleton, Thomas Cotter, Carrigtwohill, John Fitzgerald, Ballinbrittig, Knockraha, Martin Fitzgerald, Knockraha, Denis Lynch, the Bench, Cobh, William Sheehan, Brook Lodge, John Long, Knockraha, Charlie Reid, Harbour Row, Cobh, Paddy Leahy, Patrick's Square, Cobh, Danny Leahy, Ballywilliam, Cobh, Jerome Grayley, St Colman's Square, Cobh, George O'Reilly, French's Avenue, Cobh, Paddy Daly, the Mall, Cobh. Mick Burke was initially taken to Midleton before being transferred to Cork Gaol.

While in Midleton, the officer in charge of the prisoners gave an order to the sentry on duty outside of Burke's cell, to have the Cobh man's boots polished for the morning. The officer told Burke about this and asked him to leave his boots out for the sentry. The rebel leader scoffed at the offer however, and naturally declined. It was plain the officer was aware of who Burke was by reputation, and either out of respect, or just as an attempt to sweeten him up and win him over, made the futile gesture. Burke was soon moved to Cork, but didn't plan to stay there for long. In September, along with thirty-eight others, Burke decided to make a bid for freedom. The prisoners in a particular section of the prison had discovered that there was a disused ventilation shaft beneath the building.

They immediately started digging until they met the shaft, and then broke into the narrow passage. A man was sent down to explore and came back with the news that the tunnel was just passable, and that it led out through a larger shaft beyond the jail premises. One by one then, the men who had access to that certain section of the County Jail went into the cell from which the tunnel had been started and disappeared through the narrow hole in the back cell, through the ventilation shaft, and up through a manhole in the centre of the road outside the jail walls. As each man made his way out, he quickly disappeared from view. It was not until a considerable time afterwards that the escape was discovered and by then the thirty nine had got clean away. Among the other thirty-eight escapees with Burke, was fellow Cobhman John Moore of Ticknock. The two men discreetly returned to Cobh where Burke quickly resumed control of what was left of his old company.

In early September, a small-scale attack was carried out on a Free State outpost in Carrigtwohill, those involved were Patrick and Maurice Twomey of Cloyne Terrace, Cobh, Charlie Cullinane and Charles Bell both of Cobh Junction and Michael Galvin of Cobh. No serious injuries were reported. Still in Cork Gaol a month later however, was Seamus Fitzgerald. From there, he received a letter from his friend and Cumann na mBan member Ciss O'Connor. Writing from the Rob Roy Hotel, Cobh, she told him that while she was in England visiting her sister, she learned through the *Irish Independent* that he had been arrested. She said the *Daily Mail* also ran a piece about him but she didn't elaborate. She expressed relief that he was now safe as it would put an end to the suspense of his mother and father. 'What a tragedy this whole business is, it seems unthinkable and dreadful. I can always remember how human you've been through all this and someone told me since I last saw you that during the reign of the Black and Tans, you often gave your coat on a cold night to some pal in need of covering and you never bothered about yourself.'[68]

While in England I came into contact with several people and always liked to hear what the general feeling is from England. Needless to say, they have nothing to voice in our favour and everything is for England's noble in giving what has been given. I ended each argument with this reply, 'if Mr Lloyd George & Co had such a mighty love for England, why all the bloodshed, before she became so D..... unselfish', I won't write the adjective knowing your dislike for strong language. Coming home on the Celtic on Saturday night last, some of the Americans were very anxious to know all about the Irish troubles. I asked a few had they been over at all and they said "Say what do we want in such a crazy country" another lady who had been all over Europe said to tell us when your finished fighting and we'll come right along. I said you've got a wrong impression altogether of the Irish, sure we are a most peace loving race (to myself I uttered God help us). You may or may not be surprised to hear "Machushla" is still here and she has done something very serious during my absence. Words fail me at this point, and they say each of us has a guardian angel, I hope her's is right, in directing her for the future. It's no business of mine. All I wish for her is happiness. I have not met him yet. Are you surprised? [69]

Throughout the autumn the IRA continued its guerrilla strategy of ambushes and flying columns, forcing the Free State to increase the size of its army and import more weapons. Although the Free State had expected a quick victory, it soon became clear that its troops had only superficial control over large areas and especially Munster proved to be something of a headache. A General Army report commented on 22 August: 'The irregulars in Cork and Kerry are still more or less intact. Our forces have captured towns, but they have not captured irregulars of arms on anything like a large scale and until this is done, the irregulars will be capable of guerrilla warfare.'[70] Meanwhile, gaols all over the country were starting to fill up. From his notes, Seamus Fitzgerald leaves us with a glimpse of what prison life was like for Republicans in Cork Gaol, when he briefly stayed there before being transferred to Kildare in late 1922.

Routine for Republican Soldiers while in Cork Prison

1. Men turn out of bed (except sick men) at 8.30am.
2. Breakfast 9.00am-9.30am.
3. Sweep out cell and make beds 9.30-11.00am.
4. Exercise and wash 10.00-11.00am.
5. Men on fatigues duty, clean up landing 11.00-12.00pm, give out parcels.
6. Lunch 1.30 clean up after.
7. Exercise 3.00-4.00pm.
8. Supper 5.00pm, clean up after.
9. 5.00-11.00pm all recreation, Irish Classes.
10. The wing Adj is to see the above mentioned is maintained and must tell off men for orderly fatigue duty.
11. The wing P/M is to see after men's fitness and further requirements.
12. All complaints, requests, applications to see doctor to be made in writing to Adj. at his cell between 10.00am and 10.30am.
13. Men to wash cells once a week at least.
14. Men on fatigue to wash themselves once a week at least (see if committee can help to do more with this in time).
15. Men to have bath once a week at least.
16. Any indiscipline to be dealt with under the attention of the Wing Commander, who will see that all duties are performed.
17. Men guilty of insubordination to be tried by the Wing Council and sentenced to extra fatigue duty or deprivation of food, or such like inflicted on him. After ratification of such by general Commandant.

Refuse after meals to be put in bins at end of corridors. Bins to be forwarded for that purpose and emptied each evening by convicts.

On 6 October Seamus Fitzgerald issued a notice of instruction to the men of wing two, in Cork Prison.

1. 'Your Free State guard has decided to impose a strict surveillance of the prison for fortnight only' – as stated to me by Captain Murphy.
2. A Free State sentry has his rifle levelled at you continuously. Similarly with wings four, six and one.
3. Even your Commandants are not allowed free movement.
4. I call on everyone of you therefore to stand disciplined tonight, (a) no man

to leave a cell without shouting 'Sentry' going out such & such a place. (b) no shouting or indulgence in rising or firing or such like.

5. Don't believe for a moment that I do this to facilitate the Free State guard. We still have weapons left us and we will use them against and despite of Free State militarism if necessary in our own time.

(Signed) Seamus Fitzgerald

Vice/Commandant – Prisoners

Around this time, Fitzgerald had also scribbled a note about the treatment of prisoners by the Free State authorities. It is not clear if this was intended to be smuggled out for general publication (as a statement or letter to the newspapers) or if it was something he meant to pass on to his superiors on the outside.

Treatment of Prisoners

It is the most shameful of regulations that could be imposed upon internees and prisoners of any description as is now being imposed upon Republicans by the Free State Government. It is that non recognition of the right to parole under even the most harrowing circumstances. Prisoners have from time to time made applications for parole to visit a dying father or mother, wife, sister, brother or children and parole has been constantly refused them from the very beginning. It is barely necessary to bring before the public mind the pictures of the death bed scene of one nearest and dearest, and departing of me never to be seen again, the shattering of a home, the complication of business and family matters ensuing, and made tragic melancholy by the refused. Abuse of a prisoner that would be behind the suffering and uplifting when it would be most required: death bed and final scene enacted …

Unfortunately, most of Fitzgerald's letter was illegible, but nevertheless gives a clear impression of the tensions and strains which existed in the prisons at the time.

Between September and December a kind of military stalemate existed, the Free State army holding the towns and the IRA holding the mountain vastnesses from which they carried out raids on the towns. The IRA in Cobh had effectively two enemies, the Free Staters and the British, the town being one of the treaty ports retained by the British (a British garrison was stationed on Spike). Burke and his officers had seen at first hand how the British had facilitated and helped the Free State arrival in their harbour. The latter was an enemy in waiting as far as the IRA was concerned, but for now they had others to contend with. The Cobh Company staged several ambushes from September onwards, and although these attacks were mainly small-scale due to their now limited resources, it was enough to make things uncomfortable for the Free Staters. British naval vessels anchored in the harbour also came under attack, as a reminder that they were still unwelcome in Cobh or in any part of Ireland. By targeting the Royal Navy ships, Mick Burke was calculating to appeal to those in the town who were wavering and considering joining with the Free Staters.

The symbolism of attacking the British also had the effect of reminding people of who the real enemy was. Regular attacks continued from Carrigaloe hill down upon the old RIC barracks at Passage West which was now in Free State control, but such attacks had no serious value and were mainly token acts of resistance. On a Sunday evening in early September there was a lot of reported firing going on in the Cobh area, but the reason behind it could not be discovered, or was not admitted by the Free State forces. A lot of troop activity followed the shooting and several arrests were made, but the names of the arrested men were not published in the papers.

On Monday 25 September a party of four soldiers, proceeding in a car from Cobh, were ambushed near Brook Lodge, but NO ONE was injured. A grenade was thrown at the car, blowing off the back wheel when it exploded. The soldiers at once engaged their attackers, seeing that there was little other choice now that the car was out of action, but by the time they started shooting the attackers had already dispersed. A passing car was then hailed down by the soldiers and a messenger sent to Cork on it, where a wheel was procured. Before long the stranded soldiers were back on the road again. A couple of days later another ambush in the same Glanmire area, saw two lorries of Free State soldiers ambushed. On this occasion, three soldiers were killed with many more injured. Jack Kiely of East Hill, Cobh was in charge of the operation and was joined by Martin Corry's Knockraha Company.

Others from Cobh involved with Kiely were, Seamus Fitzgerald, Michael Kidney, Tom Hayes, Jack Kilty, Liam O'Doherty, William Walsh, and Frank Coakley. Local man Michael McCarthy from Brook Lodge was also involved as was Michael Hudson from Lisgould. On the 5 October, at about 11.15pm a grenade was hurled at a motor patrol of Free State soldiers as they passed Leonard's Lodge on the High Road. Heavy rifle fire rained down on the patrol, as the explosion brought down telegraphic wires, but apart from that, no casualties were reported. Later that night, an explosion in an area high above the water of the inner harbour was heard to echo all around the harbour. A British cruiser, the *Castor*, kept a search light on the area of the ambush for some time afterwards, but no arrests were made following the attack. A total of twenty-four Volunteers were involved in this first Leonard's Lodge attack under the leadership of Mick Burke. Martin Corry was also present, as were the following Cobh officers and men: George Geasley, Michael Kidney, Peter O'Shea, John Moore, Andy Butterly, William Walsh, Tom Hayes, William Glanville, Tom O'Shea, John Glanville, Paddy Twomey, Dan O'Halloran, Jack Damery, Ned Mulcahy, Michael Moore, Jack Kilty, Frank Barry, Maurice Twomey, Richard Ahern, Moss Ahern. Patrick White of Midleton and William Kelly of Castlemartyr were also present.

Two nights later, there was an exchange of fire between the IRA and Free State troops at Belvelly Bridge. The Volunteers had been trying to plant a bomb beneath the bridge, when the Free State guards heard the commotion and foiled the attack. However, the Republican Volunteers managed to escape, when their retreat was covered by another unit of men lying in wait close by. The faulty bomb exploded some time afterwards with a spectacular noise that was heard in Cobh, but the only known casualty of the incident was that of a donkey found dead nearby. The High Road, particularly around Leonard's Lodge was to become a regular spot for Republicans to launch ambushes against Free State patrols as they regularly passed to and from their guarded outpost at Belvelly.

On one particular occasion, Mick Burke was in charge of one such ambush team lying in wait for an enemy patrol. Some of the party had rifles trained towards the Rushbrooke direction in wait, while others were armed with grenades. Burke, with revolver in hand, watched with steely eyes as the expected patrol appeared in the distance. As the noisy engines of the enemy patrol motored along the High Road towards them, the Volunteers braced their weapons at the ready. But as the patrol came within firing range, the only order that Burke gave to his men was a loud 'hold your fire'.[71] To the astonished Volunteers, who watched in bewilderment from behind a wall as the Free Staters passed safely by, Burke told them that he would order NO ONE to attack a patrol which had the brave Jack O'Connell among its ranks. Burke had recognised O'Connell in the lead car of the patrol from about eighty yards away. He knew for some time that it was always possible he would one day face some of his former comrades in the field. But Jack O'Connell was someone he had the highest respect for. Jack had been out in 1916, a year before Burke joined the Volunteers himself, and of course O'Connell carried the enormous burden of seeing most of his comrades slaughtered at Clonmult after he had broken out from the ambush. O'Connell had also commanded the Cobh Company for a short period while Burke was in Cork Gaol in 1920. But if Burke had now saved O'Connell's skin from attack because of loyalty and respect, then a similar gesture by O'Connell would soon show that a mutual respect existed between him and his old comrades.

This happened one day when Free State forces were well in control of the town of Cobh. Jack O'Connell paid a visit to the home of the Hawes family at King's Square. The Hawes were one of those rare families who played a brave and Trojan role during the Tan war by feeding and sheltering Volunteers on the run. Their own daughter Lily was interned herself as a leading member of Cumann na mBan. But when Civil War broke out, the family refused to take sides, leaving their door open to whoever called on them. When O'Connell called on one particular day, he told Lady Hawes, as she was affectionally known, to tell George O'Reilly and his Republican colleague to leave the house and get away as it would soon be raided. In October, things started to heat up further as local Republicans started to vary the areas of attack. On Saturday 21 October, at 2am in the morning, a bomb was thrown at a Free State patrol as it was passing near Small's Well at the Top of the Hill area, about 100 yards from the old RIC barracks. An exchange of fire between the two forces lasted about half an hour with the Republicans having the advantage of being concealed behind a wall. After the exchange, Lieutenant Watson and Privates Harding and Cotter of the Free State Army were wounded, while there were no casualties on the Republican side. The next night, Sunday, another mobile patrol came under attack as they were returning to Cobh from duty at Belvelly. The troops were in a lorry, with the officers following behind in a touring car.

As they were passing Carrigaloe, at about 10pm, a single shot was fired

Posthumous medal issued on behalf of Volunteer Danny O'Halloran.

at them, immediately followed by a number of bombs being hurled down at the soldiers from the hilly ground above. The Free Staters returned fire in the direction of what they thought was the source of the attack, and fire was kept up for about half an hour on both sides before the attackers finally dispersed. One of the Free State soldiers had sustained several shrapnel wounds to his side, and Lieutenant Ryan had been hit in the knee. The wounded men proceeded into Cobh to get reinforcements. On their way to town a man suddenly appeared from behind a telegraph pole and ordered the car to stop, pointing a gun at them. However, the Free Staters were faster on this occasion and one of the men in the touring car fired, hitting the man in the jaw. He fell to the ground and the car went over him, but when the Free State troops later set out to find the body it was gone.

Once in Cobh the incident was reported to a Captain Browne who, with another officer, led a party of soldiers to the scene of the ambush, where several neighbouring houses were searched. But the IRA had anticipated that this was what the troops would do and had already dispersed and gone home. There was one exception, Volunteer Danny O'Halloran, who lived near the scene of the encounter. He thought that instead of going into Cobh for reinforcements, the Free Staters might turn left at Ballynoe, head up the hill and circle up behind the IRA position and possibly searching his house on the way if they suspected his involvement in the ambush. So instead of returning home, O'Halloran aged thirty-four, moved down the hill to see if there were any Free State casualties. When he got down near the road, the Republican was surprised to find the Free State patrol back on the spot. The soldiers catching sight of O'Halloran immediately gave chase. O'Halloran started running for his life, but realising that his chances of outpacing the Free Staters in the dark were slim, probably decided to seek protection in a tunnel under the railway line which divided the road from the hill. The soldiers, not sure if they were being led into another trap, remained outside. Two officers first fired a number of shots into the tunnel with their hand guns, then got a Lewis machine gun into position on the road and sent a volley up the arch of the tunnel, also sweeping the surrounding hillside with the Lewis for good measure. Satisfied that whoever had been there wasn't there anymore (or at least not alive), the troops then returned to their barracks in Cobh.

The following morning it came as a great shock to the comrades and friends of Daniel O'Halloran to learn that he had fallen victim to the Free Staters in the previous night's action. His body had been found by neighbours who had gone to the hill, where all the firing had been, to investigate. They found O'Halloran's body, which had a bullet wound in the back, and removed it to a nearby shed before the Free Staters could claim it.

The funeral later took place from Danny O'Halloran's home directly to the Old Church Cemetery. At the time the bodies of Republicans were not allowed into Roman Catholic churches for a requiem service before the funeral, the Catholic hierarchy having previously excommunicated all Republicans, and the remains of O'Halloran were barred from St Colman's Cathedral.

At the subsequent coroner's inquest the brother of the deceased IRA Volunteer, Mr Patrick O'Halloran, stated, 'I think he was killed in a fair fight.'[72] While Patrick O'Halloran was obviously distraught at the loss of his brother, he probably also displayed something which burdened so many Irish families at that time, having to disagree with the political position that was adopted by a relative. The conclusion of the military court of inquiry was that Daniel O'Halloran had died, 'from a bullet wound caused by national troops'. The certificate of death which was released to the family two weeks later (13 November 1922) from the registration of Births & Deaths office at 5 King's Square Cobh was signed by the Registrar Margaret Walsh, stating that Daniel O'Halloran died from gun shot fired by National troops in the execution of their duty. Under the heading 'Signature, Qualification and Residence of Informant' on the certificate, was the name S. Browne, Captain O. C., Cobh. Today a Celtic cross stands in the spot where Danny O'Halloran fell defending the ideal of an Irish Republic.

A street built in the 1950s at Newtown, Cobh, was named in honour of Daniel O'Halloran. One aspect of the O'Halloran killing doesn't seem to add up however and this relates to the account which some Free State officers gave to a *Cork Examiner* reporter following the incident. These seem to raise one big question. What became of the so-called gunman that allegedly jumped out from behind a pole and attempted to hold up the touring car? The Free State officers said they shot him in the face and then drove over him with the touring car. Why is it that there were no follow-up reports in the newspapers relating to this man? Surely the man couldn't have survived such an ordeal and just disappeared without trace or record afterwards. We know that Daniel O'Halloran is the only Republican Volunteer from Cobh on the Republican Roll of Honour to have died in battle during the Civil War. Could it be that the other reported incident never really happened, and that maybe it was invented to divert attention away from something more sinister (the manner in which Danny O'Halloran was killed)? If we are to look at how O'Halloran was killed on its own, even by the accounts given by the Free State officers, and if we were to remove the other incident about the second alleged gunman, then perhaps there is a case to answer that the O'Halloran killing was unlawful. We know that the Republican ambush party had departed before Danny O'Halloran went back down the hill to examine the scene. It is almost certain that someone among the retreating ambush party was delegated to collect and dump the unit's weapons, and that O'Halloran would have been empty handed when he returned down the hill. There was no mention by any of the Free State officers that the man they had chased was carrying a weapon. Neither do they mention any return fire being directed at them from the railway tunnel, and of course there was no mention of O'Halloran's neighbours finding a weapon when they discovered his body the next morning.

There can be little doubt that the Free State patrol was sure that O'Halloran was part of the ambush party that had earlier attacked them, when he suddenly appeared on the scene. It is therefore very likely that he was pursued with the intention of being made an example of. The fact that he most likely was unarmed would have been a minor consideration in the overall scheme of a shoot-to-kill and reprisal policy. The circumstances under which O'Halloran died were by no means unique. The Free State Army had by this time, in an attempt to force an end to the IRA's guerrilla tactics, set aside any scruples over Irish blood, and throughout the Civil War several atrocities against IRA Volunteers occurred, particularly in Kerry, where men were chained to mines and blown to pieces, interrogations were conducted with the aid of a hammer leaving several Volunteers going mad at the hands of Free State troops. The Army was fully supported by the Free State Cabinet who resorted to equally harsh measures. Mulcahy, the Minister for Defence, obtained emergency powers from the pro-Treaty Dáil to set up military courts for a wide variety of offences. Unauthorized possession of a gun was now punishable by death under the new 'Murder Bill'. The courts began operating in the autumn and during the first month several rank and file IRA Volunteers were executed by the Free State. Altogether, in just over six months the Free State executed seventy-seven Republicans by firing squad, more than three times the number executed by the British during the entire Tan War.

Erskine Childers was one of those executed, having been arrested in possession of a gun that had been given to him by Michael Collins. The four IRA leaders captured following the seizure of the Four Courts (Rory O'Connor, Liam Mellows, Joe McKelvey and Dick Barrett) were shot without trial in the yard of Mountjoy in December. The war continued throughout the winter, as did the executions of Republicans. There were over 12,000 Republican prisoners in camps and jails. On the morning of 24 November the Cobh Company once again went into action when they destroyed the Electrical Power House in the town. As a result of the attack, extensive operations were carried out on the Great Island by the Free State Army troops stationed at Belmont and Belvelly, during which two Cobh men were arrested (afterwards described in the press as 'prominent irregulars'), John Moore who had earlier escaped with Mick Burke from Cork Gaol some months earlier, and Tom Foley.

These men were very lucky to escape execution, as they were found to be in possession of a considerable amount of bomb-making materials. By now, Free State forces had all but neutralised Cobh, with most of the Republican leadership having been rounded up and back in Gaol. Although Mick Burke and John Moore had earlier broken out of Cork Gaol together, Burke was back in custody again and Moore, one of the last experienced veterans of the Tan War, was now taken out of circulation too. With only a small group of inexperienced recruits left on the Island, the Civil War was virtually at an end in Cobh. On the 1 July 1923, Seamus Fitzgerald received a letter from the Female Prison in Cork. The swelling and overcrowding of prisons and Internment camps all over the country meant that male prisoners were now been placed in female gaols also.

Jim,

Your letter of the 16 July received. Glad to hear yourself and all the lads are well. It's about five weeks now since I last saw Mick, John and Garrett. They're over in the other wing you know. I'm the only representative of Cobh in this wing, as a matter of fact, of East Cork. There is a good sprinkling of Fourth Cork fellows here, all fine fellows. I am quite alright here, making the best of it, but would like a shift to some camp. You seem to be making yourself handy, making rings etc. There is no scope to make those here. I'm just starting a new style of macramé bag, which some former Limerick Internees have begun here. I made already and sent home 4 macramé bags, 4 frames, 4 mats, a ring for mother and a ring for little John. Remember me to Duggan, Count Bonger, Johno and all the Cobh lads. I suppose you heard Jacko Harding was released. Poor beggar was sick a long time, was since the hunger strike in Cork Jail. I hear he is in Cork District Hospital. I was speaking to him twice before he was released over in the other wing and he was looking bad. Paddy White and Gerry Daly are over there too. They were brought into the Grange early the morning of the day we were brought up here. Tom'O is in the County. It must have been great fun at the sports. I hope Cobh wasn't let down. I suppose ye have some sport with Leo, as of before. Both City hotels [prisons] are full up, we may have a shift soon and the sooner the better. I can't complain regarding form, keeping in good health since arrested. What about our compensation claim Jim, I see in the paper where Careys and Flemings [I think of Midleton] are getting paid soon. Eva is carrying business on alright. She writes me as I told her if she'd be in doubt about anything, I'd explain to her. Just before I was arrested I ordered 3 doz copies of 'The Sheik' direct from the publishers [Lyo Leivens]. The picture of it was coming to the Coliseum and I got notice from Mr Paton of it coming.

I got a letter here from Eva where she said she sold 5 doz copies and had to order more. Any big picture like that I always get notice of and get advertising for same and the Coliseum advertise on the screen for me. I suppose you heard of Alec and the strike. The poor beggar is all the time falling in for it. Will now close with best of luck.

Don't forget to remember me to all the lads, Michael. [73]

Although he doesn't sign off with his full name, it is very evident that this letter was from the younger brother of Seamus, who was also his business partner. Although Cobh was now virtually neutralised, the war was far from over in other areas however. In January 1923 alone, thirty-four Free State executions took place, and they only ended when De Valera, recognised as the political leader of Republicanism, issued (with IRA agreement) a call at the end of April to suspend IRA aggressive action.

However, William Cosgrave, leader of the Free State government, refused to negotiate, demanding an unconditional surrender, and in May, De Valera ordered the Volunteers to dump arms. The war was effectively over. The Free State had lost 580 men; this was later revised to 800 men. Republican losses were much higher and there were no accurate figures of civilian casualties. The Free State was faced with a bill of £30 million in physical damages to property. It had already spent £17 million on its war which was around 30 per cent of national expenditure. There were by this time some 12,000 Republican prisoners in the twenty-six counties. Despite the dump-arms order at the end of May, the war didn't come to an end immediately: brief clashes, arrests and Free State raids continued mainly in the south of the country, these areas being noted for their Republican support. However, despite the governments claim in June 1923 that it was back in control of the country, its policy of coercion continued. The prisons and interment camps remained closed, and life was still unbearable for those who had taken the Republican side in the Civil War; there would be no forgetting and forgiving as far as Cosgrave was concerned.

His anger was particularly fuelled by the fact that Republicans had steadfastly refused to recognise the legitimacy of the 'victorious' Free State. There had been no official surrender as demanded by Cosgrave, only a dumping of arms. On 3 August a deputation of parents and relatives of Cobh Republican internees were received by Cobh Urban District Council. They presented a petition signed by a large number of the public, demanding that the Council should make an immediate and definite protest against further internment and demanding a general release of internees. The members of the Council, one after the other, expressed their agreement and the Council passed the resolution proposed by Cllr John McCarthy (Sinn Féin), seconded by Cllr Telfer (also SF):

That we, Cobh Urban District Council, emphatically demand that the political prisoners detained without trial or charge be released immediately and that we request all the County Councils, Corporations, Urban District Councils and Rural District Councils of Ireland to cease to function until such time as the above demand is carried out.[74]

The resolution was sent to Cosgrave, Thomas Johnson (the leader of the Labour Party, which was the opposition in the Dáil), General Mulcahy (the Minister of Defence) and the Deputy Lord Mayor of Cork. In the run-up to the General Election in August 1923, the harassment of Republicans continued. Sinn Féin decided to participate in the election on an abstentionist ticket, to show that they were still a significant force to be counted with.

Several candidates were put forward, including men on the run or in prison. De Valera won a seat from his prison cell, having been arrested during an election speech) and despite several raids and the beating up of Sinn Féin workers by Free State forces, the Republicans did surprisingly well: forty-four of their candidates were elected. Cumann na Gaedheal (the new name of the pro-Treatyites) won sixty-three seats, the rest of the seats being divided between Labour and Farmers. From his cell in Newbridge prison, Seamus Fitzgerald learned how his campaign for election was going from the outside. He had been in regular receipt of letters from Miss Ciss O'Connor, a local Cumann na mBan member. O'Connor who had written from the Rob Roy Hotel on 26 August told Fitzgerald that there had been a very successful meeting in Cobh the previous week. She wrote of how great it was to hear Mary McSwiney put the Republican case and what a fine speaker she was. Mr Sean Nolan also spoke very well, she wrote. She wished Fitzgerald well with his bid to be elected and told him that whatever was best would turn up; such was her faith in the Holy Souls and she had not forgotten to go to Mount Mellary this year.

Tomorrow, she wrote, would be a general holiday all over the country. I think with all the strikes, some have more than enough holidays. All the big shops in Cork are closed down and from what I hear, hundreds of men are parading the streets with banners etc, things seem very upset everywhere. Quite a number of our good fellows are leaving our lovely country every week.[75] To Republicans the significant number of seats won by Sinn Féin proved that not all Irish people had swallowed the treaty line.

Meanwhile the IRA had gone underground following the dump arms order. The only visible sign of Republican activity at this time was the 'release the prisoner' campaign. The conditions in the prisons and internment camps were very poor and the treatment of the prisoner was more often than not brutal, with beatings by warders occurring frequently. Cosgrave turned a blind eye and a deaf ear: he was not going to be humanitarian, let alone release, prisoners who had consistently refused to recognise his regime. In October 425 men including ten TDs started a hunger strike in Mountjoy jail, which spread quickly to other prisons and camps around the country. The strike was initially meant as a protest against the appalling living conditions in Mountjoy, as well as the prolongation of internment. Thousands of prisoners joined in the protest that eventually ended after thirty-five days in the Tintown Camps of the Curragh. Two men were to die on the protest, while the Free State government tightened the reins of the media, suppressing news about the hunger strike or publishing statements defamatory of the imprisoned hunger strikers. The strike started in Mountjoy on 13 October, and a week later some 3,200 men in Tintown Camp had joined in the protest, as had Cork City female jail (which, curiously enough, held male prisoners) and some in Gormanstown.

Two of those who were among the first to join the strike, were from Cobh: Frank Oakley of Bishop Street, and Tom O'Shea of Carrigrena, Ringmeen. By 23 October the hunger strike had extended to prisons and camps in Cork, Kilkenny and Gormanstown. Cork District Council at this point passed a resolution demanding the unconditional release of all political prisoners or a general amnesty. The next day the following letter appeared in the *Cork Examiner*:

Comhairle Ceantair, Sinn Féin, 56 Grand Parade, Cork 23-10-23,
A Chara, kindly publish the enclosed names of Cobh men at present in various camps on hunger strike, Mise, le meas mor Rúnaidhe Ónórach.
Tintown: M. Rafferty, Mick Fitzgerald, J. Murphy
Harepark: Ernie Fowler, W. Hannon, Jack Stack, Der Kilty, B. McGinn, Joe Halloran, M. Keohane, J. Higgins, J. Kiely, Robert Verling, M. Murphy, P. O'Keeffe, Phil O'Neill, J. O'Keeffe.
Newbridge: Andrew Butterly, Mick Burke, John Kilty, Seamus Fitzgerald, P.Galvin, J. O'Connor. P. Rafferty, B. Cavanagh, B. Murphy, Richard Murphy, George O'Reilly, Tadgh Lehane, W. Palmer, D. Dennis, J. Grayley, M. Twomey, W. Walsh, Pat Leahy, Donal Leahy, John Glanville, W. McCarthy, G. Geasley, J. Scott.
Gormanstown: P Dalty.
Mountjoy: Tom O'Shea, Frank Oakley.
Female prison: John Daly (from Belvelly).

By 26 October, sixty women of NDU (North Dublin Union) had joined the strike and in Mountjoy 1,050 of the 1,100 prisoners were now on the protest. At the end of the month Sinn Féin claimed that some 9,000 men and women were on hunger strike. However, from then on, the number of hunger strikers gradually decreased for several reasons. Firstly the government had made considerable concessions to the hunger strikers, judging by the thousands of releases during the immediate aftermath of the hunger strike (though the Free State government denied that any concessions had been made to the prisoners). Another reason was that some prisoners had signed a bond in order to gain freedom from hunger and prison: the government used the strike as a convenient opportunity to apply pressure on Republicans to sign the pledge; some of those who signed afterwards claimed that they were deliberately misled concerning the numbers of those who had gone off the strike or who had gained release. Another reason that the protest was eventually called off at the end of November was that the hunger strike had been poorly planned – too many prisoners had been allowed to go on the strike when it should have been limited to the selected few who could be relied upon to follow the hunger strike to the end, whatever that might be.

In the week prior to the calling off of the strike, some 1,000 prisoners were released, among them were the following from Cobh: Richard Murphy, Dermot Kilty, John Glanville, Michael Dunne and Pat Leahy. The releases continued throughout December. Nita Murphy, the Secretary of the Cumann na mBan in Cobh, sent a telegram to the Governor of Harepark prison in the Curragh during the hunger strike: 'Mothers distracted – Intense anxiety – How are prisoner – Awaiting reply.' [76] On the 23 November she received a reply: 'All off strike here since Saturday –Governor Harepark.' On 8 November a statement on the hunger strike was sent to all Republican prisoners. It was signed by Mary McSwiney, sister of Terence, and was clearly intended to lift the men's morale.

Collapse of Hunger Strike

Comrades, some foolish people are talking about the 'collapse of the hunger strike' and a few have been silly enough to say harsh words to some of those who broke. And so, to all of you – to those I know and those I don't know – I want to send a greeting and a word of encouragement. I know something about hunger striking both from trying it myself and from what is much harder - watching one I loved endure it to death. You will therefore I know pay more attention to what I say than to those who speak in ignorance. First, the hunger strike has not collapsed, even though the great majority have ceased. That was bound to happen for several reasons; the first being the fact that very, very few men can stand starvation - deliberately endure it when food is in sight. Another reason is that the great majority who undertook the hunger strike did it in sympathy with the men in Mountjoy and under the impression that it would be only a matter of a few days. If you are really going to succeed in a hunger strike you can only do so (1.) by having some great motive and (2.) by taking it for granted that you are going to die, or at least that there is a good likelihood of it. A sympathetic hunger strike will not succeed, simply because 'self-preservation is the first law of nature'. Those who know about it are the least surprised that the majority have already stopped. There are three different classes of you, comrades, to whom I want to say a word separately: (1.) those who broke first from sheer hunger and because they couldn't stick it any longer, (2.) Those who came off strike reluctantly and in obedience to orders, in order to preserve or restore discipline in the camp, and (3.) those who are still on, and mean to continue to 'Victory or the grave'. I have not much to say to those last. They have only to go with me in spirit to Brixton and by that bed-side they may hear me tell them they are one and all my brothers, and that I pray for them and think of them hourly that they may have the strength and endurance to continue to the end, but that the end for them will, I am confident, be Victory with Freedom. One thing more I would like to say, I am fully sensible that you suffering is greater and for that reason cannot last so long – because you have not the comfortable bed, warm clothing, fire and careful attention which made the physical suffering easier, nor have you the consolation of relatives constantly with you. God grant you a speedy release. To you who obeyed probably the hardest order you ever got in your life – hardest to your noble spirits at least what ever relief to the body, and who reluctantly abandoned the hunger strike for the sake of the weaker ones; the most understanding sympathy is due. It is you who are suffering most, whose hearts are almost broken. Won't it help you a little to know we who understand most have no blame for you. Will you not try to complete your sacrifice by cheering up, and not spoil it by getting bitter? For you may be inclined to get bitter both ways; against those whose failure called you off and against those who when ordered refused to come off. And without discussing your right to feel bitter, or to get discouraged, I want to plead with you to make up your minds not to do either. You will get your chance yet to do something big for Ireland and you will prove yourselves. The more sure you are of your own ability to have gone on to the end, the more easily you will realise the truth of what I say. I could name several men I know myself and many more I only know by reputation, who have obeyed orders in this matter, whose courage I would no more doubt than I would my brothers. Some people, ever your friends, in the first shock of surprise were disappointed, but not when they understood. If the Government, your Army H.Q. and people like myself who have some knowledge of what is necessary for organisation and discipline, all agree that you did right, you may be sure the country will accept our verdict. No one who knows me will give me credit for having patience with cowards and slackers. I have not. But then you are neither the one nor the other. I am proud to call you all my friends and I feel sure you will do the big thing now and help in the re-organisation of the camps cheerfully, patiently and with no grudge of any kind against anybody. Ireland wants us all, those who have limitations as well as those who have not. And now for the poor boys who may be feeling a bit down-hearted because they broke away under the stress of hunger. Some of you perhaps declare you don't care, you could stick it; and some others of you are feeling sore and ashamed and sorry you did not try harder. Never mind! You all did your best and if you were not able to fight against the pangs of hunger as well as you fought against the enemies of the Republic remember we are not all asked to do the same kind of work for Ireland. I can do a hunger strike but I would be a poor hand in a fight, and if I had to do a forced march you would beat me to fits in five minutes. Don't be afraid that you will even be reproached with a breach of discipline. There is only one kind of discipline that hunger will obey and that is self discipline and self control. If you are disappointed with yourselves, work all the harder now; acquire self-discipline; study to make yourselves more fit to serve Ireland. I have read the cheering message sent you by the C/S. That will cheer you up above all. And if some foolish people don't understand at first what a terrible thing hunger is, well don't get discouraged. Ireland has plenty work for us all. If you don't do one kind you can do another. No torture inflicted from the outside must ever make you give up the Republic. And I am sure it never will. Cheer up now. Get into good working order again at once. If you are released, join your Sinn Féin Club and work for the Local Election and work hard; if you are not released, yet, go ahead inside to make yourself better citizens of the Republic. And if you don't know Irish study that first. If you do know it, teach it to those who don't and talk nothing else.

Beannact Dé óraibh go léir,

Mary MacSwiney. [77]

In the winter of 1923-24 the prisoners started being released gradually. There were no jobs for the released men and women, no social welfare, leaving many with little choice but to emigrate and find a new life without hunger and harassment. Those who stayed behind and brazened it out very often suffered harassment by the new police force, An Garda Siochána, who had replaced the RIC. This new eager police force were constantly on the door steps of Republican homes, very often with good reason as they saw it, as some ex-internees returned to reactivate their local units. However, in the main the police activity was totally unjustified and was merely meant to harass and make life miserable and unattractive for Republicans to remain in the new state. It soon became very clear that the Free State government had little appetite for undertaking a national programme of reconciliation where they could encourage at least some Republicans to join and work with them in a new shared future. The words Forgive, Forget and Heal, were not ones that came easy to a deeply bitter and short-sighted administration. But because the Free State administration had deviated so considerably from how Michael Collins had intended to use the treaty, they were neither in the mood nor position to hold out olive branches. Those on the losing Republican side, who were left feeling deflated, cheated and sold out, believed there was little hope now in hanging about in a bitterly divided country which fell far short of the Republic they had fought to establish. Many from the Cobh Company took the first opportunity to get out and make a new life for themselves abroad. Three of the most senior officers from the Cobh Company to emigrate were John Moore of Ticknock, whose brother Maurice had lost his life to the struggle, and whose family had more than once been targeted for assassination by British forces. Daithí O'Brien, the former commander of the Cobh Company and leader of the 4th Battalion during the Truce and Civil War, was another who made a new life for himself on the other side of the Atlantic, as did Tom O'Shea and many other of their former comrades.

As reality began to sink in and the new political administration sought to deal with mass unemployment, emigration began to soar once more. Cobh, like in times past, began to thrive on the misery and misfortune of others as it was one of the main ports of departure for those seeking a new life in the New World. A local man who worked as a porter at this time, witnessed one Irish man bidding his country farewell in a rather original way. The man in question had received a great deal of harassment from the Garda Siochána for his Republican sympathies and had consequently decided to take the boat to America. Saying goodbye to a friend on the morning of the departure, the man mysteriously added that he had one more job to do before leaving. This was an hour or so before the tender was due to depart, and the next hour the Republican spent waiting in a shop entrance until finally a particular policeman came along. He grabbed his suitcase, took a deep breath, and then rooted the shocked Garda with his boot from behind. Having fought his last battle on Irish soil, he then made a run for the tender, becoming another emigration statistic.

Around this time, a former police sergeant by the name of Thomas Cahill was released from Cork Gaol after serving a lengthy sentence for treason and collaborating with the IRA. Cahill was a serving officer in a West Cork RIC Barracks when he was found out by the British some time around 1919. He not only forfeited his career for his alleged crime, but was ostracised by his former colleagues, arrested and imprisoned. While in Cork Prison, Cahill was singled out and subjected to beatings and torture. One such beating was so severe that it resulted in the former policeman losing his eyesight. But if Cahill thought he had it rough in prison, he soon learned that life outside as he knew it would be very different from that he left behind before he went to gaol. Home was no longer in West Cork but in the East Cork coastal town of Cobh where his Unionist wife had taken up a position as Post Mistress of Rushbrooke post office. The family lived over the post office near Rushbrooke Tennis and Croquet Club (today the premises is occupied by Murphy's Day Market). Thomas Cahill lost not only his eyesight in prison but also his marriage.

His wife never forgave him for selling out to Republicanism and bringing disgrace to the family, and remained married to him only in name. Cahill's new home was a cold place to be and this led him to turn to heavy drinking. The broken former policeman very often slept on the benches of Rushbrooke railway station, rather than what should have been home over the post office. Then one morning after one of his drinking sessions, Thomas Cahill's body was found on the railway tracks across the road from his home. It is almost a certainty that the victim, a blind man, could not have climbed over the 4ft high safety rail of the footbridge to jump to his death. It was more commonly felt at the time that the unfortunate man was accosted by people lying in wait for him before being thrown off the bridge. No one was ever charged with the crime. Following the incident, fingers were pointed in a number of directions over responsibility for the killing. The family which Thomas Cahill left behind never spoke of the incident. That all changed however in the late 1990s when one of Cahill's grandnephews learned of the family's hidden history and decided to examine it further. However, all attempts to discover the facts of the case came to a dead end.

In the year 2000, relatives of Thomas Cahill held a small prayer service and commemoration at Rushbrooke railway station, where this author was in attendance. It is very likely that the identity of Thomas Cahill's killers will never be known, but it is the opinion of this writer that the only people who might have had a motive for taking the poor man's life, were those who he previously had worked with in the British police force. It is also very likely in the background of a Civil War which had just at the time ended, that there was an absence of political will amongst the fledgling Garda Siochána to properly investigate the case.

28. The American Connection

The part played by Mick Leahy in the Civil War is relatively sketchy. We know that he was promoted to officer, commanding the 1st Cork Brigade in the days following the Free State attack on the Four Courts, after Sean O'Hegarty resigned, wanting to play no part in the Civil War. It would appear however, that Leahy didn't stay around for long and whether he fled to avoid arrest and or was sent as part of an authorised delegation by the Republican leadership to seek recognition and funding for the alternative Republican government, there is a record of him being in New York in March 1923. It is very likely however that he was in the USA before then; we know for example that when Mick Burke made contact with Brigade HQ after the Free Staters landed in Cork Harbour, it was Mick Murphy he had spoken with not Leahy. A number of documents originating from the US make it clear that he was working there on behalf of the Republican government.

One letter sent to him on St Patrick's Day 1923 from Sean Moylan of the 4th Cork Brigade, also from a New York address, informs Leahy that a recently released Volunteer Dan Leahy from the Four Courts (released on health grounds) was now being put at his disposal to assist him with his work. Moylan then jokingly chastises Leahy for having the Cork habit of not sending in his reports. He told him that he spoke to his sister the day before and had arranged transport for the reserves. He added that they were doing well in spite of all the sore heads and the people at home were pleased with their progress.

> The war goes on. Things seem at a deadlock. Both sides unaided and the side that pulls a new stunt gets there. We may be the old firm you know, depended on for the novelties. Special Easter show always. So if the news doesn't filter through in the end woolly vest will only because we don't control the press or have shares in it.[78] It is clear that Moylan's letter was in part written in code and that he, Leahy and others were busy working for the war effort back home.

Another undated and unsigned document with a headed address of Eight East Forty-First Street New York City, and which seems to have belonged to an Irish American Republican support group, appears to have been written with the purpose of raising funds in the USA for an alternative Republican government in Ireland. The letter which appeared rushed and written in long-hand is as follows:

> It is understood that the delegation headed by Mr O'Kelly and the army men Messrs Moylan and Leahy shall work in harmony and that the entire delegation Messrs O'Kelly, O'Doherty, Moylan and Leahy are to work as a unit to secure money for the army, for the working of the Republican Government. Now that the work of the military and political sides of the Republican Movement has been co-ordinated it is agreed that all moneys collected shall be sent to Ireland

until the instruction that any money necessary shall be used for army purposes. And as long as money is required for defence purposes that the defence department shall have first call on all moneys in preference over any other department. A copy of this understanding shall be sent to the President and to the Chief of Staff IRA, with the request that they immediately send approval or an alternative agreed upon by them both. [79]

One means of how these much wanted monies may have been raised can be seen through the following document. Again, it is not very clear who the author of the document is but it is very likely that it was made on behalf of a Trade Union or the USA Labour Movement, and was composed with the intention of raising funds for the Republican cause back in Ireland:

Dear Sir and Brother: One of the leading men of the Irish Republican Army who has just arrived from Ireland will be present at the next meeting of our Camp. The enclosed card gives date, place and hour of meeting. This soldier of the Irish Republic has been in communication with the officers of the Camp and has directed that a special request be sent you to be present at this meeting so that you may have an opportunity of a personal talk and of hearing first hand the true story of how the war for Ireland's Honour and Independence is progressing. The name of Michael Leahy should convey to the mind of every member and worker for an Independent Ireland the thought that an opportunity to meet and greet this young hero if neglected would be an insult to the unbending spirit of Irish nationality. The story he will tell you will be a very modest story that you will treasure while life lasts. He makes a special request that you bring to the meeting any and all prospective members of your acquaintance, so that they may be added to our ranks and imbibe the spirit of confidence and victory that this winner of victories will be present in answer to his invitation and grasp his hand as a comrade and brother. [80]

It is unlikely that Mick Leahy returned to Ireland at anytime throughout the remainder of the Civil War (secretly or otherwise), we do know however that he remained on in the United States long after the war until 1935 when he returned to settle back in Cobh.

29. The Free State Army Mutiny

The Civil War was barely over when signs of unease and strain within the Free State army began to surface. It was always inevitable that some senior

Republicans who Michael Collins had previously won over to join his stepping-stone strategy, would one day question its lack of progress. After a bitter and bloody Civil War that had cost countless more lives than the previous Tan War, there was now little to show for it except bitter wounds that would take generations to heal. In the absence of their dead hero Collins' leadership, these officers were well aware that if they didn't take the initiative to further his aims, their political masters certainly would not. Cosgrave the President/Taoiseach appeared far more interested in suppressing Republican sentiments in the Free State than showing any concern for the welfare of beleaguered Nationalists in the North.

In January 1924, the Dáil once again gave the government emergency powers. However, Cosgrave failed to hear the rumblings coming from within the Free State Army itself and on 6 March he received an ultimatum from a group within the army calling itself the Old IRA, warning that they had only accepted the treaty as a stepping-stone to more than what their government was giving them. What later became known as the Army Mutiny was put down before it even took off, when Cosgrave had the signatories of the ultimatum arrested, several other plotters and 'unruly elements' sacked and Eoin O'Duffy (the future leader of the Blueshirts) appointed as Commander–in-Chief of the Army. Around the same time, 138 rifles, 9 Lewis machineguns, 41 hand grenades, 2 revolvers, 20 sets of web equipment, 24 rounds of .450 revolver ammunition and 34,400 rounds of .303 ammunition, went missing from army stores. Cosgrave and his government may have been content that they had nipped the dissent in the bud, but it soon became apparent that some kind of an alliance had been made between at least some of the dissenters and senior Republicans in Cork. It also became apparent by the target that was chosen by the plotters, that there was a common believe abroad which felt that military action taken against any remaining British forces in Ireland would have a unifying effect on national morale. However, when some of the missing Free State weapons turned up in Cobh on the 21 March, their use against an unsuspecting and unarmed British target, had anything but a unifying result.

At around 7pm on that evening, as a British military launch pulled into the pier at Cobh, a yellow Rolls Royce car halted about fifty yards away on the road at the front of the pier. The five-man IRA attack team waited patiently while the passengers were disembarking and then, when the soldiers from Spike Island had disembarked, the windows of the car rolled down and out came two Lewis machineguns. There followed rapid fire for about thirty seconds, after which the car sped off out the High Road. About a quarter of a mile away the yellow Rolls Royce stopped again and this time fire was opened up on a British gunboat, the *Scythe*, which

Wanted poster for Cobh shooting suspects, 1924.

was anchored in the harbour. The attackers in the Rolls then sped off towards Rushbrooke and off the Island. No one was injured aboard the ship, which did not return fire, but back at the pier, the site of the original shooting, one officer and eighteen soldiers were wounded, one of them fatally. One eyewitness, who was looking out from one of the shops facing the pier (Joseph Grogan's Establishment), recalled seeing the machine guns in the back of the car, and the shots fired at the crowd on the pier.

What he remembered most vividly about that day was how the companion of the dying soldier never left his side and stood by him throughout the firing. Also injured were two seamen and three civilians (one of which was a local boy who was delivering groceries to the boat). Other witness reports in the *Cork Examiner* the next day, said the soldiers froze for about thirty seconds when the firing started before reacting. Then they dived down for cover to avoid being hit. One young soldier who was slow to react was blown back into the tide by the force of the bullets, but his friends managed to pull him out to safety. In the panic, the soldiers were at a loss to know what to do and started heading towards the town, but then a sidecar arrived on the pier with a young female doctor on board (Dr H.A. Ledlie) who ushered them all back onboard the launch. The boat immediately made back for Spike but was instantly called back as another

Jack O'Connell in Free State uniform.

sidecar arrived on the pier with another wounded soldier. The driver of this second sidecar was later identified as Mr Walter Barry, a well-known local coal importer and undertaker. When Dr Ledlie reached Spike with the wounded, another party of troops boarded the launch for Cobh.

A second *Cork Examiner* report stated that by 8.30pm gunfire could be heard from a number of local streets in Cobh, leading many civilians to hurry to the Town Hall to take cover. It was eventually discovered that this firing was the result of the second group of British soldiers who had come ashore from Spike Island looking for their wounded and lost comrades. They were said to be under the charge of an officer. It was also reported that a number of National (Free State) troops arrived in the town at 8pm in search of the attackers, who by then were long gone. There was no report of what took place when the British and Free State troops met up with each other in Cobh, especially as the original attackers were also wearing Free State uniforms, and as the British soldiers who were now shooting wildly in the streets of Cobh, had no jurisdiction there. When the attack car left had earlier departed from the Great Island it was followed by two covering cars at the rear and headed at speed towards Fermoy using back roads and then headed west to a safe hiding place. The Free State and British armies were thrown into confusion and panic by the attack from the polished, well maintained Rolls Royce. The attacking party had worked so quickly and assuredly that they must have been familiar with the town and the various times of activities of the British base on Spike. But most disturbing of all was that the attackers were wearing Free State uniforms, a thing that implied at least passive involvement of Free State forces.

No theft of uniforms had been reported and as an army mutiny had been suppressed only weeks before, suspicions were rife. Cosgrave put out a £10,000 reward for information on the incident, but despite the substantial reward and an intensive police investigation, the five men were never found. Cosgrave naturally blamed the IRA, claiming that they had wanted to provoke the British, but Frank Aiken, the IRA's Chief of Staff, denied any Republican involvement, an indication that the operation may not have been sanctioned. Nevertheless, the names of the attackers were well known in Republican circles, and soon became known to the Free State authorities. The £10,000 reward issued was for information on the whereabouts of five named individuals. They were Dan 'Sandow' O'Donovan, Frank Busteed, Jim Grey, his brother Miah Grey, and Cobhman Peter O'Shea of King Street. No one in Cobh talked with the authorities, despite the lure of the reward money, or at least not immediately, though there were enough people around at the time of the shooting to recognise a face or two. The Free State government apologised and later paid the British government compensation for the attack, the British accepted and the matter rested at that. In a *Sunday Press* article in 1965 a former *Cork Examiner* reporter gave his account of the incident which he had partially witnessed. Mr Dan O'Connell recalled how he was attending a Council meeting in the Town Hall (Casement Square) at the time when he suddenly heard the rattle of gunfire.

As the councillors dived under the table for cover, the reporter ran out to investigate. He saw people gathering a couple of hundred yards away on the Admiralty Pier and when he began to make inquiries, O'Connell was told that men in Free State uniforms had opened fire on British soldiers getting off the boat. The reporter at the time believed the attack to be a Free State operation. Seamus Fitzgerald gave some details of the incident to his cousin some years later. Not only had there been cars to cover the escape of the Rolls Royce off the Island at Belvelly, but there had also been three cars at the eastern end of the town to cut off any possible counter-measures by the Free State Army at Belmont hutments. Local man Peter O'Shea of Kings Street, was said to be a driver of one of the cars used in the attack, and was said to have fled to the United States in the weeks that followed. Sandow O'Donovan was also said to have fled the country and travelled to the USA with another Republican, Connie Neenan. O'Donovan, however, resurfaced in Cork in 1928 and is said to have turned up in disguise at St Finbarr's cemetery where his young niece was being buried. The Special Branch were also said to be at the funeral watching out for the wanted fugitive, but the illusive 'Sandow' calmly left the cemetery after the ceremony from under their very noses.

It is not very clear if Seamus Fitzgerald had any direct involvement in the Cobh operation, but it was clear that some local Volunteer Company members played a part in the action. The Rolls Royce car used in the operation was said to have been owned at one point by Lord French (the

British Viceroy), once the King's own man in Ireland, but somehow came into the possession of Republicans. In sporadic raids against the military over a prolonged period, the car was used entirely during the hours of darkness, thus earning the name of the 'Moon Car'. It is very likely that's its driver, Jim Grey, who for years had organised transport for brigade purposes, had come by the Rolls upon his travels. Some years later in quieter times, Jim Grey would settle to live at Carrigaloe in Cobh. Some eyewitness accounts had stated that the big yellow touring car had been seen in Cobh prior to the attack. Immediately after the operation, the car was driven to a small, uninhabited farm in Donoughmore, where it was burned out and buried in a bog. In order to allay local suspicions about the lights used on the farm by men digging the grave, rumours were spread that the place was haunted. The big 'Moon Car' lay buried there until it was eventually found in 1981 by a local historian Liam O'Callaghan from Waterfall. A medical orderly who was at the scene shortly after the Cobh shooting, told of how most of the wounded were put back on the launch and taken to the military hospital on Spike Island. The more seriously wounded were taken to hospital in Cork, including the soldier who later died from his wounds, Private Herbert Aspinall. When he was put into the ambulance, the soldier was cushioned with hot water bottles to help his body deal with the shock, but by the time they reached Cork he had drunk most of the water from the bottles. The medical orderly noted that he had an insatiable thirst due to a massive loss of blood.

Following the attack there was a special meeting of the Council called on Saturday 22 March. A special seat had been placed along side that of the Chairman for the Bishop of Cloyne, Dr Browne. The purpose of the meeting was to issue a condemnation of the shooting of the British soldiers on the previous evening. The Council and Bishop Browne described the incident as a 'horrific crime' and it was decided that the Councillors should visit the injured soldiers on Spike to disassociate the townspeople from the shooting. Two days later the Council received a letter from Captain Halfparney of the Royal Service Corp (South Irish Coastal Defence) thanking the UDC on behalf of Private Aspinall's family for their sympathy and their floral tribute. There was a general fear of reprisal among the local population after the 'Moon Car' attack, and to soothe whatever misgivings the British may have had about the loyalty of Cobh, a telegram was sent on behalf of the women of Cobh to the family of Private Aspinall, expressing their deepest sympathy.

In fact the women of Cobh were largely unaware of the contents of the telegram: it had been sent by two local men. Apart from reminding people of the shortcomings of the Treaty (in relation to the possession of coastal ports) and exposing unease within the Free State army, the Cobh attack by and large helped the Republican cause very little and probably caused more harm than good. A bounty was put on the heads of some senior Brigade officers in Cork. At least one of which and a local Cobh Volunteer were forced to flee to America. Another pitiful aspect of the fallout from the shooting was that some Republican councillors found themselves in the position where they felt it necessary to condemn the action and this despite them probably having some private knowledge of who had carried it out. It would appear the bounty placed on the heads of the attackers was left to lapse when a new Republican party (Fianna Fáil) came to power in 1932, as some of those previously wanted were living openly in Cork in the years that followed, and at least one who earlier fled to American returned home to settle down.

Aftermath of Free–State Army Mutiny

A report in the *Cork Examiner* newspaper on 22 March, the morning after the Cobh attack, stated that the following Free State Army officers had been released from custody on parole:

It is officially announced that Colonels Patrick McCrea, Francis Thornton, Christopher O'Malley, John Slattery, and Commandants Joseph Dolan, Patrick Griffin, Charles Byrne and Robert Halpin, and the following three civilians, namely: Joseph Shanaghan, Ml. Collins and James Leahy, who were arrested on Tuesday night last at 68, Parnell Street, have been released on parole under open arrest, having previously expressed acceptance and approval of the position laid down by the government as outlined in the memorandum of the 18th inst by the Minister for Defence, which reads as follows - The President has instructed that all persons who left their posts or unlawfully took away stores during the recent mutiny be dealt with from the point of view of arrest on the lines indi-cated in the following paragraphs (1 to 5) – (1) By Thursday, the 20th inst, at 6pm all arms and equipment received from barracks to be returned to the place or places from which they were taken. (2) Persons concerned in the removal of such material to surrender at the place from which it was taken to officer now in charge of that place. (3) After such surrender, on presenting parole to this officer in charge, such parole will be accepted, and persons concerned allowed out under open arrest. (4) Absentees from duty shall also surrender by 6 pm on Thursday, the 20th inst, and their parole being presented it will be accepted. They will also be allowed out under open arrest. (5) Thursday is only mentioned as a convenient date to allow a certain amount of time, but it is desirable that no delay should be occasioned in giving effect to the terms of paragraphs, 1, 2, 3, and 4. Suitable instructions should be wired immediately to al G. O.C.'s and by them to their officers concerned to secure that. (Signed) Sire Chosanta

Note – The date mentioned in paragraphs 1 and 4 in the memorandum as announced by the Vice-President in the Dáil on Thursday, the 20th inst, has been extended to 6pm on the 22nd inst. Commandant Ashton, who was arrested on Monday, the 17th inst, has also expressed acceptance and approval, and has taken steps to comply with the special requirements in this case.[81]

The mutiny, if it could really be described as such, was now truly put to bed and the Free State government was satisfied that it had matters firmly under its control. It still however, had to solve the matter of the Cobh shooting. In this regard it was quite satisfied to pin responsibility for the entire military operation upon the five named Republicans that it had issued a proclamation against. There was no question of seeking from those who had aligned themselves with the attempted mutiny, the names of those who had supplied the weapons and uniforms for the Cobh attack, or even to establish who had suggested and set up the target. Neither was there any evidence offered publicly to back up the proclamation offering a very hansom reward for information leading to the capture of the five named Republicans. It might well have been that the public outrage caused by the attack, was enough to persuade the Free State authorities, that there was an ideal opportunity to get rid of some of the 1st Cork Brigade leaders in one swoop. But if that were the case, or even if the authorities had identified the right people with responsibility for the attack, they would soon learn that they were not going have it all their own way. On 15 May, the following statement was issued to the *Cork Examiner.*

We the undersigned officers of Cork No. 1 Brigade, wish to give an absolute and emphatic denial to the allegations made against us in the Free State Governments Proclamation, which appeared in your issue of May 14th. We had nothing to do with the Cobh shooting. The reasons which prompted the Free State authorities to accuse us are obvious. We have been 'on the run' for the past two years, and they assumed that we would not be in a position to defend ourselves. We have no intention of facilitating the Free State authorities to get out of their difficulty by allowing this charge to rest on our shoulders. "It is our considered opinion that the proclamation as issued is an attempt to justify the shooting of us in the event of capture. It is clear that we are not presently in a position to proceed against those people responsible for the issuing and publishing of such libellous statements. We, therefore, demand of you to give as much publicity to this denial as you gave to their accusation.

Dan Donovan, James Grey., Jeremiah Grey, Francis Busteed, Peter O'Shea.[82]

30. Cumann na mBan in the Republican Struggle

In all struggles and revolutions the part played by women rarely gets the mention and credit it deserves. However, no struggle can succeed without the support and participation of women. The women of Cumann na mBan contributed to the Republican struggle in many ways. The women's organisation was founded in Dublin in 1914. Although some male Republicans were reluctant to let women participate in the fighting (Eamon De Valera for example), the women of Cumann na mBan and the Irish Citizen Army stood side by side with the men who fought British Imperialism and declared the Irish Republic at Easter 1916. The 'Declaration of the Republic' drawn up by Pearse and the Volunteer leaders was ahead of its time in that it guaranteed equal rights to Irish men and Irish women. Credit for this is widely given to the influence of James Connolly, whose Citizen Army admitted women on an equal footing to men. One such woman was Constance Gore-Booth, better known as Countess Markievicz. She founded na Fianna Éireann, the Republican boy scout movement, in 1909, was associated with the trade unions and James Larkin in the 1913 lock-out, and took part in the 1916 Rising as one of its commandants, a participation for which she was consequently sentenced to death but the sentence was commuted.

In the 1918 General Election Countess Markievicz became the first woman to be elected to the British House of Commons, but like the other Sinn Féin deputies she refused to take her seat, believing that the Dáil was the rightful parliament for Ireland. When in 1921 the anti-Treaty TDs left the Second Dáil in protest at Griffith's election as President, she was vociferous as always in expressing her beliefs. When Michael Collins, one of the treaty defenders, called the anti-treatyites 'deserters', Markievicz snapped back, 'oath-breakers and cowards'. But of course Countess Markievicz wasn't the only Irishwoman to throw her weight behind the Irish cause. There were many others and their bravery passed the test many times throughout the struggle. The importance of Cumann na mBan is shown by the fact that they were recognised as being a threat to the authorities, first to the British, then to the Free State, and the organisation was banned on several occasions along with the IRA.

The duties of members of Cumann na mBan were manifold and including such activities as intelligence gathering, the carrying of dispatches, the raising of funds, the carrying of arms and ammunition through enemy-occupied areas, nursing the sick and wounded, carrying out propaganda work and helping Volunteers on the run as best they could. The women also worked to keep up the morale of Republican prisoners by regularly writing to them in prison and the internment camps. Unfortunately the important records of the local women's organisation were accidentally destroyed by its secretary, Nita Murphy. But some years later, while applying for a Republican pension, she presented a broad outline of some of the activities she engaged in during the earlier struggle. In 1917 she and the other members of the local branch, drilled in first aid and accompanied the Volunteers on the training. They catered for some 130 men who were attached to the No. 1 Brigade, and collected great sums of money, Murphy going to the United States herself for the purpose. 1918 was mainly taken up with campaigning and distributing anti-conscription literature. They carried dispatches, fed and clothed a number of men and their families.

In 1919 the girls collected for Republican dependants, carried dispatches, held public meetings in support of the struggle, and monitored the enemy for the IRA. When 1920 came around, the girls kept arms and ammunition. They also organised safe places for Volunteers to stay while on the run. They collected money for the prisoners in Wormwood Scrubs and kept the Clonmult boys, four of whom were murdered. They carried dispatches about fourteen miles. 'When Captain of IRA was arrested, I managed an interview from Jocks and managed to get important verbal message from him about dispatches hidden in his house.'[83] This latter deed mentioned by Murphy was probably a reference to Mick Burke's detention at Belmont Camp shortly before the Truce, when he was mistakenly released. It is also worth noting that as former O.C. of the 'A' Company, Mick Burke wrote a letter of verification in support of Nita Murphy's application for a Republican pension, as he also did for many other former Volunteers seeking the pension.

Ironically, Burke never sought the pension himself as he personally didn't recognise the legitimacy of the State and felt there would be time enough for people to give themselves pensions when the Republic was established. Nita Murphy's home at 21 Bishop Street (Formerly Ferry Street) was the centre of the Cobh Cumann na mBan operations. A music teacher and book-keeper by profession, the British did not at first appear to take much notice of Murphy. Her home was regularly used to hide Volunteers and arms. Some of those who were killed or captured at Clonmult in February 1921 had stayed at Murphy's home in the weeks leading up to the tragedy. But No. 21 Bishop Street, was not the only house on the street to have had an attachment to the Republican struggle.

The street in fact was home to quite a few members of 'A' Company and also had one or two discrete sympathisers in its midst. One such house was still occupied by an old lady in 1969 when the war re-erupted in the north. This writer was reliably informed that at least two firearms were made available to the Official IRA in Cobh from this source. In 1998, I was contacted by a man who then resided at rented accommodation at 19 Bishop Street. The man told me that while he was looking out from his back window the previous day; his attention was drawn to a number of Gardaí and soldiers swarming around the back garden of a neighbouring house. On closer examination of the situation, the man then saw a number of soldiers carry what looked like a long box through the gardens and onto the street out front, before placing it securely in an armed vehicle.

From such an account, it sounded like a number of old weapons, probably old Lee-Enfield rifles had been left buried in the backyard of the premises for many decades, and this certainly made sense to me and would not have surprised anyone who would have been aware of the history of the location. The man, who witnessed and reported this incident to me, probably did so believing what he had seen was the uncovering of a modern IRA arms dump. However, when I spoke with a retired Garda who had been present on that day, some years later, he had a totally different explanation for what had gone down that day. The first part of what he told me, I already knew, that building contractors digging a foundation had uncovered a suspicious looking box and reported it to the Gardaí. This I was told coincided with a complaint that was made by another man who had not long before had two shotguns stolen from his home in the town. The man was fairly sure he knew who had taken the firearms and suspected they were buried close to where the suspect lived at Bishop Street. When the Gardaí received the second call from the building contractors, they immediately acted and found the stolen shotguns buried in the garden.

There is much about this second explanation however, that doesn't quite add up. For a start, the suspect lived at least three doors up the street from where the box was located. Why would he bury stolen shotguns in a neighbouring garden where he knew there was building works being carried out? Secondly, if the Gardaí knew they were dealing merely with the actions of a common petty criminal, why all the cloak and dagger activity and why was the army brought in? It is quite probable in my view, that while the Gardaí and army were digging to remove the discovered box, they may have also stumbled across the missing shotguns somewhere close by.

During the height of the Tan War, 21 Bishop Street was used to prepare food parcels and messages for prisoners on Spike Island, Cork and other Gaols. The parcels mainly got to the prisoners on Spike through a sympathetic Englishman working on launches to the Island. A Republican priest by the name of Fr Fitzgerald also communicated between the prisoners and the outside. Nita Murphy and others also provided a vital link in obtaining messages from sources on the transatlantic liners that passed through the harbour. The Cobh Cumann na mBan girls, like their counterparts in the Volunteers, were also pivotal in building up the organisation in other parts of East Cork. In the early days when the organization was weak in Midleton, Cloyne and other outlying areas, the Cobh girls organised concerts and other fundraising events, firstly to help the Volunteers with finance for the purchase of weapons, and latterly to support the dependants of Republican prisoners. The make-up of Cumann na mBan personnel were just like those of their male counterparts in the IRA. Some were very talented, others were not. Some were very eager, dedicated and brave, while others preferred to play a more low-key and safer role. Some like Nita Murphy, Cathy Crowley, Eva Dinan, Ciss O'Connor, Mary O'Shea, Liz Quinn and Patty Murphy, had no problem going door to door collecting money for Republican dependents, despite being constantly harassed and arrested by the RIC. Others like Nell McCarthy and Lily Hawes played for higher stakes while working closer with local IRA members. McCarthy's home at Mount Eaton House which was used as a training camp was less than a hundred yards away from Belmont Military Hutments. The home of Lily Hawes at King's Square which was an open house to many Republicans was situated next door to Miss Kinnear's bar (later called the Welcome Inn), the local of many RIC members from the nearby Westview barracks. Volunteers James Ahern and James Glavin had visited the Hawes home on the Tuesday before they were killed at Clonmult. The late Geraldine Norris (*née* Hawes) recalled the occasion for this writer some years ago. She told me that young James Glavin was affectionately known as Fintan Lalor, because of his admiration for the nineteenth-century patriot. James Ahern also made a surprise visit to his mother at Oreila Terrace, which would be the last time they would see each other. As fate would have it, whether it was by coincidence or the result of a tip off, a Britsh raiding party pounced on the Ahern home that evening, but the fugitive had made his escape over the back wall and into St Mary's Girls' School, where he hid until it was safe to depart again.

Geraldine Hawes was a member of Cumann na gCailíní, the youth wing of Cumann na mBan, and was therefore too young to be considered a threat by the authorities, but one of the reasons why her older sister Lily ended up as the only female from Cobh to be interned, was because of the exceptionally close and dangerous role she played in the struggle with her male counterparts. It is far more likely the reason why Nell McCarthy played a low-key role within Cumann na mBan, was because she was probably instructed to do so by the local IRA leadership who didn't want to spoil access to her family home by allowing her to draw attention to herself.

When the Civil War broke out, the women of Cumann na mBan took the Republican side (they had in fact been the staunchest opponents of the treaty, having rejected it by 416 votes to 63). They continued the same kind of activities as during the Tan War and according to Seamus Fitzgerald, the Battalion Quartermaster, a small army could have been armed at one stage from what was stored in Nita Murphy's back garden. After the Free State Army had landed in Cork and Republicans began to retreat from the Great Island, the women of Cumann na mBan kept watch on the Fota Road while the Volunteers slept for their last time at their Fota House Headquarters. Nita continues with her diary of events as part of her application for a Republican pension:

> 1922 – Kept men on the run. Kept arms on my person, under my bed and out in my garden. Got American dispatches regularly which I had to get to Miss McSwiney's in Cork. That was very risky as the detectives were always around Miss McSwiney's. My house was raided many times; about 50 soldiers were on guard back and front. At 6am one winter's morning I had to travel seven miles to meet an IRA man with money. I constantly visited jails. Kept watch all night while the boys were sleeping. We stood on duty for all of one night waiting for the Staters while the boys slept in Fota. Meetings were held regularly in my house. In fact it was practically headquarters for the boys.

As the war continued, the Free State army grew increasingly impatient. They had expected the war to be over in a few months at the most, but although the IRA had been forced to abandon several strong points, they continued to wage guerrilla war against the Free State forces. The latter soon started relying more and more on the use of dirty tricks, and no exception was made for the women of Cumann na mBan (though they did not suffer the same ill-treatment as their male comrades). Nita Murphy as secretary came in for special attention in Cobh, and her house was raided frequently by Free State troops. In 1923 she often received threatening letters, and on the night of her father's funeral one of the threats was actually carried out when her house was burned down.

However, Nita was not around as she was in Carrigtwohill delivering a message, 'that night I had to travel four miles with a dispatch. I hurt my foot getting shelter for the boys. It was so dark, I missed my footing and the bone is still displaced.'[84] Any time an IRA operation was carried out in the Battalion area, the detectives would call on Nita, asking repeatedly where the Volunteers were. Their questions were always met with silence. Then as now the British and Irish police forces collaborated on 'security matters' and Nita's sister, who lived in Plymouth, was one day visited by Scotland Yard detectives because Commandant Mick Burke had called at the house some time earlier. The Yard men made it abundantly clear to Nita's sister that they knew all about her sister's activities in Ireland. Yet although the Free State forces tried very hard to break the resistance of the Cumann na mBan women (to us Nita's own words, 'in fact I was persecuted'), their efforts met with little success. Geraldine Norris later recalled how in one night in 1921, two Volunteers were staying at their home at Kings Square, while another two were sleeping at another house across the square. Suddenly, the house was alerted to loud banging on the front door.

Lily and Geraldine immediately hurried up stairs ahead of the raiding party and managed to clear all incriminating evidence by concealing the Volunteers revolvers under their skirts before the soldiers arrived in the room. The raiding party left empty handed on that occasion and also passed by the other house across the way without calling. At the time of interviewing Geraldine Norris in 1988, she also told me the then familiar TV scenes of British army and RUC saturation of Republican funerals in the North, reminded her so much of the funerals of the Clonmult boys in Cobh in 1921. The gloating presence of the Jock Highlanders all over Cnoc hill looking down on the funeral cortèges on its way to the Old Church Cemetery, attempted to not only criminalise the dead volunteers and their cause, but also anyone who dared to mourn them. As mentioned earlier in this book, Geraldine's older sister Lily was interned after it became apparent to the British that she had been working a lot closer with the Volunteers than they had earlier suspected. This came to light when they had found a nail file with her name on it among the possessions of dead Volunteer James Ahern. This soon led to her arrest and internment where she spent the following nine months in Waterford prison. She was only released in December 1921 after her superiors advised her to sign a bond and get herself out of there. Upon her return back to Cobh, the streets were lined with burning tar barrels, giving her a fitting homecoming matched by any afforded to her male comrades.

When Fianna Fáil was founded in 1926, some prominent members of Cumann na mBan like Countess Markievicz and Mary McSwiney joined, but the bulk of the organisation remained solidly behind the IRA and its activities for the next few decades. During a reorganisation of the Republican Movement in the 1970s Cumann na mBan was incorporated into the IRA on an equal footing with the male Volunteers so that Irish women could play a full and active part in defeating British imperialism and ending the occupation of the six counties.

31. Rebuilding for the Next Round

Gradually the country returned to a state of normality after the Civil War. Cosgrave felt confident that the Free State was by now well in place and by July 1924 most Republican prisoners had been released. Although it was still open season for IRA men, Sinn Féin was now reluctantly allowed to function as the political party that it was, albeit under constant surveillance.

By the end of the year Cobh was once again represented in an IRA operation, this time by Volunteer Frank Barry of Harbour Row. Like John Duhig, he was a seaman with experience of ships and navigation. In November of that year, Commandant Mick Burke was approached by Sean McBride, who inquired if he had someone reliable capable of handling a big boat, for use in a prison escape in the North. Burke assured McBride that he had just the right man for the job. Barry had already had some experience with prison escapes, having taken part in one of the Spike Island escapes three years earlier. The Cobh Volunteer was immediately sent to Dublin to familiarise himself with the proposed operation, in which an ex-Canadian ML submarine chaser was to be used, which McBride had purchased in Belfast. The boat crew for the proposed escape were McBride himself, Frank Barry, Tom Heavey and Tony Woods.

As there were still a few changes that had to be made to the boat, the crew and their vessel first stayed in the Belfast dockyard for a while, where they had a fitter helping them to carry out the works on the boat. The Volunteers had a pass for moving in and out of the docks area, and of course concealed identities. Their mission was to leave for Larne as soon as the boat was ready and collect fifty prisoners who were working on a tunnel out of the military camp there. While they were waiting, the four-man crew resided on the boat and before long the harbour police got to know the four very polite and well-behaved Irishmen, even to the extent that they would come aboard for a drink now and then. The night before the *St George* (thus named to avoid suspicion) was due to sail, the men decided to invite the superintendent and a few others onboard, much to the resentment of Frank Barry.

Although (or maybe because) Barry was a Cobhman, and should have been well used to fraternising with the enemy, he strongly disliked this sort of camaraderie and usually kept in the background. While Barry was upstairs in the boat preparing food, the other three Volunteers were below drinking with the superintendent and his men. McBride decided to call a toast for St George, probably with the next day's mission in mind, and the superintendent, impressed by McBride's sudden chivalry, responded by calling the next toast to the King. As the crew raised their glasses to the King, Frank Barry, who was still upstairs in the galley, was so appalled on hearing the toast that he dropped the tray with a clatter. However, McBride's toast didn't benefit the mission, which had to be called off shortly afterwards as the tunnel at Larne had been discovered.

32. Sinn Féin and the Republican Press

Sinn Féin in Cobh was keeping itself busy in 1924. On 2 December, Seamus Fitzgerald received notification of a meeting of the 'Comhairle na dTeachtai' due to take place on 11 December at 23 Suffolk Street Dublin (Sinn Féin TDs did not recognise the Free State Dáil, but met separately). The note also informed him that the President would preside over the meeting. Also enclosed with the letter was a cheque for £2.11.0, to cover his expenses towards a third class railway ticket, for his previous attendance at a similar meeting held in November. The letter was signed by Mary McSwiney.

Fitzgerald was also working hard locally trying to raise finance for a Republican Press project. It is not clear if this was the seed that would eventually blossom in to De Valera's and Fianna Fáil's 'Irish Press' project of some years later, or if the money collected in 1924 by Fitzgerald and Sinn Féin was held over for that purpose. On 18 December 1924, Fitzgerald issued a receipt to J. Barrett of 6 East Beach Cobh, for the sum of £1 towards the Republican Press project. On the 29 December he issued another receipt for £3 to Michael Doyle of West Beach Cobh. Others who contributed to the fund were Diarmuid O'Rahilly of Casement Square, giving £10; John Murray also of Casement Square gave £1;. Timothy Cronin of 24 Roches Row, £1; Robert Buckley 7 Harbour Hill, £5; Kathleen McCarthy of Mount Eaton House, £3; Pad Daly East Beach, £3; James Downey 2 Brighton Terrace, £1; James Long Spy Hill, £10; J. Colman, Cobh, £5. The last receipt stub with Mr Colman's name on it was numbered 5010, leaving one to assume that Seamus Fitzgerald and the local Sinn Féin organisation must had collected quite a large sum of money for the Republican Press project by that stage.

On 12 February 1925 Seamus Fitzgerald received two bills with a covering note from J.J. Healy Builders for outstanding services. The combined bills amounted to £781 for furnishings and other material issued to the Quartermaster of the 4th Battalion Irish Republican Army at Belmont Hutments in July 1922. Healy's note is as follows:

Dear Sir,
I beg to enclose herewith my bill for materials supplied to the 4th Battalion 1st Cork Brigade IRA when in occupation of Belmont Hutments and Military Hospital in July 1922. This account has not been furnished to any body except to the Q/M of the Brigade but without result. I shall therefore be obliged if you will please forward the bill to the proper quarter as I understand these accounts are now being collected with a view to payment.
Yours faithfully,
J.J. Healy

Fitzgerald found himself in the unenviable position of receiving bills from all over East Cork for services provided to the Republican Army during the Civil War, as well as election bills to Sinn Féin for the same period. One such bill was for a cow requisitioned from a farmer in the Glanmire area by 4th Battalion Volunteers in 1922. On 6 January 1928 while now a member of a new political party, Seamus Fitzgerald wrote the following letter from his business address at 74 Grand Parade, Cork:

Dear Mr Eager,
I have your note of the 4th Inst, and regret my inability to let you have a remittance before now on foot of Election Bill of 1922.

My position is that I am not a free agent in the whole matter. I have been inundated with bills from people all over the constituency for every election. The amounts due in East Cork alone would eat up my deposit, leaving Mr Kent or Mr Hunter to settle up North East Cork, and the balance divided still further afterwards. If I pay debts incurred in N. East will either of the others pay debts incurred in East Cork? I am more than anxious to settle every debt in the whole constituency, and have several times informed Mr Corry of the necessity of meetings to arrange for same in our area, and then combine with our people in N. East to finish off the matter. He has not even called to see me here since he was elected, although it was his practice to call several times every week prior to the election. He has ignored my communications. He placed me in a position of not being able to make a financial return to the Sheriff for my election, because he secured all the bills, receipts, etc there were. He similarly ignores Mr Twomey the Hon Sec of East Cork. It is imperative that I know exactly where I stand myself financially, as I have lost as much as any individual in every election. I can assure you that I mean to fix things, but want you to recognise my right to protect myself by making other responsible people do there part. I will write you next week as to the outcome of the meeting, which I now intend to demand of Mr Corry with Twomey and myself, failing which I will place the whole matter in the hands of my headquarters.

Yours Sincerely, [85]

Two things from the above letter seemed to betray the frustration from the legacy Fitzgerald then faced. Not only was he determined not to carry the burden of debt for the entire East Cork constituency for the 1922 election, especially for his former comrades who hadn't joined him in the new political departure, but it was equally clear that he wasn't going to let Martin Corry off the hook for his neglectful behaviour. The seed of division and bitterness that was sown and expressed towards Corry in the letter was one that would blight their personal and party relationships up until the time of their deaths. It was probably also true that Fitzgerald wasn't exactly over the moon that Corry was holding the Dáil seat that he believed was really his.

Two months later on 5 March 1928, Fitzgerald wrote another letter from his Cobh address at 19 East Beach, to a Mrs Ryan in relation to another outstanding bill from 1922. This particular bill appears to be for goods received by the IRA during the Civil War:

Dear Mrs Ryan,
Your husband called tonight respecting the matter of your letter to me claiming payment of a sum for goods obtained from you in 1922. I was surprised to see him, for although I admit not having replied to your letter, and feel sorry for having appeared so discourteous. I had gone to see Mr Ml. Burke that very evening I received your note, and he said not to mind replying, that he would see you or write you at once, about the matter. It seems, now, that he didn't, and as I have not seen him of late, and heard nothing further I thought the whole business was settled. I can assure you, Mrs Ryan, that I could not but feel that I should do everything to see that any rightful claim you have should be settled, and am prepared to try to do so as soon as possible. I do indeed believe that it would take a good deal to make up for all the good turns we all received at your hands. If you will let me have more definite details I will act immediately.[86]

It seems clear from the above letter, which was written in 1928, that Fitzgerald the politician had probably severed personal links to the Republican Army by then. It is also clear from the Ryan's direct contact with him, that he, as former Quartermaster of the 4th Battalion, was the person whom had requisitioned the goods from them in 1922. Whether by clear intention or not, Fitzgerald was also letting the Ryan's know that Mick Burke, who also seemed to be known to them, was very much still a significant player with the IRA and the person who was now carrying responsibility for the outstanding debt. It is not clear if the Ryan's were from Cobh or some other part of East Cork.

In several by-elections during 1924 and 1925 the Sinn Féin vote increased, bringing the total number of TDs to forty-eight. In his annual report to the party in 1925, the Director of Organisation Eamonn O'Donghaile, gave the strength of the Munster organisation as follows:

East Kerry -20 Cumainn -17 of which meet regularly.

West Kerry - Only one report of reorganising meeting in January.

North Kerry - February.

South Kerry - Notice of appointment of C. Ceantair on 1 Feb, no report received.

Cork City - Nominally 22 Cumainn under 3 sub-executives.

East Cork - 21 Cumainn - 10 meeting regularly.

Mid Cork - 20 Cumainn - 17 meeting regularly.

North Cork - 29 Cumainn - 21 meeting regularly.

North-East Cork - 1 report of reorganisation meeting held on 8 Feb.

South Cork - no definite report, organisation very unsatisfactory.

South-East Cork - 1 report of reorganising held on 1 Feb in Kinsale. Progress seems good.

West Cork - No reports. Organisation seems very unsatisfactory.

North Tipperary - 1 report.

Mid Tipperary - 3 reports - 16 Cumainn - 15 meet regularly.

East Tipperary - 2 reports - 19 Cumainn.

South Tipperary - 2 reports.

East Limerick - 1 report - nominally 39 - Org unsatisfactory.

West Limerick - 1 report - 39-5 meet regularly.

Limerick City - 1 report of reorganisation meeting on 8 January 1925.

East Clare - 1 report and number of Cumainn reports, organisation poor.

West Clare - 2 reports - 35 Cumainn -13 meet regularly.

East Waterford- no reports - recently reorganised.

West Waterford - 2 reports -32 Cumainn - 6 meet regularly.

This gave a total of 307 Cumainn throughout the province of Munster. While it was undoubtedly true that some of those Cumainn were inactive and not all registered, it nevertheless created a big improvement on the previous year, where there was a mere 148 Cumainn registered. In addition, also reported for 1924 were 132 Cumainn in Leinster, 50 Cumainn in

Connaught, while the relatively recent divided and partitioned Province of Ulster had a mere 27 Cumainn registered. The same report also noted that Scotland had 18 registered Cumainn while England had 6.

A notice sent to all Comhairle Ceanntair Secretaries (constituency area secretaries) from Sinn Féin Head Office on 8 May 1925, stated that the Standing Committee had given serious consideration to the question of large amounts of outstanding debts which was hampering progress in almost every constituency.

It advised all areas to hold Constituency meetings to estimate the total debts due in the area. To devise and consider the best means of raising funds in order to liquidate the debts. It also gave some advice on how finances should be spent, i.e. no funds should be spent on large engagements such as building of halls or memorials, until debts are paid and working funds created. It also advised that any debts predating the period of the Treaty, should not be considered for payment unless those pre-treaty Sinn Féin funds were made available by local treasurers and some of the Officer Board of the Standing Committee who accepted the Treaty.

With only ten active Cumainn in the East Cork area, it was easy to see why Seamus Fitzgerald and other Sinn Féin election candidates were coming under serious pressure to settle campaign debts, even after some of them had left Sinn Féin to join Fianna Fáil. But while Sinn Féin may have had a temporary bounce in its electoral step in 1924-25, the IRA on the other hand, distanced itself from politics. At an Army convention held in November 1925, a resolution was accepted to withdraw allegiance from the second Dáil. The resolution had been proposed by Peadar O'Donnell, who felt that there was no longer a place for the 'theorists' of the second Dáil and that the IRA should involve itself in the lives and present-day struggles of the Irish people. There had been talk within the Republican Movement about entering the Free State Dáil, a thing that was felt by many IRA men to be totally at odds with their principles. Mick Murphy, O.C. Cork No. 1 Brigade, made an emotional appeal to support O'Donnell's motion, to save the IRA from the jaws of Leinster House. The dispute about whether the policy of abstentionism should be dropped or not continued within the Republican Movement.

In 1926 De Valera proposed that Sinn Féin should enter the Dáil once the oath had been removed. However, many Republicans felt that to do so, oath or no oath would dishonour the ideal of the Republic proclaimed at Easter 1916 and De Valera's proposals were rejected, his most stubborn opponents being the women of Cumann na mBan. De Valera consequently resigned as President of Sinn Féin in March and set about organising his own party, Fianna Fáil. De Valera explained to everyone willing to listen, would only enter the Free State Dáil once the oath of allegiance to the

Mick Burke with bike, reorganising the Volunteers.

British Crown had been removed. Only a year later, following the June (1927) General Election, all elected Fianna Fáil TDs, including De Valera, took the oath and entered the Dáil. Although he insisted that he was not taking the oath but merely putting his signature in a book, De Valera chose to ignore the fact that the only physical requirement for taking the oath was the signing of the book.

While De Valera failed to bring the majority of Sinn Féiners along with him, he succeeded in attracting many Republicans who were or had previously been TDs. But more importantly, for the future of De Valera's new party, he had accurately judged the mood of the Irish people. Now that the killing of the Civil War was over, people were prepared to vote for a party that would actively campaign to unite the nation through parliament. The Free State Cumann na Gaedheal Party had clearly failed on that account. While Sinn Féin was saying the right things and meant well, they were never going to deliver on their policies while they continued to boycott the State Parliament, so when Fianna Fáil arrived on the scene, it seemed to be offering what people were looking for. For many others, particularly many former Republicans and their families who had suffered at the hands of the brutal Free Staters, they saw the opportunity to enter Leinster House as a means to re-fight the Civil War by other means. Prominent Republicans from all over the state began organising rallies to win support for the new party.

In Cork, Seamus Fitzgerald was to the fore among those in winning people over to Fianna Fáil. On 31 May a public meeting was called at the Coliseum in the City where the party leader De Valera was present as the main speaker. Presiding over proceedings Seamus Fitzgerald spoke:

The purpose of the meeting is to put before the people of Cork the aims and objectives of the new organisation, Fianna Fáil, which is a purely Republican Organisation, and which aims at uniting the people of Ireland for the purpose of restoring the republic as a functional State as it was prior to 1922.[87]

As a Republican on that platform, Fitzgerald said he was one who believed that Ireland was entitled to be completely free, nationally, politically and economically, of the interference of any other country, and as one who gave allegiance to the only Sovereign Irish Assembly that functioned in this country, the assembly of the Second Dáil Éireann – an assembly still undissolved which was holding a certain a certain *de jure* position of authority which they would safeguard as much as possible until that authority could be handed over to a worthy successor. The aim of Fianna Fáil was to create such a position that such a worthy successor could be brought into being as speedily as possible. He said it might be said that this was the same as Sinn Féin Policy. It was and could be so. The Sinn Féin organisation had not adopted it officially, but the majority of its members had adopted it and had banded themselves together in the new organisation to prosecute its aims and objectives to fruition.

1926 was not only the year when De Valera finally packed his bags and left Sinn Féin, but also when Mick Burke got up on his bike to blow some new life into the Republican struggle. Mick felt that there had been enough lying around and that something had to be done to change the situation. One summer evening he began visiting some old friends and comrades-in-arms. He soon discovered that those who had not emigrated and refused to be sucked into the Free State machinery had been waiting for someone to call on them to resume the struggle, and before long he had most of Munster organised and on its feet again. Tom Kelleher, who had been a commandant with Tom Barry's famous flying column, later recalled how Mick was the first person to call on him after the Civil War to reorganise the IRA. Meanwhile there had been a considerable change of tone in the Cobh UDC. The position of chairman from 1924 to 1928 was held by former Sinn Féiner and old political rival to Seamus Fitzgerald, Michael Hennessy. There appeared to be an easing of attitudes towards the Free State in the town; the economy of the country had improved slightly and most people, including the new Council, just wanted to forget about the past, the North and the fact that Cobh had ever had a Republican-dominated Council.

The British military stationed on Spike Island were a lucrative source of business and a contract to supply them with groceries and goods was considered by the local traders to be, if not an honour, then at least a fast way of earning some good money. Within five years of the Civil War, the Council had begun to lose its bite on the national question. As elsewhere in the country, Fianna Fáil gained influence by styling itself as the 'respectable Republicans', as opposed to the 'unprincipled' Free Staters of Cumann na Gaedheal and the and the 'unruly' Republicans of Sinn Féin.

However, few in Fianna Fáil saw any contradiction in taking seats in the Free State parliament while at the same time using the names and traditions of the men and women who had fought from 1916 onwards. While being despised and castigated by many of their former comrades in the IRA and Sinn Féin for operating with this new diluted brand of Republicanism, the Fianna Fáilers pushed ahead with their plans to achieve their goals. This new approach was best demonstrated on Friday 15 July 1927 when the Fianna Fáil members of Cobh UDC joined their old Civil War enemies in sending a vote of sympathy to the family of the Justice Minister, Kevin O'Higgins, who had been executed by the IRA.

There had been no mention or acknowledgement of the fact that O'Higgins had been responsible for the executions of many of their former colleagues (many of whom were prisoners) including Rory O'Connor who had been his highly praised secretary and even the best man at O'Higgins' wedding. The Cosgrave government reacted to the shooting of O'Higgins by introducing military courts which sentenced to death or imprisoned for life anyone caught in possession of a gun. The members of Cobh UDC remained silent on the issue. However, three days earlier on the 12 July, an irate Seamus Fitzgerald found himself in dispute with the Editor of the *Cork Examiner* over its biased reporting of his comments at a Harbour Commissioners meeting the day before:

Sir, Your leading article of Yesterday's date contains a most insidious attack on those who do not see eye to eye with you politically. I was quite content to ignore it, but your report of my remarks at yesterday's meeting of the Harbour Commissioners seems to me so unfair, considering the same leading article, that I ask you to append to this letter in the next issue of your paper the full text of my remarks. It will show, in addition, that while associating myself with the vote of sympathy to Mr O'Higgin's wife and family, I could not but refer to the National position as I see it, and the execution of Mellows and his comrades. I gave your reporter a typewritten copy of my remarks.

The remarks referred to are as follows:

In associating myself with the vote of sympathy I have to say that few of you know Mr O'Higgins as I did. In the struggle in 1920 and 1921 I was associated with him and I sat on committees with him, and a crossfire of words often passed between us. At that early period I formed a very high opinion of his forcefulness and great intellect. I disagreed with him on the issue of the Treaty, conscientiously, as I believe, he disagreed conscientiously with me. I will remember his attitude at that time. It is not for me to asperse his motives. I looked upon him as a great Irishman according to his lights. He was a political opponent of mine who did put the Treaty at its face value only. He stood by the Treaty, realising its limitations. I could not stand with him in the execution of Liam Mellows and his three comrades; I could never reconcile my conscience with such an act. I do not stand for the act of assassination of yesterday; I could not ever reconcile my conscience with it. Irishmen are not given to such a policy, no matter what the Press may say, and such and such acts do not inspire fear in the public; they speak out their minds as we do here today. This assassination may have bad effects for the country. I hope not, but if it does it will be our common duty to minimise them. We can all work together if each one is allowed to serve his country according to his lights. The wife and relatives of Mr O'Higgins have my sincere sympathy in the appalling blow that has fallen on them.[88]

As the months passed by political harassment of Republicans increased, leading Fitzgerald and his Fianna Fáil colleagues to challenge the Gardaí and government openly. A council meeting held on 9 November heard

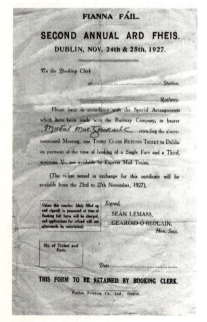

A 1927 travel voucher belonging to Seamus Fitzgerald, for the Fianna Fáil Ard Fheis.

some vocal protests by Fianna Fáil members over raids on Republican homes in the town. Cllr J. O'Connor said that the townspeople were being persecuted day after day and that the council, as a representative body, should protest. He pointed out that councils elsewhere had protested because the people were not criminals. Seamus Fitzgerald, once again Chairman of the Council, said that there was no use in protesting because the raids were of a political nature and the majority of people knew this. Cllr Downey agreed with the Chairman, saying that the authorities were working in the wrong direction. He added that they should be congratulated on their stupidity. The fact that Fianna Fáil protested against the raids is quite noteworthy if one takes into account that only a few years later the party enthusiastically took up where Fine Gael had left off, coming down on Republicans in a way that would have made Lloyd George look like a human-rights campaigner.

33. The Poppy Day Affair

On the 10 November 1928 (the eve of Poppy Day and the tenth anniversary of the ending of the First World War) Mick Burke and Mick Fitzgerald, the younger brother of Seamus, were on their way to a battalion meeting in Midleton. As the two men were cycling through Carrigtwohill they noticed a couple of men leaning against a wall, one pointing in their direction. As Burke and Fitzgerald were well-known Republicans, they were used to being the topic of conversation and thought nothing more of it. The next morning they heard about a raid on a house near Carrigtwohill the previous night where a quantity of poppies, the fundraising emblem of the British Legion of War Veterans was stolen along with money and other goods. They then remembered the suspicious demeanour of the men they had seen lounging about earlier. Later that day, on the 11 November, Mick Fitzgerald was visited and ordered to report to the Cobh Garda Barracks at Westbourne Place by Detective Breen. Breen interrogated Fitzgerald for some hours before Superintendent O'Driscoll took over the questioning. Fitzgerald however, refused to answer the questions of his interrogators, believing his presence in the barracks was nothing more than the continuation of the campaign of political harassment that had plagued the town for months.

After he had agreed to make himself available at the barracks for further questioning the next day if required, he was released to his home. He was not contacted the next day, nor the next, but two weeks later on Christmas Eve, he and Mick Burke were arrested in the town at midday. They were immediately brought before Peace Commissioner William Murphy of Cobh, who at the request of Superintendent Collins remanded them in custody to the County Jail, for a subsequent trial. Three days later, at Cobh District Court, the two men were brought before Justice Patrick O'Sullivan. The men were charged with having on the 9 November 1928, at Greenville, Carrigtwohill, with two others, conspired while armed with revolvers, to assault Thomas Barry by presenting revolvers at him. They were further charged with stealing from Mr Barry a Woolsey motor car valued at £300; a Glick portable typewriter, valued at £15; a double-barrelled shotgun, valued £5, and a collection box containing 28 shillings, belonging to the Earl Haig Poppy Emblem Fund.

The third charge was having been in possession of firearms without the necessary certificates. Detective Officer Breen tendered formal evidence of their arrest. The two men were remanded to the Midleton District Court on the 3 January after bail was refused. It was not clear at that point if the Garda authorities really believed that Burke and Fitzgerald were responsible for the Carrigtwohill raid, or if they were just using Fitzgerald's connection to Burke to take one or both of them out of circulation, but it was clear that many in Cobh believed the whole episode was a set up and the culmination of months of political harassment by the police. Whatever the truth may have been, the Garda authorities were soon to learn that they too had questions to answer, after UDC Chairman and brother of Mick Fitzgerald demanded a meeting with Superintendent O'Driscoll. The meeting which happened while the two accused were on remand took place at Union Quay Barracks in Cork. Seamus Fitzgerald immediately challenged O'Driscoll for failing to take any steps to ascertain from his brother's friends and family his whereabouts on the night in question. The Superintendent immediately took umbrage and said he refused to be told his duties by anyone. Fitzgerald then reminded the Superintendent that his brother held himself in readiness ever since the occasion of his first interrogation to be further questioned, always being available at his home in Cobh, and that his arrest and the arrest of Michael Burke on Christmas Eve was unpardonable. Superintendent O'Driscoll then replied that while he knew Michael Fitzgerald was always available, such would not be the case with Michael Burke. This was probably the first hint given, that Burke had been the real target of the Gardaí.

Shortly afterwards, Seamus Fitzgerald made contact with a number of prominent Cork people who agreed to offer bail for the men, as the authorities for some strange reason had now agreed to accept it on the men's behalf. When however, Mr Hugo Flinn TD accompanied Seamus Fitzgerald to see the men that evening at the County Jail, Mick Fitzgerald refused to accept bail, protesting his complete innocence of the charge, and claiming his arrest was petty political persecution. He also stated that at an identification parade, both Mr and Mrs Barry failed to identify either of them as having been on the raid on their house. Prior to the trial at Midleton District Court a week later, signed statements were placed in the possession of Superintendent O'Driscoll by W. Ronan & Son, Solicitors, acting on behalf of Mick Fitzgerald's mother, setting forth her sons whereabouts during the time of the raid for which he was charged, and setting forth the willingness of the signatories to satisfy the Authorities that he was in Cobh right throughout the whole period of the occurrence. Before District Justice Farrell at Midleton, the Superintendent persisted in pushing his charge against the two men on the sole evidence that they were in Carrigtwohill, the nearest village to the scene of the raid an hour before the occurrence took place, and despite the fact that a second identification parade that morning had resulted in the Barry's inability to identify the men.

During Michael Fitzgerald's cross-examination of Detective Breen, the Justice stopped the case and refused information, despite the protest of the superintendent who asked for a further remand to seek fresh evidence.

Reports of the trial didn't exactly go into the minutiae of Fitzgerald's cross-examination of Detective Breen, but it did appear the accused extracted enough background details from the Detective Garda to alarm Justice Farrell, leading him to stop the trial and throw the case out. By now, it was generally believed by most people in Cobh and around East Cork that the two men were being framed and that the two other men that Fitzgerald and Burke had earlier seen acting suspiciously in Carrigtwohill on the day of the raid were probably working at the behest of the Gardaí. It is also worth noting that on Friday 28 December, four days after the two men were arrested, and one day after they were first remanded to Cork County Jail from Midleton District Court, a photograph of Mick Burke appeared in 'Fógra Tora' a weekly internal Garda Bulletin. It noted that he was sought for the Carrigtwohill raid. His address was given as 4 Donnell Terrace Cobh; he was a Grocer's Clerk, aged thirty-five but looked thirty. He was described as 5ft 8ins, eleven stone, with blue eyes, fair hair and clean shaven. Normally has hands were in his pockets, wore soft collar and tie, brown soft felt hat, black boots.

Of all the wanted people referred to in the three page bulletin, Burke was the only that had an accompanying photograph featured. This would also add to the suspicions of those who felt that Burke was always the real target of the Gardaí, especially as there was no mention of Michael Fitzgerald being sought in the same issue of 'Fógra Tora'. After the case was thrown out of Court, Cobh UDC congratulated the men on their release. Seamus Fitzgerald, the Chairman, said that every country with full governmental institutions was desirous of having a Justice Department that would merit the respect of every citizen, but when officers acting in the name of such a Department were guilty of persecuting men under the guise of unfounded criminal charges, the country had a right to call a halt to their activities. The case also prompted the Town Chairman to keep a diary of Garda harassment of local citizens which he later passed on to Hugo Flinn TD, to take up with the Justice Department. The short file of such activities for the months January and February of 1929 was presented as follows.

Diary of Arrests, Searches, Etc, By Civic Guards and C.I.D. of Certain Cobh Citizens

Jan-Feb: Ml. Burke and Ml. Fitzgerald held up in meter-ears at various dates journeying to and from, and while in the town of Midleton, including five hold-ups on Sunday, 27 January 1929.

21 February: Liam O'Doherty, Maurice Twomey and Joe Stockdale, entered the Bus outside GPO at 7.15pm in Cobh to go to the Cork Opera House. At Dunkettle C.I.D. who seemingly motored down from Cork to intercept them, halted the Bus, asked all passengers for their names, took the three Cobh men out, and held them while the Bus proceeded to Cork. After searching them and interrogating them the C.I.D. allowed the men go. They had to walk the remaining distance of 3 miles to the Opera house.

22 Febuary: Michael Fitzgerald got on the 12.15pm General Bus at Cobh to go to Cork to report to his employers on his completion of work on which he had been engaged in Co. Waterford since 11 February, and to receive his wages and further instructions. At the 'Coliseum' corner, and before the Bus had arrived at its stopping place, two C.I.D. took him off the bus, brought him to Union Quay Barracks, and questioned him as to where he was going, and where he had been since 11 Febuary. When searched correspondence showing that he had been working in Co. Waterford was found, this he corroborated. He was then released.

23 February: Michael Burke got on the 3.15pm train at Cobh to go Cork. At the next station, Rushbrooke, a detective got on the train and on arrival at Cork Michael Burke was arrested by C.I.D. and brought to Union Quay Barracks. Here he was searched, a return bus ticket being taken from him and a photograph of himself. He was then put in a cell, uncharged, and kept there for 4 hours. He was then taken out, interrogated, refused the return of his bus ticket which he requested, also the photograph and released. Half-an-hour later, when proceeding to a restaurant to get some tea, he was again arrested by three

C.I.D., brought back to Union Quay Barracks, put in a cell, and only released at 11.25pm when it was too late to catch a train or bus to Cobh. He asked how he was to get home, and they replied that he could home the best way he could. He had to stay in Cork that night.

24 February: In the evening, as is customary with him on Sundays, Michael Fitzgerald set out in a motorcar to go to the usual Sunday night dance in Midleton, accompanied by Patrick Kilty and another friend. Mr Brierley's band, Cobh, is engaged for such dances, and the customary arrangement is that the motor car which conveys the Band to Midleton returns and in this case brought Ml. Fitzgerald and the others to Midleton. On the completion of the dance the same procedure obtains, and in this case the Band got into the motor car, to go back to Cobh, the driver intending to return to bring Fitzgerald, Kilty and their friend back later. At that point the three men were arrested and the driver warned not to return for them under any circumstances. The men were brought to Midleton Barracks and subsequently released one by one at intervals of 30 minutes. The driver of the car was seemingly afraid to return, and the men, tired of waiting, had to procure a car in the early hours of Monday morning (it was after 1am when the last man was released, and did not arrive at their homes until near 5am Michael Fitzgerald having to be up from bed again at 6.45a.m. to catch the 7.45am bus to work.

The salient feature of all those arrests is that on every occasion individuals concerned were deprived of means to get to or from their destinations or homes. None of the men have been searched or arrested while in his own town. In no case has any charge been preferred against any of the men.

On 6 May, Seamus Fitzgerald received a reply from the Department of Justice, via Hugo Flinn TD.

A Dhuine Uasail, Adverting to your letter of the 28 February last enclosing a communication received by you from Mr J. Fitzgerald, 19, East Beach, Cobh. I am directed by the Minister for Justice to state that he has made careful inquiries made concerning the arrests of Michael Fitzgerald, Michael Burke, and others and he has ascertained that there are good grounds for believing that these persons are engaged in armed and other treasonable activities against the State and against public and private security.

In these circumstances, the Garda Siochána have no alternative but to deal with them as they have been dealt with and the Minister is not prepared to interfere with the discretion of the police who have a primary duty to prevent outrages and to keep in check persons who are not prepared to abide by the laws of the country.

Mise le meas agat,

Rúnaidhe

Mick Fitzgerald, Mick Burke and Derry Kilty late 1920s.

Meanwhile in 1928, the Fianna Fáil organisation in East Cork was experiencing some organisational problems. On 22 May, Seamus Fitzgerald received a letter from Hon. Sec. Sean Lemass at Party Headquarter at Lower Abbey Street, Dublin. The letter stated that as Mr M. Twomey, the former Secretary of the East Cork Comhairle Ceantair, had moved to the city and no longer has contact with the Comhairle Ceantair; the organisation had fallen into a very weak state. Lemass said there was an urgency to get the organisation back into shape and working properly in advance of coming County Council Elections. He then asked if Fitzgerald was prepared to act provisionally as Comhairle Ceantair Secretary until a proper Comhairle Ceantair had been established, and added that they believed he was the only man available there who could make a success of the job. It was also proposed that Eamon Donnelly TD would be sent into Cork during the month of June for the purpose of co-ordinating the various constituencies for the County Council Elections.

On 5 June, Fitzgerald replied to the Head Office letter and in doing so, didn't hold back with his sharp criticisms of Martin Corry:

A Chairde,
I apologise for delay in replying to your letter to me of the 22nd. I believed that Mr Corry had had some chat with you about the matter of strengthening the

F.F. organisation in East Cork, and put off my reply from day to day thinking he would call on me at my business premises in Cork to discuss matters with him. He did not, although the press shows him to have plenty time to attend meetings and write letters on his pet aversion, namely the Cork County Council.

I can assure you that I would only be too pleased to help in reorganising East Cork, despite any inroads made on my time, which I have to devote to earning a livelihood under very difficult circumstances. It would however, be impossible for me to work with Mr Corry. Outside his attitude during the two recent elections; his having left me with no opportunity of making an Election Return of Expenses, but instead a legacy of unpaid debts; he has never made the slightest endeavour to approach me to discuss any matter concerning the F.F. organisation. Although I refrained from taking measures to justly exclude Mr Corry from the organisation, and was quite prepared to give of my very best to make the best of the situation I must now say that that time has passed. I do honestly believe that Mr Corry would prefer to work single-handed rather than with men who would place the organisation above him and themselves. I am not in a position to recommend any other name, i.e. for such an important position. Several times I wrote to Mr Corry and requested him to meet Mr M. Twomey and myself in Cork to arrange matters, and reorganising work with him from Cork City.

I would ask you to kindly inform Mr R. Brennan that I am handing in my National Press Share moneys to Mr Brady and Mr Dowdall of Cork, as I find it more convenient. I would be glad if Eamon Donnelly called on me when he comes south as I would like to have a chat with him. I have intended very much, of late, writing you a long letter giving my opinion of the F.F. position here in the South, as I have been much concerned and disgusted with events as they have panned out. Perhaps I may have to speak out some time, but I hate scandal for petty purposes, and my attitude may be greatly understood. I have no objection to having this letter read by Mr Corry.

Do chara,

Seamus Fitzgerald[89]

It was clear by this time that Fitzgerald's painful differences with Martin Corry, and to a lesser extent with the Fianna Fáil Party, was having an adverse affect on other areas of party activity, i.e. the collecting of funds for the *National Press* (later to be known as the *Irish Press* newspaper). On the 19 June 1928, Fitzgerald fulfilled his promise to Sean Lemass to send Mr Brady of Dowdall & Co., New York House, Cork, with £3.10.0 the amount of thirty-five shares for the Press Fund. In the letter, he enclosed the names of those who subscribed to the fund. Mr James Long of Spy Hill Cobh, £2.10.0. ;Patrick Collins, Belvelly Cobh, £0.10.0: and Timothy Cronin, Roches Row, £0.10.0 with an amended reminder that the latter had previously provided 10*d* for five shares. Fitzgerald also points out that he really should have collected much more, but had his time had been taken up with other matters. He said he would secure more amounts immediately after the Local Elections. Again, it is worth noting that at least two of the named subscribers to the 'Press Fund' were the same as those who contributed in 1924 while Fitzgerald was still a member of Sinn Féin, making it very probable that those in positions of control over the fund, were all followers of the De Valera/Fianna Fáil faction of Sinn Féin in 1924.

In a follow-up letter to Seamus Fitzgerald, Mr Brennan of the *Irish National Press* thanked him for the monies received and reminded him of the commitment he gave Mr Brady to collect more funds immediately after the Local Elections. He then asked, 'I wonder what am I to do about East Cork generally?' – a reference to the appalling state of affairs there. 'So far I received only eight per cent of the quota from the area, which is miserable. It is the lowest on the list for all the Constituencies in Ireland. The fact of the matter is that the Project is now being held up because half a dozen areas will not get in the work, and it is hard lines on poor areas like Kerry, Mayo, Monaghan, etc., which long ago put up their quota.'

Brennan then went on to say something which indicated the concerns that Fitzgerald had expressed about Martin Corry were not exaggerated or biased, 'During the past couple of weeks, North Cork has increased its percentage of quota collected from 10 to 50% simply because Dan Corkery TD has gone out after the money, and we could do the same in East Cork if the TDs did their work. I have however, lost all hope that Corry will do anything. I think Mr Kent is willing enough, but he does not seem able to lift the subscriptions. Can you suggest anything that could be done?'[90]

Gun Running
Prison for Irishmen Found with Thirty-Five Revolvers.
Sensational Record
Sinn Féiner Who Organised Several Ambushes

The above headline is what the people of London awoke to one morning in March 1928, after Mick Burke was sentenced to three months imprisonment for gun running with two other Irishmen in the city. It showed that the London Metropolitan Police had far more luck than the Garda Siochána in getting to grips with catching Burke involved in an actual crime, rather than having to invent one. It must have also been a source of great annoyance to those of the Irish authorities watching the case, that the three Irish Republicans received a mere three-month sentence for the gunrunning offence. Along with Burke at Marlborough Street

Police Court, were twenty-four-year-old Laurence Joseph Godfrey, a tailor, of Goodge Street, West London, and twenty-nine year old Michael O'Flanagan, a labourer of King's Cross.

The court was told that the men were apprehended in Goodge Street in possession of thirty-five revolvers wrapped in separate parcels, without the necessary certificates, and that Burke had refused to give his name initially. Detective Inspector Clancy said that when he approached the men and asked them what the parcels contained, none of the men made a reply, and as they made an endeavour to run away, they were taken into custody. A Mr Knight appeared for the prosecution and O'Flanagan and Godfrey were defended by Mr Edmund O'Connor. O'Connor told the court that as far as his two clients were concerned, they had pleaded guilty, that he didn't represent the other defendant but understood he (Burke) too had pleaded guilty. Mr Knight said that Burke and O'Flanagan were each found with a parcel of ten revolvers. Godfrey didn't have anything but at his premises another fourteen revolvers were found. Burke had £20 and 6d in his pockets when he was arrested. 'My point is that none of these men has offered any information as to where they got them or what they intend to use them for' said Mr Knight. 'One can only infer that they procured them for an unlawful purpose, and that was as serious as it can be under this section.'[94] Detective Inspector Clancy said that Burke was a native of Queenstown, Co. Cork and that he was thirty years of age and that since the establishment of the Irish Free State Burke has organised several ambushes. He was arrested in September 1922, but escaped from custody shortly afterwards. He was again arrested in March 1923 under the Public Safety Act (Internment) and classed as dangerous. At this time he held the rank of Battalion O.C. in the Irregular forces.

He was released in 1924 under the general amnesty. Since then he has taken a leading role in the IRA organisation in Cork, and although arrested on several occasions by the Free State police it was not possible to charge him with any specific offence.

He first came to the notice of the Metropolitan Police on 29 February 1928, when he attended a Sinn Féin Club in the Peckham district. It was ascertained that he was passing under the name of Smith, and made the pretence that he was in London seeking employment, 'His family is highly respectable, and undoubtedly unaware of Burke's revolutionary activities. Burke, Dt. Inspector Clancy said was described by the Free State authorities as an active revolutionary, with a dangerously violent creed.'[92] He said that O'Flanagan was also known under the name Desmond, alias Duffy. He was a native of County Fermanagh, was a labourer, and had been in the country for the past five years, 'He is an ardent Sinn Féiner and one of the most prominent members of the Sinn Féin Club at Peckham. He has been associated with prominent Republicans in this country for some time and in January 1925, was adjutant of the border battalion of the IRA.'

'Godfrey had been in England for some years', said Clancy, who added that after leaving school he was apprenticed as a tailor for several years. Nothing was known to his prejudice, other than his close association with certain young Irishmen in London who called themselves Republicans, and who were suspected of being involved in gunrunning. Regarding Godfrey, Mr Knight asked the witness if when the detectives went to his premises he said the firearms were for other people. The witness replied positively. In reply to the Magistrate, Burke had nothing to say, but on behalf of O'Flanagan and Godfrey, Mr O'Connor said that although there was no getting away from the fact that they were found with firearm in their possession and without certificates, that was all that concerned them.

'It has been said that one of these men is an ardent Sinn Féiner. I submit that it is possible for a man to be an ardent Sinn Féiner and at the same time to be a respectable man' said, Mr O'Connor.

'Nobody can say that they had these arms for an unlawful purpose if these revolvers were found without ammunition. A man who has one revolver loaded in six chambers is much more dangerous than a man with twenty-five revolvers, and without any ammunition.' Mr O'Connor submitted that notwithstanding what Detective Clancy had said, both the men were respectable men, in respectable employment and without any previous convictions. What they were doing with the revolvers he could not suggest. [93]

The Magistrate: 'I don't agree with you.'

Then turning to the three men in the dock, Mr Cancellor said, 'Three months imprisonment with hard labour.' [94]

On the 5 March 1929, Seamus Fitzgerald found cause to write again with some hostility to his party colleague Martin Corry TD at Leinster House. The letter, which was also sent simultaneously to Sean Lemass at Party Head Office, showed how much trouble the Fianna Organisation was in East Cork, particularly in Cobh:

A Chara,

Following the last Convention held in Mallow, and presided over by E. de Valera, Esq. T.D., I had hoped that you would call to see me at my premises 74 Grand Parade, Cork, to discuss the formation of Clubs and a Comhairle Ceantair in East Cork. You did not call on one occasion, although you have been in Cork regularly at County Council meetings and have passed by my door. I am, therefore, writing you direct to Dublin, also sending Mr S. Lemass, T.D. a copy of this letter, so that both of you will receive my letters at the same time, and he will be enabled to discuss the matter with in a proper light.

I have always stated that a good club can be formed in Cobh at any time, despite the fact that their enthusiasm waned following the last election, when they were left to face numerous bills incurred by the Election Committee of the Dáil Ceantair, and were completely ignored by their representative. On Cobh will depend to a huge extent on the formation of an active Comhairle Ceantair.

I am prepared to take the necessary steps to form the club, but only on one condition, namely that you give me the letter received by you from Mr Sean Hegarty on the occasion of the recent Senate election selections. In conversation with you you repeatedly promised me that you would give this letter to me. If there is any bit of loyalty in you I should not have occasion to write you for it at all. I do not know if you say one thing to one person and another thing to another, but I trust I have made the position clear to you without further amplifying matters.

Do Chara[95]

With the onset of the world economic recession in 1929, Ireland's flimsy prosperity quickly evaporated. The country once again became little more than an exploited agricultural province of Britain, with Irish exporters dependent on the British market and the Irish economy dictated by the British one. Factories were closed, wages decreased and unemployment and emigration soared. In the wake of the worsening economic situation a certain radicalisation took place and there was a sensitive swing of the country away from the policies of Cumann na nGaedheal towards the left. In several rural areas campaigns against the payment of land annuities (the sums paid by Irish farmers to the Free State government, who in their turn passed the money on to the British government to meet the loans raised for buying out the landlords in the 1891-1909 period) were embarked upon.

It was during those years that a three-year campaign began in Cobh against one of the landlords who owned much of the property on the Great Island. The titled gentleman, Lord Rushbrooke, owned several houses and small businesses, charging high rents that enabled him to maintain his high standard of living and mini-empire. For the people in the grip of Lord Rushbrooke nothing had changed with the establishment of the Irish Free State in 1922, and against the background of an economic depression and increasing poverty in the country, it was decided to start a campaign to have the rents reduced. The campaign had the townspeople united in one force, but once again the age-old mistake was made of leaving the leadership to the propertied middleclass. Although Sinn Féin members and IRA men were increasingly taking part in land and industrial agitation, they largely remained behind the scenes, not sure about what role to assume.

Had the Republicans shared some of the leadership positions, the demands of the campaign would most likely have centred on the re-confiscation of the properties and the title to them. Such a policy would have been in accordance with the Easter Proclamation of 1916. Many in Cobh felt that now was the time, to stand up to Lord Rushbrooke and eliminate his and other titles to Irish land granted by the British government. Public opinion had fallen foul of Cosgrave, and Rushbrooke was part of the conservative elite so favoured by Cumann na nGaedheal's policies.

After a few years Rushbrooke eventually decided to reduce the rents, a decision which in fact only benefited the business class; they would be comfortable enough, as would the owners of the big houses on the Beach, Harbour Row, Harbour Hill and parts of Top of the Hill districts and Rushbrooke, all the property of His Lordship. There was not much improvement in the lot of the working classes though; especially for the families that were forced to call home to overcrowded, unsanitary slum tenements, many which stood on grounds belonging to the absentee Landlords. It would be from many of these same tenements, along the Holy Ground, Cottrell's Row, Top of the Hill, Atlantic Quay, and Harbour Row that an up and coming TD from the new Republican Party would build his base in Cobh. Through his position on the County Council, Martin Corry would lobby vigorously for a campaign of local authority house building in Cobh. Starting with the streets of Belmont and Glenanaar, the next number of decades would see hundreds of families housed in new modern estates by Cobh UDC and Cork County Council. Corry and his party would largely take the credit for this great achievement of Local Government.

One person who was certain to have borne a grudge against the old Lord Rushbrooke was Mrs Coleman, the woman who kept pigs in the Quarry near Bishop Street. After the attack on the Cameron Highlanders in the Quarry in August 1920, the Jocks looked upon many living and working in the area of Bishop Street with deep suspicion. This was to lead to Mrs Colman falling foul of the Jocks one evening. Normally the Jocks would allow the woman to break curfew in order to collect waste from her neighbours to feed her pigs.

One evening after the attack however, the morale wounded Scotsmen decided to stop her and demanded that she threw out the contents of her bucket before them. In amongst the waste scraps, the searchers found sandwiches wrapped in a tea towel with two revolvers (most likely for some Volunteer on the run). In the subsequent trial which followed, Mrs Coleman was found guilty and as a punishment, much of her property was confiscated and ended up in the Rushrooke's Estate. A number of properties on Bishop Street and Thomas Street were confiscated, as was a property at the Anchorage and a public house in Oliver Plunkett Street in Cork, which traded under the name of Murphy's. For some strange reason, the Crown never targeted the land around the Quarry which remained in Coleman's possession long after the British had departed. In 1920 however, the Crown was determined to hit Mrs Coleman where it would really hurt, but above all wanted to make an example of her for offering support to the rebels. Seventeen years after the Free State came into being; Mrs Coleman took the King of England to court in an attempt to have her properties returned to her. She may have been prompted and encouraged to take the case after the British had not long before handed back the Harbour Forts, including Spike Island, Camden and Carlisle, to Irish control. Unfortunately, Mrs Coleman lost her case, learning that the King and his subordinates had acted within the law in taking the actions they did against the plaintiff in pre-Treaty 1920.

By 1930, the new Fianna Fáil party was slowly gaining ground and steadily moving towards a position where it would take power in the state after the next general election. Despite this new energised and vibrant Republican Party, its East Cork organisation could best be described as rudderless, and without proper leadership. In spite of his open differences with Martin Corry TD, Seamus Fitzgerald was plainly making efforts to build the organisation in advance of the election. It could also be argued that he was attempting to establish himself as an additional candidate on the Fianna Fáil ticket before the election.

On 9 December, Sean Lemass wrote to Fitzgerald at his Bellavista home in Cobh. He informed him that he was forbidden by party rules from supplying him with the names of Cumainn Secretaries, only an Officer of the Organisation was entitled to such information. It would appear from such a remark, that Fitzgerald and the Cobh Cumann was not a properly registered and a functioning arm of the organisation at that time. He was also informed that no speaker will be accompanying the Chief (Dev) to Cork for a planned trip and therefore it would not be possible to arrange a meeting for Cobh at this time. Lemass further informed him that provisional arrangements were being made for a public meeting in the New Year where he would be present to address it. He said they would love to see a Cumann established in Cobh at once but in a manner that would not cause disharmony with the other Units in East Cork. This could have been construed as meaning Cobh had been behind some of the problems experienced in East Cork. Noting that the East Cork Comhairle Ceantair was not functioning properly and without an organiser, Lemass then boldly suggested that Mr Corry should be asked to participate in any action taken for that purpose, clearly siding with the local TD in preference to Fitzgerald.

The next day, 10 December, Fitzgerald replied to the Honorary Secretary of the party with a very stern letter. He stated that he had half expected the refusal of the Cumainn Secretaries names but had expected a more helpful letter. He also said he resented very much the suggestion that forming a Cumann in Cobh would have been out of harmony with other units in East Cork. He had already stated that Mr Corry would have been invited to any organisation meeting, despite the fact that he is very much responsible for the absence of a Cumann in Cobh and elsewhere. He said it was never suggested in the past that his actions might be out of harmony with the proper working of the Organisation when ever head office required him to act on their behalf. He then asked if there was any responsible officer, or Secretary, of the Organisation in East or North East Cork, to whom he could send the formal request for the organisation of Cumainn.

Not to be outdone, Lemass wrote back to Fitzgerald personally the next day. He told Fitzgerald that head office could not ignore the fact that considerable friction existed in East Cork and they had no reason to believe the causes had been removed. He said that if they were wrong about that they would be glad to hear. Holding the view that the friction centred on Cobh, they were very concerned that any reorganisation there should be well thought out beforehand so that the organisation established will be available and willing to work for the success of the selected candidates whoever they may be. To that end, he said, they had provisional arrangements made for a public meeting in Cobh on the date of the convention or subsequent to it. He said no useful purpose would be served by getting a Cumann going before it, if it had to be done all over again when the selections were known. He then told Fitzgerald that although he felt satisfied that his attitude will be correct in any eventuality, that may not apply to all the prospective members. He then again suggested to Fitzgerald that he should work with Martin Corry to strengthen the organisation.

The next day, 12 December 1931, Fitzgerald received a rushed handwritten note from someone at Leinster House, maybe De Valera. Unfortunately it is not clear who the author was but it was clear that they wished to apologise for any hurt caused to him by a previous letter:

My Dear Seamus,

I regret very much that the letter sent in reply to yours was so worded as to make it possible to suggest that you were thinking of something out of harmony with the organisation. I am quite satisfied Sean Lemass had no such intention. I would not have agreed to allow my name to be signed if I had seen it. What happened was that although it was addressed to me personally, I handed your earlier letter to Sean to deal with, as he is director of elections and the acting Secretary. I deal more with Party matters, and could not have done anything about the meetings you mentioned. I was not shown the reply to your letter. [96]

On 15 December Seamus Fitzgerald made a further reply to the honouree Secretaries. He told them they were wrong in assuming that the considerable friction which existed in East Cork centred on Cobh. He said in practically every town and village the success of present-day organisation depends chiefly on the efforts of one energetic person, and when I took merely a passive interest in the Fianna Fáil organisation for the past two years, the other supporters of Fianna Fáil in Cobh apparently did likewise. There was no Comhairle Ceanntair to send delegates to, no attempt was made at public or organising meetings, and no TD ever visited them. Cobh has thus been just passive, as, indeed, Youghal, and many other important centres appear to have been as well. Fitzgerald then informed the Secretaries that he had called a meeting for the next Sunday in Cobh Town Hall for noon for the purpose of constituting a Cumann, and making application to them for registration. He then asked that they should contact Messrs Kent and Corry about same before they would receive his letters. He also suggested that Head Office might deputise someone acting

Na Fianna at Carrignafoy around 1930. Front: Daddler Kelly, John Hegarty, Oliver Twomey, Sean Ryan, Terra Twomey, John Buckley. Back: James O'Donoghue, Charlie O'Donoghue, Sean (?), Mattie Griffin and Tommy Keating.

for the North East or Cork City Executives who might attend on their behalf. He finished by saying Cobh will act honourably by its Republican principles as it has always done.

However, a final reply from Fianna Fáil Head Office on 18 December, might have suggested to Fitzgerald that Corry had their support and was determined not to allow him to organise Cobh before the Convention, possibly out of fear that he might have had his name added to the ticket at Convention and damaging Corry's chances of re-election. The letter said that because the two TDs Kent and Corry were unable to attend the Cobh meeting on Sunday, head office was requesting that the meeting would be postponed until another date was fixed with the two Teachtaí (TDs). It also suggested 10 January as a provisional date for the Cobh meeting. It is clear from these series of letters from Head Office and Fitzgerald's stern replies that the Cobhman was outmanoeuvred in his attempts to give Cobh local representation in the Dáil again, though he wasn't quite prepared to give up the fight yet.

Realising that its grip on power was slipping, the Free State government tried to protect itself by introducing an amendment to the constitution in October 1931. A military tribunal replaced the normal courts and several organisations were proscribed, among them the IRA and Cumann na mBan. But it was too late and Cosgrave's party suffered a defeat in the 1932 election. Ironically, De Valera's new Fianna Fáil party swept to power after many members of the now proscribed IRA openly canvassed for them. Even though they were clearly acting in breach of their own Army Constitution (in supporting an election to a Free State/Partitionist Parliament), in doing so, it would appear the main motivation of the rank and file IRA Volunteer in canvassing to elect their local Fianna Fáil candidates, was to see their Free State enemies thrown out of office. In the end, it was an easy winnable Republican combination that saw the Cumann na nGaedheal/Free State party off.

Several of the government's policies had been counterproductive: the 'red scare' had been more smoke than actual fire, the suppression of the IRA now had Fianna Fáil candidates roaming the country with the all-emotive 'release the prisoners' cry and it was also Fianna Fáil who had benefited from the land annuities campaign. The IRA indeed did see Cosgrave off, but they soon learned that the devil they knew or thought they knew wasn't necessarily better. At first things looked bright. The military tribunal was suspended and the prohibition of the IRA was lifted. The oath of allegiance was also abolished and Republican prisoners were released.

In short, things looked better than they had for a long time, and the IRA stepped up recruiting. More arms were imported, many of them arriving into the country through Cobh. Slowly but surely the Republican Movement regained strength. Timmy Leahy, the nephew of Mick Leahy, remembers assembling at the bush field near Norwood/Newtown for na Fianna Éireann training around this time, and often remembered marching on later towards the railway station. In 1931 Gerry 'Daddler' Kelly was the Fianna Company bugler, while Jim Brady was the Scout Master. Kelly and Brady would later join Paddy and Seanie Walsh, Simon Donovan and others when progressing to the ranks of the IRA.

By 1939, all but Brady would end up interned in the Curragh's Tintown Camp. But not everyone who had served in na Fianna automatically moved on to join the IRA. Some opted to support the new Fianna Fáil party. One young man who would later join Fianna Fáil in Cobh was Tommy Keating. Tommy went on to become a committed party member, giving a lifetime of service to the organisation, but in the early days he would, like many others have a foot in both Republican camps. In the early 1930s when local Republicans had to play a vigilant game of cat and mouse with the Gardaí to avoid having their Easter Lily money boxes confiscated, the boys had a system where some of them would lead the Guards on a wild goose chase, thus allowing Tommy Keating to speedily drop off the box containing the collected money to an unsuspecting Mrs Kelly on her doorstep on Thomas Kent Street, where the contents would be kept in safe keeping for the Movement.

Another founder member of Fianna Fáil and former member of the Fianna in Cobh was Pat (Pakie) O'Mahony. Pakie, who went on to be elected to Cobh UDC for a record thirty-eight years, was also a founder member of the 'Erin's Own' Pipe Band which initially had more Fianna members than non-members in its ranks. The IRA began applying a policy of denying Cumann na nGaedheal speakers a hearing at meetings, thus in May, Cosgrave was prevented from speaking in Cork by the howls of IRA men in the audience, and increasingly the ACA (Army Comrades Association: an organisation of Free State Army ex-officers formed in 1931, partly in response to the several left-wing movements then on the political stage, partly to counteract the soaring popularity of the IRA) started providing bodyguards for Cumann na nGaedheal speakers. Although Cosgrave had not succeeded in getting his point across in Cork City, he had more success in Cobh in that same year. In fact, Liam Cosgrave had spoken in Cobh on several occasions already, and in 1932 he was much welcomed by Bishop Browne to the town.

The former President led a march from the Bishop's Palace to Casement Square, where he then spoke from the window of the Gardenia Bar and Guest House. The ACA and IRA also clashed over the latter's boycott policy of British goods (Bass Ale for example). By the end of 1932 there had been several street fights and small scale riots between Republicans and ACA men. In Cobh, these riots would take place in Casement or Pearse Square, where one group would organise a rally and the other would arrive to smash it with a counter one. When in January 1933 a General Election took place, called by De Valera to consolidate his position, Cumann na nGaedheal lost even more seats to Fianna Fáil.

The following month De Valera dismissed Eoin O'Duffy, the Commissioner of the Garda Siochána. O'Duffy immediately took his revenge by entering into negotiations with the ACA, who were very much anti-Fianna Fáil, and became its leader. A few months later the ACA adopted the blue shirt as its uniform and renamed itself the National Guard. The organisation had by now become more than just ultra-conservative, styling itself on the fascist movements that were blossoming throughout Europe. The fascists were given undue credit and an air of respectability by two sources; first of all there was the Catholic hierarchy who hated the IRA and anything that whiffed slightly of Republicanism (including De Valera) and were calling on young Irishmen to go out and fight with General Franco, the Spanish fascist who claimed that he was saving Catholicism by trying to topple the democratically elected socialist government. The other source was Cumann na nGaedheal, who later merged with O'Duffy's Blueshirts and unionist rancher farmers to form Fine Gael. Eoin O'Duffy became leader of the new party and in August 1932 he announced his intention to organise a fascist march on Dublin in an attempt to follow the example of Mussolini, who had seized power in Italy by marching on Rome. Fianna Fáil, wary of what the Italian fascist had achieved by his march, banned O'Duffy's march and declared the National Guard an unlawful organisation (a move that was counteracted by the Blueshirts through merging with Cosgrave's party and adopting the name of Fine Gael). The military tribunal was once again revived.

Throughout the winter of 1933-1934 the clashes between Republicans and the Blueshirts grew more violent, particularly in Co. Cork where under the leadership of Tom Barry the rank and file of the IRA threw itself enthusiastically into the struggle. This was not very surprising, with the presence in the Cork area of many of the bigger farmers who if not actively, then at least passively supported the fascist movement. By this time the Blueshirts had organised themselves in most towns in Ireland, but almost everywhere that they organised a meeting, they met with strong opposition from Republicans and violent clashes were by now commonplace. Cobh was no exception to this.

Pearse and Casement Squares were often the scenes of scuffles between the Blueshirts and the IRA after demonstration and counter-demonstration. De Valera had at this stage realised that he could hit two birds with one stone by allowing the Republicans to fight it out and eliminate the fascist threat from the Blueshirts, while at the same time expending the energy of the IRA. When he came to power in 1932 and lifted the prohibition of the IRA and released Republican prisoners, De Valera had no idea it would quickly flourish and become very popular amongst the Irish people, soon to the point where it greatly out numbered the States Irish Army. But now De Valera had a clear strategy to outflank this Republican threat to his position of power. He therefore left the IRA with a free rein to clean up the fascist problem, taking the credit himself afterwards, while at the same time cutting off potential recruits to the IRA by forming Broy's Harriers. Republicans were encouraged to join this special group of Garda Detectives led by Ned Broy, with promises of a steady income, a pension and a chance to smash the Blueshirts.

One such incident of Republicans clashing with the Blueshirts in Cobh took place at the Presentation Brothers School. A local woman who lived on the outskirts of the town was a staunch O'Duffy supporter, so much so that she could often be seen parading through town dressed in the fascist uniform and clutching a baton on a white horse. But the woman's desire to flaunt her fascist credentials didn't end with her imitation of Napoleon or Mussolini on a white horse. She also insisted on dressing up her sons in the Blueshirt uniforms and sending them to school in such attire. At first, this was seemingly tolerated by the Presentation Brothers at the school, some of whom were no doubt supporters of O'Duffy, and probably in the knowledge that such behaviour wouldn't have upset the Bishop too much. The problem began however, when the presence of the Blueshirts started to infuriate other boys at the school who were Fianna Éireann members, and their parents. While some might have seen little distinction between young fascists and young Republicans in uniform, they did see a big distinction when it was allowed to be brought into the schools. People were only too aware that there would have been uproar and maybe even expulsion if a young Fianna member showed up one day in school in a Republican uniform.

The matter came to a head one morning when at the 11.00am break in the playground, all the boys fell in military file (word had been passed around through the classes previously by na Fianna members) and marched out of the school grounds to the Top of the Hill area, where they were met by Tom Stockdale, a local Volunteer and Fianna scout leader at the time. Stockdale, along with other Republicans had ready prepared banners and flags for the occasion. The march then proceeded down to the centre of town, where by then a large number of angry parents had assembled. They too joined in on the march and rally to denounce the action of the woman and the school authorities and to ensure it wouldn't be allowed to happen again. It didn't, and apart from achieving their goal, the march was also used by local Republicans to re-assess their support in the town. Republicans fared less well on the local Council showing the non-effectiveness of Sinn Féin in Cobh at the time. In the local elections of June 1934, only one non-Fianna Fáil Republican had been elected to the UDC – Mick Fitzgerald, the brother of Seamus, made it on after standing as an Independent Republican candidate. One other former IRA Volunteer, Dermot Kilty, who had been interned and on hunger strike in Harepark with Fitzgerald, also made it on to the UDC, but as a Fianna Fáil member. Ned O'Regan, whose launch had been used in the 1921 escape from Spike Island, was also elected on as a Fianna Fáil member. When the Spanish Civil War broke out in 1936, Ned O'Regan was appointed as a naval observer by the Fianna Fáil government.

In January 1932, there was some confusing behind the scenes activity taking place within the East Cork Fianna Fáil organisation. On the 8 January, Seamus Fitzgerald received a letter from a Mr Joe Power of 29 MacCurtain Square, Fermoy. Mr Power was responding to a letter sent to him earlier by Fitzgerald which might have indicated that the former had some influence within the Fermoy organization. He said that he honestly believed a fourth candidate should be selected. He warned Fitzgerald however, that some of their supporters would be lukewarm about the prospect, given the large area that they would have to cover, and it would be a hard slog for any candidate to arouse enthusiasm. Power said he would feel more convinced if Fitzgerald would throw himself wholeheartedly into the fight, a remark which might have indicated that the Cobhman was merely putting out feelers to see what kind of support there was for a fourth candidate, but more particularly for him. Despite his own favourable support for Fitzgerald, Power told him that he wouldn't expect a lot of enthusiasm for a fourth candidate in Mitchelstown, but considering that he was based so far away in Cobh, he wouldn't anticipate any objection. Power then finished by saying that his local club in Fermoy were unanimous in their support for a fourth candidate.

It would appear that the exchange of letters between Fitzgerald and Power had followed a convention held in Fermoy which may not have made a clear decision on whether a fourth Fianna Fáil candidate should contest the forthcoming election. The following unsigned letter from Party Head Office dated 1 January 1932 appears to confirm this:

A cara dil,

When speaking to the members of the Cobh Cumann on Sunday evening, I was under the impression that there had been no meeting of the National Executive since the Fermoy Convention. But when I got home I learned that there had been a special meeting on Thursday 7th inst, and that after a very full discussion it was unanimously decided to nominate only three candidates for East Cork. I raised the matter again last night when the letter from the Cobh Cumann was read, but was informed that as the matter had been fully discussed and a decision taken it could not be raised again. I realise how disappointed the Cobh people will be especially as I left them under the impression that there would not be any difficulty about the matter. [97]

The above letter appears to have come from the hand of Sean Lemass after his promised visit to Cobh. A letter from Fitzgerald to a constituency colleague prior to the Lemass visit appears to put the picture in a clearer context:

Dear Jerry,

Many thanks for the letter, which I just have time to reply to briefly, before post goes. I believe the Nat. Executive are all wrong in deciding against the wishes of the Convention, and against the large majority of opinion in each Comhairle Ceanntair. I have been dunned from Youghal, Fermoy and Mallow C.C. areas to stand, and Cobh has me persecuted.

I believe Lemass will find a genuine demand for the 4th candidate. It will not be me however. Paddy has just been directed to take up duty for R.O.P. here in Cork, so it would be completely impossible for me to stand, or even sit if elected, as Paddy will have to leave the business almost entirely in my hands, and I can assure you that it is some business to look after.

Will write you later, at length, but I want this letter to reach you before Lemass leaves for Cobh, so that you may tell him. [98]

Whatever may have been the reason for the National Executive turning down the option of running a fourth Fianna Fáil candidate, it would appear by the ensuing results of the election, that their feet were placed more firmly on the ground than that of their East Cork party activists.

The result ensured that Patrick Murphy and Martin Corry were returned safely, receiving 5,518 and 4,939 first preference votes respectively, while William Kent lost his seat after trailing with 4,870 votes. Also losing his seat was Cobh man Michael Hennessy (Seamus Fitzgerald's old nemesis) for Cumann na nGaedhael, after he received just 2,703 votes.

Fitzgerald and the Cobh Cumann might have been correct in their expectations of Cobh turning out in big numbers to vote for Fianna Fáil in this election, but it's worth noting here that it was not a Fianna Fáil candidate that topped the poll, but an Independent candidate in the guise of a Mr Brooke Brasier. Less than a year later on 24 January, 1933, when the people of Cork East went to the polls again however, Martin Corry had taken the election by the horns and secured his place as the poll topper with 10,923 votes. This time William Kent came in second place with 7,712 votes but not as a Fianna Fáil candidate but for the National Centre Party. Patrick Murphy had also held his Fianna Fáil seat, polling 5,092 votes. It is interesting to note however, that William Broderick and Patrick Daly of Cumann na nGael (the forerunners of Fine Gael) had each managed to secure a seat from just 4,432 and 3,645 first preference votes respectively. A clear pattern which was beginning to emerge of how people were voting along party lines, was pointing towards the non-viability of the proposition of Seamus Fitzgerald and others in the local Fianna Fáil organisation, of running a fourth candidate.

If things weren't going his way in terms of making it onto the Fianna Fáil ticket for the Dáil elections, they were also turning bad for Seamus Fitzgerald on the local scene in Cobh. A number of letters between the secretary of the Cobh 'James Ahern' Fianna Fáil Cumann and Seamus Fitzgerald in June and July 1933 shows that the latter was fast losing the confidence of the local organisation. The President (chairman) of the Cobh Cumann was Sean P. Barry. The Vice-President was Dermot McGrath. The joint Treasurers were Tadgh Cronin and Eamon O'Regan, and the Secretary was Cormac Kilty. Kilty's first letter to Fitzgerald was sent to his place of business at the Grand Parade in Cork on 6 June. He informed the Councillor that his Cumann was not at all happy with the position he was adopting towards the disposal of lands at the military hutments at Belmont Cobh. It is not very clear what form Fitzgerald's role in this matter was supposed to have been as the initial hand written letter was not very legible, but presumably the councillor was being brought to account by his local party because of his position as leader of the party on the Town Council.

Cormac Kilty told Fitzgerald that his position was at odds with that of the Cumann and that they in turn had adopted a resolution seeking the mediation of Mr Finn TD to resolve the matter. There is no available evidence to show how Fitzgerald responded to this initial letter or if he responded at all, but a second letter sent to him by Cormac Kilty on 27 July might indicate that Fitzgerald had not responded positively and as such had fallen foul of his Cumann completely. Addressed to presumably his new abode at 'Villa Ronan' Cork, the short letter read as follows:

A Cara, at a meeting of the committee of the above held on Tuesday 25th inst, the following resolution was passed. Resolved – 'That owing to the action of Mr S. Fitzgerald in connection with the position of Bone-taken [*sic*] of its Cobh Military Hutments, he no longer has the confidence of the members of this Cumann. We therefore call on him to resign membership of the Cumann.' Mise le meas, Cormac Kilty. [99]

Again, it is not exactly clear what or who 'Bone' or 'Bowe' was, or whom it represented. Perhaps it was a government appointed body that was set up to decide what should become of many of the old run-down military barracks' and establishments left over from the British. One must bear in mind that Fitzgerald himself, was one of the last to vacate Belmont Hutments as it was burning in flames eleven years earlier, while Free State forces were advancing up through Cork harbour. He and other members of the Council were clearly of the view that the old burnt-out hutments were of no real benefit to the army or the community and the transfer of the land beneath it would serve the town better in some other way. Fitzgerald's own local organisation obviously felt otherwise and presumably saw the retention of a military installation in Cobh as a must for jobs and business. One can see where the local Fianna Fáil organisation was coming from when one considers that the backbone of the local economy had always come from the military and naval forces in Cobh, albeit the British forces. Despite the clear internal difficulties which the local Fianna Fáil organisation had experienced over this issue, there is no evidence to suggest it would be a long lasting one. One year later, Seamus Fitzgerald would again become Chairman on the Town Council and would retain that position until 1943 when he would again be elected to the Dáil for the Borough of Cork. Six years after the Belmont Hutments controversy in 1939, Cobh Urban District Council handed over the keys of ninety new local authority houses to ninety families who never knew what it was like to have a house of their own. It was largely due to the foresight of Seamus Fitzgerald and others when they had earlier taken the unpopular decision to take over Belmont, that these tenement families could now have their own homes. What's more, it was also due to Fitzgerald's stubborn foresight that ensured the local Fianna Fáil Party would take the lion's share of the credit for housing the ninety families.

34. The Many but Divided Strands of Republicanism

Despite the initial thaw that the arrival of the Fianna Fáil government brought about, thus allowing for a new lease of life to the IRA, Sinn Féin by the 1930s was virtually a dormant force. Its own policy of abstentionism towards Leinster House and its refusal to recognise the State had placed a straightjacket over its growth and of it having any real meaning for the people. For now at least, Fianna Fáil was offering them everything that the pre-Civil War Sinn Féin used to. The people could also see that prominent IRA volunteers were supporting Fianna Fáil and that many of its TDs and ministers were themselves former IRA men. Fianna Fáil on the other hand, while initially being quite happy to enjoy the highs of power at the expense of Sinn Féin, soon became concerned that it had unintentionally boosted the prestige of the IRA, thus leading thousands of young Irishmen to join its ranks.

The time ahead would see the Fianna Fáil government introduce many desperate and harsh measures to counter the IRA, some every bit as harsh as they had faced from the Free State government more than a decade earlier. 1934 saw a new initiative surface in an attempt to bring all the different streams of Irish Republicanism together. It was organised by mainly left-wing Republicans and Trade Unionists, some serving IRA members, some former. Its aim was to bring all the progressive forces in Ireland together North and South under one umbrella in the hope of bringing Irish unity and the principles of the First Dáil's Democratic Programme centre stage once again. This new alignment would be called the 'Republican Congress'. Invitations went out to all Republican bodies and trade unions throughout the Island. Many of the Fianna Fáil Cumainn across the state received invitations to send delegates to the Congress in September.

Among the many northern trade unionists (some from Protestant communities) who supported the Congress idea were: Mr William McMullen, Belfast; William Craig, D.C., A.E.U.; Murtagh Morgan, Belfast; J. Swindenbank, Belfast, Central E.T.U. member; John Campbell, Councillor, Belfast; John McConnell, Northern Ireland Socialist Party; Daniel Loughran, Belfast and P. Hadden, Northern Ireland Socialist Party.

From the south, the list of trade unionists supporting the Congress was enumerable. Resolutions to the proposed gathering were many and varied.

There were Anti-Fascist motions, motions supporting the Irish working classes, motions re-declaring support for the Irish Republic. There were industrial resolutions and agricultural resolutions, and on housing and on the Irish language.

Invitations to attend the Congress were sent out by its joint secretaries, Michael Price, Nora Connolly-O'Brien (daughter of James Connolly) and Frank Ryan. Among its many other sponsors were Sean McGuinness of Offaly; Maire Laverty of Belfast; Peadar O'Donnell, Donegal; George Gilmore, Dublin; Patrick Gralton, Leitrim; Seamus McCann of Derry; Patrick Lynch, Offaly; Tom Maguire, Westmeath; Brian Corrigan, Mayo; Patrick Norton, Athlone; John Joe Holy, Leitrim; Michael Feely, Roscommon; Sean Mulgrew, Mayo; Liam Kelly, Dublin; James Cahill, Galway; Peter Doolan, Offaly; Robert Emmet, Dublin, and Joseph Doyle of Dublin. Alas, nothing meaningful ever came of this once promising initiative, mainly because it was not supported by that element of Republicanism which already had a grip on power in the south and was not about to start sharing it with others. It is not clear if there was a general instruction sent out to all party members by the Fianna Fáil leadership to boycott the Congress, or if it was left to individual Cumainn to decide, but it seems the party were more than happy to let what they saw as a possible new political rival fall by the wayside.

That is not to say however, that individual members of Fianna Fáil were not interested to learn what Congress had to say or what it was trying to promote. Amongst the vast amount of papers belonging to Seamus Fitzgerald at the Cork Archive institute, is a full copy of the agenda for the Republican Congress, inclusive with all its proposed resolutions, along with a delegate form to attend. This might indicate that people like Fitzgerald in the middle leadership of Fianna Fáil, were at least tacitly interested in what Congress had to say.

But while Congress was allowed to fail on the political front, the IRA was still flourishing throughout the State. As early as 1933, people among the leadership of Fianna Fáil were trying to devise ways to counter the IRA. If they could at all neutralise this phoenix-like rival without been seen in open confrontation with the Republican Army, they could then keep their own Republican credentials intact and maintain popular support amongst the people. Before long, an internal party document offering a possible solution to the problem surfaced. Its opening paragraph read, 'Every country possesses a system of military training, voluntary or otherwise, that serves dual purpose of maintaining a trained reserve of young manhood in case of national emergency, and satisfying the country's youth in its desire for youthful organisations with military ways and uniforms.'[100] From here the idea of the Volunteer Defence Force was born. It first became known as the LDF, later the FCA and today it's known simply as the Army Reserve. In 1933 however, the Irish or Free State Army as it was better known didn't require a reserve wing, and its formation was designed only for a political purpose. The second paragraph of the Fianna Fáil document read, 'Irish youth has a strong desire for organisations with military ways, and uniforms, but these it is denied in a legitimate fashion as the State has made no provision for them, and refuses to countenance their existence.'[101] It goes on:

> The IRA is an organisation with military ways, but in addition it purports to act as an army with a definite purpose to achieve in the re-establishment of the Irish Republic as a functioning state. It is attracting to it increasing members of youthful supporters of the policy of Republicanism. It has as its command a certain supply of arms.[102]

The document also focused upon the activities of the Fascist Blueshirt Movement and noted how it too was behaving in a military fashion. It said the IRA was not prohibited by the government but the display of arms and military manoeuvres was. It said the vast majority of the IRA including its officers, were maintaining confidence in the policy of Fianna Fáil as a gradual means to the end of an Irish Republic. It said that the ACA (Blueshirts) believe the IRA intend carrying out a coup when strong enough to form a Republican Government, while the IRA believed the ACA intended carrying out a coup against themselves and the present Government when sufficiently strong.

Alternatively they seek to create such a position that the Government will be forced to prohibit them and before doing so, must of necessity prohibit the IRA also. The document also stated that the senior officership of the IRA was mainly composed of old IRA Officers. The rank and file comprise of some old IRA men and others, with Tone's gospel who hearken to the teachings of An Phoblacht. It said, recently a drive has been made to attract membership from Fianna Fáil clubs and to weaken the latter by making stringent their rule that a member of the IRA must not remain a member of Fianna Fáil at the same time. The document went on to admit that people were leaving Fianna Fáil to join the IRA and this in part was due to the inattention of TDs and the Government of their grievances. It proposed as a suggested course of action to have TDs and the Government to work more closely with the youthful members of Fianna Fáil, and the setting up of a State Volunteer Force under a council of its own officers, sanctioned by and functioning under the Minister of Defence, with a simple test declaration of allegiance to the principle of Irish Independence to be taken by all members. The Volunteer Force to work under proper Training Constitution, with no use of arms, except say, during a fortnightly period of camp training once a year. Although this would prove to be an ingenious initiative on Fianna Fáil's part to draw away recruits from the IRA, it would only take effect gradually and in the long-term. In the short-term it would have its drawbacks.

Firstly, the idea of young men being able to handle a rifle once a year at a summer camp was hardly more appealing than the offer to be able to use one in real action with a Republican army that had a definite and meaningful purpose. Secondly, by requiring new recruits to declare allegiance to the principles of Irish Independence was hardly something new or different to what was expected of IRA recruits. It must also have caused some confusion in the minds of young men who were being told the IRA was out to overthrow the state, when their own oath to the republic by its very definition was aiming to do just that and abolish the state in favour of a thirty-two-county unitary one. It must also have left them asking the question of how they were to react if by chance the two Volunteer armies ever came face to face in a confrontation. It would only be when a national emergency was called at the outbreak of the Second World War in 1939 that the LDF would come into its own. This would coincide with the IRA being rounded up and interned, while many former IRA men would offer their services to De Valera's Government for the duration of the Emergency. Only then, did the threat to the neutrality of the state by the axis and allied forces become more important than what the IRA had to offer or was hoping to achieve.

Five years earlier however, things were very different and despite being in power for two years already, Fianna Fáil wasn't feeling as confident as it might, or at least it wasn't in Cork. On 4 August, a letter of appeal was sent throughout the city to IRA Tan War veterans, appealing to them to come on board and support the party. It is clear that amongst the aims of the letter was to bring the veterans on board before they would be attracted back to the IRA. The letter which was couched in very strong Republican rhetoric called on its readers to attend a Fianna Fáil rally for the following week at Corrigan's Hotel at MacCurtain Street, and was signed by three other Tan War veterans; Tom Crofts, Seamus Fitzgerald and Seoirse Ua Buachalla. It read as follows:

A Chara, the Fianna Fáil organisation in Cork City needs an infusion of strength and thorough reorganisation, and we, the undersigned, have agreed to their request on us to help them. The first aim in the Constitution of Fianna Fáil is "To secure the Unity and Independence of Ireland as a Republic"[103] Amongst others is 'To carry out the Democratic Programme of the First Dáil.'[104] We are confident that this constitution is one that can readily be accepted by all

Republicans. Fianna Fáail has to bear the brunt of the highly organised attacks by the Blue Shirts and allied movements, and we believe the support of every loyal Republican is required by Fianna Fáil. We therefore invite you to a private meeting of old fighters in the Republican Cause to discuss the best means of helping them to bring their movement to speedy victory.[105]

It is interesting to note that the three signatories of the above letter seemed to give the impression that they were merely helping out the Fianna Fáil party, while in reality they were very much involved with the Fianna Fáil movement, Seamus Fitzgerald infact had only been elected a TD for the party two months earlier for the Borough of Cork.

In Cobh as elsewhere in 1934, the IRA and Fianna Fáil were competing hard with each other for recruits. This was a period when Seamus Fitzgerald TD, was concentrating most of his energies towards his new constituency in Cork City. The local organisation in Cobh was meanwhile kept busy working with and for their own TD Martin Corry, who was himself building an electoral empire that would last for another four decades. The IRA on the other hand was also building and training in the locality. Much of this training and range practice would take place on isolated farm land at the back of the island. This location was chosen because it was generally away from public view, it could be easily scouted and was difficult to be raided by the Gardaí. The weapons used by the local IRA were maintained and kept at number of different locations in the town. Some were hidden at a Republican pipe-band hall at Cottrell's Row near East Hill. Others were sometimes kept beneath the floorboards of a Volunteers home at the nearby Albert Terrace.

The Company Quartermaster also kept weapons at a safe house near his own home at the Old Street, while Mrs Walsh of Ticknock often allowed the IRA to use her house to store weapons. Another veteran of the Tan War, John Duhig often helped to hide weapons onboard an old disused coal hulk at French's Bay near Cuskinny. Duhig was also the caretaker at the Republican pipe-band hall at Cottrells Row. This was a period when the IRA had a flourishing youth wing (Fianna Éireann) in Cobh. The Fianna initially lost members to Fianna Fáil when the latter came on the scene, but the attraction to military ways, albeit in a scouting capacity, saw the Fianna numbers rise steadily again throughout the middle and late 1930s. One Fianna member from this period, Seanie Walsh recalled for this writer how while employed as a grocer's delivery boy to Mick Burke, he would often find himself carrying more revolvers than groceries around in his bicycle basket, to different locations in the town. By now the Garda detectives were more interested in Walsh and his family than his employer Mick Burke, who by now was married for a number of years and with a healthy grocery business in operation at a premises at East Beach, appeared to give the impression that his role in the Republican struggle was over. Burke married Angela Ahern in 1932. She was the younger sister of martyred IRA Volunteer James Ahern, who was lost at Clonmult. Although Burke was beginning to settle down to married life in the mid-1930s, he still played a limited role in local IRA affairs from behind the scenes.

Seanie Walsh recalled how on one occasion while he was passing down Midleton Street (Top of the Hill) on his bike, he noticed a local Garda eyeing him up from a street corner. Although he had a basket full of eggs on the bike, Seanie had two revolvers hidden beneath them and so began to pedal away furiously. On seeing the young lad pick up speed, the Garda waved his hand and called loudly after him to stop, but Walsh only pedalled harder and soon faded from sight at the bottom of the hill. Two days later, Seanie again encountered the same Garda in the same place but was unable to give him the slip this time as he was proceeding uphill on this occasion. The irate Garda demanded to know from Seanie why he hadn't stopped the last day he shouted after him. The young Fianna member assured the Garda that he tried to but his brakes had failed. This explanation seemed to ease the Garda's curiosity enough to send the young lad on his way without further questioning, and it was a lucky thing he did as Walsh was again carrying revolvers and ammunition in the bottom of his basket.

35. Pipe Bands in Cobh

Besides clashes between Blueshirts and Republicans, the 1930s in Cobh were marked for their disagreements between Fianna Fáil and the IRA over the town's pipe bands. Both the 'Cove Pipers Band' based at Cottrell's Row and the 'Belvelly Pipe Band' had their origins in the Republican Movement, and as that movement split from mainstream Republicanism into Fianna Fáil, some band members' allegiances changed with it. When a third pipe band arrived on the scene in the early 1930s, it mainly comprised of members of the Fianna. The young Erin's Own pipe band was trained by some of the older members of the Cove Pipers band, particularly by Tommy Murphy who was an IRA Volunteer. The band had its headquarters at an old garage near the Lake Road. Dinny Doody and Simon O'Brien were its caretakers. Although the band was non-political, it did play at Republican commemorations in Cork City and County during the mid-1930s. Other sources contradict this and say the band was firmly under the influence of the Republican Movement. Appropriately enough, the band's banner, a Tricolour with a Harp in the centre, had been

Erin's Own Pipie Band, 1933.

made aboard a British destroyer by the father of one of the band members, Bunny Howard.

One of the most memorable rallies the band played at was probably for the Cork County Cottages Society where Eamon De Valera spoke. On this occasion an old Fenian from the Tay Road, John Mellerick, marched out front and led the Cobh contingent. Seanie Walsh of Ticknock was also present on the day as a piper. Within a few short years, Seanie would find himself interned and tortured at the Curragh's Glass-House Camp. Among the long-term scars he would receive from his stay at the Curragh would be damaged hearing after having his eardrums burst. He would also see many other colleagues tortured and murdered there by De Valera's regime. He would not be released until after the 1939-45 Emergency. But as a young Fianna member in the mid 1930s, he had no idea that De Valera or his Government was going to resort to such brutality. He later said had he known back then when he played for him at the County Cottages Rally how Dev would turn out, he would have packed his bagpipes with gelignite, lit the fuse and thrown them at him. Although Seanie remained true to the Republican cause up until his death in 1989, other band members eventually went their different ways. Raymond Oakley for instance, from Bishop Street (a brother of Frank Oakley, who was a Republican internee in Mountjoy, and one of the first to join the 1923 hunger strike) later joined the British Navy, but his ship, the *Glorious* was sunk by the Germans early in the Second World War, taking its crew with it to he bottom of the sea. Another member, Dicky Homer, opted for dry land and joined the British Army. One of the band's drummers, and founding member, Pat O'Mahony, later made history by becoming the longest serving councillor in Cobh. Another remarkable man connected with the Erin's Own Pipe Band was Tommy Murphy. Tommy was a Pipe Major for the adult Cove Pipers Band. He worked for Ned Regan's coal business and used to drive the Erin's Own pipe band around East Cork for Republican commemorations during the early 1930s. Tommy was very familiar with East Cork having worked throughout the area as an IRA courier during the Tan and Civil Wars and later. That Tommy could be a persuasive man with his pipes was demonstrated by an incident which took place in the 1920s.

Following a collection made by some White Cross member for the relief of the families of Republican prisoners, it was brought to the attention of the local IRA that some money collected had not been handed over to the White Cross committee. A meeting was called, at which the guilty party was identified without any difficulty as the guilty man had been spotted living it up at the expense of the prisoners families, who hardly had bread on the table. Several suggestions were made as to how the money could be recovered and the guilty party dealt with, some drastic and none pleasant. At this point Tommy Murphy, a mild mannered and devout man, cut in and asked if he could be left to deal with the guilty party as he knew the man and knew exactly how to recover the missing money. He also gave a guarantee to the meeting that when he was finished such an occurrence would never happen in Cobh again. Nobody knew what Tommy was up to, but they knew he was a man to be trusted and so he was given the grateful job. The pipe major immediately started tracking down the lost sheep. He was soon tipped off as to which of Cobh's many bars he was drinking in. Tommy immediately set off armed with his bagpipes. Like a scene from a 'western' movie the doors of the bar swung open and there in the crowd the black sheep of the White Cross was seen lowering back his drink. Tommy immediately started up the pipes and proceeded to march inside towards the guilty party.

Others in the bar were at first unaware of what was going on and thought Tommy had come along to provide a bit of music and so began to clap. Encouraged by the warm welcome, Tommy proceeded closer to his target and parked himself alongside the guilty man's barstool. The crowd were by now beginning to wonder if maybe they were missing out on something here, or if there was some sort of message in the music. People knew that both men were connected with the Republican movement, but it nevertheless seemed strange that Tommy should circle the stool of this particular man, who obviously wasn't at all comfortable with the situation.

Soon the red-faced and embarrassed man quickly finished his drink and rushed out to another bar. But no sooner had he called for a drink in what he thought was to be blissful peace than the door swung open behind him and in marched Tommy playing another tune. This time the man didn't wait to finish his drink, but ran out and made for the safety of a bar at the far end of the town where he was sure he had given Tommy the slip.

At last he could continue his spending spree in a nice, quiet location, but only for about twenty minutes. Soon the sound of the pipes was heard in the distance, then drawing nearer, with the man's hand beginning to tremble as he tried to hold his glass. The haunting sounds were getting louder and the pressure was building up, when into the bar came none other than Tommy and his pipes. The man, who by now looked like he had seen a ghost, gave up the fight and threw all the money he had on the counter in front of Tommy before dashing out of the bar. Tommy returned the money to the White Cross committee, and later when he reported back to his O.C., he did not have explain how he retrieved the money, as by then the whole town were talking about the case, which had been Tommy's intention in the first place. The last time the Erin's Own Pipe Band played was at the festivities surrounding the takeover of the harbour forts on 11 July 1938.

The 'Cove Pipers Band' had years earlier been established with the assistance of the older Belvelly Pipe Band. The band had initially been aligned to the Republican Movement, with many of its members either being IRA Volunteers or supporters, but when the new Fianna Fáil party emerged, the bands allegiance tilted towards the fledgling Republican party. Along with the band, went control of the band hall situated at Cottrell's Row overlooking the Holy Ground. This new departure caused some difficulties and tensions between mainstream Republicans and local Fianna Fáilers, not least with the band-hall caretaker John Duhig. Duhig, a veteran of the Tan War and famous for his skippering skills during the capture of the British arms ship the *Upnor* and brought back to Ballycotton in 1922, lived next to the hall, having been given permission to do so by the IRA years earlier. The problem for him now, was that while many of the band members had now changed allegiance to De Valera's new party, he remained loyal to the IRA. At first these differences seemed minimal and were overlooked, but by 1936 they could no longer go unchallenged. This was the year when De Valera outlawed the IRA and banned mainstream Republicans from attending and commemorating the father of Irish Republicanism, Wolfe Tone, at his graveside in Bodenstown. Republicans ignored the Fianna Fáil proclamation and turned out at Bodenstown in greater numbers than in previous years. This was just one of many ploys undertaken by De Valera which would sour relations between him, his party and their former comrades.

Earlier in the year, the IRA in Cobh had learned that the local Fianna Fáil organisation was planning to upstage them by organising an alternative Easter commemoration at the Republican Plot at the Old Church Cemetery, where the bodies of Volunteers James Ahern and James Glavin lay buried. What annoyed them more than anything else was that Mick Leahy, who had returned home the previous year from the USA after an absence of thirteen years, had thrown his full weight behind Fianna Fáil and was now one of the prime movers behind the commemoration plan. The former First Cork brigade commander was clearly eyeing up a career for himself in politics and would unsuccessfully contest along with Martin Corry for Fianna Fáil, in the new three-seat Cork South-East constituency in the 1937 General Election.

For now though, Leahy and Fianna Fáil had raised the ire of the IRA with their plans to hold an alternative commemoration in Cobh. Tom Barry, who was now O.C. of Leahy's old brigade, sent Tomás MacCurtain Jnr down to Haulbowline, where Mick Leahy worked to try and talk him out of causing further confrontation. Leahy was in charge of the Fianna Fáil aligned 'Old IRA' association in Cobh, the umbrella under which the alternative commemoration was being called. To mainstream Republicans, particularly to Tom Barry, there was no such thing as an 'Old' or 'New' IRA, there was just one Republican Army of which some of its number had left to form a new political party and whom was now trying to adopt a new high moral ground by distancing itself from its former colleagues. When he came face to face with him, Tomas MacCurtain Jnr addressed Leahy as 'Commandant', an obvious sign that his old associates still maintained some degree of respect for him. The young MacCurtain asked Leahy to call off the commemoration in the interest of peace. Leahy however, was at first furious by the request that he should even be asked to reconsider, but then he began to realise that it was only for the rank he previously held in the IRA and his service to the republic, that he was now being afforded the courtesy of a visit and an opportunity to reconsider his position in advance of a showdown. He brazened it out with MacCurtain however, and insisted that the commemoration would still go ahead. MacCurtain was not about to leave Leahy off the hook though, and told him that he and anyone else who wanted to honour the memory of those IRA Volunteers in the Republican Plot, could do so by attending the Republican Army commemoration at their graveside each Easter, and reminded him that Volunteers Ahern and Glavin didn't give up their lives so that some of their colleagues would later split their movement, dilute their Republican principles and go on to disown their former comrades. He forcefully added that he was under strict orders to have the alternative commemoration called off or to prevent it from taking place. The next day, the Fianna Fáil adherents met and laid their wreaths, but at a different venue: Smalls Well (Top of the Hill area) had been selected for the occasion, about a mile away from the Republican Plot at the 'Old Church' cemetery.

Tensions remained high between local Republicans and Fianna Fáil members throughout the remainder of the year and this was mirrored in the local pipe band. When the Cove Pipers were invited to play at a Republican commemoration in West Cork, the local IRA were more than just a little annoyed. The band, which had in it many guises Old IRA and Fianna Fáil, was initially tolerated but now that these bodies were openly sneering at the IRA and trying to undermine it, they were looked upon as little more than traitors. Fianna Fáil, by now was seen by all intents and purposes as just another Free State government. Again, approaches were made to the band leaders and to Fianna Fáil, asking them to cancel their proposed trip to West Cork. The band organisers refused and insisted that they had every right to play at any event which they were invited to. Then at 9.20pm on the eve of the commemoration, three armed men marched into the band hall at Cottrell's Row where the band was in the middle of practise. One of the gunmen ordered the members up against the wall while the other two began slashing the instruments with a knife. About eight sets of pipes and drums were destroyed, while one of the gunmen sarcastically announced, 'Of course you can all still play at your commemoration tomorrow.'[106]

The bandsmen were then told not to leave the building for an hour, while the gunmen made good their escape in a car. A local IRA Volunteer from the period, Simon Donovan, told this writer many years later that the armed Volunteers took the instruments with them and dumped them at Ballyleary near the Tay Road. However, though the gunmen didn't wear masks, NO ONE was arrested following the incident, despite the fact that Gardaí had saturated the Great Island as soon as they received word of what had happened (exactly one hour later) and stopped all cars passing several traffic control points, the most important being Belvelly Bridge, leading off the island. A lot of fingers were pointed at John Duhig, the Republican caretaker, accusing him of setting up the band for the IRA raid, although it may just as well have been Jim Brady, another Volunteer who lived in the house next door to the hall at Cottrell's Row. Others within Fianna Fáil believed the real intention of the raid was the beginning of a move by the IRA to regain control of the premises, and shortly afterwards the Fianna Fáilers made their own pre-emptive strike by setting fire to the building. Fortunately, and thanks to prompt action of John Duhig, the building was saved. By the late 1930s many who had earlier supported and given Fianna

Fáil a chance to bring about the Republic their way, had completely lost faith in the constitutional party. Now that the fascist threat was a thing of the past (albeit away fighting in Spain) De Valera decided it was time to deal with that other threat to his grip on power. When the IRA subsequently executed Admiral Somerville at his home near Skibbereen on 24 March 1936, De Valera was handed on a platter the excuse he had been thirsting for.

Somerville had been the Admiral in charge of British naval forces in Cork harbour in 1922, which allegedly passed onto the Free State authorities, information regarding the whereabouts of Republican mines in the harbour. On this occasion however, that little detail was not the issue and Somerville's alleged recruiting of young Irishmen to the Royal Navy was the declared crime against him.

The action had been ordered by the O.C. of the Cork 1st, Tom Barry, and sanctioned by IRA headquarters in Dublin, but it is not clear if the actual order was given to shoot him dead or whether he merely should have received a warning. In any event the Admiral ended up with two bullets in him, one going straight through his heart, and a small card was left by the body, saying:, 'This British agent has sent 52 Irish boys to the British Navy in the last seven weeks; he will send no more.'[107]

Sean Russell, an IRA leader at the time, later commented in a *Daily Mirror* interview in August 1936, 'Admiral Somerville was recruiting for the British Navy, and we won't tolerate a foreign power recruiting for its navy or army. I plainly warn the British people not to interfere with Ireland.' [108]

The shooting caused a storm of uproar, which was further fuelled by the establishment press, who were appalled that such an eminent Englishman should have been shot dead on Irish soil. The newspapers referred to as the murder of an inoffensive old man, with one journalist, clearly shaken, reported that the white shirt-front of the deceased was coloured with a 'ghastly red stain'. All Garda barracks in County Cork were notified to keep a sharp look out on all cars, and motorists all over the county were held up and questioned, some no less than three times. A special police task force was set up and a chief superintendent was sent from Dublin in search of the culprits. However, NO ONE was ever charged with the actual murder owing to a lack of evidence.

The Dáil expressed its sympathy with the relatives of Somerville, adding that it was determined to bring those responsible for the shooting to justice. But time dragged on and while several arrests were made in Dublin and Cork during April and May, NO ONE was ever able to pinpoint the man who had fired the shots, or his accomplices in the getaway car. Among those arrested for alleged involvement were two Cobh men, Jim

Brady and Joe Stockdale then O.C. of the 4th Battalion. At the end of April some thirty-one men were picked up in Cork City and County, including Stockdale and Brady. Likewise the Free State forces also swooped down on Republican homes, searching them in the hope of finding incriminating evidence. However, one of the men wanted was not at home on the night that the Gardaí raided his house – at the time Tom Barry was in Cobh, busy organising an attack on a British destroyer in the harbour. Others arrested were Tomas MacCurtain Jnr (ironically, at the time, De Valera's government were planning to erect a monument at the City Hall of Cork in memory of MacCurtain's father) and Sean McSwiney, brother of the other martyred Lord Mayor of Cork. The prisoners were all transferred to Arbour Hill. That 'Rebel' Cork had not let its reputation slip over the years was shown by the reports carried in the newspapers, 'In the small hours of Thursday morning a state of siege outside a house in the Ballyclough district lasted nearly six hours before a member of the family was removed by the raiding police', 'Early morning workers in Mallow streets saw a motor car pass with a struggling mass of humanity inside and heard an occupant shout "Up the Republic"' (it later transpired that the man in the car had been Vice-Chairman of the GAA's North Cork Divisional Board) and 'After midnight the Gardaí made a demand for admission which was refused, a member of the household stating the hour was unreasonable.'[109]

Two of the prisoners missed the train to Dublin. The rest of the men, guarded by an escort armed with machine guns, got onto the train cheering, but not before one of them had forced his way out of the train again through a small carriage window in an attempt to escape. The *Cork Examiner* reported, 'As the train moved out from the station there were shouts from the prisoners of "Up the Republic" and all appeared to be in the best of spirits.'

Obviously Brady and Stockdale were in good company. Some of the men were released shortly afterwards, and one of them, Sean McSwiney, spoke at a meeting held in Mallow at the end of May, to protest against the arrests of Republicans that were taking place. He said he had never received such harsh treatment from the British or Cosgrave government, which were 'supposed to be worse than the present Fianna Fáil government.'

De Valera had one time told the youth to take Ireland, and the youth would take it. The movement would go on. There was no such organisation as the Old IRA, according to McSwiney, and the men who styled themselves as the Old IRA were really quitters. 'The Old IRA are forming up for the Pension Bill, but I say Republicans can't be bought.' He ended with the emotive, 'If you exercise your vote, don't vote a Fianna Fáil man. He is as bad as a Blueshirt.'[110]

The late Lord Mayor's sister Mary McSwiney, attended a meeting held in Bandon on the same day, where she ridiculed the Minister for Defence, who had sworn that he would search every house in Ireland to find Tom Barry. Also on that day a meeting was held in Cobh, at which Mick Fitzgerald, the Republican UDC councillor and brother of Seamus, presided. One of the speakers was Annie McSwiney another sister of the martyred Lord Mayor and she referred to the other late Lord Mayor of Cork, Tomás MacCurtain, who had been murdered by the RIC in 1920, when his son was only five years old. However, she said, as there was no army who would take babies, he (the son) had to wait until he reached a military age and then he joined the IRA, of which he was 'always proud to be a member'.[111] It was hard to imagine that the Corporation in Cork were erecting a bronze monument in the City Hall to the memory of MacCurtain, and the government were coming down for the opening of the hall, while at the same time they had interned his son.

A few days later the trial of several of those arrested a month previously took place. Most of the men had been charged with IRA membership and refusing to answer questions put to them by the Gardaí. During the men's appearance before the military tribunals in Dublin it became clear that many of them had been asked to account for their movements on 24 March, the day of Somerville's execution, and 26 April, when a man named Egan (a suspected informer) had been shot dead. Joe Stockdale was found not guilty of being a member of the IRA, despite when asked how he wished to plead, he said 'As a soldier of the Irish Republican Army, I deny the right of this court to try me',[112] but he was found guilty to the charge of refusing to answer questions when demanded to do so by the Gardaí. Stockdale was sentenced to three months imprisonment. A Cobh Garda explained before the tribunal how he had arrested Stockdale on 29 April at his home, and that he had found a bullet in the pocket of the man's coat. Furthermore, the Garda had found a military drill book and several letters between the mattresses of a bed occupied by the accused 's brother Tom Stockdale. Two of the letters were signed William Conroy of Carrigtwohill and Denis Conroy of Carrigtwohill,[113] and requested that the writers be transferred from the 4th to the 1st Battalion IRA. Elsewhere in the house incriminating documents had been found, one of them concerning the parts of a gun. It is not very clear why Stockdale was cleared of the IRA membership charge, or if the Gardaí were sitting on information they had on him and were under instructions to play the situation down due to fear of alienating public opinion, but whether the authorities were aware of it or not, Joe Stockdale was O.C. of the 4th Battalion at the time of his arrest, while his brother Tom was O.C. of the Cobh Company. The letters from the two Volunteer brothers from Carrigtwohill seeking transfers should have told the Gardaí that they were dealing with at least one senior IRA officer.

On Wednesday 29 April, just before midnight, the Cobh Company went into action again, this time under the command of Tom Barry. During the previous night a number of Fianna Éireann members collected a quantity of rifles from an old coal hulk which was moored at French's Bay, near Cuskinny at the eastern end of the town. The rifles were taken to the home of Seanie and Paddy Walsh at Ticknock and kept there overnight. Early the next morning, they were moved again, this time to a vantage point near Leonard's Lodge on the High Road, which overlooked the harbour. Later that night, eight Volunteers under the command of Tom Barry assembled at the prearranged point of attack. Barry, who had every confidence in the Cobh Company under its leader Tom Stockdale, was happy to allow the local Volunteers to do the direct firing with him. Other Battalion Volunteers from Midleton and Cloyne had taken up covering and scouting positions along both ends of the High Road and around the railway station below. Motor transport was also hidden close but well out of sight, for to transport the weapons and men, immediately after the operation.

When all had taken up their positions and after ammunition was distributed, an order was given by Barry to open fire on a British destroyer that was anchored in front of the town, the HMS *Tenedos*. [114] After keeping up constant fire on the ship for some time and when Barry was satisfied that the British had received sufficient notice that they were not welcome, he called a halt to the firing and ordered the volunteers to disperse and return the rifles to their dump.

Following the attack, there was renewed activity throughout the night on the part of the Gardaí and Free State troops. Within the next twenty-four hours, every square inch of the great Island was combed in search of the weapons, but the weapons were not on dry land but concealed back onboard the coal hulk at Cuskinny. The coal hulk, which in a previous life was used in penal times to imprison convicts (including some who had participated in the 1798 Rebellion), while awaiting transportation to the penal colonies, was the last place the authorities suspected of being used for rebellious purposes. At the time of the attack on HMS *Tenedos*, the hulk's prime purpose was for refuelling steamboats in the harbour. Its foreman was none other than John Duhig, and for some strange reason, he had slipped away down the Gardaí's list of Republican suspects.

In June the IRA was again declared an unlawful organisation and the annual march to Bodenstown to the grave of Wolfe Tone was banned. On the day of the commemoration, 1,000 troops and some 500 Gardaí were out in force all along the route and inside the cemetery. Trains and buses

Simon Donavan with Stockdale
brothers of the Fianna.

heading for the commemoration in Kildare were stopped. A young teen-age piper from Limerick, named Tom Conway, recalled for this writer what he experienced that day while he and his fellow pipers were travel-ling to Bodenstown. The truck on which they were travelling was stopped and the whole band was arrested and detained overnight. Tom said he couldn't sleep properly for months later after listening to the screams of grown men being tortured and beaten by the Free State army and police. One of those Tom recalled as getting a bad beating in a cell next to him was fellow Limerick man Sean Glynn. Glynn, along with other prisoners was detained and sent to Arbour Hill where he was later found hanging in his cell. Tom Conway, who later joined the Irish Naval Service and mar-ried and settled down in Cobh, told me that he could still often hear the screams of those men like they happened only yesterday.

De Valera had finally shown his true colours. While the Blueshirt/IRA struggle took itself off to Spain at the end of 1936, De Valera continued his constitutional innovations. The governor-general was removed in December of that year and in 1937 a new Constitution was enacted after being passed by referendum. The name of the Irish Free State was changed to Éire or Ireland, though in reality these were merely cosmetic changes; under the surface everything remained the same and in practice the posi-tion of the partitioned six sounties remained equally unaffected. The Catholic faith was given a special place in the new Constitution which was greatly at odds with the true principles of Republicanism.

It would appear that De Valera, who had earlier lusted after the special relationship and moral blessing with which the early Cosgrave Free State Government had received from the Catholic hierarchy, was now eager to grasp for himself. De Valera's and Fianna Fáil's brand of Republicanism was now purely aspirational, with some arguing that his new Constitution had in fact copper-fastened the status of the two partitioned states on the Island. One can only wonder what De Valera must have actually been feeling at this time. Did he for example ask himself, if he was right to have opposed the Treaty with Britain fifteen years earlier, and should there really have been a Civil War? Was his policy towards the eventual reunification of Ireland through the aspirational clauses in his new constitution, the same if not less than what Mick Collins had been offering back in 1922 through his stepping stone strategy? Collins, many historians would argue was offering much more than a fancy slogan and appeared far more serious about what his real intentions were.

One sign of how serious he had been was demonstrated by his sending weapons to northern IRA units via the Four Courts garrison, for the defence of nationalist areas under attack from Orange mobs and the sectarian RUC police force. Collins was bold enough and intelligent enough to have carried out that initiative well after the treaty had been accepted with Britain and well after the Northern State was a functioning one. It would appear he clearly understood the necessity to do so, and understood his own position of leadership as going further than addressing the needs of the people of the southern state alone. All that De Valera was now offering Nationalists, who were effectively second-class citizens in the relatively new one-party sectarian state, was a couple of clauses in the new southern constitution which in effect read as nothing more than, 'You are still part of us, but for the foreseeable future, you must remain the property of Britain. Behave yourselves and we won't forget you.'[115]

It was around this time that the IRA started preparing for a bombing campaign in England, a campaign that was to take place in 1939 and to a lesser extent in 1940. With many left-wing and progressive Republicans now away fighting fascism in Spain, the leadership of the IRA at home would soon come under the control of conservatives. This new leadership would itself gravitate towards another fascist regime in Germany when it went to war with Britain in 1939. The new Republican leaders totally underestimated their new allies, who bore little resemblance to the regime which assisted Roger Casement and the 1916 leaders twenty-three years before. The German Nazis had in fact played a big part in helping to crush the democratically elected Socialist Government in Spain, where many Irish Republicans died fighting to defend it. This obvious contradiction in positions didn't influence the conservative IRA leaders away from the Germans; again they only saw Britain's difficulty as Ireland opportunity.

Meanwhile the people of Cobh, and indeed the rest of the state, had their minds preoccupied by other things in 1938. Following talks between the British Prime Minister and De Valera, the Anglo-Irish Agreement was concluded in April of that year, granting Ireland possession of the British 'Treaty Ports'. The 1921 treaty had permitted military and naval bases to British forces in three Irish Ports, one in Cobh, and the rights to these ports were now abandoned. It was a move the British would soon regret, for when subsequently the Second World War broke out, Ireland remained neutral, with the British government desperately yearning for the Irish bases that had proved so valuable during the Great War.

From noon onwards on the 11 July, buses and trains were arriving in Cobh, and by that evening some 40,000 people had gathered at vantage points all around the harbour to witness the handing over of the forts. The town had been decorated with flags and several pipe bands made a brave attempt to be heard over the bustling crowds.

At the Deepwater Quay a guard of honour of the Free State army was lined up to await the arrival of Eamon De Valera, who was on his way to raise the tricolour over Spike Island at 8pm. At sundown, the Union Jack flag was lowered for the very last time on Spike. De Valera and his entourage which included his military top brass and some cabinet ministers also had Seamus Fitzgerald among its number as they made the journey to the island on a military launch which now flew the Irish flag. As he looked on from a distance with other Republicans, Mick Burke must have watched and remembered with some irony the last time he journeyed from the Island with a number of escaping prisoners and how he flew not the tricolour but the Union Jack from his boat mast on that day. Once there, De Valera ceremoniously hoisted the flag amidst jubilant cheers from the crowds all over the harbour. Once the ceremony had been completed, the Taoiseach then returned to Cobh, where he was reminded in a speech by Seamus Fitzgerald, the UDC Chairman that 'the unity of the entire country under the flag was the fervent wish of the people of Cobh.' [116] A copy of a welcome speech to De Valera, on headed council paper and bearing the name of Arthur J. Powell, Town Clerk (probably prepared for the Chairman in advance), gives a fair impression of the mood and atmosphere of the day:

> On behalf of the people of Cobh we extend to you a heartfelt welcome on your coming to this Cathedral Town, not as a second Westmoreland to declare open these forts in the interests of a foreign power, but to restore to them this important portion of their ancient heritage. The Flag raised by Pearse over the GPO in 1916 will today be as proudly broken by your hands, and these bold

defences, won for us by your great Statesmanship, will be a living symbol to the world of our Independence and Nationhood. The unity of our entire country under that flag is the fervent wish of the people of Cobh. May God guide you to that greater fulfilment. [117]

The local Fianna Fáil organisation also had a special four page Spike Island souvenir programme with De Valera's picture on the front printed for the occasion. There was hardly any doubt in the minds of most people but that De Valera had pulled off a master stroke in diplomacy, in having the harbour forts returned to Irish control, though some would say they're return had more to do with the weakness and incompetence of Neville Chamberlain, the British Prime Minister, than the negotiating skills of De Valera. One man who wasn't as enthusiastic in his reception of the Taoiseach was another councillor, Mick Fitzgerald, brother of Seamus. During a Council meeting held a few days before the festivities, the Republican councillor had expressed his caution of De Valera's real intentions in taking over the harbour defences. He said that he would like it to be made clear that there was nothing behind the taking over of the forts; that they were taking them completely and that there was no idea of any alliance with England. If he thought there was any such alliance or obligation he would certainly not attend the ceremony. The Chairman moved to assure his brother that there was no obligation whatsoever and that the Irish people had given a very definite answer on the matter at the recent election, to which Mick answered that the election figures did not convince him in the least, adding significantly, 'We know what happened in 1921.' [118]

Elsewhere in Cobh on the day of the takeover of the forts, another gathering was taking place. This time a public meeting was held at Clifton Place near Small's Well at Top of the Hill. A big crowd had gathered to hear Mick Leahy speak in support of De Valera's leadership in gaining possession of the forts. Fresh from his defeat at the polls the previous year, Leahy was very impressive and fired in what he had to say, leaving many to wonder why he hadn't spoken in public before now. Firing up the hundreds of gathered listeners who already were in jubilant spirits for the day that was in it, the former IRA brigade O.C. said:

there was much talk by some in England of a threat looming against peace in Europe by dark forces and that war was maybe unavoidable. Well, I would like to remind those people in England who are so partial to peace and justice that dark forces still insist in controlling a part of our country, and we too demand peace and justice. [119]

Following his speech, which was excellently delivered and reported widely in the press, many people wondered why Mick Leahy had not been elected to the Dáil at the election of the previous year. Some said it was because he had spent too much time away in America and people had forgotten who he was and the fact that he was previously the IRA's Brigade O.C. and Martin Corry's Commanding Officer. While that may have been true in part, the fact that he and Corry were competing with each other and Fine Gael and Labour in the new three seat constituency of Cork South-East, was probably his main obstacle to becoming a TD for Cobh. The election which was held on 1 July 1937 saw the previously independent (unionist) candidate Brook Brasier take the first seat for Fine Gael with 8,594 first preference votes. Martin Corry of Fianna Fáil took the second seat with 7,567 votes and Jeremiah Hurley of Labour took the third seat with 6,720 votes. William Broderick of Fine Gael with 4,818 votes and Mick Leahy (FF) with 3,315 votes were each eliminated.

Sixteen days before the next General Election of 17 June 1938, an internal party document was submitted to the Fianna Fáil South East Convention which was very critical of its sitting TD Martin Corry. This was by far the most critical attack and exposé made against Corry to date, albeit internally. As the entire document is not available in the Fitzgerald Papers at the Cork City and County Archives, it is impossible to know for certain who its authors were, but one must assume that Corry's old rival, Seamus Fitzgerald himself, had some input and, guiding hand over it, perhaps with the support of the Cobh Cumann, and even the Comhairle Ceanntair. As one line among the list of complaints below, refers to the Constituency of Cork City, it can probably by assumed also that Fitzgerald had enlisted the help of some of his old contacts in the City organisation, to help bolster their case against Corry. Some of the complaints against the TD were as follows:

1. We believe the attitude of the outgoing Deputy, for the past 12 months, should be considered before again selecting him.

2. For 4 months after the last Election he completely ignored the Organisation. The Dáil-Ceanntair Secretary resigned as a consequence.

3. Over the whole period the Dáil-Ceanntair obtained little or no assistance in its work; Comhairle Ceanntair Secs Complained of continued lack of attention, clubs became disorganised. A special Convention was ordered to be held last December, and was presided over by Mr Tom Crofts, representing Headquarters, Dublin. The delegates from the entire Constituency unanimously declared that the Deputy was ignoring them. At the Chairman's request he promised to do the organisations bidding, and the Chairman said he would report accordingly.

4. His attendances at Dáil-Ceanntair meetings, fixed to suit his convenience, were not one in four.

5. On the Dáil debate on the Anglo-Irish Agreement he uttered a statement for which the President found it necessary to apologise. The Deputy has not since offered an explanation, and the Dáil-Ceanntair has had under consideration the necessity of convening a full meeting to disassociate itself from his public utterance.

6. In general the selection once again of the Deputy would give serious dissatisfaction to your principal officers in the Constituency, and the neighbouring Constituency of Cork City, and tend to greatly reduce our strength at the polls in each of these two areas.

7. These statements are not made in the sense of any personal attack on the Deputy. It is recognised that he has given good service in many ways that may be hard to equal. It is, however, believed that he is unsuitable under present circumstances to gain us the confidence of the electorate, and the confidence of the Organisation in South-East Cork.[120]

It is clear that this critique of Corry's character failed to have the desired effect. What is not clear however, is how representative it was of the actual membership on the ground. It would appear from the recorded resignations of Secretary's in the organisation that Fitzgerald and others were not exaggerating about Corry's shortcomings. Perhaps the matter wasn't even debated at Convention and perhaps Head Office rubberstamped their popular vote catcher as they often did in the past. What we also know, is that when the votes were counted on 18 June, the final result mirrored exactly that of the previous election, With Brook Brasier topping the poll for Fine Gael, Corry again taking the second seat and Hurley taking the last one for the Labour party. One might rightly conclude that there was some merit in what Corry's critics were saying that he should have taken the lion's share of the votes for the Fianna Fáil party in the Constituency.

For all of De Valera's public posturing and great statesman-like achievements, particularly around the return of the Harbour Forts, and even in relation to the test of Irish Neutrality a couple of years later, there are some aspects to these issues which De Valera and Fianna Fáil could never afford to let the public to hear about. During a Cabinet discussion for instance, in advance of De Valera's negotiations with London over the Treaty Ports in 1938, a Northern Fianna Fáil member, Joe Connolly argued strongly that there should be no agreement on the issue of the ports without the ending of partition first. Sean Mac Entee disagreed however, and in doing so, betrayed the hollowness of Fianna Fáil's Republicanism. 'In relation to partition we have never had a policy'. he said. 'The government consistently maintained that it did not wish to coerce northern Protestants into a United Ireland, but it did nothing to win them over. With our connivance, every bigot and killjoy, ecclesiastic and lay, is doing his damnedest here to keep them out.'[121]

Later, during the Second World War while Britain faced a perilous situation and looked like invasion by Germany was imminent, Churchill through an envoy, made a number of attempts to reason with De Valera. On each occasion, the Envoy would make an offer on behalf of his government to end partition in return for the use of the Treaty Ports. On each occasion however, De Valera refused the offer.

Historians will probably speculate and debate for years to come as to why De Valera turned down these offers, and if he had missed a great opportunity. The common wisdom of those who have so far written about this relatively new information, is that De Valera didn't trust Churchill, and wasn't up for uniting the country if northern Protestants didn't want it, and therefore was probably right to have declined the two offers made to him. Perhaps that is a fair assessment of the situation, but then again maybe there is an equal and alternative view which says De Valera had indeed squandered a golden opportunity to resolve our national differences once and for all, and to improve and naturalise our relationship with our nearest neighbour across the water.

Suppose Churchill hadn't been bluffing and was prepared to hand over the six counties in return for the use of the southern ports so desperately needed against Hitler's U-Boat war in the Atlantic in 1941. Had we in the south been seen to come to Britain's aid with the use of these ports at that time, then perhaps, it wouldn't have been a great stretch of the imagination to expect northern Protestants to accept the nation they were now being asked to become a part of as a friend of Britain. Also, why was it okay for De Valera to dismiss Churchill's offer out of hand, partially because he didn't want to force Protestants into a united Ireland, yet without giving it a second thought, was prepared to condemn northern Nationalists into a sectarian State which they never wanted to be part of? Did the following forty years or so, of terrible conflict and loss of life justify De Valera's decision to stick with partition? And finally, is it not also true, now knowing what we do about the real facts surrounding De Valera's policy of neutrality, that we were never really neutral at all?

In the early 1930s while Tom Barry was in command of the Cork 1st Brigade, he had cause to work closely with the members of the Cobh Company. This was not just because the British presented themselves as an occasional target in the harbour region, but because the port was also one where weapons could be smuggled into Ireland, particularly from the USA on board the busy trans-Atlantic Liner traffic using the port. Barry would have direct control over this issue later as Chief of Staff of the IRA, but earlier on, he would also have some input, and would often show up in Cobh. Many of the weapons smuggled in at this time, used to find their way to Ireland in small quantities, mainly small Thompson machine guns and short arms, buried in people's suitcases and landed by tender at the Atlantic and the Deep Water Quays.

There was always a Garda posted at the Railway Station alongside the Deep Water Quay to monitor the comings and goings and to keep a particular eye out for noted Republican activists. One morning out of the blue, the Garda on duty at the station was stunned to see someone disembark from a train which he hadn't seen for many years. Garda O'Donovan had to take a second glance to make sure he had the right man. Tom Barry approached the gate confidently but was also taken back by who he saw behind it. When he arrived in front of the policeman the two men's eyes had locked on each other. Immediately, they both reached out to shake each others hands, before handshakes turned to hugs, not having met each other since 1921. The two chatted for nearly an hour about the old days when they soldiered with their old Flying Column. O'Donovan had completely forgotten about his post and his purpose at the station, but more importantly, he had forgotten who he had been speaking to and neglected to question Barry about the purpose of his visit to Cobh.

Within a few short years however, Barry would become public enemy number one, or at least he would in the eyes of the Fianna Fáil Government, with its Minister for Justice vowing that every house in Ireland would be searched to locate the dangerous Republican. But such animosity towards Barry would be short lived. He would later resign as Chief of Staff of the IRA while refusing to countenance its proposed bombing campaign of Britain, favouring instead, a full all-out attack to recapture the six counties. Furthermore, he would later offer his services to De Valera as an officer in the Free State army for the duration of the Emergency. Barry saw no contradiction in such a position and saw a threat to Ireland's neutrality, from either Britain or Germany as amounting to the same thing. Barry would only be one of many former IRA men who would make the same offer to De Valera, with Mick Leahy, Seamus Fitzgerald and Florrie O'Donoghue being among the others.

From his place of business, on headed Cork Harbour Commissioners paper, Fitzgerald sent a handwritten note to De Valera at Government Buildings on 1 September 1939, 'A Chara, in the present crisis, I offer you my resources and services to command as you may require them for our country's need. Le mór mhease, do chara, Seamus Fitzgerald.'[122]

Meanwhile, the IRA was also gearing up for action. At the latter end of 1938, intensive training was underway at the back of the Island in Cobh. On one particular occasion, a unit of Volunteers were engaged in target practice with rifles in what they thought was a secluded and isolated field at Ballydanielmore. After firing had been in progress for some time, two armed scouts who had been standing guard from a distance were seen approaching with a third party. The officer in charge of the training exercise immediately recognised the stranger as the owner of the farm land they were on. On seeing this, one young Volunteer panicked, threw down his rifle and ran off.

The young farmer, who himself had only recently returned from service with the British army abroad, took serious offence to the presence of the IRA being on his property and insisted they depart immediately. The training officer however, tried to reason with the man and insisted they were doing no damage to his lands and asked if he would let them stay. The infuriated farmer objected most strenuously however, and wouldn't give an inch. He again ordered the intruders to get off his land. The irritated officer relented, and ordered his Volunteers to gather up their rifles and belongings. He then turned backed to the farmer and warned him that if any of his men received a visit from the Gardaí over the matter, he would have him shot with immediate effect. Nothing further came of the incident, the farmer apparently receiving the message. The young Volunteer, who had panicked and ran off was obviously not soldier material and quickly realised so himself. Fortunately, the above incident gave him the opportunity to find out the easy way, thus sparing him the possible future ordeal of internment or worse. He did however, remain a firm Republican supporter for the remainder of his life. He was also a lover and practitioner of the Irish language, and a stalwart of the local GAA club.

Also in 1938, on the 7 February, Captain S. Lehane of the South Cork Area Volunteer Force, wrote from Collin's Barracks Cork, to the local Fianna Fáil organisation. In a patriotically worded letter, the Captain engaged in selling the new Volunteer Force to its members and asked that they would do all in their power to promote the organisation and help to find it new recruits. The letter stated that although it had made progress since it was founded four years earlier under the Fianna Fail government, it was meeting with some recruitment problems due to emigration of many young men. It said Éire was rising from her knees, and at these critical moments should look better with her Forces around her, strong and well organised, 'I would ask you therefore, to remind your members, that we should heed the wave of her summoning wand, because, we and our young Brothers and Sons, are again beginning to hear the Bugle call of Foreign Armies within our Shores.'[123]

On Saturday night 11 May 1940, Seanie Walsh was among a number of local IRA Volunteers that were deployed at Carrigaloe to cut the telephone lines linking up to Cobh. The signal to do so was the passing by of a certain car, after which they were to cut the lines twenty minutes later. In the car were a number of Brigade Volunteer officers whose mission was to blow up the Royal Yacht Club, the oldest in the sport of yachting. The target was chosen simply for its symbolic value. The building was situated near the quays and overlooked the harbour between Spike and Haulbowline islands. The very exclusive yacht club, formerly a symbol of the British presence and connection to the town, was now frequented by old unionists and those who still longed for and wished to imitate the British upper class way of life. As Seanie Walsh later said, 'they were the kind of people bitterly opposed to any Irish national aspirations'. The club building which was once visited by King George 1st, Queen Victoria and Winston Churchill, was situated about sixty yards away from the Garda station at Westbourne Place.

According to reports at the time, a car believed to be a taxi pulled up near the building and five men got out. They rang the bell at the front door of the club and when a maid opened the door, the men pushed their way past her and preceded into the club; one man was left on guard at the door. The other four volunteers went downstairs, where the staff's quarters were situated, and asked how many persons were present on the premises. As it happened there were no members in the club at the time, only the manageress and her maid, both of whom were strongly advised by the Volunteers to get out as fast as their legs would take them as they were going to blow the place up, a mistaken move one might say, as it gave the two women time to alert those outside.

Unsurprisingly, the suspicions of the Gardaí from the barracks across the way had been aroused, leading two of them to pay a visit to investigate. When one of the Garda officers decided to step into the club building, he stumbled upon the Volunteer who had been left on watch above and arrested him. The arrested Volunteer was Michael Lucey of Cork. When the same Garda was about to descend the stairs to the staff quarters, he heard footsteps. On shouting, 'Who's there?,'[124] the only answer he heard was the click of a revolver, soon followed by a bullet whizzing past him. This reality check for the Garda allowed the intruders time to gather themselves and get out. Reinforcements arrived shortly afterwards, but by then the remaining Volunteers had already made their escape through the side doors of the building. When the club was searched a little later, a landmine was found in the staff's quarters. The explosives had been placed in a cemented kettle, the fuse lit but gone out again.

Although it looked crude enough, the mine held enough explosives to blow the building to pieces. Official reports later stated that the bomb had been placed in a bucket of water and removed to the bush field (today Norwood Park), situated remotely above the town, where a ballistics expert from Dublin arrived the next day to examine the device. Crowds had gathered in the hope of seeing an explosion in the wooded Bush

Field area, but were disappointed when the army officer took the device back to Dublin with him. Some local Republicans give a slightly different account of what later happened to the bomb. They agreed that the device had failed to detonate, and this they attributed to the gelignite weeping and being unstable. The Volunteers instantly realised this when they went to place it in a room downstairs. In fact, its instability made them more anxious to flee the building than the arrival of the Gardaí. Later, from a secluded location across the street, a volunteer watched as a lone Garda was seen carrying the lethal device back across the street to his barracks.

The Volunteer broke his cover and silence and shouted after the Garda to put it down as it was unstable and could detonate at any moment. His appeal however, apparently went unheeded; he then made his own departure to safety. During the next number of days, three other men were arrested in connection with the incident. They were the Conroy brothers from Carrigtwohill, Denis and William. Daniel Bullman of Cork City was also arrested. Also a couple of days later, a local Volunteer, Simon Donovan, was visited by three Gardaí demanding that he'd account for his movements on the night of the Yacht Club raid. Donovan smiled back at the Guards and sarcastically told them, 'go away and check your prisoner log book',[125] for he had a good nights sleep in one of their master-suites (cells) that night. Simon had been the local Company Quartermaster at the time and keeper of the Cobh Company's weapons, though it's not clear if the Garda were aware of that fact when they had him in their custody. There was to be further fall out from the Yacht Club raid though. As a result of extensive searches made throughout Cobh and Cork City in the days and weeks that followed, detectives discovered a fully equipped premises for the manufacturing of grenades in the City, the largest of its kind found in Cork in years.

In April 1939 one of the largest attended and most impressive Easter Commemoration parades in the Cork area took place in Cobh, when over 3,000 people, accompanied by seven bands (among them the Cove Pipers Band) took part in a procession from the town to the Old Church Cemetery. The parade had been organised by the 'Old IRA' members of Cork No. 1 Brigade and the comrades directly honoured were the men who had fallen at Clonmult. In addition to those in the procession, hundreds of others accompanied them to the cemetery to witness the laying of wreaths by former Brigade officers and relatives. The IRA at the time seemingly had given up on its quarrel with the local Fianna Fáil/Old IRA organisation, probably having a lot more important things to attend to. It more than likely would have also instructed its Volunteers to lie low and not to bring Garda attention upon themselves. It also allowed Fianna Éireann members to attend the ceremony and to act as a guard of honour at the Republican Plot. Among those present were Seamus Fitzgerald Chairman of the UDC and Chairman of the Harbour Board, Martin Corry TD and former Volunteer officers, brigade officers Tom Crofts and Mick Leahy, and several former battalion officers. Kevin Murphy and Tom O'Shea, who had returned from the USA for the occasion, were in charge of marshalling. Seamus Fitzgerald presided at the oration ceremony. He thanked the 'Old IRA' for the honour they conferred on Cobh that day and pointed out that the town had long been in association with Republican principles. It still cherished these principles deeply, according to the UDC Chairman, and would continue to do so until Ireland was a complete and sovereign independent Republic. When the procession had returned to Cobh, an oration was delivered by Mick Leahy at Clifton Place.

The following is a newspaper report of his speech:

It was the taunt of the British that the Irish fought everybody's battle but their own, but the men whose memories they were honouring had given the lie to this because they proved they were capable of fighting their own battle when it came to the point. Cork No. 1 Brigade was known as the fighting Brigade; Irish freedom was not yet achieved and it never would be until the Six Counties of North East Ulster were united in an Irish Republic. They were at present living in an atmosphere of war hysteria: they were told that war was imminent when as a matter of fact it had been in progress for months unofficially if not officially. They were told that England was out for peace and that she was horrified by the terrible things being done to small nations in various parts of Europe. Let England prove to them in Ireland that she was in earnest, by withdrawing her soldiers from the Six Counties.

Earlier in the afternoon a wreath had also been laid at Carrigaloe Hill where Volunteer Danny O'Halloran had been killed during the Civil War. When one reads the newspaper reports of the 3,000 plus people who turned out for this parade, and the Fianna Fáil/Old IRA people who so enthusiastically organised it, one cannot but wonder where all those people were nine years later when a new and more fitting memorial stone was erected to the martyred Volunteers in the Republican plot. On that day in Easter 1948, the only prominent Republicans present from the 1939 Easter procession were Ned Butler of Belvelly and Mick Fitzgerald, the latter continuing to throw his weight behind the Republican Movement up until his death in 1986.

On 5 April 1939, a meeting was held in Cork City to establish the 'Cork Anti-Partition Council' among the delegates present were Mrs Lehenagh of the 'Old Cumann na mBan', Maighread DeBarra and Treasa Bean Ni

Bhriain of the Women's Industrial Development Association. A further meeting was called for the following week Thursday 12 April at 83 Grand Parade. The agenda circulated for that meeting included a number of points already raised by various contributors. It was signed by joint secretaries, T. Mac Thighearnain and Maighread DeBarra.

The contributors, though some were of a Fianna Fáil bent, were varied in their views as to how partition should be dismantled. Mr P. Brady for example was very blunt in his opinion that 'force was necessary to secure the six counties'.[126] He felt that economics shouldn't be allowed to cloud the issue, and stressed the necessity of putting clear-cut principles to people. He advocated complete severance from England and advised Council to Action.

Mr P.J. O'Brien in contrast, discounted the idea of force. He believed there should be concentration on constitutional and intellectual lines to direct minds of people into a desired channel, and that a militant organisation could be developed later if found necessary.

Mr Seamus Fitzgerald recommended the formation of County and Provincial Councils with a view to forming a National Council. He also believed that serious propaganda campaigns should be launched in the North and the USA. Public meetings and lectures should take place and a common line should be found along which North and South could proceed towards a new Ireland.

Mr J. Barry felt that sacrifices were necessary, and the people of the North needed to be shown that unity was of an advantage to them.

Professor J. Busteed compared the economic position in the North and South to the detriment of the latter. He recommended that a statement be secured from the Government declaring their awareness of the position and that steps were being taken to ensure that no one would suffer as a result of the inclusion of the six counties in Éire. He suggested that similar guarantees be made to manufacturers in the South. He also felt that the national question was the primary issue while the economic one was secondary.

Mr Frank Busteed suggested that Branches should be organised in every parish and the youth should join semi-military organisations to remove the border by every means possible.

Mr S. Mitchell said that talks were a complete waste of time. They should complete the organisation and tell England to get out.

Mr E. Wall called for the break of the connection with England. He said the world situation favours propaganda in England and that Radio should be used.

Mr A. Healy suggested that not enough attention was being paid to propaganda in England. He also called for the conscription of young men to be trained nationally.

Mr S. Neeson felt that no inducement will entice Orange Lodges in the North as they were being subsidised by the Tory Party. He felt the North could not survive alone without British subsidies.

Despite the varied views of those above and others, it was nevertheless interesting to find a coming together of so many from different backgrounds, but yet united in one common view of wishing to see an end to partition. It is unclear if the Council progressed any further with its goals. More than likely it did not, as people's attentions were probably directed towards other matters with the arrival of the 1939-45 Emergency.

Meanwhile in 1939 the IRA embarked on a bombing campaign in Britain, in line with the age-old strategy of England's difficulty being Ireland's opportunity. However, it was not the British government that came down on the IRA first, but the Dublin government. In June 1939 the Dáil passed the Offences Against the State Act (OASA), setting up military courts which allowed for imprisonment without trial, and declaring the IRA an unlawful organisation. The annual Bodenstown commemoration and march was again proscribed, and at the end of the month Gardaí and military clashed with Republicans who were trying to make their way to Wolfe Tone's grave. One of the most serious explosions to take place during the English campaign was the one in Coventry in August. Five people were killed and the two Irishmen that were subsequently arrested, Peter Barnes and James McCormack, were found guilty and hanged on 7 February 1940. Their hanging caused a storm of uproar in Ireland, as the actual involvement of the two men had never been proven. The day following the execution of Barnes and McCormack in Birmingham, Ireland went into national mourning, with flags flying at half-mast all over the country. Cobh UDC was only one of many public bodies that protested against the fate of the two men. Referring to the execution of the Manchester Martyrs, the Town Council on 2 February passed a resolution that the two Irishmen under sentence of death arising out of the Coventry explosion were not guilty, saying that it hoped the Irish government's efforts to save their lives would be successful. They weren't.

In September 1939 a national emergency was declared by the Dublin Government and the Garda Special Branch was reorganised in an attempt to make it more effective against 'internal enemies' (the IRA). De Valera dusted off the 'German Plot' conspiracy theory that had been used against him and other Republican leaders in the past by the British, blew new life into it, and exaggerated a plot by the IRA and Nazi Germany to take over the state. It was somewhat strange however, that if De Valera really felt so threatened by the Germans, he would have refused the British the use of Irish ports. A mere six months earlier the Department of External affairs in Dublin had advised Seamus Fitzgerald on the etiquette surrounding the visit of a German Commander and his staff when the vessel called on Cobh. The advice given was to welcome the foreign visitors, and consequently when the courtesy calls were made, the German Commander and his staff visited Cobh, Fitzgerald and the Town Clerk boarded the vessel. If former IRA man Fitzgerald was conspiring with the Germans, at least the action had been sanctioned by Dublin. In any event, De Valera now had the instruments and excuse to round up his nemesis, the IRA, and from September onwards several large-scale arrests were carried out.

When in December the IRA caught the Government and the army napping by seizing the bulk of its ammunition in the Magazine Fort raid, the Minister for Justice, Boland, demanded additional powers to crush the IRA and in January 1940, internment was extended to Irish citizens. The first internees were locked up at the Curragh military camp in Kildare. Boland could now intern people on suspicion and Cork was especially badly hit by the arrests that followed. In the first week of January some twenty-four arrests were made in County Cork under the special emergency powers of the government. One of the cases, that of a Macroom man, was heard at Cobh Court. Cobh, although not targeted in the first wave, was just like many towns around the country and would soon feel the blow of internment. Taken from the town in early morning swoops were: Tom Stockdale, Paddy and Seanie Walsh, Simon Donovan and Gerry (Daddler) Kelly.

Given the level of Volunteer activity in the town at this time, it is hard to understand why the authorities settled only on five from Cobh to be relocated to the Curragh, along with 800 others. It is probably safe to say that Garda intelligence was not as good as it may have assumed. While among the prizes they netted, was the local Company Commander; Tom Stockdale. His removal from the scene could hardly be regarded as much of a coup, since he virtually handed himself to them on a plate as early as four years before, when he sloppily left incriminating documents under his bed mattress to be found. Simon Donovan they may well have regarded as a better catch, since he was in charge of maintaining and storing all of the Company's rifles. This was a job he previously shared with Mick Mulcahy from the Old Street, but when Mick left for England to find work a couple of years earlier, Simon was left with total responsibility for the Company's ordnance. Simon organised a network of houses and safe hiding places for the weapons to be kept at different locations around the town and island. Assuming and probably hoping that he and his O.C. Tom Stockdale had not taken measures to have someone new take over control of this position in the event of a big round-up, the Garda and military authorities probably thought they were about to neuter the Cobh Volunteers by removing

Donovan from the scene. The Walsh brothers from Ticknock were a different kettle of fish. While Paddy was a few years older than Seanie, who at seventeen would be one of, if not the youngest internee in the Curragh, had some experience as an IRA Volunteer, his younger brother was relatively new to the ranks of the army.

The Walsh brothers however, were no more or no less active than many other Volunteers in the town who were not picked up and shipped off to the Curragh. Maybe it was just mediocre intelligence on the part of the authorities that they fingered the Walsh's while ignoring others. The brothers both had flaunted their Republicanism for years while parading around in Fianna uniforms, and there was also Seanie's known relationship with Mick Burke, albeit on a semi-employment level. But perhaps the real reason why the two brothers were singled out though, was because the authorities wished to teach their mother a lesson, for continuingly allowing her house to be used by the IRA. Then there was Gerry (Daddler) Kelly. Like the others, Daddler would have spent his childhood activities as a member of the Fianna.

He came from the same part of town as Simon Donovan on the east-end. Again, he was no more or less active than many other Volunteers, like the O'Donoghue brothers who lived nearby, but after coming up through the ranks of na Fianna Éireann and going on to train others, he probably had caught the eye of the Free State authorities. Like that of the possible thinking behind the removal of Simon Donovan from Cobh, with Kelly too out of the picture, there probably would be no one left to attract and train other young ones coming up. Kelly in later years would go on to become a popular Branch Secretary of the ITGWU in Cobh.

Of the five Republicans from Cobh that were shipped off to the Curragh, four would eventually sign a bond and be released early. Only one, the youngest, Seanie Walsh would refuse to sign and remain interned for the duration of the Emergency (the Second World War). Yet he alone would be the one to return to Cobh with physical scars that would remain with him for the rest of his life. Seanie recalled for me how when each morning they would have to queue up in line for a piece of bread and a kipper, they would have to run the gauntlet of a number of Military Policemen before getting back to their table and by the time they would reach the table, there would rarely be anything left on the plate. In an interview with one of the military guards that served in the Curragh Camp at the time, a recent documentary made for Sky's History Channe' titled Tin Town explained that ordinary soldiers like him were picked for the job of guarding the internees. He said it was a very attractive position to volunteer for because they were paid almost double what a normal soldier would get each week. It was clear that the soldiers loyalty was bought through this money as they weren't about to do anything that would jeopardise their double week's pay. The soldier didn't admit to the brutality of the camp regime which he was a part of, nor did he deny it. The History Channel documentary likened the camp regime to that of one of Stalin's 'Gulags' especially as no one outside knew what it was like or what was going on inside, because the De Valera government was able to use the Emergency to censor newspaper reports. The conditions were deplorable with damp overcrowded huts, rations were minimal and poor, and lice and dysentery was widespread. The prisoners had no choice by to take action themselves to try to force the authorities to introduce better and humane conditions.

In February, several men went on hunger strike in Mountjoy Jail. Two of them, Darcy and MacNeela, were to die before the protest was finally called off, but one of those who survived, Tomas MacCurtain Jnr would play a leading role in the later 1956–62 border campaign. Their main argument was that as they had been brought before a military tribunal for engaging in military activities, they were political prisoners, yet they were thrown in amongst the criminal population in Mountjoy Prison. During the hunger strike, the prisoners on the protest were soon removed to St Bricin's military hospital. A resolution was received by Cobh UDC from the Secretary of the Cobh Cumann na mBan, asking the Council to protest against the treatment of the prisoners on hunger strike at the military hospital. It was unanimously decided that, 'This Council protests against any political prisoners not receiving political treatment.' [127]

On 3 April, Blathnaid Nic Chárthaigh and Padraigín Ní Chochlainn issued the following statement through a flyer on behalf of Cumann na mBan Headquarters in Andrew Street, Dublin. It's heading went, 'De Valera Forbids Prayers For Hunger-strikers'. On Monday of this week the following letter was sent to all the daily newspapers, but was refused publication by the censor:

We ask the people of Ireland to unite with us in a Triduum of prayer, including Mass and Holy Communion, beginning Wednesday, 3 April, and ending on the First Friday for the intention of the Republican prisoners.

On Tuesday another letter was sent to the papers in which we deleted the words 'intention of the Republican prisoners', and substituted 'the happy solution to a certain tragic situation.' Again the censor refused to allow one single word to be published; consequently we have to resort to the distribution of these handbills in order to get prayers for the prisoners in their terrible agony. The original intention was to close the Triduum on the First Friday, but as De Valera decided otherwise, we ask you to commence the Triduum immediately you receive this. Also please ask as many as possible to join with you in this campaign of prayer.

In Cork similar flyers were being distributed by the women of Cumann na mBan. One headed, Citizens of Cork.

Men are praised all over the world to-day for the standing for their Countries Rights. Pole and Finns are especially everyone's Heroes. Men are being treated as criminals in Ireland for standing for Ireland's rights. They have gone on hunger-strike, not for release, but against being treated as criminals. Tomas Ashe died in Mountjoy in 1917 to vindicate that Principle. Will you stand idly by, while his successors die in 1940 to vindicate the same Principle? You know Republicans are not criminals.

The flyer went on to say that dozens of letters of protest had flooded the desks of newspaper editors over the previous weeks but were stopped by De Valera's appointed censor. It then finished with the words, 'The Fool, The Fool, The Fool! De Valera thinks that he can let these men die unknown to the Irish People. He thinks that he has pacified Ireland. He thinks he has purchased half of us and intimidated the other half.' [128] As IRA suspects were being rounded up in nationwide swoops during June 1940, several former Cork Republicans were lining up to join the army that would incarcerate, torture and in some cases murder some of them. Among them were Tom Barry, Liam Deasy, Tom Crofts, and Florrie O'Donoghue. From Cobh, Mick Leahy and Seamus Fitzgerald would also step up to the plate. In one week in June when 390 were interned from all over the State, Cork prison was converted into an internment camp in order to be able to handle the big influx of internees. Meanwhile in the Curragh things were heating up.

When in December the butter ration in the camp was reduced, it was seen as the last straw, and the prisoner's leader decided that the time had come to take action. He posed the question to them, 'Are we men or mice?' [129] He then gave the order to burn down one of the camp huts. However, failing to take into account the prevailing wind that was blowing that day, the fire spread with a number of other huts going up in flames too, one of which covered an escape tunnel that was being dug at the time. The tunnel was consequently discovered and all the prisoners were locked up under armed guard and not allowed any food from Saturday evening until the following Monday morning. The suspected ringleaders were taken out from among the others and forced to run the gauntlet of the baton wielding military. The badly beaten and bruised men were then put in solitary confinement in the bitterly cold 'Glass House' for ten weeks. The remainder of the prisoners were allowed out for breakfast on Monday morning. Seanie Walsh recalled:

> We came out of our huts as usual to fall in military file. Our hut, the Cork one, was the second facing the guards. The men from the first hut had already fallen in as we were coming out, and they were about to march to the cook house for breakfast when the rattle of machine-gun fire roared out. Nobody seemed to know what was happening, but one lad from Cork, Jerry Cronin, screamed, 'Hit the deck', which we all did. After a few minutes the firing stopped and we began to pick up our wounded. Barney Casey was badly wounded and later died. Bob Flanagan received a couple of wounds to his chest. Art Moynihan, Martin Staunton and Walter Mitchell were also wounded. Only for the quick thinking of Jerry Cronin, there would have been far more casualties. [130]

Bob Flanagan, one of the wounded, had acted as a bodyguard to Gerry Boland when the latter was elected to the Free State parliament in 1932, and when Boland and his Fianna Fáil colleagues entered Leinster House with revolvers in their coat pockets. Now Boland as Minister for Justice was responsible for internment and the death of several internees, including hunger strikers. Less than twenty years earlier, in December 1922, the then Minister for Justice, Kevin O'Higgins, had betrayed a friend in a similar manner when he agreed to the execution of four men captured after the Four Courts episode, one of them Rory O'Connor, having been his personal secretary and the best man at his wedding. (Bob Flanagan was a brother to a Presentation Brother in Cobh, Brother Chrisistum, who later taught this writer.) If the History Channel documentary about Tin Town as the Curragh Camp was more commonly known, exposed another reality, it was the manner in which the general public were hoodwinked about how all internees were treated during the Emergency. Away and out of sight of the Republican section of the camp, were two separate compounds for German and Allied prisoners respectfully.

In stark contrast to the treatment of Irish (Republican) prisoners, these foreign prisoners were treated humanely, were well fed, and were even given an allowance to go to dances and the cinema in the nearby towns in the evenings. All were happy to return to camp at night and none wanted to escape, as Ireland was literally a holiday camp away from the war in Europe. Such was the contrast of how De Valera's Government was operating different camp policies for the different sets of prisoners, that he secretly released the allied (RAF) prisoners as early as 1944. From such a background, and when one considers how Republicans were treated and how the vindictive cutting of the butter rations to prisoners who were already half starved, one cannot but conclude that the regime deliberately went out to provoke a situation where serious damage and deaths would result.

But where De Valera, Boland and their Government did succeed, was in breaking the men's morale. After the initial camp leaders were taken out of the camp and thrown into the Glass House, a new and more conservative leadership assumed command. This new leadership was far more disciplinary and short sighted. It failed to focus on the struggle outside and discouraged attempts to plan an escape. This new regime, soon led to splits and factions forming within the camp, eventually leading to a breakdown of morale. It was because of this dead-end leadership that some internees took up the offer to sign the bond and get out of the place. Others waited for a time to see if a change in leadership could be brought about to swing things back on the right track again. No change came however, leading to more and more men throwing in the towel and signing out. In the end, what was left could best be described as the unbroken remnants of resistance. Seanie Walsh was one of those that held out to the bitter end. When he returned home to his mother's house at Ticknock, there was a message waiting for him from the local Garda Sergeant asking him to call to the barracks to see him. Seanie was suspicious about the request so he first paid a visit to Mick Burke to get his advice on the matter. Burke advised his former helper that it would be best to go and see the sergeant, to play along but always to be one step ahead of him in his own mind. Seanie took Burke's advice and proceeded to the local barracks. When he met the Sergeant, the first words out of the policeman's mouth were, 'Why was Seanie Walsh the last Cobhman out of the Curragh? Why had he refused to sign the bond like the others?' Seanie however, thought that such questions did not deserve an answer, feeling as the sergeant had the latest information on him, he must already know the answers. But the policeman obviously did not see the logic in this and when Seanie refused to co-operate, the Sergeant furiously called him a 'hardliner that would be quietened one day'.[131] Seanie thought to himself and decided that now was the occasion to be quietened and stubbornly remained silent to the annoyance of a deep-red-faced Sergeant. The Republican then left the barracks with a broad smile on his face. He immediately reported back to the 4th Battalion for active service.

Some time during the years of internment in the 1940s, a local person showed their disgruntlement with events by throwing a bottle of ink at the Union Jack when it appeared on the screen prior to the showing of a film in one of the Cobh cinemas. They didn't reckon on the ink stain remaining on the screen long after the Union Jack disappeared however, which resulted in the annoyance of many other viewers. The local Council, on the other hand, did little to distinguish itself during the Emergency years, and remained ambivalent where Republican-related issues were concerned. Although motions had been passed on the plight of Barnes and

McCormack, and the Mountjoy hunger strikers, a public meeting was also called in August 1940 to encourage recruiting in response to the governments appeal for men to join the Free State Army. During a monthly meeting held on 6 February 1942, a circular letter from Sinn Féin was discussed, asking that a resolution be adopted by the Council demanding the withdrawal and annulment of the Emergency Powers order 1941, but although adoption of the resolution was moved by Cllr Mick Fitzgerald, (Independent Republican), there was no seconder for the motion.

In August 1942 there were new elections to the local Council, on which occasion one of the recently released internees from the Curragh, was successfully elected on the Republic ticket of Aiseirghe. Tom Stockdale's comfortable election produced some evidence that there was support in the town for the Republican cause, and perhaps some evidence of disenchantment also with the government's policy of internment. In the 1945 local elections, Stockdale was again re-elected on the 'Aiseirghe' ticket. Also that year, another former internee from the Civil War period, Phil O'Neill was elected, representing National Labour. O'Neill had earlier worked undercover for the local Volunteers, while working as a writer at the Admiralty buildings. He later took the oath and became a Volunteer during the truce, and found himself interned after the outbreak of Civil War. At the time of his election, O'Neill worked for the local gas company and was the local Branch Secretary of the Irish Transport and General Workers Union. Tom Stockdale's popularity on the Council saw him elected Vice-Chairman in 1945, after which he eventually became Chairman in 1950-51.

St Patrick's Day 1942, saw a group of fourteen former officers of Cork's number 1 Brigade meet in Cork to discuss a grave and for some, an embarrassing situation. They were meeting to formulate a letter of appeal to the Minister for Justice and his government to intervene in the plight of Tomas MacCurtain Jnr who was in solitary confinement in Maryborough Prison (Portlaoise) under sentence of death. He had earlier received the death penalty for the shooting dead of Detective Sergeant John Roche in Cork. At 9.15p.m. on Friday 3 January 1940, Roche along with three other armed detectives moved in to arrest MacCurtain on St Patrick's Bridge Cork. In the confused struggle which followed, Detective Sgt.Roche received a gunshot wound from which he died from some hours later. Twenty-two-year old MacCurtain was immediately taken in to custody, charged and remanded to the Special Court (military tribunal) in Dublin. His comrades under Mick O'Riordan of the City Battalion, of which he previously commanded, had hoped to rescue him from the Courthouse in Cork, before he could be moved, but their plans never amounted to anything. MacCurtain had good reason to believe the Special Branch (Broy Harriers) were not interested in taking him alive. They had been shadowing him for months, particularly Sergeant Roche, leading him to think they had ample opportunity to arrest him peacefully if they had wanted to. He also had a deep suspicion of armed plain-clothes law-men from the time he saw them gun down his father (the Lord Mayor) twenty years before. At his subsequent trial, the State produced a hand gun with the name MacCurtain scratched upon the stock. His counsel Mr Albert Ernest Wood failed in an attempt to have the charge reduced to man-slaughter, claiming that he had been hounded by the Cork detective unit for months and believed his life to be in real danger. However, both the State and the Cork Detective Unit were determined that MacCurtain would swing. Now two years on, the former brigade officers, who had served under the command of MacCurtain's father, were attempting to spare the neck of the young Republican. Their letter of appeal didn't call for MacCurtain's release, not even for his sentence to be commuted, but for the easing of the conditions in which he was incarcerated. This softly-softly approach was probably made because many of the signatories were supporters of the government and didn't want to be confrontational or cause embarrassment for the Fianna Fáil party. They possibly also believed they would have more success by broaching the matter with the Minister in a non confrontational manner, though there were at least two names among those of the signatories, Mick Burke of Cobh and Tom Kelleher of West Cork, who if had their own way, would probably have composed a far more harshly worded letter to the Fianna Fáil government. The even-tual letter decided upon was as follows:

We, old members of the IRA, who served under Tomas MacCurtain, first Brigade of Cork City and County, view with grave concern, the appalling position of his son in Maryborough Prison. He has already spent twenty-two months in Solitary Confinement. During all this time he is wearing blankets only. He is denied the right of attending Mass. He is not allowed communicate with his family or they with him.

In view of this treatment, which must have already caused grave and perma-nent injury to his health, we believe that the time is opportune for you to bring theses conditions to an end.

(Signed) Tom Hales, Peter O'Donovan, Patrick Whooley, Patrick Twomey, Sean McCarthy, Thomas Kelleher, Mick Burke, Tom Canty, Liam Ivers, Patrick Ivers, Willie Hales, Liam Murphy, Denis B. Coughlan, Sean S. MacCárthaigh. [132]

Perhaps the letter from these former Brigade officers had some influence on government thinking around the MacCurtain saga, but probably more than anything else, Fianna Fáil's own intelligence on the ground, which had always been a close barometer of public opinion, would have told them, that it would have been the ultimate act of political suicide in Cork to execute MacCurtain. Not only that, but it could also spark a mini rebellion in the area and drive people to join the IRA in their droves. The Government just didn't possess enough internment camps for such a scenario. It was a no win situation for the De Valera's Government, which had already crossed over the Rubicon by executing Republicans, allowing them to die on hungerstrike, and giving its forces a free hand to murder them in cold-blood, as had happened in the Curragh. When they eventually withdrew the death penalty and commuted MacCurtain's sentence, no one in Ireland was in any doubt but that they had acted out of political cowardice and expediency. De Valera's government may have finished up with egg on its face, but at least for them, the Fianna Fáil Party in Cork would remain intact.

35. Back to the Drawing Board

After the years of sweeping arrests and internment, the IRA slowly but surely began to rebuild its strength. The men and women who were being released from the camps and prisons, and those who had evaded arrest and kept the movement going through the years of internment, now began to reorganise the Republican Army. In Cork it was Mick McCarthy, along with several other dedicated Republicans, who got the movement back on its feet. The uniting cause was, once again, the campaign to release the prisoners. Ex-internees returned to their hometowns with harrowing accounts of the living conditions and ill-treatment they had to endure at the hands of the government, whereas several of those regarded as hardliners were still kept in prison. Several of them had been kept in Solitary in Portlaoise for years. However, the De Valera government refused to give into public appeals on behalf of Republican prisoners, and this was to be one of the factors in the subsequent defeat of his party suffered in the 1948 General Election. In fact it wasn't until the ousting of Fianna Fáil in 1948 that the last IRA men were released from Portlaoise Gaol.

Meanwhile in Cobh a committee was formed to raise funds for the erection of a monument at the Republican Plot in the Old Church Cemetery. Tom Stockdale, UDC, was its Chairman, and T. W. Cronin, also a former Volunteer and Fianna Fáil councillor, was its Vice-Chairman; while Nita Murphy and Lizzy Quaine, both former members of Cumann na mBan, were its joint secretaries. Mick Fitzgerald and A. Collins were joint Hon.

Treasurers. The committee circulated letters appealing for funds, but failed to achieve their objective. The original committee eventually faded out and was replaced by a new committee with Joe Stockdale as its chairman. Rosie O'Neill (Phil O'Neill's daughter) as secretary. Other members included Danny Dinan, Paddy Coakley, Mick Fitzgerald, Cllr Phil O'Neill, Ned Butler and Simon Donovan.

One of the contributing factors to the success of this committee, was that it had among its membership, individuals who were active Volunteers, Commanders and Internees, from the previous three decades of struggle, and while some of those had ties to the existing IRA, it was clear that the old argument over who had the moral authority and rights to the Republican Plot, had now given way to a united approach in the greater interest of the establishment of a fitting memorial to those buried there. Much of the monies raised, came from the Kilty brothers (former Volunteers) in the USA. This time the project met with success, leading to a big limestone engraved Celtic Cross monument being erected over the plot in time for Easter 1948. On that day, a big parade left the town-front and marched the two mile journey to the Old-Church Cemetery, many more lined the streets to watch and offer support. Shops and businesses along the town and up through the 'Top of the Hill' areas, flew tri-colour flags and hung green, white and orange bunting from their premises. The oration at the Plot was given by Mary McSwiney, sister to the late Lord Mayor. Gerry Cronin represented the IRA's Cork No. 1 Brigade staff, while Seanie Walsh represented the Cobh Company Volunteers. Mick Fitzgerald and Ned Butler represented Cobh IRA veterans. The event was a resounding success and helped put a bounce back in the step of the local Republican Movement. One aspect of it also highlighted a problem for the local Fianna Fáil /Old IRA organisation which failed to show up or participate in the commemoration.

This time, they couldn't blame the IRA for ordering or intimidating them away from the Republican Plot, but simply distanced themselves by their own choosing. Whether the local organisation took a calculated decision to boycott the commemoration, or if Seamus Fitzgerald, Mick Leahy and others came under pressure by a national directive to steer clear of such events is not clear. What is clear, is that the Fianna Fáil party and by extension its brother organisation, the Old IRA, had openly ceded its moral claim to be the rightful adherents to 1916 Republicanism, and to the ideals and memory of those buried in the Republican Plot.

A serious consequence of Fianna Fáil turning its back on those who made the supreme sacrifices, and laid the groundwork for the very existence of their party, came later that year in the General Election when it was thrown out of government. After sixteen years of uninterrupted power, the De Valera

Seannie Walsh and Paddy Coakley 1945.

regime was forced to make way for the unlikely alliance of Fine Gael and Clann na Poblactha, a new radical Republican party under the leadership of Sean McBride, a veteran of 1916, and more recently, Chief of Staff of the IRA. Since its formation twenty-two years earlier, Fianna Fáil had become increasingly conservative and had lost its radical edge, so much so that the desire to hold on to power, had replaced their desire to appear Republican. There can be no doubt that the often brutal, degrading and unnecessary treatment of Republican prisoners over the previous number of years had now caught up with the De Valera regime in terms of electoral support. Ironically, De Valera and his government had unintentionally opened the doors of office to his old foes that previously and similarly had mistreated many of them when they were the ones behind bars.

The new incoming Taoiseach John A. Costello would within a year, steal some of Fianna Fáil's thunder and embarrass the party by declaring the southern state a Republic. De Valera must have wondered why he hadn't thought of that in any of the previous sixteen years he held power. However, whether it was intentional or not, history has since shown us that the notion of regarding a single part of Ireland as a Republic has misleadingly led many Irish people including some political parties to regard the twenty-six-county state as a fully sovereign entity, which had filled the criteria of the Republic for which many fought and died since Easter 1916.

The success of Clann na Poblactha, who had ten members elected to the Dáil, helped to revive Republican sentiment at the expense of Fianna

The old monument at the Republican Plot in around 1946.

Fáil. Although many Republicans regarded McBride's party as Treaty Party number three, others saw it as a great opportunity to address the fundamental issue for which they had supported Fianna Fáil sixteen years before, namely the matter of re-uniting the country.

Sean McBride had earlier trawled the twenty-six-county state for suitable candidates to take on what he saw as a discredited Fianna Fáil Party in the upcoming election. When it came to the Cork East constituency, he immediately made for Cobh to see one of his long time friends Mick Burke. McBride believed he would be onto someone good by getting Burke to stand for election. He felt that the Tan War veteran and Civil War Commander, was a well respected figure in Cobh and was a well known name throughout East Cork, and therefore would be well positioned to challenge Fianna Fáil for one of its seats. Mc Bride was right about Burke being a well liked and respected figure in Cobh, but he overlooked the fact that the Cobh man's military exploits in other areas of East Cork had long ago faded from peoples memories. He also underestimated the challenge that Burke would face if he was to unseat his old friend Martin Corry. Had such a challenge been attempted ten years earlier, they might have caused problems for Fianna Fáil and Corry, but by 1948, Fianna Fáil and its East Cork ambassador Corry, had firmly established themselves among the electorate as its fitting representatives and guardians.

The party, and by extension Corry, were seen in Cobh as being responsible for the construction of two new housing estates of Belmont and Glenanaar which had taken over 130 families out of the squalor of run-down tenements in the town and provided them with new homes. The building of two other local authority streets were also about to come

The unveiling of the new
monument 1948.

on stream. They would be the new Connolly Street along the Holy Ground under Cobh UDC, and Maurice Moore Place on the north side of Villa Park by the County Council, both streets would be named after Republican martyrs. A few years earlier, the Fianna Fáil government also attracted a new industry to the area when a Belgian company opened up a Steel Works that would later become Irish Steel on Haulbowline Island. Corry and his party were careful to make sure people knew who were responsible for bringing about these positive changes to their lives.

When McBride initially approached Mick Burke to stand for his party, the Cobhman instantly rejected the offer. Burke had always had a deep distrust of politics and saw how it had destroyed good men in the past. He also believed that no candidate could unseat Corry as he had had too much of a free run in the past and had soundly consolidated his position with the Cork East electorate. McBride didn't give up though, and kept working on his old friend and comrade, eventually managing to convince him that there was a serious mood for change out there among the people. Both men believed that if they were to have any real chance of taking a seat, they would have to make a serious challenge in Cobh. Speaking soon afterwards to a crowded street from the balcony of Burke's own business premises, at the oddly named, Imperial Hotel on the town-front at West Beach, McBride tore into the Fianna Fáil government for turning stale and worn from too many years in office. He ridiculed their Republican record and said they should be run from office by the people for the way they had treated Republican prisoners during the Emergency years. He also spelled out the radical changes that his new party would introduce if elected to government, but promised above all else to not shy away from the issue of national reunification, as Fianna Fáil had done for most of its time in office. McBride and his party were clearly hoping to capitalise on left-wing voters rallying to them, in addition to attracting Republicans and disenchanted Fianna Fáil supporters. McBride had also secured a second running partner for Burke, in Garrett Roche from further down the constituency in Mitchelstown, displaying a sign of his overall confidence. One man who recalled his first introduction to the policies of Clann na Poblactha was a young school lad named Johnny Dorrity. Johnny remembers Burke, a local grocer and hotelier and, Roche, a farmer, each taking a side each of the balcony windows to address the crowd below. He also recalled that for some reason, a lot of school teachers were drawn towards Clann na Poblactha.

But when the votes were counted on 5 February, the news didn't look good at all for McBride and his party in Cork East. The big problem for McBride and Burke was that they were contesting for the first time in a three-seat constituency. They were also contesting from a field of ten candidates. This very unusual and some might say suspiciously high number of candidates, split the vote so many ways that it was sure to suit the bigger and established parties. As a result, Corry not only held his seat but topped the poll with 7,172 votes. Unlike the previous election however, when the constituency went under the name of Cork South East, Fianna Fáil didn't hold its second seat. Patrick O'Gorman of Fine Gael took the second seat on this occasion with 4,072, with the last seat going to Sean Keane Snr. of Labour, coming in just 6 votes behind O'Gorman with 4,066 first preferences. Mick Burke came in with a poor 1,638 votes, while his running partner Roche, received a derisory 838 votes. Leo Skinner of Fianna Fáil polled 4,013 votes but failed to be elected, while Joe Ahern of Fine Gael polled 2,170 votes. Daniel Cashman, the Clann na Talmhan candidate polled extremely well and picked up much of the farmers vote in the constituency with 3,352 votes, while the two Independent candidates, William O'Dwyer and Pat O'Brien polled 1,167 and 823 votes respectively.

The news was better for McBride and his party elsewhere in the state as they had managed to get ten candidates elected, including McBride himself. But no sooner did the new radical Republican Party receive this gift, than it began to squander it. So eager was McBride and his party to get into office and oust De Valera, that he was prepared to do a deal which would briefly turn the notion of Civil War politics on its head. Fine Gael who were also lusting for office, didn't give a second thought to the fact that they were about to go into office and share power with a Republican party led by a man who only twelve years earlier was the IRA's Chief of Staff. Not only that, they were so eager to take up office, that they were prepared to change its leader from Richard Mulcahy, the Free State leader responsible for overseeing the executions of scores of Republicans during the Civil War. McBride let it be known that he wouldn't serve with Mulcahy. and John A. Costello took over as leader of Fine Gael. Fianna Fáil was six seats short of an overall majority but refused to consider going into coalition, and although the new alternative coalition was made up of six different parties and independents, it was really the relationship between Fine Gael and Clann na Publachta in Government that would grab the public imagination. It was a gamble on McBride's part, for it was clear that if this relationship didn't work out, only one of these two extremely contrasting partys would survive to fight another day. McBride and Clann na Poblactha never got to make the big impact on the national question that they had hoped for, nor could they ever have seriously expected to while they were junior partners to a party that practically regarded the partition of Ireland as one of its proud personal achievements. Fianna Fáil for its part just waited patiently in the wings, knowing that these unlikeliest of coalition partners would create the conditions for their spectacular return to power after the next election. It is probably true to say, that many people had just used both their votes and McBride's party to give Fianna Fail a temporary shake up and warning, not to stray far from the Republican principles they had started out with.

Easter 1959 at Republican Plot Youghal. Centre holding flag: Eddie Collins. Drummer: Dessie Swanton who was killed a few years later by an explosion in Cork.

36. Operation Harvest

One of the policies that emerged from the reorganisation of the IRA after its disastrous English campaign and the fall-out from internment was that henceforth the military campaign was to be directed solely against the occupation forces in the six counties. The main objective of the Republican Army was defined as driving the British forces out of Ireland and its Volunteers were forbidden to use any force against the twenty-six-county police or military. In May 1951 a Military Council of the IRA decided on a campaign in the North and in the following years several raids were made on barracks along the border.

It was around this time that a young Republican from Mogeely in East Cork named Eddie Collins, moved to Dublin to find bar work. Before long, he came into contact with Cathal Goulding, Paddy McLogan, Sean Garland and Seamus Costello. Collins was eventually persuaded to move to England on a fundraising exercise for the movement. Once there, he first made contact with the Wolfe Tone Society and with other Republicans. Although he had no idea that a decision had already been taken for the up-coming Border Campaign, Collins over the next two and a half years raised a substantial amount of money which found its way back to Dublin. It was through such fundraising ventures abroad, particularly in Britain and the US, that the leadership was able to purchase the weapons needed for the upcoming campaign. But purchasing the weapons was only half the battle. They also needed to be smuggled into the country undetected. This was done in a number of ways and not always with a successful outcome.

One such unsuccessful landing occurred in Cobh in 1956, when the then veteran Republican Mick Burke took his family for a short drive into town from their Rushbrooke home. Not explaining to his family the reason why he had taken a detour from the normal route, he headed for the Deepwater Quay. Once they arrived there, his family instantly realised why. His youngest daughter Emer said as soon as they arrived onto the quay, they saw a crowd of Gardaí and Customs men gathered around what looked like a big wooden box or chest. When her father quickly swung the car around and sped away from the quayside, she instantly knew that all the excitement had something to do with him. It was only years later that it all came together for her. Emer couldn't quite remember or pin down which year the incident happened, but her older sister Nuala, is certain that was in 1956, the year in which the IRA's Border Campaign was launched.

The campaign which was not launched until 12 December 1956, became known as 'Operation Harvest' by the IRA, but was generally

Easter parade Cobh 1961.

known simply as the Border Campaign. The campaign initially met with a degree of success in that its participants managed to scoop and build up their supply of weapons captured from the raids. They also seemed to have a good supply of recruits from most of the twenty-six counties and some from across the border itself. The most famous of these raids took place on the RUC barracks at Brookeborough on New Year's eve 1957, when two IRA Volunteers were killed and a number of others wounded. The names of the two dead Volunteers, Fergal O'Hanlon and Sean Sabhat have since entered the annals of Republican folklore, with a number of songs written about them. In a recent documentary interview to mark the fiftieth anniversary of the raid, six of O'Hanlon's and Sabhat's surviving comrades from that night, explained what happened but also painted a broader picture of the campaign itself. They told of how Sean Sabhat arrived up for active service from Limerick in his FCA uniform (he had been a Lieutenant in the reserve army force). Others also turned up at the border in FCA uniform and like Sabhat, were ordered to remove all the insignia relating to the southern state uniform. Some men just opted to wear British uniforms which were made available to them to avoid implicating the southern state in the conflict. Regardless of which uniform or semi civilian dress they chose to wear however, all had to stitch an Irish tricolour badge to their coat sleeve, which was then displayed as a common requirement under the Geneva Convention by all guerrilla movements around the world. When they arrived in Brookeborough village that night and pulled up on the street on the back of the Bedford truck, the local RUC Sergeant had just crossed over the street to his barracks, and probably saw who and what was on the back of the truck. Almost immediately machine gun-fire began to rain down on the men from a top window of the barracks before they could do anything.

One Volunteer who was designated to plant a bomb outside the barrack wall managed to creep up towards the building. He could see that the Sergeant had been in such a hurry to get inside, that he had left the door open behind him. The Volunteer neglected to take advantage of the opened door as he had not trained or prepared for such a scenario. Instead he left it on the outside as he had done so many times in the drill practice, but because of the intense fire-fight, didn't get a chance to set the detonator. Meanwhile back at the truck, most of the others were pinned down and weren't sure of exactly where the fire was coming from. Sean Sabhat was already dead beneath the lorry and Fergal O'Hanlon was also badly hit. The Volunteer in front of O'Hanlon had already taken three hits to his front and the side of his leg. He later claimed that some of these shots had passed through him and into O'Hanlon. He also knew that they were under attack from a number of different points in the village, probably from other off-duty B-special RUC men who immediately began firing on the truck from their homes after they had been alerted by the initial gunfire.

The RUC soon realised that they had the upper hand and were determined to finish off if not capture the entire Republican force. Realising that the RUC were trying to knock out the driver of the truck, thus prevent any chance of escape, the Volunteers quickly hauled their wounded and dead onboard the back of the truck and quickly exited out of the village at speed. They eagerly headed through the darkness for what they thought was south towards the border, but it soon became clear that they weren't exactly sure where they were going. After some time they pulled up on a quiet roadway near a disused farm shed. They decided they would have to abandon the truck and make the rest of the journey on foot as they would probably soon run into armed check points. One of the Volunteers, Sean Garland, who was himself wounded, asked another wounded Volunteer to stay behind with him to fight a rearguard action. This would probably mean certain death for them but would at least allow their comrades time to escape. Daithí O'Connell spoke up then and said he was assuming command and that no one was staying behind, that he was determined all surviving volunteers would make it back across the border. The two dead volunteers were then laid out in the farm shed, before their comrades took a bearing with a compass and headed south through the fields towards the border. They had hardly reached the second field when they heard the engines of their pursuers pulling up on the road behind them. Within seconds they heard machine gun fire fill up the night sky over them. They then took cover in the ditches until the RUC expended another few magazines of ammunition into the surrounding countryside. A few seconds later they heard a short sharp burst of fire, which they knew was aimed inside the door of the farm shed. The dead bodies of their two comrades were now in the hands of their enemy. The men struggled on in the darkness for a number of miles, the RUC having given up pursuit in their direction. Some of the wounded were using their rifles as crutches and using the shoulders of their comrades for support. As they were without any drinking water, and the wounded were parched with thirst from the heavy loss of blood, they occasionally stopped to take scoops of snow off the ground before swallowing it.

Eventually, the unit could see the lights of a town in the distant which they took to be Monaghan. They kept heading towards that light in the hope that it would take them to the right side of the border. After a time when they stopped for a rest, a Volunteer spotted a dim light flicker from a nearby cottage window. He decided to take a gamble and go and see if he could get some assistance there. When he knocked on the door, the man of the house came out and confirmed that they were on the southern side of the border. He told the Republican to go and get the others and he and his wife would see what they could do to help the wounded. The man's wife tore up some bed sheets to wash and bandage the men's wounds as best she could. One of Volunteers who was losing a lot of blood was laid out on top of the kitchen table while he was being attended to. Some of his comrades didn't think he would make it either. Daithí O'Connell ordered a few of the able-bodied Volunteers to gather up the weapons and get them away to a safe place. While they were gone, the man of the house was sent out to seek a doctor and help. When he eventually returned, he was accompanied by the Gardaí and the army. One of the wounded Volunteers later recalled how when a young army officer entered the cottage and saw the wounded men laid out on the floor and table, he broke down crying. It was the first sign some people in official Ireland were in sympathy with what the Volunteers were doing. The second sign came when the wounded men were dispatched to hospital and allowed back to their homes after they had recovered.

Another Volunteer recalled how it was some months after the event before he received a visit from the Special Branch and arrested. He said he remembered being in a Garda cell with some other Volunteers when they were visited by a particular Judge who told them, 'Don't worry boys, you'll be out of here in no time.'[133] This was the same judge who had earlier thrown out a case against Tomas MacCurtain Jnr, and Harry Gough, after they had been found in possession of weapons by the Gardaí. He had told the court that the act to which the charges were brought against the men was an old imperial one from the days of the British Empire, and said 'Sure we are no longer part of that Empire, so I'm dismissing the case.'[134] The men from the Brookeborough raid waiting for trial in the Garda cells were not so fortunate though, as the Fianna Fáil government took swift and prudent action in replacing the sympathetic judge. Another judge who just happened to be a former British Army officer was given charge of the Brookeborough case and had no compunction about giving the men a jail sentence, though it was minuscule by the standard and size of sentences that would later be issued to Republicans in the decades that would follow.

The Brookeborough story was one that awakened something in the national psyche. The Volunteers from the south who made the sacrifice to go up north to recapture that which had been taken away by threat of force were seen as heroes, while their two fallen comrades were regarded as martyrs in the same mould as Pearse, Connolly and Kevin Barry. Their funerals were attended by tens of thousands of people from all over Ireland. The IRA was flooded by young men wanting to join up and do their bit for the Republican cause. This rise in support for Republicanism was again causing worry in the Fianna Fáil government which had been returned to office only in the previous March. Not only was support on the rise for the IRA once again, but a number of Sinn Féin TDs had also been elected, though they refused to take their seats or recognise the Dáil. Even though their election helped to remove the Clann na Poblachta and Fine Gael parties from office, as far as Fianna Fáil was concerned, the seats they had won rightfully belonged to them and no Republican Pretenders had any right to make a claim to them. By July De Valera had re-introduced the Offences against the State act. Internment was again rolled out and by the following March 131 internees were back in the Curragh Camp.

For Cobh, the 1950s campaign would be the first time since their inception in 1913 that local Volunteers would not play a direct and leading role in the East Cork Volunteer Movement, have influence in Brigade matters, or take part on active service where the action was happening. Just before the campaign had begun in 1956, Seanie Walsh had married and emigrated to Canada. Many of the former Volunteers, who had been active with him in the preceding decades, were now settling down and taking a back seat in the struggle. In 1950, a recently married member of Cork City Cumann na mBan Mary O'Halloran (née Coughlan), had just moved to Cobh. Mary's family was steeped in Republicanism. Her father Jeremiah had survived the Dripsey ambush, while her two uncles, John and Pat O'Donovan had fought at Kilmichael. Mary however, had more important things on her mind with married life in the 1950s, and didn't know any local Republicans in the town. In later years, she joined the local Fianna Fáil Cumann of which she is still today the Secretary. Throughout the Border Campaign of the 1950s, Sinn Féin and Fianna Éireann were still active in the town and to a lesser extent the IRA, though the latter organisation was really only a shadow of its former self.

After the short lived high, which followed the Brookeborough raid, some efforts were made in Cobh to recruit new blood into the local movement. This was mainly carried out by a well-dressed and respectable insurance clerk from Kinsale, named Tim Fitzgerald. Tim and two of his brothers had been active Volunteers during the Tan War but had taken opposite sides during the Civil War. Never a subscriber to the myth of an Old IRA, Tim saw the present generation of fighters as nothing other than young Irish men attempting to finalise the nation's unfinished business. He also felt, just like Tom Barry did, that a missed opportunity had been wasted by the border campaign not having been launched decades before. The smartly dressed insurance man was in an ideal position going door to door around the town to meet and arrange for young men to make contact with the IRA in Cork. One young man, who had such an encounter after taking the initial steps to join up, was Tim Hayes. Tim would later make history for holding the World Guinness Record for remaining buried alive below ground. In the 1950s however, Tim was sufficiently influenced by what had happened at Brookeborough to encourage him into joining the ranks of the Volunteers. When he reached Cork for the initial meeting, after arriving by train, he and some others were met by a contact who soon after issued them with blindfolds. They were then guided to walk a relatively short distance to their meeting place, but Tim being the curious man he was, managed to peep below his blindfold and see that they were entering the Imperial Hotel.

Later when he was leaving the building, Tim received another big surprise when he noticed a local Garda from Cobh trying to walk past as discretely as possible. Apparently the policeman had a special interest in the meeting; not as a Garda but rather as a parent, for his son was one of the recruits inside. However, it would appear the military careers of both Tim and the policeman's son never extended beyond that of good intentions. Meanwhile, the authorities in Cobh were not about to sit back and be complacent that the Republican Movement was at its weakest point in the town for decades. Gardaí kept the pressure on those found to be involved in any form of Republican activity. The boys of Fianna Éireann were hunted from church gates while trying to collect money for Republican dependants, the women of Cumann na mBan were equally intimidated while attempting to hand out literature, while the men of Sinn Féin took the heaviest blows. When it came to selling Easter Lilies, the Gardaí didn't hold back or show mercy. This would turn into an annual game of cat and mouse between the Gardaí and local Republicans who had always to be one step ahead of their pursuers in other to protect what money they had collected for the cause. When ever the Gardaí would get lucky and manage to apprehend a collector, they would nearly always receive resistance against handing over the collection box. It would normally be at that point that the Gardaí would let their batons do the talking, and as one incident demonstrated in Cobh in the 1950s, a Ballymore Republican by the name of Jimmy Rowe had an arm shattered to pieces when he defiantly refused to release a collection box from his grip.

The custom of wearing the Easter Lily was begun by Cumann na mBan under Constance Markievicz in 1926. The design was inspired by the Easter Lily used as a decoration in churches during Easter. The lily is a symbol of rebirth and resurrection. The Easter Lily was also regarded as a symbol of endurance of the Irish freedom struggle, and the rebirth of the Irish nation after the sacrifice of Easter 1916. In 1929 the relatively new Fianna Fáil party attempted to challenge the Republican Lily with a badge of its own. De Valera's party used another Republican symbol in an attempt to wean people away from wearing the Easter Lily. The 'Rising Sun' emblem which was also used on the flag of Fianna Éireann failed to resonate with the Irish people and faded out soon after.

An incident which took place in Cobh during the late 1950s led to a poor unfortunate priest pleading with God to spare the young men of Ireland from the insanity of war. The incident happened as three young workmen were about to take a wooden ferry boat named the *190* to Whitegate where a new national refinery was then under construction. The men had some difficulty starting the petrol engine of the launch and because daylight was poor at the time, one of them decided to light a match to overcome this problem. The men soon found themselves in a ball of fire. A few hours later, as a priest was doing his evening rounds in the wards of a Cork City hospital, he nearly broke down by the sight of three men lying in their beds with severe burn injuries to their heads and limbs. 'Oh God, why do your do it, why do you insist in blowing yourselves and others up with your bombs?', he cried out to the three unfortunates before him.[135]

By 1959, post–Brookeborough when its memory began to fade from the public mindset, the IRA's campaign began to peter out. This was mainly due to a lack of interest and complacency by Nationalists on the other side of the border who, for the time being at least, were prepared to accept their lot as second class citizens in the six county State. The fact that the

IRA in the North wasn't as organised as might have been, also added to the problem. Because the Republican leadership had always been a southern based one, was also starting to come into play and cause difficulties. Within another ten years this Dublin based leadership would be caught completely off guard when the conflict exploded onto the streets of the North. They would neither have the arms nor trained men on the ground to deal with the crisis, but worse of all, they wouldn't see it coming, leaving hundreds of nationalist families homeless after being burnt out of their homes by orange mobs and B-Specials.

Back in 1959 though, the Dublin Government was confident enough that the IRA was on its last legs, to allow it to close down the Curragh Camp again, after releasing the last of its internees. The Border Campaign made a slight revival in 1961, and after an RUC man was killed in an ambush at the end of that year, De Valera and his new Minister for Justice, Charles Haughey, decided to put an end to the IRA once and for all by reintroducing military courts. Harassment of former prisoners was also stepped up, as were raids on the homes of Sinn Féin members. This was nothing new for Republicans and was easily tolerated. The main reason however, for the eventual ending of Operation Harvest, was a shortage of funds and a lack of popular support from the nationalist community around the Border. The campaign had cost the British Exchequer £1 million in outright damages (official figure) and approximately £10 million in increased police and military patrols. However, it was mainly Republican Volunteer causalities that made up the bulk of the human cost of the campaign.

While customs huts were being blown up along the border, Cork was once again making the headlines in June 1958, in a more peaceful way. In that month the remains of two patriot priests of the Capuchin Order, Frs Albert and Dominic, were brought home from the United States to be laid to rest in their native soil.

Together with Fr Michael O'Flanagan (a former Sinn Féin Vice President), these two priests had not been able to reconcile their conscience with the policy of their bishops, who were excommunicating Republicans during the Tan and Civil Wars. For example, in Cobh Bishop Browne would not allow the body of Volunteer Danny O'Halloran into St Colman's Cathedral in 1922. Father Dominic had been the Civic Chaplain of Terence McSwiney and Tomas MacCurtain, and in 1918 he had been appointed Brigade chaplain of the 1st Cork Brigade. He was arrested together with Fr Albert in early 1921 and after being tortured by British officers in Dublin Castle; he was sentenced to five years penal servitude and sent as a convict to an English prison, but was released again the following year under the General Amnesty. At a time when the Bishops, particularly Bishop Cohalan of Cork and sections of the press were telling the Volunteers that they were sinners and criminals, Fr Dominic would regularly give assurances to the brigade explaining that they were engaged in a just war.

On 15 December 1920, Fr Dominic sent a letter to the Brigade Adjutant Florrie O'Donoghue, to clarify Canon Law and reassure his Volunteers of the justness of their military campaign. The following section of the letter explains this position very clearly,

> Now, kidnapping, ambushing and killing, ordinarily would be grave sins or violations of Law. And, if these acts were performed by the I.V. as private persons (whether physical or moral) would fall under the Excommunication. But they are doing them by, and with, the authority of the State — the Republic of Ireland. And the State has the right and duty to defend the lives and property of its citizens and to punish, even with death, those who are aiming at the destruction of the lives or the property of its citizens or itself. It has, moreover, a right and duty to protect by every means in its power, the liberty of the State and its citizens against the Army of Occupation of a Foreign Power unjustly present in the country. [136]

When the Civil War broke out, both he and Fr Albert brought spiritual aid to the besieged IRA garrison in the Four Courts. The Catholic hierarchy soon made life very difficult for the priests to carry out their duties according to their calling and before long they were forced to leave for the United States. They continued to interact with the Irish community in the United States particularly with the many exiled Volunteers from the Tan and Civil Wars who had also been forced to leave Ireland.

In 1953 veterans of Cork No.1 Brigade set up a committee under the Chairmanship of Sean O'Hegarty to have the remains of the two priests repatriated and re-interred in Irish soil, but it wasn't until 13 June 1958 that the coffins of Frs Albert and Dominic were taken off a liner in Cork harbour and loaded onto a US Merchant Navy vessel to be landed at Cobh from where they had left Ireland more than thirty years before. The funeral cortege passed through the streets of Cork to Rochestown Cemetery, where one of the biggest funerals in Cork since those of MacCurtain and McSwiney took place. Present at the funeral were not only members of the Church and several politicians of the southern State, including Mr De Valera. Cumann na mBan was also well represented and over 500 members of the old Cork No. 1 Brigade as well as members of the Dublin Brigade were in attendance.

37. The Calm before the Storm

Following the disaster of the 1956–62 Border campaign things were relatively quiet everywhere, particularly in Cobh. The only activity keeping Republicans together was the annual Easter commemoration and the selling of Easter Lilies and Republican papers. The IRA was hardly active during this period, being more preoccupied with building itself up again, than paying attention to the rumblings of nationalist dissent beginning to surface in the Sectarian State across the border.

On Saturday 21 November 1964, on the eve of the Manchester Martyrs commemoration, a number of Cork Volunteers decided to pay their own tribute to their martyred comrades by opening fire on a British Frigate, the HMS *Relentless* as it was leaving the harbour. The ship had made a courtesy visit to Cork and was on its way to Derry when it came under attack on its way down river, just as it was clearing Passage West. Six Volunteers under the command of Gearóid Mac Cárthaigh had earlier taken up positions near the river, and although they could hardly see the *Relentless* because of the dense fog in the harbour that morning, the vessel itself solved this problem by sounding its fog horn. On the instruction of Mac Cárthaigh, the Volunteers opened fire at the British symbol of war at 8.35am, announcing that its presence was an unwelcome intrusion in an Irish harbour. About ten rounds from the Volunteers .303 Lee Enfield rifles and a couple of .22s were reported to have hit the vessel. Despite being shot at, the *Relentless*'s skipper Captain Watson later declared he would be 'delighted' to go back to Cork again. He also told reporters that not only were they shot at but his vessel had been picketed by a number of young men during her three day stay in Cork. Initially, Watson tried to excuse the shooting incident by claiming he thought it was someone engaged in duck shooting, but later admitted that whoever it was had been firing in the direction of his ship.

The Gardaí took the incident more seriously than a duck-shoot and posted men on all main roads to Cork; each car that passed was held up and searched, without result however. The only things the Gardaí did find were empty .303 and .22 shells near the scene of the firing. Later that day a note was handed into the offices of the *Cork Examiner* newspaper, in which Cork No. 1 Brigade claimed responsibility for the shooting incident. On the next day at the Manchester Martyrs commemoration the Republican Movement once again accepted responsibility for the attack. In a reaction to the incident, questions were asked by an Ulster Unionist in the British House of Commons, who wanted to know what the Irish government had to say about the matter. The British Minister for Defence

(Navy) answered: 'I think it is too minor an incident to expect protest', a remark that sparked several shouts of 'ooh' in the distinguished house, to which the Minister quickly added, 'The action was outrageous, but the Navy has faced more difficult engagements than this.' [137]

A Labour MP, obviously annoyed at the fuss the Unionist was making about the whole affair, asked with a touch of sarcasm whether the Minister thought it useful to consider a declaration of war in order to satisfy Ulster. Significantly enough, the British Minister failed to give an outright yes or no to this query.

Two years later a Carrigtwohill Republican, Jack Hartnett, expressed his attitude to the British influence in Cobh in a different though no less effective manner, when during the European Angling Championships in 1966, held in Cobh, he decided to act.

The flags of the participating countries, including that of Britain, had been raised for the occasion. However, Hartnett took a particular dislike to the Union Jack and tore it down, dumping it in the mud. For the next few years the British ensign was the odd one out on several international festivals held in Cobh, for fear that it would come in for special treatment again and thus embarrass not only the neighbouring nation, but also those living in the town who still had loyalty to the old empire.

In East Cork, Daithí O'Connell had already placed Eddie Collins in charge of the East Cork Volunteers. In 1968, a dispute developed at the E.I. factory in Limerick, where fifteen scabs were brought in by management to undermine a strike by the aggrieved workers. CIE bus drivers refused to ferry the scabs to the factory site, leading management to hire the services of a private bus company. After appeals by the men's union for the bus company not to transport the scabs fell on deaf ears, contact was then made with Cathal Goulding, the Official IRA Chief of Staff to intervene. Shortly afterwards, the company which took up the contract to ferry the scabs, lost six buses through fire. Eddie Collins and another Volunteer were later arrested and charged with causing more than £50 worth of damage to the vehicles. However, when the case later went to trial, the jury had by then come under the influence of another senior Republican, Sean Garland. 'We had a strong sense we were going to walk from that trial.' The jury later found the men not guilty. [138]

38. The Final Conflict

In the second half of the 1960s the Civil Rights Movement started gaining ground in the Six Counties. With the inequalities in housing, gerrymandering, and anti-Catholic discrimination, it is no wonder that it was in the North that the Civil Rights Movement mushrooned. In 1968 it gathered enormous international publicity when a civil rights demonstration was batoned by the sectarian police force. The brute force used by the RUC against the peaceful demonstrators spurred Republicans from all over Ireland including Cobh back to life, while also attracting new members to the movement.

The Republican Movement North and South became deeply involved in the events in the six counties, though the leadership didn't at first envisage a situation where armed force would be needed. It soon became clear however, that the Stormont Regime couldn't or wouldn't resolve the situation, while responding in the only way it knew how, to baton-charge the Civil Rights Movement into the ground. Nationalists had by now however, had enough of the life of the second class citizen and were determined to resist whatever the state threw at them. A massive boost in Nationalist confidence was delivered in 1969 when the people of Derry fought the RUC for two weeks with sticks and stones and petrol bombs, before beating them back out of the Bogside. Barricades were soon erected all around and the area which had by now become a no-go area for the RUC was named Free Derry. Panic soon spread right throughout Stormont. London, eager to keep its little sectarian Statelet away from international eyes on TV, sent in its first troops to Derry to keep a lid on the situation.

At first the troops were welcomed by many Nationalists who genuinely believed they had arrived with good intentions. Downing Street after all was making the right noises while speaking of introducing reforms and justice, though it plainly refused to accede to a demand by the Civil Rights leaders to abolish Stormont. Then the real test came when Orange mobs backed by B-Special RUC men started attacking Nationalist homes along the Falls Road in Belfast. Hundreds of families had to flee their burning homes, many ending up across the border in the south seeking sanctuary, some even settling as far south as Cobh. Meanwhile, when the first shots were fired into Nationalist homes, panic began to set in when it was realised there were few weapons available to a totally unprepared IRA for which to defend its communities. Despite this, some local Republicans managed to keep the joint Loyalist and RUC gunmen at bay with the little firepower they possessed. Causalities started mounting on both sides, though nationalists were clearly on the back foot from the ferocious boot of the Orange State. It was war, but clearly from a Republican/Nationalist perspective, it was a desperately cobbled together defensive effort. Before long, British troops started pouring into the North in even greater numbers. Soon the strain of being caught totally off guard with few weapons to defend their communities put enormous pressure on the southern Republican leadership by its northern members who were desperately trying to hold the line. Slogans began appearing on street walls with the words 'I Ran Away', in relation to the poor Republican response to the murderous activities of the Orange state. The demand for weapons was loud but they weren't forthcoming, or at least not quickly enough.

It was said that most of the army's weapons had been sold off to Welsh Nationalists after the failed Border Campaign had ended in 1962. Then in December 1969 matters came to a head when the Army split; the mainly northern faction becoming the Provisional IRA while the remaining southern faction now calling itself the Official IRA. In the South, where Republicans were somewhat removed from the hostilities, their inclination was to support the leadership they already knew and remain with the Officials. In the North, the first priority and preoccupation of Volunteers was to defend their communities. Desperate efforts were made in the South by many to secure weapons for the defence of Nationalists. Old veterans from the Tan War came forward with old Lee-Enfield rifles and machine guns that had been buried for many decades. Farmers handed over their shot guns and hunting rifles to both IRAs, later claiming them to have been stolen.

In Cobh, a prominent business manhanded over a pair of shot guns to the Officials. Mick Leahy the former 1st Cork Brigade O.C. produced an old Lewis Machine gun and handed it over to the Provisionals in Cork. The Officials, who were by far the dominant faction in Cobh, even reverted to the old tried and tested method of securing weapons as the first Volunteers in post 1916 did, and in at least one reported incident raided one of the old big houses on the Great Island in the hope of securing much needed arms. Even the Southern Government was doing its bit in defence of Northern Nationalists though it would later deny it. Secret trainings camps were taking place at Army Camps in Donegal. Some from the northern defence committees availed of this training, while many IRA volunteers declined, feeling Dublin could sell them out at anytime and leave them at the mercy of the British as it had done before. Weapons were also made available by the Dublin Government to the defence committees, with the right hand of the Government claiming not to know what the left hand was doing. All would later deny any knowledge of such gun running operations and despite a subsequent high profile court case, all would soon be forgotten, including the plight of northern Nationalists. As the two Republican Armies got their acts together and went from defensive to offensive mode, particularly against the British Army, the North would quickly become an embarrassing nightmare, and for successive Irish Governments, it would effectively become an albatross around its neck. Their responses to what would become a long war of attrition between the IRA and British forces, was to let the British get on with it and hope that they wouldn't engage in too many big killings or human rights abuses. But despite what would follow, the Dublin and Monaghan bombings and the long catalogue of murders by the British and its secret services in the South and the North, every Government that held power in Dublin during the conflict, would refuse to accept that the British were part of the problem. Not only that, but they would go on to openly collude with the British under a sanitised term they would call 'Cross Border Cooperation'. Citizens on the southern side of the border including elected representatives would be kidnapped and shot; others would be assassinated in their beds, with little or no follow up investigation by the Gardaí. Because of what would eventually become the long-term, backward policy of all Dublin governments towards the North, it effectively removed any chance of an easy or swift solution to the conflict. What could have been a relatively small and short conflict with the prospect of being resolved in less than five years was often horrific and went on to last for more than twenty five.

As far as Dublin was concerned, the IRA and Loyalists equalled bad, the British equalled Honest Brokers, and they themselves were just trying to keep the lid on things. It didn't seem to occur to them, no matter how distasteful it might have appeared, that the Nationalist people saw the British Government and its army as anything but honest and neutral, and it was partially because of that, that people saw the IRA as their legitimate and only defenders. Further more, if Dublin saw the IRA as being the problem and if Northern Nationalists saw the British Government and its military forces as being the problem, then surely there could never be a solution found, unless both of those parties were part of it. It therefore beggars belief as to why successive Dublin Governments went tacitly along prolonging the agony for all involved. The censorship which Dublin introduced in the early years of the conflict and which was specifically designed to silence Republicans and stifle any debate which might offer an alternative view of the conflict from that of the official government, in effect increased the ignorance, paranoia and one sided view of official Ireland towards the North.

In late 1969, Sean MacStiofáin, the first Chief of Staff of the Provisional IRA asked Eddie Collins of Mogeely to report to the border, and from

Republicans Denis Murphy (left) and Tom McGoey (centre lead). The funeral of Vol Martin O'Leary 1971 – picture by *Cork Examiner.*

there, to carefully work his way into the six counties by organising safe houses for the coming campaign. At first Collins found it difficult as he received some hostility from families who had earlier looked after and fed Volunteers during the 1950s Border Campaign. Some of those families went hungry themselves so that the Volunteers didn't, now they complained they hadn't even received a Christmas card from some of them since. Collin's task was not an easy one, but with every passing day, the situation on the ground ensured that more and more doors were opening to the Volunteers, and before long, most of the Nationalist Community, particularly around the border had become part of the war effort.

By 1970, Eddie Collins was back in charge of his own unit in East Cork again. Earlier they had received a visit from a number of those in charge of the Cork Command including, Jack Lynch, Tom McCarthy and John Madden, appealing for them to remain on with the Officials. The meeting took place in Collins' house and every one of the East Cork volunteers present declined the Officials offer and declared allegiance to the Provisionals. Earlier, the Volunteers had attended an Army Convention in a Dublin hotel, and were partially influenced by the fact that many other units from around the country had also declared for the Provisionals. Later that year, Eddie Collins' East Cork unit had some early successes in their hunt to acquire much needed weapons.

Their first success was when they raided the FCA Barracks in Dungarvan and scooped a number of .303 Lee-Enfield rifles. That was later followed by a raid on the Slua FCA Hall in Midleton. Mac Stiofáin was aware of these two operations and offered to supply personnel from up the country to assist the locals, but Collins insisted on picking his own trusted team from the East Cork Volunteers for the operations. From Midleton, he had received good intelligence that all the local weapons were kept in a strong-room under the stage in the Slua Hall. When they moved in to remove them, they discovered all the weapons and supplies of ammuni-

Official republican colour party 1971.

tion were exactly where they were told they would be. The Volunteers quickly cleared out everything they could find. Their only difficulty they had on the night, was the huge effort they had to make to load a big mortar gun in to the back of a van they had had positioned across the street near the local cinema. The joint Dungarvan and Midleton raids, netted the Volunteers a total of eighteen rifles, six Bren machine guns, eight Gustav sub-machine guns, two .303 rifles converted to fire .22 ammunition for training purposes, thousands of rounds of assorted ammunition, and other military equipment. They were immediately taken to a safe hiding place, from where they were moved across the border by Mac Stiofáin's people two days later. Collins held on to the two converted .22 rifles for Volunteer training in the locality.

For reasons of security, Eddie Collins resided in Youghal at this time and would only visit his own home at Mogeely during the hours of darkness once a week. This would usually take place on Thursday nights when he would undertake training exercises in the locality with Volunteer recruits using the two new converted rifles taken in Midleton. The two rifles were kept in the possession of another Volunteer who was unknown to the authorities at the time. He would bring the weapons to Collins home earlier in the evening and conceal them in a wardrobe in the house. The next day when training was completed, he would collect the weapons again and return them to their safe hiding place. One Thursday evening while he was otherwise detained, Collins sent a message to the Volunteer contact

Protest march through Cobh, West Beach after Bloody Sunday.

that he wouldn't make it that night and training would have to be deferred until the following night.

The Volunteer however, had already delivered the rifles to Collins' house earlier that day. The next morning, people awoke to hear news reports of a big arms find uncovered on a farmhouse in Mogeely in East Cork. The Special Branch in fact, had only netted the two converted training rifles and not the entire haul of weapons taken in the Dungarvan and Midleton raids, which they were publicly claiming. Neither did they get the man responsible for organising those two operations. Shortly afterwards, the Gardaí arrested Collins as he was passing the local station in Youghal on a motorbike. He was charged with possession of the two stolen rifles at his Mogeely home and of stealing all the others taken in the two raids. For some strange reason though, they then released him pending his trial. Collins knew there was nothing he could do but to go on the run. He then reported back to the border for active service.

Meanwhile in Cobh in 1970, divisions in Sinn Féin were about to split the local organisations along the same lines as the Army had earlier done, though the issue of recognising Leinster House would also come into play. A meeting held in the ITGWU Hall at East Beach, saw Joe O'Neill, Paddy Collins and Seanie Walsh, leave the party to set up a Cumann of the Provisionals. Those of the majority who stayed behind remained loyal locally, to Dan Collins and Tom McGoey and to the leadership of the

Official republican Anti EEC rally in Cobh 1972.

Official organisation nationally. Another source belonging to the Officials claimed the local split didn't materialise but rather was one where those who went on to form a Provisional Cumann, had earlier drifted away. In an interview with Seanie Walsh some years before he passed away in 1989, he told me that when he returned to Cobh in 1971 he was initially approached by the Officials to join that organisation but he declined in favour of the Provisionals. This might indicate that Seanie was not present at any walk out of a previous meeting. This was later expanded upon by the late Paddy Collins however, who explained that Seanie had initially returned from New York in 1969 and went back to the United States shortly afterwards to wrap up his final business there before returning to Cobh with his three sons in 1971. Paddy insisted that Seanie had earlier decided which way he would align himself, and following the local split, that's exactly what he did. For Seanie, the position was very clear and straightforward, there could be no sell-out by recognising Leinster House and this was a position he never relinquished up until the day he died. I had a heated discussion with Seanie one morning outside of the Post Office in town, after Sinn Féin had shortly before taken a decision to recognise Leinster House. That was in late 1986, sixteen years after Seanie had first offered his services to the Provisional leadership. I endeavoured to explain to Seanie of the tactical position of where the then leadership was coming from and that there would be no winding down of the military campaign until its final goals were met. Seanie however, wouldn't budge an inch on the issue of Leinster House, but he did agree to keep supporting the movement as long as the war effort was maintained.

Although the Officials continued to meet at the Union Hall on East Beach (with permission from its Branch Secretary and former Volunteer Gerry 'Daddler' Kelly), it was mainly preoccupied in military matters. The provisionals on the other hand who were far less organised, had only a handful of members, with nothing of a military organisation. This poorly organised group who were virtually starting out from scratch, used to meet at a rented room at Harbour Hill. Those individuals from Cobh who decided to join the Provisional Army were guided towards the organisation in Cork City, while those who opted for the more popular and public Official IRA, did so locally. The local Official Movement was well organised, earning itself the respect of those in command at the Tomas Ashe Hall in Cork. Although the military structures of the Officials were not entirely the same as those when Mick Leahy or Mick Burke commanded the Cobh Company, they were never the less a well led unit of Volunteers, and although they may have had in their ranks, one or two who could be best described as impulsive and reckless like their former predecessor Daithí O'Brien of a previous generation, they were in fact, equal to their predecessors in terms of knowhow and commitment. During the course of a conversation I had with the late Jack Lynch (former O.C. of the Officials in Cork) in 1982, the Veteran Republican whose military exploits stretched back to the 1930s, told me that of all the Volunteers he had ever operated with, none had matched the bravery he had seen of Cobhman Tom McGoey.

On 22 September 1970, a meeting was held in Bantry West Cork of IRA veterans and Republicans from the North and South. Some 150 people attended the meeting, and among those veterans present were Mick Leahy, Liam Deasy and Criostóir de Baróid. The meeting was called to see what assistance could be given to the Provisionals efforts up North.

Back in Cobh, the Officials were continually building. A local former British Soldier was even recruited to assist with the training of Volunteers. This weapons training would take place at the sand pits at the back of the island, close to where the Volunteers trained in the 1930s and 1940s. Such was the level and standard of training undertaken by the Cobh Volunteers that by the time Internment was introduced in the North in August 1971; the leadership sent a special VIP on a mission to the area. The VIP who was to act as an Envoy to the Canadian people was sent by the 'Officials' leadership. He was to engage there in a public speaking tour, outlining the real state of affairs in the North including the human cost of Internment and the British presence. The tour was also hoped to raise much needed funds for their military campaign back home in the North. The Envoy was also expected to explain how Republican Freedom Fighters back in Ireland were responding to the British Governments War on the Nationalist Community, and this was why he had first visited Cobh. When he arrived in the town, he was taken to the back of the island where he was given a demonstration of the first Armalite rifle to have reached Ireland. It was clear that the Officials were away ahead of the Provisionals in terms of getting much needed weapons into the country.

The Officials also had the added advantage of not having to limit themselves to where they would acquire such weapons. Their links to the Soviet Union, though limited at first, would prove to be fruitful in terms of acquiring much needed weaponry and money. In addition to the effectiveness and capability of the Official organisation in Cobh, another likely reason why they were chosen to give a demonstration of the first Armalite to arrive into Ireland, was because it more than likely arrived through the port of Cobh. Later that year in October, another effort to smuggle arms in through Cobh by the Provisionals was less successful however. On the 19 October, the tender serving a liner from the United States, the QE2, docked at the Deepwater Quay. All the luggage was unloaded on the quay and was subject to Customs Inspection as usual. However, at the completion of the examination six large blue suitcases were still unclaimed. One of the Customs officials subsequently went to lift one of the cases to bring it the Customs' lock-up for the night. But on trying to lift the suitcase found it was too heavy, and called a big twenty-stone 6ft-3 baggage handler to do the job for him. It was this baggage man 'Sharkey Griffin' who later claimed that he had said to himself, 'It is heavy enough to contain arms' when lifting the cases, but he nevertheless brought the six cases to the Customs' shed and thought no more of the matter. However, a Customs official who subsequently checked the contents of the cases made what the media referred to as 'the sensational discovery,'[139] contacted the Gardaí, and the cases were duly taken to Cobh Garda Station. Volunteers who had earlier turned up to claim the suitcases immediately withdrew when they found the Deepwater Quay area in pandemonium. Not only had the local police been called in, but so had the Special Branch and even an Army Captain. After the initial examination in Cobh the cases were removed to Cork under heavy army escort, with the lorry in which the arms were transferred being surrounded by soldiers armed with Gustav machine-guns.

Later there was a full check of the contents of the cases at Union Quay Garda Station. Then to add a bit of drama to the already exciting events, the investigation of the cases was interrupted by the firing of shots near the Union Quay. The detectives hadn't had this much excitement for a while, and carloads of them rushed off to investigate the shooting. Then there was a phone call a few minutes later, stating that a bomb had been placed in a Cork cinema. Out rushed the detectives again only to learn it was a hoax. The Gardaí later stated that the IRA must have planned to raid the Customs lock-up during the nigh to remove the cases, not aware that IRA Volunteers had in fact been there, under their noses, to collect the cases in the normal way. Gardaí in Cobh spent the day searching for a person by the name of Walsh, which was the name on the suitcases. They questioned a passenger family by that name on board the QE2 but later dismissed them as not having any connection to the affair. It didn't seem to occur to them, that a well known Republican by the name 'Walsh' had only returned from New York with his family a few months beforehand, and that he may have had something to do with the cases. Two kitchen porters of the QE2 Liner were later charged with possession of two rifles, two Springfield rifles, seven Armalite rifles, fourteen magazines, one rifle butt, five telescopic sights, 7,390 rounds of ammunition and thirty-seven hand grenades. During the trial which took place in England, the two Belfast men denied any involvement in the attempted arms-smuggling, one of them claiming that he had been tricked into keeping the suitcases in his cabin by an assistant steward. The steward, appearing as a witness in the trial, naturally denied this, claiming that it had been the other way around.

On 2 April 1971 the people of the coastal town of Baltimore in West Cork were awoken to a loud explosion. A Royal Navy launch which was moored in the bay for some time was seen no more. The 35ft motor launch which was said to be worth between £15,000 and £20,000 was engaged in a marine survey of Baltimore Bay on behalf of the Irish government. The launch was attached to the HMS *Hecate* which was said to be on its way to the scene (well inside Irish waters). While one launch alongside the British naval vessel avoided damage, another did not, with one of the two taking the impact of the explosion being later discovered grounded near Sherkin. A Volunteer of the Official IRA, who participated in the operation, later claimed that a British Duke had been observed onboard the launch in the days preceding the explosion, and was their main target.

Later in 1971, with the national outcry caused by the introduction of Internment in the North, two Sinn Féin Cumainn were formed in Cobh. The first one was started up in August by the Officials, and adopted the name of local patriot 'Maurice Moore'. It elected Dan Collins as its Chairman, Tom McGoey Vice-Chairman, Denis Murphy Hon. Secretary and John O'Brien Hon. Treasurer. A month later, a Provisional Cumann was established which also adopted the name of a Clonmult martyr, 'Seamus Ahern'. Joe O'Neill was elected its Chairman, Liam O'Brien elected Secretary, and Mick Leahy (grand-nephew of the former brigade O.C.) was elected Treasurer.

When internment was introduced in the North in August, people awoke one morning to find hundreds of men taken in dawn swoops. Later that night several people were killed in incidents of shooting, rioting, burnings and looting. Within two days the official death-toll had risen to twenty three. It was clear that the internment round-ups had been solely aimed at the Nationalist community. In the wake of the riots and the consequent deaths, Cobh UDC passed a vote of sympathy to the relatives of those who had been killed or injured, with Cllr Pat O'Mahony calling on the Dublin Government to withdraw all Irish Troops from abroad and request immediate UN intervention. It was also decided to arrange for collections outside of all Cathedral masses in aid of the refugee fund. On 18 August, the following letter appeared in the *Cork Examiner* by a group of Cobh Protestants: J.A.D. Bird, W.T. Batson, R.H. Warbrook and Richard Ward. 'Having read the text of the "Protestant leaders" statement in support of internment, we wish to dissociate ourselves from it. It is unfortunate that the political decision to intern without trial should have applied in such a one-sided manner, and having immediately given rise to such tragic events, been supported by leaders of Christian churches.'[140]

Earlier in May, another incident took place in Cobh which caused a bit of a stir. An Englishman by the name of Robinson, known locally as the 'Count', almost had his house at Leonard's Lodge burned down on the 18 May after he covered its roof with a big Union Jack in honour of the Lord Mayor of London who was paying a courtesy visit to Cork at the time. As Robinson's house overlooked the harbour below, he knew the flag would be very visible to the Lord Mayor's passing ship as it made its way up-river to the city. Unfortunately for him, it was also visible to the general public, many of whom thought it was very distasteful and provocative. Word soon spread around the town about the Count's latest escapade and before long people began to make their way to Leonard's Lodge, mainly out of curiosity to see what was going on. As an eleven-year-old school boy at the time, I can recall leaving St Joseph's National School on that particular day, when another boy rushed up to a few of us and excitedly announced that there was trouble down at the Count's house and that we should get down there fast. We naturally headed off to Leonard's Lodge on the double, and arrived just in time to find two local men trying to set fire to the flag on the roof with a box of firelighters. After a few unsuccessful attempts, they finally got the British ensign alight.

To our utter amazement however, there was neither sight nor sound of the 'Count' or the Gardaí, only onlookers who were probably expecting the IRA to show up and take matters in hand. We couldn't understand why the owner didn't come out to try to quench the burning flag and protect his home; though in hindsight it is possible that he was at that point in protective custody at the local Garda Barracks. The flag fire eventually burned itself out with no damage to the building itself. The men responsible for setting the flag alight were later charged with attempted arson but received the minimum fine of one shilling each. The District Court Judge was obviously well versed in Robinson's activities and how he had been acting as a general nuisance in the community. One of those charged, oddly enough, happened to be the big baggage handler at the Deepwater Quay at the time of the failed attempt by the Provisionals to smuggle weapons into Cobh five months later.

Robinson, (the Count) was considered an eccentric, but his continued anti-Republican activities were seen as a nuisance by not only Republicans but by most people in the town, which probably included the Gardaí. The Englishman appeared to detest anything Nationalist and Republican and found it particularly trying to keep his views to himself. Republicans naturally came in for special attention, and Robinson would follow them around at night when they were erecting posters or painting wall slogans. He would throw sods of earth at them and try to distract them from what they were doing. Other times, he would resort to the paint brush himself and would modify the slogans that Republicans had just completed: thus the ingenuous Robinson would add a 'W' at the end of a freshly painted 'EEC-NO', changing the whole nature of the intended message. However, it was the Republicans who were to have the last laugh. One night when Robinson was having a busy time adding his 'W's, he was surprised by two seventeen-year-old youths.

The Englishman not being too popular with anyone in town, the youths decided to tip off the Republicans, who were a short distance ahead. Robinson's talent for disguises obviously wasn't as well developed as those for painting, for the Republicans were already well aware of his presence and were observing his activities in the reflection of a shop window, while the Englishman was observing them through the lens of a camera, taking snap-shots of them. The Republicans let it go for a while, but when Robinson continued, not knowing when to call it a day, they pursued him to retrieve the film from his camera. The stubborn and foolish Robinson ended up bruised for his trouble. In a subsequent court hearing, the two youths who initially stumbled upon Robinson as he baited the Republicans gave evidence in favour of the two accused, Tom McGoey and Denis Murphy. When Robinson announced to the court that he would be acting as his own counsel, no one appeared surprised. However, as could be expected, things soon got out of hand, with the Englishman becoming increasingly agitated in an attempt to convince the court of his right. Eventually the judge had to order Gardaí to remove the half hysterical man, and put him in a separate room from which he could follow proceedings in the courtroom. When the trial continued, with one of the counsels locked up safely, the two youths were called to the stand to give evidence. Robinson, they each claimed had pursued the Republicans and provoked them. Robinson, who was by this time in a frenzy, could be seen jumping up and down in the adjoining room, screaming that no such thing happened, that he had been the victim, that the Republicans were the culprits, but to no avail. Also in the courtroom was former IRA Commander and Fianna Fáil TD, Martin Corry who spoke on behalf of McGoey and Murphy. He said he was heartened to see people in Cobh standing up for themselves again, by which he obviously didn't mean Robinson. Meanwhile outside the court, there was a protest demonstration in progress. Republicans of all shades and supporters were holding up placards and chanting slogans against the fact that the two Republicans were brought to trial in the first place. McGoey and Murphy were acquitted.

Many people began to wonder and worry about Robinson as his experiences around the burning flag and stalking Republicans incidents didn't appear to teach him anything, as he continued with his obsessive anti-Republican behaviour.

One day while a local Republican was in town shopping with his wife and children, he bumped into a friend and as they began chatting, they noticed Robinson across the street taking photographs of them. Ted Noonan pretended at first not to have noticed Robinson with his camera, but as soon as he saw the man go into a nearby phone-booth to change the film, he and with his friend (a member of the Cork Volunteer Pipe Band) crossed over the street in pursuit. The two men demanded the handover of the camera's film, but when he refused, they forcibly removed it themselves. Noonan then wrapped the phone-cord around Robinson's neck and gave it a few tugs, in the hope it would encourage him to back off. After he released it again, Robinson bolted out of the phone booth and ran as fast as his legs would take him towards the nearby Garda Station, at Westbourne Place. Before he could reach the Station however, Noonan had already used the phone receiver in his hand and had phoned in his own complaint of assault against Robinson. In the subsequent court case which followed, Robinson was found guilty of assault and of breaching the peace. The indignant Englishman later appealed the case to the Circuit Court, which overturned the decision of the District Court. It gradually dawned on Robinson that he may be overstaying his welcome in Cobh. Eventually the Official IRA helped him to make up his mind when they placed a small device at the gable of his house. Although it was too small and wasn't intended to cause any serious damage, it nevertheless persuaded the man to leave the locality. The Gardaí placed a small caravan with a permanent guard on duty, outside of the house for some weeks after the attack, but Robinson, many believed, did them and everyone a favour by packing up and leaving town.

On 23 October 1971 a report in *The Irish Times* gave a report of six Official Sinn Féin men in Cork being arrested under the offences against the state act and being taken to the Bridewell Garda Station. The six were Ted Tynan, Bernard Lynch, Tom McGoey (Cobh) Derry Dineen, David Harrington and John Connors. The report failed to explain why the men were taken into custody or how long they were held.

In the North, things had gone from bad to worse. The British having long since abandoned all pretences of impartiality when they had ransacked the Falls Road in Belfast, during a two day curfew in 1970. It had then become evident that it certainly wasn't the British who would help the beleaguered Nationalist community, and during subsequent programmes nothing was done to stop rampaging loyalists. By 1971, the IRA let the troops know there was a price to pay for their unwanted presence, when it had claimed its first military casualty. By January 1972, the British decided to take off the gloves and teach the natives a lesson. Once again a Civil Rights demonstration in Derry would be the target of Paratroopers.

Before the day was over, fourteen men whose only crime was to attend the march, were dead and many more were injured. Much of the world's media was in Derry for the March and captured some of the scenes on camera. Although it later became clear that the Paratroopers had hoped to draw out the two IRAs into an open fight, neither the Officials or Provisionals took the bait, though an eye witness would later claim that an individual member of the Officials was seen to produce a hand gun and returned fire from an apartment at one stage, but soon abandoned firing when he realised its ineffectiveness in the overall situation. The British had scored a massive own-goal, and immediately launched a counter publicity campaign, blaming the demonstrators for attacking their troops; they even went as far as planting blast bombs on some of the bodies of the dead, a PR practice that would be used to perfection on many occasions in the years that would follow. The entire country went into shock by the Derry massacre.

In every corner of Ireland, meetings were held to protest and show the indignation felt over the massacre of innocent civilians. Throughout the month of February there were several reported incidents of Protestants being intimidated in the twenty-six counties. On 18 February a letter appeared in the *Cork Examiner*, sent on behalf of Denis Murphy of the Cobh Official Sinn Féin Cumann. The letter which disclaimed all responsibility for the incidents of harassment was as follows:

> It has been brought to my attention that persons unknown, claiming to be members of the Republican Movement, have been threatening and terrorising British-working-class people in the Cobh area. I would like, on behalf of the above Branch of Gardiner Place SF, to inform these people that we had nothing whatsoever to do with these sectarian acts, as they do not forward the aims of the Republican Movement towards a workers Republic.[141]

It is not clear, who was responsible for the harassment of English and Protestant people which Denis Murphy was referring to in his letter. Was he hinting that it had been the work of Provisional members, or were they ordinary members of the public who had taken a few drinks, and who were still angry after Bloody Sunday, and took it out on those they believed to be somehow connected to Britain? Or perhaps the harassment had been carried out by Murphy's own organisation, and because of some recent bad press it had received, was ordered by his Head Office to issue a statement, distancing itself from such behaviour. But regardless of who might have been responsible for the harassment, the spirit of Denis Murphy's letter is exactly how most genuine Republicans would see themselves proceeding.

Following the Bloody Sunday massacre, a special service was held at Christchurch, Rushbrooke Cobh, at which the members of Cobh UDC attended. Hundreds of workers from industries around the Lower Harbour marched in a procession to the Town Hall, where a letter was handed in to the Chairman of the UDC, Donal Casey, with a request that it would be forwarded to the Taoiseach. Then, just in case anyone local might have believed in the scare stories of Protestants being harassed, intimidated or afraid to speak out, that notion was quickly put to bed by another Cobh letter which appeared in the *Cork Examiner*. The letter which was written by a young Protestant woman named Wendy Casey, expressed her horror at 'the savagery perpetrated in the name of law and order.' She stated that 'successive British governments have lent their support to a regime of bigotry and injustice in the North of our country. I am a Protestant. The very word coined from "protest". Let us voice our protest now by condemning this latest affront to the dignity of man.'[142]

In Dublin, a protest rally which marched on the British Embassy soon got out of control and ended with the building being burnt to the ground. In Cork, an attempt was made to burn the British Rail offices in Patrick Street, when a crowd of over a thousand marched in protest over the Derry killings. The British Rail offices had also been targeted the previous May, when groups protested against the continued imprisonment of Republicans in Britain and against the visit of the Lord Mayor of London to Cork, (the same event which caused a Union Flag to be set on fire in Cobh). On 22 May, the office window was smashed by a large stone. The demonstrators had first protested outside of Collins Barracks, and when they thought that nothing more could be achieved by chanting slogans at the Free State soldiers preceded towards the British Rail offices in the city centre. What had earlier been intended as a peaceful march by its organisers (the Officials), soon got out of hand when stones started flying through the air.

The Gardaí who were present at the scene were at a complete loss and had to stand by helplessly as there was nothing they could do to control the crowd. They tried appealing to the march organisers to keep their people under control, with one asking; half pleadingly 'can't you just leave it at that?'[143] The Gardaí feared that the whole shopping street would be looted. The wine shop next to British Rail had already had its window shattered, and the policemen knew from experience that if a liquor store was the first to go, others would follow. However, the organisers would have been more than happy to 'leave it at that', but they were just as unsuccessful as the Gardaí in trying to break up the crowd. They pleaded with the chanting youths to disband, realising the adverse publicity that was sure to result from an 'Official' organised parade, ending in looting and rioting, but to no avail.

Eventually it was the Special Branch who took the first action against the protestors; when a group of people set fire to a Union Jack. This was clearly more that the Branch-men were prepared to tolerate and surrounded those burning the flag. Yet they had hardly encircled those youths when another section of the crowd started throwing fire-bombs at the British Rail offices. The fire brigade was called in, but were hindered in their efforts to quench the flames, and only with the help of Gardaí, did they eventually succeed in putting out the fire and save the building, amidst hails of abuse and jeers from the crowd. One of those in the crowd who was later charged with impeding the fire brigade from doing its work was Cobhman John Mansworth. Mansworth was consequently arrested and received a three-month jail sentence for 'wilfully impeding members of the Cork Fire Brigade'.[144]

But the biggest and most direct reaction to Bloody Sunday came from the IRA, when the Officials targeted the Parachute Regiments Headquarters at Aldershot in Hampshire. The bomb was placed in a parked car and was situated directly outside of the Officers Mess. However, when the time-release mechanism went off on the morning of 22 February (three weeks after Bloody Sunday) none of the intended target was present. The Para soldiers were then stationed overseas, including Ireland. Instead, seven civilians, including a gardener, kitchen staff, and a Catholic priest, Fr Gerry Weston, who had just pulled up behind the bomb were killed. Nineteen others were also injured by the explosion which was heard a mile away. The Officials released a statement the next day, claiming responsibility and saying it was revenge for Bloody Sunday. Anne Harris, the wife of Eoghan Harris, later wrote an article in the *Hibernia* magazine justifying the bombing. Then in November a Republican activist named Noel Jenkinson was charged with causing the explosion and received a lengthy prison sentence. He died four years later from heart failure.

Meanwhile in Cobh, the 'Officials' were flourishing as an organisation. The British own-goal of Bloody Sunday saw recruits flock to both IRAs in their droves in all parts of the country. The Officials were comfortably able to sell 240 copies of *The United Irishmen* paper in Cobh each week. They also received financial support from a number of business people in the town, and when they held social functions in the Commodore Hotel, they were able to sell the place out. When they launched a publicity campaign, they could do it with posters and leaflets, while their poor relation the 'Provisionals' would regularly have to rely solely on the paint brush to get their message across. The Officials had a political strategy and policies, the 'Provisionals' didn't, except the sole one of bringing about a British withdrawal from Ireland. As one former Provisional member from that period put it, 'We were only a few in Cobh at that time, and were nothing more than cheerleaders for the northern effort. The Officials on the other hand had it all to play for. They were big in numbers here in Cobh, were well organised and had a political strategy but their leadership blew it all, by winding it down as soon as it looked like they were going somewhere.' The former Provisional, also described a situation which was not unlike that surrounding the early Volunteers in 1913-14 where some joined up for all the wrong reasons and left again almost as soon as they tired of the image. He said he saw the same thing happen with the Officials. 'It was common for couples to join up "boyfriends and girlfriends" it was almost like it was a fashion statement at the time, but those people never lasted long in either movement.' [145]

Both groups focused mainly around the street walls and poles leading to and from Saint Colman's Cathedral, in order to sell their message as they knew everyone would have to pass by on their way to Mass. The Officials for example would erect fly-posters on walls which would ask a simple question: 'Do You Buy British Propaganda Daily?' in reference to the increasing number of Irish people who were then reading British tabloid newspapers, thus receiving only one side of the Northern story. The same Mass-goers might also have seen a simple 'Provisional' message painted on a wall which would read 'Brits Out'.

Both groups would also use the Church when it came to selling Easter Lilies. Christy Griffin, who had been a Sinn Féin member prior to the split and later remained with the Officials, recalled how it would almost be an annual ritual for the Parish Priest Fr Thornhill and Joe Sherlock to argue over the sale of Easter Lilies on church property, the Parish Priest always insisting the Republicans kept a distance of ten feet from the main gate. The Provisionals on the other hand seemed to have more trouble from the Gardaí than the clergy. They were forced to operate a system where they would have a number of Fianna Éireann members on standby behind a wall leading away from the Cathedral (The Rock) and when the Gardaí would arrive as they always did, a sprint would be made to get rid of the full boxes of collected money over the wall to avoid confiscation. Although there were big political and ideological differences between both groups, there didn't seem to be any animosity between the local members on a personal level. One former Official member reported that as he was returning to his 'Top of the Hill' home one Sunday morning at about 2.am, he walked past a group of Provisionals who were in the middle of painting a wall slogan (presumably intended for that mornings Mass-goers). He saluted and bade goodnight by name to the man he assumed was in charge of the operation, and duly had the compliment returned to him. At one point, two members of the same family were each a member of the other faction, one a short-time member of the Provisionals, the other a long-term member of the Officials and who later remained loyal throughout its various changes of political direction until it faded into the Labour party.

Around this time in Cobh, a group of mavericks with no political affiliation blasted a Garda squad car parked outside of the Garda Station. On another occasion they abducted some naval personnel and brought them to the railway station, where guns were put to their heads. The sailors were threatened and abused for being 'Free Staters' and although only starting pistols were used to add a bit of credibility to it all, the threat must have seemed real enough to them.

The Dock Bar in Rushbrooke also had its share of trouble, when a person selling the *United Irishman* (the paper of the Officials) was refused permission to sell them on the premises. The next day a suspicious looking package was found on the premises but was nothing more than a hoax. No one ever claimed responsibility, but the bar-owner, Liam O'Leary (brother of the former Labour leader, and later Fine Gael TD, Michael O'Leary) must have drawn his own conclusions.

In the early hours of Saturday 3 July 1971 a Cork Unit of the Official IRA moved in to plant a couple of explosive devices at Mogul Mines in

Silvermines, Co. Tipperary. The Volunteers had intended to blow up an electrical power station and a back up generator at the plant. The Officials were asked to intervene in a bitter dispute on the side of the workers which had then been dragging on there for months. The dispute which initially came about over the sacking of a worker, soon escalated to one involving the general safety conditions on the site. Earlier, the Canadian multinational company had been fined a mere £70 for the death of a worker killed by negligence on its part, when he fell off a roof of a building whose foundations had been undermined by the mining. Although the workers life was only worth £70, the company took $8.5 million in profits out of Ireland that same year. At the time the Officials were actively involved in the campaign to have Irish natural resources utilized on behalf of the people of Ireland and not for foreign multinationals. They were also aware that the Multinational Company had come in to Silvermines in 1968 to mine for mineral barites, but had since discovered lead and zinc deposits too.

After attempting to detonate their explosive devices on the night of 3 July, the Volunteer Unit discovered that only one had gone off successfully. The one at the main substation had detonated perfectly, completely destroying the building. The other device on the back-up generator failed to detonate. It was then that Volunteer Martin O'Leary decided to go back to check it. Unbeknownst to him, the initial explosion caused the whole area including the back-up generator to go live with an electrical current. As soon as O'Leary touched it, he received massive electrical burns to most of his body. He died three days later from his wounds in Limerick Hospital.

Volunteer Martin O'Leary was given full military honours at his funeral which had a force of 200 Gardaí walking with the hearse. Among the military Colour Party which led the funeral procession to the Republican Plot at St Finbarr's Cemetery, were two Cobhmen, Tom McGoey and Denis Murphy. When they arrived at the cemetery, mourners found it ringed by another force of 500 Gardaí. After O'Leary's remains were lowered into the grave in the Republican Plot which had been secretly dug the night before, an oration was delivered by Cathal Goulding, the Official IRA Chief of Staff. Then when the proceedings ended, detectives arrested Goulding and charged him with inciting people to 'commit indictable crimes contrary to the Explosive Substances Act, 1883.'[146] The case later collapsed in court when it transpired that those who arrested him hadn't taken notes and couldn't properly remember what he had said during his address. Goulding's counsel in court was none other than a Chief of Staff from another era, Sean McBride, who tore the Garda case to shreds.

In October, a unit of the Official IRA carried out a raid on the home of the French family at Marino Point, near Carrigaloe. Lt Colonel Robert Stuart-French was related to the family of the same name at Cuskinny who had also been raided for arms during the Tan War. He was also the same Captain French who was involved in a dispute with the Irish Transport and General Workers Union in Cobh in 1922, when the Dáil instructed Seamus Fitzgerald to mediate in the case through a Republican Court of Arbitration. However, on this occasion, the Volunteers didn't quite have the same success as their earlier counterparts, as all they could locate were some useless antique weapons. It was reported that French had been beaten during the raid and was threatened that the house would be burnt. Soon after the raid, the French family decided to sell their estate at Marino Point, and this later led to speculation in some quarters that maybe the Official IRA's visit to the house had been very convenient for others who had an interest in the estate. It is believed that a syndicate of property speculators with a connection to a politician soon gained possession of the land and subsequently sold it on to the state body N.E.T. the fertilizer industry, which immediately started work on the site of the now former IFI plant.

Immediately after the French raid, letters began appearing in the national papers, suggesting that the raid was the result of a dirty tricks operation by the SAS and MI6. One such letter which appeared in the Irish Times on 11 October 1971, from a P.F. Curran of the Catholic Ex-Serviceman's Association in Belfast, condemned the attack on Lt. Col. French, but suggested that it had been carried out to discredit Republicans.

On Thursday afternoon 24 August 1972 two men walked into the Allied Irish Bank at Westbourne Place in Cobh and cleared the cashbox and safe in the bank, adding in a Northern accent 'it is for a good cause'. The two Derrymen, Hugo Meenan and James Deehan, belonged to the Saor Éire Action Group. (A Republican freelance group which specialised in bank robberies and which normally passed on its booty to either of the IRAs for their war effort). Just before closing time on that Thursday, Deehan walked into the bank, while his partner stayed at the door, chatting to the porter, and told the bank manager that he wished to open an account. The Manager, Mr Bernal, eagerly handed the potential customer the documents required, and in return the decent looking Northerner produced a first deposit of five pounds and a gun. The bank manager later stated that 'this was like something you would see in Mission Impossible.'[147]

The second man, Meenan, had by now been let in by the porter, by telling him that his friend was inside, an argument that convinced the porter to allow him in before closing the bank for the day. Deehan then threw a knife to Meenan, and the two men then ordered the staff to lie flat on the ground. Some £10,000 worth of cash and travellers cheques were collected, after which the staff were locked in the vault. At this stage two female employees were hysterical, and it was because of their pleading that the main door of the vault was not closed by the raiders. Only the grill door of the strong-room was locked. Outside the bank the get-away car was waiting, and driving it was Cobhman Anthony Manley. Manley had absolutely no political motivation and it is still a mystery as to how he came to be driving the men's getaway car. It was Manley who eventually led the Gardaí to the men's hideout and in the subsequent trial was acquitted while Meenan and Deehan were convicted. The bank manager succeeded in opening the door of the strong room by unscrewing a panel of the lock and immediately dialled 999, while another staff member ran to the Garda Station about fifty yards away, but by then the raiders had already had twenty minutes of a head start. All over the Great Island, roadblocks were thrown up, but the Gardaí were especially handicapped by the fact that no one had seen the men arrive or leave and that they had no description of the getaway car. Shortly before that, as the raiders were about to leave the island, they spotted a Garda on duty at Belvelly Bridge. Believing he was there on the lookout for them, they immediately turned around and headed back through the country roads. The Garda at the bridge had merely been carrying out a routine check on cars for tax and insurance. Had they proceeded over the bridge, the raiders probably would never have been seen again. Instead they headed back towards a wooded area (Keeffe's Wood) about a mile and a half from Belvelly and hid out there.

The next day, some 100 Garda officers and soldiers were engaged in the search for the raiders and their efforts were partly successful in that £1,000 of the stolen money was recovered on a lonely boreen at Newtown Farm. The possibility was now raised that this money was meant as a pay-off for local assistance and that it had been hidden on the farm, to be picked up later by the local contact. On the Sunday a massive man-hunt was undertaken with the help of tracker dogs and an army helicopter. The big force of Gardaí and soldiers assembled at Cobh and were briefed at St Colman's Hall (Pillars nightclub). There was a lot of excitement in the town as the long cavalcade of jeeps, armoured personnel carriers, cars and lorries moved out. At 3pm the manhunt was started with soldiers armed with rifles and Gustav machine guns began combing an area of woods overlooking Belvelly called Keeffe's Wood. The two Derry men didn't stand a chance. Their second mistake was not to have left Cobh when they had the chance to immediately after the raid. Their third mistake was to have remained on the Great Island for longer than they had to and for not moving out during the hours of darkness. Their first and most lethal mistake though, was to have trusted their local contact. In a very short time after beginning their search, the army and Gardaí had captured Hugo

Meenan and Anthony Manley.

Soon afterwards, Deehan was caught too. The two Derry natives were sentenced to five years penal servitude in November, after all the money, except for £100 was recovered, the accused having shown the Gardaí where the loot was hidden. Manley, the men's local contact, was acquitted by the Special Criminal Court, owing to insufficient evidence.

Meanwhile new life had been blown into the Cobh Republican Memorial Committee (first formed in the 1940s) in the middle of October. This time its Chairman was Ciáran Walsh (son of Seanie), Joe O'Neill was Vice-Chair, Mick Fitzgerald was Treasurer, and Emer Burke (daughter of Mick) was its Secretary. It is not entirely clear however, why there was no Official Republican representative on the committee, if they had been invited, or had they declined the offer. The Committee's first task was to undertake a clean up and place a wreath on the memorial cross at Carrigaloe, to mark the fiftieth anniversary of the death of Volunteer Danny O'Halloran, later that month. It was the second time a commemoration was held at the hill-side monument, the previous being in 1937 when a new granite cross had been erected to replace the previous wooden one. Steps were also undertaken by the revived committee to renovate the Republican Plot on Lieutenant Joe Reid's grave at the Old Church Cemetery.

On 21 May 1972, Volunteers of the Official IRA killed a young British soldier while he was home on leave in Derry's Creggan Estate. The killing of Ranger Best (a Catholic), created a shockwave of revulsion and condemnation throughout the city and beyond. The next day 22 May, the Official's Aldershot operation, which had the potential to produce a massive propaganda windfall, also back-fired when there was no military, but seven civilian casualties left from the attack. Then nine days later on the 30 May, the organisation, through its political leader Tomás MacGiolla, declared its war was over with the British. MacGiolla made the announcement through a speech at Carrickmore, County Tyrone. The historic announcement made no reference to the army's two recent botched operations, but instead focussed on what it described as the Provisional's sectarian war as its main reason for ending its campaign. It didn't see its own targeting of Protestant policemen, or the shooting of Unionist MP John Taylor five times in the face and leaving him for dead as sectarian, but as legitimate target in a political conflict. The leadership had been veering away from militarism and heading steadily in a leftward direction since the ending of the failed Border Campaign of the early 1960s. Its contention now that only through uniting the Protestant and Catholic working classes of the North, that Irish unity could be brought about, was, if not desirable in theory, unlikely to stand up to scrutiny. It didn't seem to occur to MacGoilla and the Official Army Council that the last thing which those that partitioned their country and caused this great mess of a conflict, would allow happen was the uniting of the working classes. It didn't occur to them that in the height of the Cold War as they were, that Britain was never going to give up its foothold in Ireland easily, and it certainly wasn't going to allow a campaign involving the unity of the working classes to be vanguarded by a political movement which had a foot in the door of the Soviet Union. Nor did it seem to occur to them that neither mainstream Unionism, nor extreme Loyalism which was right-wing and ultra sectarian by nature, would oppose most strenuously the very project which they were proposing. Sectarianism and division was the corner stone of British Rule in Ireland and it was only when a British Government decided or were persuaded that it was no longer in its interests to maintain the whole sectarian apparatus of the Northern Statelet, could Irish workers be united, and this was how the alternative Provisional leadership saw things.

If the writings and example of the great Socialist Republican leader James Connolly had taught the official leadership anything, it should have been that socialism could never take root and prosper among a nation that is enslaved, divided and controlled by another. Connolly, more than any other twentieth-century Irish leader, predicted and warned against the consequences of partitioning Ireland, and he did so years before it happened. Amongst the very negative consequences he predicted, would be a carnival of reaction from various conservative and reactionary forces. The official Republican leadership, it would now appear, had fallen into the reactionary trap, by attacking the only force that was meaningfully trying to dismantle partition, and by using it to justify it's own position of abandoning its national liberation struggle. As far as the Provisionals were concerned, the British Government which were now ruling the North directly from London, and who were guarantors of the blank cheque of Orange supremacy over Nationalists, were the people for now that needed persuading, and it was clear they were not going to do the right thing of their own volition or sense of reason.

Fate had caught up with Eddie Collins one day in 1973. As a five-man Active-Service Unit approached the Tyrone/Monaghan border near Aughnacloy, they ran into a joint Army and Garda checkpoint on the southern side. The Volunteers, who were heading across the border to collect explosives for an operation, pulled up their car a distance short of the checkpoint and got out. They knew they were relatively safe from trouble but had they been travelling in the other direction on their return journey, it would have been a far more serious matter. One of the men separated from the others and tried to appear as if he had arrived separately from them. He walked a short distance close to a fence and began to relieve himself by urinating in a gap in the ditch. The other four men meanwhile abandoned the car and walked back across the border. The first man, Eddie Collins could see that the soldiers and Gardaí were preoccupied with the behaviour of the other four Volunteers, leading him to think he just may get passed them without arousing too much suspicion. For a brief time, it looked like he might just make it, but when it became clear that the others had made it away safely, all attention then focussed on him. Collins was immediately taken into custody and once his true identity was established, he was sent forward for trial for the raids on the Dungarvan and Midleton FCA bases two and a half years earlier. He was sentenced to two and half years, starting in Limerick Prison. Within a couple of days of being placed in Limerick however, panic set in by the prison authorities who feared their special guest might organise a mass breakout, and had him transferred to Mountjoy where other Republican prisoners were then involved in a protest over conditions there. After a riot broke out and the kitchens were destroyed in the prison, the men were transferred to the Glasshouse in the Curragh.

The next day, bus loads of military police and Gardaí dressed in riot gear were brought in before they stormed the men's quarters. Having been caught completely off guard, the Republicans reached for anything they could find to defend themselves. They desperately began to smash furniture, using sticks and brush handles to fend off the baton wielding MPs. Among those held with Collins in the Curragh at that time were Joe Cahill, Ruairi O'Bradaigh, Kevin Mallon and a young Martin McGuinness. When the Bishop of Kildare was brought in to intervene and examine the conditions which the men were living under, he was surprised to learn that the bedding used by the men had been in use since the British controlled the Curragh. Ruairi O'Bradaigh explained why the prisoners were on a bed strike. Using a cane-like stick in his hand, O'Bradaigh hit a mattress a flake, giving rise to a huge cloud of dust which nearly reached the ceiling of the room. In front of the Camp Governor, Commandant Enright who stood beside the Bishop, O'Bradaigh enquired loudly, 'Now Bishop I ask you, would you allow a dog to sleep on that?'[148] to which the Bishop sheepishly replied 'no'. Some time later, while the Bishop intermingled and spoke with other prisoners, a door swung open and in to the room came a number of trays of the finest smelling, delicious food. The prisoners looked on in awe, as they had hardly received a decent meal since they arrived in the Curragh. O'Bradaigh intervened once more and turning to the Bishop, declared, 'do you see all that good food Bishop, this is just for your benefit, for as soon as your good self has left this prison later, we will be back on half rationed slops again.'[149] O'Bradaigh then turned to the orderlies and told them to take away the food as they would not be playing the Governor's game. After that, conditions improved in the Curragh. Proper sleeping conditions were provided and the food improved likewise, but it wasn't long before the men were shipped off to the new Republican holding prison at Portlaoise.

While the Official IRA's war was over, it never formally stood down or decommissioned its weapons. It continued in place for a number of years to protect its members, and of course to fundraise on behalf of the party and its new political project, through armed robberies. It would also get entangled in violent feuds with the Provisionals and the INLA, and would assassinate the latter's founder leader, Seamus Costello in 1977. The Provisionals on the other hand were stepping up their campaign. They were growing numerically in the North, becoming more organised and bolder by the day. Above all, they were in the eyes of ever more people, seen as the people's 'Army of National Liberation'. Before long, people would have little further need to make the distinction between the Provisionals and Officials. From hence forward, as in times past, there would only be one IRA.

In Cobh, the situation for the Provisionals didn't progress any further from that of being one of a support group for the war in the North. The officials, who were now starting to move in a mainly political direction, continued to hold their meetings each Tuesday evening at the East Beach Union Hall. Both organisations by now had begun to feel the drop off in membership from the non-committed hangers-on who had earlier flirted with some romantic notion of revolution. As the public mood in the South changed from one of sympathy to one of apathy towards the North, it gradually developed into a situation where only the truly committed and revolutionary minded would remain involved. As the Provisionals were already weak to begin with in Cobh, they had suffered the most. The Officials, on the other hand dropped off in numbers as they had earlier been mainly a military led grouping, but still had a small core of political activists.

39. Preparing for the Long War

On 28 March 1973, the IRA Chief of Staff Joe Cahill, Sean Garvey and Gerry Murphy were arrested and taken to Cobh after been found on board the arms-ship *Claudia* which had earlier been captured off Helvick in Waterford by the twenty-six-county Naval Service. The story of the *Claudia* however, began the previous year when contact was made by twenty-nine-year-old Libyan leader Colonel Gaddafi, with Joe Cahill through the Breton artist and sculptor Yann Goulet. Goulet had been a leading member of the Separatist Movement in Brittany during the Second World War; he had many narrow escapes in the struggle against German forces occupying France. Goulet was eventually imprisoned and went on hunger strike.

On his release, his political activities again led him to be hunted by both Germans and French. Condemned to death in his absence, Goulet fled France to Ireland. Gaddafi let Goulet know that he would only deal with Joe Cahill, whom he respected and believed he could trust. Cahill's nerve in appearing at a Belfast press conference while on the run, and his high international media profile following his deportation from the United States had drawn the attention of the Libyan leader. Cahill agreed to an initial meeting and brought the IRA's Quartermaster, General Jack McCabe along with him. They talked through an interpreter as Gaddafi refused to speak English. They were surprised however, to discover how well versed the Libyan leader was on the Irish situation. Gaddafi agreed to help the Irish cause in any way he could but the Republicans refused to accept or commit to anything for the time-being, as they already had other irons in the fire in relation to the acquisition of arms. Contact was however later re-established through Yann Goulet and arrangements put in place for Joe Cahill to go to Tripoli, the Libyan capital.

The IRA put two teams into place, one making arrangements for a four-man group to travel incognito to Libya, another setting about providing passports. Cahill flew out himself from Cork in a private four-seater plane and was later picked up at a small airport in France and was taken by car to Paris. With three others, Cahill then set off for Rome and from there the group flew to Tripoli where they were met by Libyan officials. Some days later they met up with Colonel Gaddafi at a military barracks. Cahill and the others were impressed with Gaddafi's grasp of the situation in the six counties. Although the Libyan leader had good English, he again refused to speak it and was a little puzzled as to why the IRA delegation was speaking through the tongue of their enemy. He again made the offer to help the Irish cause in any way he could. Cahill made it clear that there could be no strings attached to the help being offered and Gaddafi immediately agreed. Cahill then gave a detailed list of what the IRA was seeking in terms of weaponry it felt would make an impact on British forces in the six counties. A man known merely as 'the German' organised the leasing of the Cyprus-registered boat *Claudia*. Initially, its cargo was to contain forty-tonnes of arms but it headed to sea with only a small quantity of five tonnes. The reason for the reduced shipload was that the Libyans were concerned about the ship and its reputation. Gaddafi's intelligence services had discovered that the *Claudia* had a notorious international reputation and had been involved in other smuggling operations. It was agreed that Joe Cahill and two others would make the journey back to Ireland on board the vessel, as this would be their safest route home. The ships captain was named Hans Ludwig Fluegal and his brother was the first mate. The remainder of the crew included two Turkish sailors. Cahill later said,

I have no idea what the finer details were that lay behind the acquiring of the ship. What I do know is that it we left it entirely up to the German. Our people had met the Libyans before we went out, and it was decided that a boat should be moored outside Libyan territorial waters and the stuff could be transported at sea. After I had met Gaddafi, we arranged that a radio signal from the *Claudia*, by this time just outside the limits, would let us know when to give the Libyans the go-ahead to head out to sea with the arms. When the people on board the *Claudia* could not make contact, they headed into Tripoli, which they should never have done. It was never intended that the boat would go into Tripoli. That was to be the safeguard for the Libyans, but the ship arrived in harbour and there was a bit of a panic. The Libyans were fair enough. They said they would load the ship where it was. However, for reasons which I did not discover until years later, they did not supply all they said they were going to supply. [150]

The boat reached the Waterford coast but the Republicans were frustrated when they were forced to stay at sea for another twenty-four hours due to adverse weather conditions. Equally frustrated were the awaiting groups at Helvic Head, watching out for the *Claudia*. The group on land had trouble of their own, as they were unable to establish radio contact with the vessel due to the same technological difficulties the boat experienced in Libya. A launch boat had to make numerous trips in and out to sea, watching for sight of the *Claudia* so that they could safely escort her into the harbour. To explain the trips in and out, the fishermen said that they were having engine trouble and were trying to fix the problem.

Unfortunately, one local was over-helpful and wanted to help fix the engine. The men asked the friendly local man to go and source a new lead for them to keep him out of harm's way. The land operation had its head-quarters in a house overlooking Helvick Harbour. An Abbeyside man was Officer in Command and there was also an active service unit to escort the arms to the dumps.

In all, there was a team made up of more than fifty people involved in the onshore operation. On 28 March the watchers in the harbour spot-ted the *Claudia* and the launch was dispatched to meet her. The objective was to bring Clare man Denis McInerney to shore so that he could lead up the land operation by ensuring that the arms were brought to safety, and to bring walkie-talkies on board to establish contact between all parties as radio contact was impossible. The arms were to be brought in with the help of a trawler and some specially made rope nets, which local Volunteers, who were staying in the house overlooking Helvick Harbour, had put together. These nets were designed to carry the weight of the arms shipment. The people onboard the launch informed the crew that all was clear on shore and there was not even a sign of a customs man around. While McInerney headed back to shore, one of the members of the launch, Gerry Murphy, stayed on board the *Claudia*. Séan Garvey from Kerry, Joe Cahill and Gerry Murphy from Waterford were talking about the success of the operation when they noticed three ships from the Irish Naval Service: two minesweepers, *Gráinne* and *Fóla*, and the fishery pro-tection vessel, *Deirdre*. These boats had been following the gun smuggling operation.

Earlier, fears on the part of the Republicans about a possible sighting of a submarine in the Mediterranean had been correct, as a submarine was spotted off the island in Helvick. In fact a retired Irish Naval Officer has since confirmed to me that his people were being briefed and updated by the British since before the *Claudia* had passed Gibraltar. With the help of newly-acquired radios the *Claudia* crew warned the people on the launch of the impending danger. So sudden and unexpected was the appearance of the Navy that the Republicans had no chance to carry out a pre-arranged plan to scuttle the ship if there was danger of the weap-ons being captured. Enough explosives had been provided to rip open the *Claudia*'s hull, but they were not in a state of preparedness when the twenty-six-county Navy struck. The launch quickly tried to get ashore to warn the people waiting there. A package was thrown over the side as it tried to reach land. They were able to make contact with those on land with the walkie-talkies that they had brought on board. The Navy ves-sels then opened fire on the launch, with numerous tracer bullets raining down on them. After a few minutes of firing, the Captain of the *Gráinne*, received an instruction from Lieutenant Commander Liam Brett of the Command-ship *Deirdre,* to fire a Bofors (anti-aircraft) round across the bows of the launch, as it appeared that there were shots coming from the launch. The *Gráinne* skipper paused though as he didn't feel there was fire coming from the launch. Seconds later, he received another message to act, this time from the commander of the *Fóla* who also believed there was fire coming from the area of the launch. The Commander of the *Gráinne* refused to act however, as he doubted whether they were coming under hostile fire at all. He felt instead, that the gunfire they were listening to was the echo of their own tracer fire. He was also very reluctant to engage the small launch with Bofor's fire, for fear if it was hit with a single Bofor round, (intentional or otherwise), it would blow the launch and all inside her to bits. If he fired over the bows of the launch, there was also a good chance that a round could end up striking civilian buildings beyond the vessel in Helvick.

The reluctance to act in a knee-jerk manner by the *Gráinne's* Captain, probably saved lives and prevented a lot of embarrassment that day for the Dublin authorities, for as soon the tracer fired ceased, so did the sound of all gun fire. A Gemini speed dingy was instead launched from the ship which caught up with the launch before it reached shore, and arrested those onboard. The people waiting on shore were now alerted and had to abort and set about helping the active service unit to get away. They were escorted through fields to a safe house, where they laid low until things had quietened down a few days later. The O.C. waited until a number of people gathered on the pier and headed down, along with a local fisherman, pretending to be an onlooker unaware of what all the fuss was about. The other members of the operation then slipped in the back way to Murray's pub where a party was taking place, as the owners had just returned from honeymoon. The Gardaí and Navy were all around the area. An armoured tank was placed opposite Murray's pub, with its gun pointing out to sea. Two trucks were on their way to Helvick to collect the arms when they were stopped outside of Dungarvan by an armed Garda/military checkpoint. The drivers said that they were on their way to Waterford Co-op to collect powdered milk and the Gardaí let them pass through. At the same time in Stradbally, a local man out doing a spot of salmon fishing was surrounded by armed Gardaí as he came ashore. He thought they were bailiffs, while they thought he was involved in the Helvick operation. Once the Gardaí had realised their mistake, the sergeant, a man with a thick Cork or Kerry accent, bought one of the fresh fish.

Back in Helvick on the night in question, one of the sharp-eyed Irish sailors had spotted the object being thrown over the side of the launch. A navy diver was sent down in the following days but came up with nothing.

Local salmon fishermen spotted the mystery object and marked it with a buoy. A trawler then used a grappling hook while passing it and brought it on board. The object, two suitcases tied together with rope, contained a black box, which had, £40-50,000 in it, as well as a list of contact names and addresses throughout Europe. Also inside the box were false passports, which had been used to go to Libya. The money which was a very significant amount in 1973 would have been a great loss if it had fallen into the wrong hands, as it proved very important in organising future operations. Also inside the cases were three copper plates, which had a man on camelback on them, a statue of the Arc De Triomphe, and a dagger, which Gaddafi had given to Joe Cahill. These objects never found their way back to Joe Cahill's possession and can be found in and around the Ring area. Some items of clothing belonging to Joe Cahill were among the contents of the cases. His suit and a pair of shoes were cleaned and brought up to him for his appearance in the Special Court some time later. The black box containing the money, passports and contact names, was carried up the pier by a crew member of the salmon trawler, known as having no Republican connections and straight past the twenty-four-hour guard that had been in place since the *Claudia* had been caught. The money, the passports, and the contact details were handed back to the IRA, three weeks after the *Claudia* incident, in Fraher Field, Dungarvan. The *Claudia* itself was taken to the Naval Base at Haulbowline where its cargo was unloaded and transported to Collins Army Barracks Cork. Superintendent Con McGrath of Cobh Garda Station was present on the L.E. *Deirdre* to arrest Joe Cahill, Sean Garvey and Gerry Murphy. The *Claudia* which carried 250 rifles, 246 bayonets, 850 rifle magazines, 243 pistols, more than 20,000 rounds of ammunition, 10 anti-tank mines, 500 high-explosive grenades, gelignite, TNT explosive primers, Carter fuses, electrical fuses, and material for making booby traps, was released with its crew within three hours of arriving at Haulbowline and sent on its way.

The special trial of those captured on the *Claudia* began in Dublin on 21 May 1973. In a speech from the dock of the court Joe Cahill declared.

All my life I have believed passionately in the freedom of my country. I believe it is the God-given right of the people of Ireland to determine their own destinies without foreign interference and, in pursuit of these aims and ideals, it is my proud privilege as a soldier of the Irish Republican Army, just as I believe it is the duty of every Irish person, to serve or assist the IRA in driving the British occupation forces from our shores. If I am guilty of any crime, it is that I did not succeed in getting the contents of the *Claudia* into the hands of the freedom fighters in this country. And I believe that national treachery was committed off Helvick when the Free State forces conspired with our British enemies to deprive our freedom fighters of the weapons of war. [151]

Five weeks earlier on 14 April, in a clear reference to the *Claudia* affair, the Minister for Justice, Paddy Cooney declared the IRA would not be tolerated and his government would use all the powers available to them to smash it. They would not tolerate two armies operating in the Republic and the population here would not tolerate the place being used as a base or haven for persons not prepared to accept their standards, he said. What Minister Cooney failed to say in his *Irish Times* statement however, was that two armies were already operating in the Republic with the knowledge of his government and one of those was a foreign army, whose agents would in the space of a year murder thirty-three Irish citizens and injure many more through the Dublin and Monaghan bombings. He would also neglect to mention that those who he and his government had colluded with in the capture of the *Claudia* were at that very time plotting and planning other military operations in the Republic. Above all, Minister Cooney neglected to acknowledge that it was because of the foreign army of occupation that was operating in both parts of Ireland, that people were and would continue to queue up to resist it with the weapons that were arriving into the country on ships like the *Claudia*.

Two days later in a direct reply to Cooney's statement, the IRA issued a stern reply:

Cooney's old clichés of law and order and one army are trotted out to condition the public mind for continued harassment and jailing of Republicans. The Special Powers of the Offences Against the State Act, which Cooney found so objectionable last December, were being used to the full in order to prove to the British Government that Mr Cooney was as good as Mr O'Malley in hounding Republicans. It was ironic that Cooney's statement should come at the end of a week during which the British army excelled itself in murder and brutality. [152]

The IRA spokesman issued the statement within hours of Mr Edward O'Rawe being shot in cold blood in Belfast, and at a time when the people of the North were seething with rage over other British army killings in Newry and Armagh.

While a spokesperson for the IRA and the Dublin Minister for Justice were going head to head for the hearts and minds of the Irish people through the pages of the *Irish Times*, a world away in the chambers of County Hall in Cork, the Civil War was being re-fought by the old tired parties of Fianna Fáil and Fine Gael. A motion by the latter party was hoping to change the name of the building to the Michael Collins Memorial Hall. Speaking on the legal requirement of having a two thirds majority to make the change legal, a council official added a bit of humour to the debate by claiming the building was already unofficially called the 'Corry Hilton', a reference to one of the County Councils longest serving members, Martin Corry. When he spoke himself, Corry asked that the motion be deferred until there was a full and open debate on the matter.

He then went on to declare that Tomas MacCurtain was his Brigade Commander before he was murdered, offering a hint that he would prefer to see MacCurtain's name above the building instead of Collins'. When it came to time to vote, the hostility couldn't be hidden for long. Fine Gael and Labour, the coalition parties, could only muster twenty votes against Fianna Fáil's twelve, leaving it short of the two thirds majority required. But while the old Civil War parties were trapped and fiddling in the past, they appeared oblivious and unconcerned about the burning North and the fate of their fellow country men and women a couple of hundred miles up the road.

On the 10 May a seventeen-year-old Cork City Volunteer from St Joseph's Park in Mayfield by the name of Tony Ahern was killed on active service near Roslea, County Fermanagh. Ahern, the first IRA Volunteer from the twenty-six counties to be killed in the current phase of the Republican struggle, was situated near a landmine intended for a British Army patrol when it went off prematurely. Significantly, in terms of the continuity of the freedom struggle and despite some people's claims that there was no connection between the present IRA's struggle and that of 1916, among those who attended the funeral was Joe Clarke who fought in the 1916 rising in the Battle of Mount Street Bridge.

Six weeks later on 25 June, Ahern's childhood friend and street neighbour from Mayfield in Cork, Dermot Crowley was also killed on active service along with two others, Volunteer Sean Loughran and Volunteer Patrick Carty when the bomb they were transporting in a car exploded prematurely near Omagh, County Tyrone.

In 1984 the Sinn Féin party in Cork City opened new offices at Barrack Street, which was unveiled as the Ahern-Crowley Memorial Hall. The official opening was carried out by the future Deputy First Minister in the North, Martin McGuiness after the building was first blessed by a member of the Capuchin order, whose members have had a long association with the freedom struggle.

Despite their eagerness to move in an exclusively political direction, Official Sinn Féin in Cobh didn't feel sufficiently strong enough to contest the 1974 local government elections when they came around. The party was better organised around the Cork North East Constituency though, and had made a good showing in the previous years General Election through its candidate Joe Sherlock. The former IRA Volunteer Sherlock, pulled a respectable 2,488 first preference votes in his first bid for Leinster House, many no doubt from people who believed their votes were an expression of support for the IRA's campaign.

A year and a half later on the 13 November 1974, Sherlock pulled an impressive 5,363 first preference votes in a By-Election caused by the death of Fianna Fáil's Liam Ahern. As a young fourteen-year-old full-time FCA member stationed on Spike Island at the time, I was automatically afforded the same voting franchise as all the other soldiers stationed at the barracks. I am probably honoured with being among the youngest, if not the youngest person to ever vote in a General Election in this state. Needless to say, my postal vote had a 'one' marked beside the name of the candidate whom I then believed was the IRA's choice. My second preference vote went to the eventual winner of the vacant seat, Sean Brosnan of Fianna Fáil who romped home on the first count with 19,928 votes. My vote for Sherlock was not exactly an expression of support for the IRA, but rather a belief in my then young naïve mind that his party was more serious about national re-unification, or at least more serious than Fianna Fáil had been. I also recall a private canvass going on around the barracks by some individuals who were pushing the Fianna Fáil candidates. Their line was that the Department of Defence budget is always bigger when a Fianna Fáiler was at the helm. The reality of course was that neither Brosnan's party nor Sherlock's were Republican, both having abandoned the Nationalist community in the north to whatever fate the British had in mind for them. By 1977, as a then member of the regular Irish (Free State) Army, and after having some personal experience of observing the war around the border, I found myself on transfer back to Spike Island. On the 5 July of that year and while still under the age of eighteen, I again was afforded the opportunity to cast a vote in the General Election. Once again, I made the mistake of believing that Joe Sherlock and his party were involved in opposing the British military occupation that I witnessed on the border and which sickened me to know I had assisted. Although I was acting purely on gut instinct at the time, with absolutely no political savvy, and despite his party having now diluted its name to become 'Sinn Féin the Workers Party', it would take another three years before I would realise that Sherlock and his people had sold out on the Republican cause.

Fianna Fáil in 1977 romped home throughout the State in what was the biggest ever General Election landslide. The outgoing Fine Gael/Labour Coalition took a bad hiding from the southern electorate. Among the contributing factors for their demise had been the repressive and brutal behaviour of the Garda Special Branch towards Republican activists. The infamous detective unit became commonly known as the 'Heavy Gang'. The stories coming out of Garda Stations from Republicans and other suspects were horrific and frightening. The Gardaí and their political masters often trotted out the line that prisoners were beating themselves up in an effort to discredit the Gardaí, but after a time, it became more and more obvious, particularly by the evidence of doctors, that many of the injuries received by the prisoners couldn't possibly have been self inflicted. The activities and use of the 'Heavy Gang' by the state was not exclusively directed towards Republicans however. One day in 1976, as a leading Trade Unionist from Cobh was about to enter the turnstiles for a provincial hurling match at Pairc Uí Chaoimh in Cork, he received a tap on his shoulder. When the man turned around to see who it was, he was confronted by two detectives who took him to one side. They then proceeded to warn him, telling him that he better get his act together and do something to prevent the use of strikes by his members at Marina Point in Cobh, where the then State Fertiliser Company N.E.T. had a plant under construction.

Under normal circumstances a person in such a position might have panicked and buckled to such intimidating pressure, but in this particular case, the union official was a Republican supporter and the abusive tactics of the state only lent to increase his resolve in defence of his member's rights. A year before in 1975 the Sinn Féin Vice-President Maire Drumm paid a visit to Cobh to meet with Seanie Walsh and Joe O'Neill. The meeting which took place at Walsh's home at Ticknock was organised to address the strengths and weaknesses of the local organisation. Sean Óg Walsh, who was a thirteen-year-old Fianna member at that time, remembers the presence of Maire Drumm at their home. He still has her signature which she autographed onto a piece of prison craftwork for him. Drumm was assassinated the following year as she lay in a hospital bed in Belfast, waiting on an operation, by Unionist paramilitaries, probably with the guiding hand of British intelligence.

40. The road to Republicanism

On 25 March 1976, five other Cobhmen and I passed out after finishing our military training with the 4th Battalion at Collins Barracks Cork. Almost immediately, our platoon was divided up with members of other platoons with the specific intention of preparing us for other duties to do with what we were told was the security of the state. Some of us were going to form a battalion which would be detailed to guard Republican prisoners held at the new maximum security prison at Portlaoise. The rest of us would be part of a battalion which would be sent to relieve a Limerick battalion about to finish its tour on the border. For some strange reason, I was the only one of the six Cobh recruits, to be detailed to join the border battalion. I was initially happy with this decision because I didn't want to go to Portlaoise. There had been a great deal of talk circulating around the barracks for months during our time of training, from individuals who had not long before returned from serving a term at Portlaoise prison and of claims they had sorted out the IRA during an attempted escape from the place.

One day a particular individual at the barracks was pointed out to me as the man that had shot dead an IRA man who had earlier tried to escape from the prison. Some time later, another individual was pointed out to me as being the triggerman and later another and so on. It appeared to me that if I was to believe all these stories, then the poor IRA Volunteer who was shot, and whom years later I learned to be Volunteer Tom Smith from Dublin, must have been shot a thousand times. Tom Smith in fact, died from a single gunshot to the head while taking part in an attempted escape on St Patrick's Day 1975. The Gardaí later attacked his funeral but were unable to prevent his comrades from giving him full military honours. What I found most disturbing and sickening about all these stories during my training, was that the individuals to whom they were attributed to, seemed to be enjoying the notoriety and did little to dispel them or put the record straight. Neither did the officers of our battalion do anything to stop such talk and rumours doing the rounds. I would later learn that it was all in fact, part of a pattern designed to motivate and condition up-coming recruits before they would take up such duties.

Meanwhile, my border battalion went to work training in riot control, in advance of our upcoming tour. We were given batons, shields, rubber-bullet guns, CS gas, the whole works, and began our training each day at an area at the north-west corner of the barracks close to the gymnasium. Little did I know back then, that this building where I as an Irish soldier was learning how to brutalise, if not kill my fellow country men and women, was the same building where fellow Cobhmen Maurice Moore and Paddy O'Sullivan, were Court-martialled fifty-five years earlier before facing their firing squads. The training I also found confusing. In hindsight, it is now clear to me that a decision had been made at a senior level (probably at government level) to deal in a very stern and harsh manner with rioting communities around the border. It was also clear that some of the officers put in charge of training us, were very much up for the challenge and wanted to have a go. We were being told that in a riot situation, we were to identify who ever we regarded as ringleaders, the person with the red shirt, or black jacket, the person who stood out and if the crowd didn't disperse after being called upon to do so, and after rubber bullets and gas had been fired, we were then to fire live ammunition and bring down the identified ringleaders. These instructions and indoctrination in the policy of shoot to kill, no doubt was very appealing to some recruits who joined up the army for adventure and a bit of action. It didn't ring right with me however, and in 1976, four years after the British Parachute Regiment had been given the green light to embark on a murder spree in Derry, I was now part of an army (an Irish army) that was effectively given the same licence. Then, just in case my young teenage mind was getting things all wrong and mixed up, matters were made crystal clear to us one day when our platoon was brought in for a lecture on what was expected of us when we would get to the border the following week. The lecture took place in one of our billets, a long dormitory room with a line of beds on either side. A particular captain came in a sat on one of the beds in the centre of the room and asked us all to gather around for an informal talk. He then began to fill us in on the realities of conflict, how the public might perceive things and how the army has to deal with the real world. He reminded us again that if we should find ourselves in situation where we had to deal with a riot situation and required to neutralise the ringleaders, we should aim to kill. 'Dead men don't talk', he repeatedly told us. Even, in my then sixteen-year-old naïve mind, I knew exactly what he was saying. Almost at the end of every sentence which came out of the man's mouth, he repeated the words, 'Remember dead men don't talk.'[153]

  As the youngest man in the room, I was shocked at what I was hearing, but more so that no one else questioned what we were being told. I couldn't comprehend the fact that there were many older married men in the room, who didn't seem to blink an eye about the fact that they were being schooled in murder. I also remember that captain telling us about his father. It didn't at all seem relevant at the time, but in hindsight it became very clear of what he was trying to do. He said his own father was an old IRA man with very different views about the north to him. 'Sure he's an old man with very old ideas and no understanding of the current situation.'[154] In other words, these guys today who are masquerading as Republicans haven't a clue and have some mixed up idea of history so don't you guys fall for their propaganda and end up sympathising with them, trust us, we know best.

  Almost immediately, another reality was brought home to us when we reached our new abode outside of Monaghan town. Our main purpose there was to provide security to a new military barracks that was under construction nearby but also to assist the Gardaí while patrolling the border itself. Our camp-side location was close to the border with three northern counties of Armagh, Tyrone and Fermanagh. Within days of arriving there, I found myself out on a mobile patrol and to my utter surprise, found that our land-rovers were being pelted with stones every time we passed through a border village or town. In my naivety, I at first thought the locals had mistaken us for the British Army but that illusion didn't last very long. When we were off duty and went into either Monaghan town or Cootehill to socialize, we soon discovered that there were only a few pubs where we could buy a drink. Dances were also out of bounds as they were guaranteed to end in a mini-riot. They natives or at least many of them saw us as collaborators with their enemy. Then the day came when I received my real wake-up call and saw for myself the true meaning of what was termed cross-border security. One day while on stand-to, I was engaged in a game of poker with four others in one of our camp tents. Suddenly, a sergeant arrived at the entrance to the tent and told us to report immediately to the guardroom for patrol duty. Within ten minutes we were mounted with loaded weapons and were mobile behind a couple of Garda Special Branch cars and heading into the country. We were all in reasonably good form, especially me as I had been winning money in the poker game before we were interrupted, and there was a good bit of banter going in the back of our jeep. To this day, I have no idea of what county's border we were approaching but after about twenty or thirty minutes of driving, we could hear a lot of activity crackling over our radio in the jeep.

As we neared our destination, we could also hear a lot of gunfire in the distance and it soon became clear that a fair old battle was in progress. Soon our vehicles pulled up along side a small country road where we were quickly ordered out and told to take up position a long a briar-covered hedgerow. The firefight in the distance seemed very intense for a while and then seemed to fade out. Radio traffic also seemed to get more frantic when the firing stopped, and they weren't Irish accents that were making all the noise. My three colleagues and I looked at each other with shocked gazes as I'm sure they were having the same thoughts as me. Then a broad English voice roared over a radio behind me 'They're coming your way'. I don't know if this voice was coming through one of ours or a Garda radio, but the news seemed to send the detectives standing near us into overdrive. Before long, we could see three armed figures approaching through fields in our direction. We could also hear the racket of British Army helicopters approaching not far behind them. The officer in charge of our patrol who had just been in discussion with the detectives shouted a command for us to get ready. When they came to within under a 100 yards of where we were, the three frantic looking figures threw their weapons down and continued to approach swiftly towards our location. It appeared to me that, they knew they were cornered and opted to give themselves up to us rather than the British. Then as the detectives were cuffing the men and ushering them into their unmarked cars, one of the prisoners glanced back in our direction and stared us straight in the eyes. My three colleagues and I looked on in numbed silence, and I'm sure I wasn't the only one that had a sick feeling deep in the pit of my stomach. At that very moment, I believed I knew how Judas must have felt when he kissed Jesus.

During our return journey back to Monaghan, while escorting the Gardaí and their prisoners to the local station, there was nothing but silence in the back of our jeep. The banter we had experienced more than an hour before was like it had happened an age ago. Heads were down, and apart from the career officer in the front passenger seat who was obviously feeling good with himself, it was hard to imagine that everyone wasn't having the same thoughts. After our weapons were cleared and handed back to the guard room and we were back in our tent again, we tried to resume our game of poker. There was still no real conversation though, and certainly no smiles or laughter like before. Then, before the first hand of cards was even played out, the man sitting opposite me threw his cards onto the ground and declared,

'Fuck this, the next time I'm in a situation like that, I'm going to fire on those English bastards instead.'

'Yah said another, did ya hear those fuckers giving us orders on the radios, and we're expected to jump for them in our country.'

I didn't speak myself but just nodded in agreement, I think I was still in shock by the whole experience. It wasn't lost on me also that if I had been picked to go to Portlaoise Prison instead of the Border, I would very shortly be about to encounter those three brave prisoners anyway. I spent the next number of days trying to rationalise the whole affair in my head. I was the youngest man in our camp, and kept trying to tell myself that these people, our officers and the Gardaí were my betters and must know what they are doing, but yet I kept hearing those English accents, and seeing pictures in my minds eye, of my fellow country-men fleeing from those foreign helicopters. It was like trying to force a square peg into a round hole, it just wouldn't fit.

One Friday morning about three weeks later, I and three others decided to drive into Jonesborough market in Armagh while we were off duty. We heard it was a good place to get bargains in clothing and electrical goods, cheap radios and cassette players, etc. Our driver was one of the camp cooks, who had asked the day before if we would fancy accompanying him in his Ford Capri. When we arrived into the small market village, we had only been there about five minutes and had just began to look over some stalls when we were singled out of the crowd and placed up against a wall by a British Army patrol. The soldiers demanded I.D. from us, but we didn't have any to offer. We explained who we were and why we were in Jonesborough. They didn't seem to care or be the slightest bit impressed or civil when learning who we were. Then it suddenly dawned on me that they already knew who we were. It was the mid-1970s and NO ONE in those days wore short hair unless they were part of the services. We must have stood out like sore thumbs. In the end, they left us carry on with our business, as though they had done us a favour. I couldn't help feel they were flexing their muscles and letting us know who was in charge. It was at that point that things became crystal clear to me. It didn't matter if I was standing in Armagh or in Cork; this was my country and the guys with the guns were the foreigners, the unwanted guests of my nation.

This was also at a time when there had been a number of highlighted incidents of undercover SAS activity (included among them, some relating to the notorious Captain Nairac) taking place, where they would cross over the border, snatch and kidnap Republican suspects, take them back across the border and torture them before dumping their murdered and sometimes mutilated bodies. Yet throughout our earlier training, we were never told that we should confront or shoot at such undercover British units if we encountered them on the southern side of the border and if they were engaged in illegal activity, or in the process of kidnapping or murder. We were never told that 'Dead SAS men don't talk'. Our bullets, if they were ever to be used, were meant only for other Irish people, preferably other Irish soldiers of the Volunteer kind.

A few moments after the soldiers released us in Jonesborough market and we were back at the stalls again, I received a tap on my shoulder from a very tall and big man. He demanded to know what 'those bastards' were asking us about. We told him the truth that they wanted to know who we were and what our business was there. He didn't say anymore but just turned and stormed off. Despite the man's use of colourful language, he made me feel more welcome and like I had more in common with him than our earlier foreign interrogators. The reality of course, was that the work I was doing on the border differed very little from that of the guys with the English accents. What surprised me most on this particular occasion however, was that the others who I was travelling with and who were older and more experienced soldiers than me, didn't seem to blink an eyelid or question the fact that we had been singled out by the British. While driving back to Monaghan, the only discussion they were interested in, related to the bargains they had found at the market. My apolitical teenage mind was unable to make sense of everything my eyes and ears were telling me. My gut however, was telling me very loudly that all was not right here on the border. Although I didn't quite realise yet, I was well on my

359

way to becoming a Republican.

The Official IRA in Cobh around this time had received a little assistance, unintentional as it was to its decommissioning plans. It happened
when an idling teenager hanging around an area near the old British military hospital at the eastern part of the town found a number of short arms,
when he opened a manhole cover in the ground. Believing his find to have
dated back to British times, the young lad immediately reported the contents of his bounty and later led the Gardaí to it. Meanwhile, the former
Chairman to the Officials political wing, Dan Collins, had since left the
party, some believing he had backed the wrong horse during the 1970 split,
and that he might have been more at home with the Provisionals. Christy
Griffin remembers Dan as belonging to the old traditional Republican
mould and not been very comfortable with the left-wing politics of the
new generation of activists. Dan eventually became disillusioned and left
the political scene completely. The party, now styling itself 'Sinn Féin the
Workers Party' was eager not to miss the boat again with the next local
elections and wanted to have a good credible candidate in place when they
came around in 1979. Party members first approached the chairman of the
local branch of the Irish Transport and General Workers Union (forerun-
ner of SIPTU) asking him to stand for them. Although an admirer of the
party's leftist economic policies, the chairman Mick McCarthy declined
the offer, as he could not agree with the party's abandonment of the
Nationalist people in the north, or the relegation of its policy of achieving a united Ireland to one of insignificance. Had there been the bones of
a Provisional Sinn Féin Cumann in the town at that point, it would have
been likely that McCarthy would have agreed to stand as a candidate for
it. It wasn't long before Sinn Féin the Workers Party found itself a credible
candidate from among the force of construction workers at the N.E.T. site
at Marino Point.

Leo Owens had not long before arrived back from Liverpool where he
had been a member of the British Communist Party (Marxist-Leninist).
Some years earlier Leo had had the unique experience, when standing
for the party in the local elections in Liverpool, of competing against
another Cobhman John Mansworth who stood there as a candidate for
the Conservative Party. On that particular occasion, neither the Cobh
Communist nor the Cobh Tory made it past the line. In 1979 in Cobh
however, Leo Owens had found a party with policies he could identify
and work with. He was neither interested nor cared about the North or
what political or military baggage the party had attached to it. He knew
what was important locally and what had to be done to get elected, and
elected he was.

41. The Battle of The H-Blocks

Throughout 1979, nationalist Ireland was about to react to uneasy stories coming out of Longkesh/Maze in Northern Ireland about the terrible treatment of prisoners. It had earlier been known by many people in the North's nationalist community of what was going on since the British Government had withdrawn political status from all who were convicted of a political offence after May 1976. Refusing to be branded as criminals by wearing a common prison uniform, the prisoners were forced to lie naked but for a single blanket in their cells. The prison authorities responded by removing all other privileges including, beds, mattresses, books, reading and writing material, radios etc. They were also refused visits from the outside unless they wore the uniform to the visiting area. Because of this, most prisoners went years without receiving a visit from their families and loved ones. When that didn't break the will of the prisoners, the authorities resorted to not allowing the prisoners to leave their cells to slop out their chamber pots unless they first put on the prison uniform. The prisoners fought back by throwing the contents of their chamber pots out of their cell windows. However, the prison officers then responded by shovelling up the contents and throwing them back in the windows again. They also resorted to shoving water hoses in through the windows and soaking the naked prisoners with freezing water.

Eventually, the prisoners had no option but to smear their own excrement onto the walls of their cells. Not to be out-done by the prisoners, the authorities resorted to outright naked violence against them by charging at a cell a time and physically dragging the prisoners by their naked bodies down through the corridor, battening them all the way to a central area and spread-eagling them over a mirror where they would then be forced the indignity of a body search. Then they would hose them down and physically tear their skin with a wire brush. After each severe beating, they would then be dragged back and thrown naked into their cells again. The prisoner would never know if their next beating would happen in minutes , hours, or the next day or week. Because of their refusal to wear the uniform and not receive visits, it literally took years for word of the full picture of what was happening to the prisoner to reach the outside.

This eventually happened when the prisoners took a decision to appoint a select number of prisoners to wear the uniforms and to receive visits. They also had messages written in small fine print on cigarette papers folded up tightly under their tongues. Then when they went to hug and kiss their wives or girlfriends on a visit, they would transfer the messages, known as 'Coms' (communications) to the other person. In response to the appalling stories that were now emanating from the H-Blocks, a broad-based group of Republicans, non-Republicans and human rights activists came together in an effort to highlight what the British government was up to and how it was brutalising the prisoners in an attempt to break the IRA, and by extension the will of the Nationalist community. The national umbrella-group went under the name of the National H-Block and Armagh Committee. The prisoners had earlier received a massive moral eboost in support from an unexpected quarter. When Archbishop Tomás Ó Fiaich paid a visit to the H-Blocks, he was so shocked by what he had found that he felt compelled to speak out to the waiting media as he left Long-Kesh. The Archbishop likened what he had seen in the prison to that of the sewer pipes in the slums of the Black-Hole of Calcutta, and said the H-Blocks weren't fit to hold animals in. Although the Archbishop had merely reacted in an emotional way to what he had witnessed in the prison, the net effect of his public pronouncement, which made head-lines throughout Ireland and the international community, was to put the British Government in the dock, put the spotlight on its criminalisa-tion policy in the H-Blocks, and to also expose the Dublin Government and the Catholic Church who had been sitting on the fence around the issue. The latter two, would from that moment forward, find it difficult to hide and ignore what was happening in the H-Blocks, or to pretend that the public outcry was the result of Republican propaganda. Before long, local H-Block committees started sprouting up all over Ireland and began attracting people from all walks of life in support of the plight of the pris-oners.

Petitions were circulated and rallies were held to highlight the prison-ers cause. By 1980 the campaign began to gather momentum and people started to turn out in their thousands for marches which were organised in Cork City by the Cork Anti H-Block and Armagh Committee. After a time, a number of people from Cobh who attended the Cork marches came together and formed their own local committee in the town. It wasn't long before the group started to mushroom and when it held its weekly meetings at a room at the European Hotel (Poc Fada) each Monday evening, it could have as many as thirty people in attendance. Later, as protest marches and other public events were organised in the town that number could sometimes grow to a hundred. Though the core of the group comprised of people from different shades of Republicanism, from Sinn Féiners, former Officials and Provisionals, it was basically broad-based with most members having no political affiliation whatsoever.

An independent Urban Councillor John Kidney was elected as treasurer on the Committee, and it also had a Fine Gael member and a secondary school teacher among its ranks. What was conspicuous however was the absence of either Fianna Fáil or Sinn Féin the Workers Party on the Committee, neither grouping showing the slightest interest in the prisoner's plight, or in what the British government was up to.

Mick McCarthy the Chairman of the ITGWU was Chairman of the group, while its Secretary was Eamonn O'Dea, who later went on to become an Independent Urban Councillor. What bound the group together and allowed it to work in harmony was the overall goal of achieving the 'Five Demands' of the Prisoners in the H-Blocks and Armagh prisons. The prisoners had already vowed that they would not cease their protest until the British Government granted their Five Demands. After 1976 the prisoners demanded that certain rights be restored to them. These five demands were as follows:

1. The Right to wear their own clothes.
2. The Right to refrain from prison work.
3. The Right to free association with fellow prisoners.
4. The Right to organize educational and recreational facilities with one letter, parcel and visit allowed per week.
5. To have remission lost, as a result of the blanket protest, restored.

As the campaign started gathering momentum, with more and more people attending marches in Cork, Dublin and Belfast, as well as in many local communities around the country, there was a feeling in the air that the Taoiseach, Charles Haughey would intervene with the British behind the scenes to have the prisoners' demands restored. Then at a Rally in Cork just before Christmas 1980, the Chairman of the Cork H-Block/Armagh Committee, Jim Lane announced to those gathered at Daunt Square, that the British Northern Ireland Office had agreed terms with the prisoners, which appeared to meet the basis of their Five Demands. This was after seven IRA and INLA prisoners in the H-Blocks led by Brendan 'Dark' Hughes and three women in Armagh prison had been on hunger strike to restore political status, but not before one, Sean McKenna had come close to death after going fifty-three days without food.

There was a great sense of achievement and triumph around Daunt Square and the city centre after the announcement was made. When those of us from Cobh, headed back towards the train station with our banners and placards, I recall listening to a conversation where some had concluded that Charlie Haughey must have pulled off a master stroke behind the scenes with the British and was destined to have his name in the history books. The national sense of euphoria and achievement following the announcement was short lived however.

Within weeks of the ink going dry on the document that the British had agreed with the prisoners, it became very clear that Mrs Thatcher and her government had no intention of honouring it. The civilian-type clothing the government had agreed to, turned out to be nothing more than another uniform. The game was up; it had all been a ploy to get the prisoners off the hunger strike. The British government didn't want to back down, yet it didn't want the further embarrassment of deaths in its prisons broadcasted around the world. Mrs Thatcher and her government had totally underestimated the will and resolve of the Republican prisoners though, and the prisoners, now under the command of a new leader named Bobby Sands, were determined to resume the strike and not to be out-manoeuvred this time. Sands began the strike himself on 1 March, and was followed by others at different intervals.

In Cobh we all knew it was a case of back to the drawing board. We had a strong sense that there would be bodies coming out of the H-Blocks this time, as Thatcher had already demonstrated taht she didn't understand the meaning of compromise. We also wondered if it would be possible to mobilise the masses onto the streets again.

Around this time, I immersed myself in reading a wide range of books on Irish history, some of which involved the build up to the then present troubles and not all written from a Republican or nationalist perspective. Much of this new information gleaned from these books, made me at first wonder why it had been missing from our school history curriculum, but the more I read, the more I understood why it was been hidden and out of bounds to the education system. The more I read, the more I also developed a left-wing outlook and began to see the overall Republican struggle in a left-wing context. It was also around this time that I had my first encounter and visit from the Special Branch (political police). Three officers called to my parents' home one morning and arrested my brother and I, and about a half dozen other committee members from around the town. To the best of my knowledge, none of us arrested at that time were members of any political party or organisation and our only reason for being arrested under the Offences Against the State Act, was because we had offered moral support to the hunger strikers. These arrests for nothing more than political expression, helped to strengthen my growing politicisation and view that the Dublin Government's approach to the North was nothing short of being politically bankrupt if not corrupt.

If the government, through its political policy believed it could frighten people away from supporting the H-Block prisoners, it was greatly mistaken. What it did achieve through these unjust arrests and attempts at criminalising innocent people, was to force many who might otherwise have faded away from politics after the hunger strikes had ended into revolutionary political parties and in some cases, armies. My overriding memory of that first experience of being arrested was one of being in the back of an unmarked Garda car and of one of the three detectives trying to belittle me with his thick superior attitude.

As things progressed and it became more and more obvious that Thatcher was boxing herself into a corner and that deaths would therefore be unavoidable, members of the local H-Block/Armagh Committee desperately began to contemplate a more militant and bolder approach towards highlighting the plight of prisoners. There had been a suggestion to try and stage a protest on top of Lismore Castle in Waterford, by hanging a huge banner from the top of its walls. It was felt that it would attract huge publicity, especially since Lismore had a big passing tourist industry. The plan was later dropped however, after it was learned that the owner of the Castle, the Duke of Devonshire, had a Special Branch Unit guarding the castle. A number of Committee members who worked on the construction of the new extension at the Irish Steel Plant at Haulbowline, had arranged with shop-stewards there to have a couple of speakers from the National H-Block Armagh Committee address the workforce.

One of the speakers, an emotionally distressed mother from Belfast by the name of Mrs Greene, gripped the attention of hundreds of workers who were crowded into the site canteen, when she began to explain the daily routine that her son had to endure while on the blanket protest in the H-Blocks. At the end of her address, Mrs Greene was in tears as she received a standing ovation from those who had packed the canteen. It was probably the first occasion in a long time that the Belfast mother had been given a ray of hope from people in the South. The campaign had also received a much welcomed injection of financial help, when collectors who hand passed through the crowd with collection buckets, had them filled to the top. In the meantime, committee members reverted back to basics in generating publicity and to getting the message of the prisoners out there. Wall slogans with the words 'Smash H-Block' were painted in various public locations around Cobh. A long stretch of wall overlooking the harbour at the High Road had the words 'Victory to the Prisoners of War' painted in bold three foot tall letters, visible to all traffic entering and leaving the harbour.

One of the boldest paintings to appear around this time went up on the then derelict Martello Tower at Belvelly. The tower was the first thing a person saw when they arrived over Belvelly Bridge and came onto the Great Island of Cobh. The painted sign, read 'Cobh Salutes the Hunger Strikers' in letters four feet tall. On the night that this sign was painted, a pair of double extension ladders were used, and even then, they only reached a little more than half way up the huge tower. As I made my way up the ladders to start painting, I had another man below holding them steady. Two other men were posted on the other side of Belvelly Bridge to keep an eye out for the local Garda squad car on its patrols. I'm not sure what they were supposed to do when they spotted the Garda car as it would have been on top of us at our side of the bridge before they could even whistle. The tower was the property of the Board of Works, whom I'm sure weren't even aware of its existence at the time.

Meanwhile, the painting of each letter was a slow process as we didn't want the sign to look sloppy or uneven, and I had to rely purely on moonlight to allow me to see my work. Then by the time I was on to my third or fourth letter, I heard a whistle sound in the distance. I didn't turn around to look from where I was, as I was in the middle of painting a long letter T. My friend below, holding the ladder, Cionnaith O'Cinneide (Ken Kennedy), shouted up to me, 'Don't look now but we have company – stay put and keep painting.'[155] I had no intention of looking around or of leaving the job. I was having a Magnus Magnuson moment, 'I started so I was determined to finish'.

As my friend shouted up those words to me, I noticed the area of where I was working had lit up brightly. When I glanced around, I noticed a squad car parked by the side of the road with a spotlight on its roof beaming up on my location. I also noticed that the occupants of the car didn't appear bothered about getting out to investigate and seemed more interested in what was being written and or who was writing it. Whatever the reason for doing what they were doing, I was suddenly provided with a blast of light which made my job a whole lot easier. After a few minutes more, I couldn't resist the urge to turn around and give the guards the thumbs up for their assistance. At that point, and probably after seeing and learning all they needed to know, the squad car pulled off again, no doubt with a couple of smiling faces inside.

The Committee had also taken a decision to make a recording about the H-Blocks which it hoped to broadcast to the people of Cobh and Cork. The recording was to include some history to the prisoner's dispute, some update information on how the campaign was progressing and the eventual aims of what the campaign was hoping to achieve. It would broadly appeal to people to come out and support the prisoners. A local DJ with the appropriate recording equipment and who happened to be the grandson of veteran Republican Mick Fitzgerald, agreed to make the recording for the group. He mixed the vocal political text which contained the voice of one of our group, in between songs, music and poems from the then recently released H-Block album which featured many prominent artists including Christy Moore. After the final tape was completed, the man who produced it had no idea of how or where it would later be used.

The Committee had already taken a decision that the recording should be broadcast on one of the pirate radio stations which operated throughout Cork City. We had decided there would be no point in approaching and asking any of those stations to play the recording, as they were already operating unhindered but illegally and would only bring the authorities down on them if they were to be seen to adopt a political position, particularly a pro-Republican one. It was therefore decided to call on one of those pirate stations unannounced and insist on playing the recordings ourselves. That way if there was to be any fallout from the authorities, the pressure would be taken off the disc-jockey and staff at that particular station. Eventually a station in Paul Street was selected and on the Saturday morning in question, when we moved in, a number of us entered the building in a commanding manner.

One of our number shouted an order that we were taking the place over for a time. I recalled the DJ in the room looking very frightened and shocked. The recording was broadcast for the entire forty to sixty minutes of the tape as planned and later we left the building and went home. During a recent reference to that incident, on his local morning radio show, 96FM radio broadcaster Neil Prendeville, who happened to be that unfortunate DJ, recalled the incident with some clarity. Until he

Author after painting the H-sign at Carrigreine H.

was recently informed otherwise, Neil had always believed his little pirate station had been taken over by the IRA. I can well see how in his shocked state at the time, he may not have been listening to the content of the tape recording as it was going out on air. Perhaps he was listening and maybe he believed that anyone who supported the H-Block prisoners must have been in the IRA themselves. For all our efforts though, and for all the political protest by tens of thousands of marchers up and down the country, the Haughey government remained silent, and sixty-six days after he had embarked on hunger strike, Bobby Sands MP died.

Sands had earlier been elected to the constituency of Fermanagh/South Tyrone after the seat had become vacant by the death of Nationalist MP Frank Maguire, and after securing over 30,000 votes. There was a lot of anger expressed when Sands died and much of it directed towards Charles Haughey and his government. There was a common belief abroad, that although Haughey may not have moved Thatcher to give in to the prisoners diplomatically, he certainly should have at least issued a public statement offering his truthful opinion that Sands, and his comrades were indeed political prisoners. Whatever alternative strategy Haughey was working with, if indeed he had a strategy, it wasn't helping to curb the intransigence of Thatcher and her government and it certainly wasn't leading towards the saving of lives. The death of Bobby Sands was also a turning point for many people who up until then were mere supporters of the Republican struggle. For many of them, it was now time to become part of that struggle.

As the prison struggle continued with one hunger striker after the other making the supreme sacrifice, more and more recruits flocked to the ranks of the IRA and INLA.

Meanwhile in Cobh, there was a growing sense of unease in the town, particularly among the political establishment. A public meeting which had been held in the Commodore Hotel was addressed by a former Blanketman from Belfast named Harry Flynn. Flynn, a leading member of the Irish Republican Socialist Party, and former INLA prisoner was a gifted orator and had everyone in the hall hanging on to his every word as he spoke graphically of what it was like to be a prisoner in the H-Blocks, and what it broadly meant to be a Nationalist person living under British Rule in the North. After the meeting had ended, two local Fianna Fáil politicians, Pat O'Mahony and Kevin Foster walked up to Flynn and promised to do what ever they could to support the prisoners cause through their positions on the local Urban Council.

When the opportunity finally arrived for the Fianna Fáil majority on the Council to support the memory of the hunger-strikers by giving permission for a monument in their honour to be erected in the town promenade, they refused outright to give it their support. The Council did, however, support an earlier motion by Cllr John Kidney which called for support to be given to Cardinal O'Fiaich in his search for a solution to the prison impasse.

When the H–Block Committee made a decision to erect an 8ft high sign with the hunger strikers names on it in front of an existing monument which commemorated the Lusitania disaster at Roger Casement Square, it brought out the worst from the local political establishment. The Committee's decision to place the sign in front of the Lusitania monument was arrived at after some careful consideration. The move was made in the height of a critical situation when Bobby Sands life was ebbing away from his fading body. The prime reason for locating the big H–sign there was because it was ideally situated in the centre of town and was felt it would grab maximum publicity. Secondly, the Committee viewed the existing Lusitania monument with some cynicism, especially the manner in which a previous British government had exploited the tragedy, with some historians believing the then 1st Lord of the Admiralty, Winston Churchill, had deliberately let the big passenger liner cruise into the German U–Boat trap, with the cynical purpose of bringing America into the war. The placing of the H–sign at the monument was always intended to be a temporary measure, though how temporary was really dependant on other forces. The big 8ft x 4ft plywood sign was removed more than once and dumped.

On one occasion it was found about fifty yards away on the harbour shore, having been thrown into the tide the previous night before washing back up on the camber again. When it was returned to its original location again, the sign was secured in such a way that those who were intent on vandalising it could not do so without damaging the Lusitania monument also. Rumours were by now circulating about the town that those responsible for the vandalism were regular drinkers in a certain bar in the square situated close to monument. This not surprisingly led to some concern if not panic by some customers frequenting the premises. The British tabloid newspapers soon took up the story, decrying what it termed the 'desecration' of the Lusitania monument. These tabloid reports appeared to be politically driven and grossly exaggerated the ill-feeling which existed in the town because of the presence of H–sign in Casement Square and of the vandalism caused to it, claiming there was a great deal of intimidation taking place in the town. One paper went as far as to suggest that a man wearing a black beret and dark glasses was permanently positioned by steel railings across the street from the H–sign in case any brave person dared to interfere with it. The people of Cobh however, were well aware that the man with the dark glasses and a black woolly hat and who always hung around by the waterfront bar-railings was a local character by the name of Willie (Waloo) O'Donoghue. Willie as everyone knew locally, was totally apolitical and was about as intimidating as the Easter Bunny. This simple truth didn't prevent the tabloid papers from pursuing its political agenda or of like-minded locals feeding in to it. The Fianna Fáil Chairperson on the local Urban Council, Ita O'Reilly then made a public statement backing up such claims, saying she had received reports of intimidation taking place in the town. The Council Chairperson however, failed when confronted to produce or name a single person who had experienced such intimidation.

The lies and deceit which spewed from the British tabloid papers was aimed at serving only one side in the H-Block dispute and the British government wasn't complaining about it. Individual committee members confronted their friends and people they knew wouldn't take offence by pointing out that they shouldn't support the British war effort by buying and reading its propaganda. For their efforts, the committee members nearly always received the same standard answer 'Sure I only buy it for the sports section, the Irish papers are useless for sports.'[156] The sensational stories and half truths printed about the Cobh situation not only attempted to undermine the overall prison struggle, but probably also increased paper sales. It also helped to provide the local political establishment, particularly Fianna Fáil with a fig leaf to cover its impotent prison policy. Around this time, there had been a discussion by some members of the committee regarding the possibility of holding up the newspaper delivery van as it attempted to arrive onto the island some morning and of removing all the British tabloid papers and disposing of them. It was felt at the time that if such a move achieved nothing else, it might have at least made people question why they were buying and reading such papers. The idea never went beyond a discussion though. As the Garda Special Branch continued to raid and arrest members of the Cobh H-Block Committee throughout the summer of 1981, no one arrested was every asked a single question about intimidation. The detectives were probably well aware of the truth about such matters, as I'm sure they were about the vandalism caused to the H-sign or the black flags that had been removed from poles lining the main road onto the Great Island near Belvelly. The last time the people of Cobh experienced controversy over a Republican hunger strike was after the death of Cork's Lord Mayor Terence McSwiney in August 1920, when some scab workers broke a work boycott at the Haulbowline Dockyard.

On that occasion, the workers who passed the picket-line were jeered and pelted with stones upon their return to Cobh. A more militant faction in the town also replaced the Union Jack with the Republican tricolour on the flag-staff at the Admiralty pier, and greased the pole the night before, so it couldn't be removed. If a person was to compare those actions, with the later ones of 1981, they might well conclude they bore more of a resemblance to the actions of the vandals who tried to destroy the H-sign, the very ones who were making claims of intimidation. The Special Branch must have come under a lot of political pressure to deal with the high-profile Cobh H-Block Committee, and this must have taken them some time to get to grips with, identifying who was who and which particularly Republican faction if any, people were aligned to, especially as more and more people were coming forward to support the campaign as it developed. In the June General Election, the Haughey government received a stern message from the electorate over its handling of the H-Block situation. The National H-Block/Armagh Committee had fielded prisoner candidates in many of the twenty-six-county constituencies with all receiving substantial votes. In the Cavan/Monaghan constituency, hunger-striker Kieran Doherty was elected, as was blanket-man Paddy Agnew for the Louth constituency, while in the constituency of Sligo/Leitrim, hunger-striker Joe McDonnell just missed out on being elected after receiving 5,639 first preference votes. Other prisoners fared well also, wherever they stood, including Armagh prisoner Mairead Farrell, (who would later be shot from behind and murdered in Gibraltar by the SAS), after receiving thousands of votes from the people of Cork North-Central.

There had earlier been much excitement in Cobh while parties were on the canvass. Charlie Haughey decided to pay a personal visit to Cobh while supporting his local candidate Joe Dowling. The local Committee had earlier learned of the route which Haughey would take when approaching the town. He was first due to arrive on the grounds of Cobh Community College by helicopter, then he would be led, by a motor cavalcade from the Carrignafoy School down through Bishop Street and on towards the centre of town before addressing the crowd from a platform erected outside of the Commodore hotel.

About sixty H-Block protesters were lined up on opposite sides of the road on a hill leading on to Bishop Street when they heard the helicopter coming in to land in the distance. A short time later when Haughey's open-top car was spotted coming over the brow of the hill, the protestors began shouting 'Smash H-Block'. The Fianna Fáil leader with his arms stretched high in air like a Pope, at first seemed to think he was being greeted by loyal supporters. Then as his vehicle got closer and he noticed the faces of hunger-strikers staring up at him from the rows of placards lining the road, he made a bold and dismissive gesture with his hand. The Taoiseach's driver also stepped into action once he noticed they were in the middle of a protest and quickly picked up speed. This was Haughey's first sign that he was not going to receive an easy time in Cobh. It also did not bode well for his local candidate who could have done without the agro, but people were dying while his leader was parading around the country like a rock star, rather than a national leader who was prepared to defend his people. Once the motorcade had passed, the protestors, with placards under their arms, ran down the town trough Lower Midleton Street (the old street) and onto an area in front of the Commodore platform before Haughey's arrival.

There they were met by other protestors, making themselves very unwelcome to the local Fianna Fáil organisation. When Haughey took to the platform, he was greeted by the sight of hunger-strikers faces everywhere in the crowd beaming up at him, and of a barrage of vocal protests throughout his address. In the end, his presence in Cobh did little to win support for his local candidate who while joining two others on the Fianna Fáil ticket in Cork East, probably split the vote anyway, something his predecessor Seamus Fitzgerald was not allowed to do all those years before. Apart from its blatant lack of support, interest or understanding for what was happening in the H-Blocks, there probably was another reason why Fianna Fáil didn't do as well as it might have in Cork East in 1981, and that was because of the Joe Sherlock factor.

From his early days in Sinn Féin, Joe Sherlock worked hard cultivating his Republican image. Throughout the 1970s he steadily made progress with every election and by-election he contested in Cork-East. One thing Sherlock had mastered to a fine art was his ability to continue to sell himself to that Republican section of the electorate who believed he was with them, even when his party had long since abandoned its Republicanism. In that sense, Sherlock and Haughey had something big in common. One of them knew there were votes to be won by keeping up the pretence of being aligned to the gun-man, while the other built and mastered a career on the image of being a gun-runner. In the height and tensions of the hunger strike during the lead up to the June election of 1981, the H-Block Committee in Cobh made a conscious decision to lobby all the sitting TDs in Cork-East regardless of which party they belonged to, as well as candidates that held constituency clinics in the town, in support of the prisoners' five demands. All of the sitting TDs expressed horror about what was happening in H-Blocks but none would support the prisoners' five demands. A deputation belonging to the local H-Block Committee expected a little more understanding and compassion from Joe Sherlock though, when they went to visit him at his clinic at the European hotel one Saturday morning. The former Republican Internee was anything but understanding or sympathetic to the prisoners' cause however and blatantly refused to support their five demands. Some who attended on the deputation, later claimed that Sherlock refused to see the big picture and was blinded by his hatred for the Provos and the INLA the organisations which earlier split from his and whose prisoners were now dying in the H-Blocks.

A month after the election, Sherlock's party leader Tomás MacGiolla would claim that his party had already supported the prisoners' demands more that a year earlier. That claim would come in a statement, not in support of the prisoners but one that effectively called for the ending of their protest, without expecting a blink from the British Government. The statement by the party of former Republicans probably had more to do with their concern that Sinn Féin, who were learning about the virtues of electoral politics North and South through the prison campaign, might decide to drop its policy of abstentionism towards Leinster House, and in doing so make them irrelevant to the southern electorate. In the weeks leading up to the June election, a couple of former members of the Official IRA in Cobh who became disgusted with the position adopted by Sinn Féin the Workers Party towards the prisoners, particularly that of Joe Sherlock, began distributing leaflets around the town, in an attempt to expose the connection of that party to the murder of Larry White in Cork in 1975. These former colleagues of Sherlock were only too aware of how he had often played the Republican card when it suited him at election time, and now wished to expose him before the electorate. The people of Cork-East didn't quite see things in such straight forward black and white terms though, and certainly weren't up to speed on the minutia of inter-Republican differences and policies. As things transpired, Sherlock had his

Sinn Féin election poster 1985.

373

Funeral of Mick Fitzgerald 1986.

greatest election result yet, after winning 6,241 first preference votes and snatching the fourth seat from Fianna Fáil. There can be little doubt but many of the votes that were cast for Sherlock, came from traditional Fianna Fáil supporters who wished to give the government a message about the H–Block situation, and thought by voting for a party with the words 'Sinn Féin' in its name, was the best way to do that.

As the summer dragged on and more hunger strikers made the supreme sacrifice, other prisoners lined up to replace them on the fast. The British Government it seemed had dug its heels in and didn't appear to know how to row back or compromise. Throughout the International Community, Mrs Thatcher's name was pilloried and was seen by many as one of a stubborn old tyrant, while Bobby Sands had streets named after him. Thatcher had earlier introduced legislation in the Commons prohibiting other prisoners from standing for election. This was probably after someone had made the point that Bobby Sands had received 11,000 more votes from his people than she had as British leader from her Finchley constituents. When the by-election came around to fill the seat made vacant by Sand's death, the H–Block/ Armagh Committee decided to nominate Owen Carron who had earlier acted as Bobby's Election Agent.

To the horror of Thatcher, Unionists and probably many in the Dublin establishment, Carron had maintained Sands vote and held the seat. In Cobh, wreaths were placed at the H-sign at Casement Square every time a prisoner passed away. Solemn processions were then made from the Square to the Republican Plot at the Old Church Cemetery by supporters of the prisoners. One man, who had himself endured a hunger strike while a prisoner during the Civil War, was Mick Fitzgerald. Although being very elderly at the time, Fitzgerald made a determined effort to attend every-one of the commemorations each time a hunger striker died. Not only did he personally lay a wreath on the plot of his former Company comrades each time a commemoration was held at there, but he also addressed the gatherings and told those assembled that there was no difference between the attitudes of the British government which tried to deny political status to the Lord Mayor of Cork, Terence McSwiney when he was a young man, and the British Government which tried to deny that same right to Bobby Sands and his colleagues today.

By September, after ten prisoners had already given their lives to the protest, a Catholic cleric who had been working and massaging the emotions of the hunger-strikers families for some time, had a breakthrough when one mother took the momentous decision to disregard her son's wishes and took him off the strike as soon as he entered into a coma. This had a domino effect and was soon followed by other heartbreaking mothers who had been watching their son's fading bodies. In the circumstances, the prisoners had no choice but to call an end to the hunger strike. While there was a considerable feeling of anger, treachery and resentment throughout the prison for the way the protest had been undermined, not by the British, but by one of their own priests, it would very soon become clear that the prisoners had won, with all of their five demands being put in place in a short period of time.

Without having the benefit of a crystal ball, Bobby Sands could not have known how matters would transpire after he was gone. The only thing he was absolutely sure about was that he or some other prisoner would have to die before the British government would be moved. As the elected O.C. of the prisoners, he had long before taken the decision that it would be him. The hunger strikers were political prisoners before they undertook the fast, they were certainly political prisoners now and the whole world was in no doubt of that fact. Mrs Thatcher and her Government's reputation and its role in Ireland paid a high price for that lesson. So too did the two Dublin administrations which held office throughout the period of the hunger strike. The IRA and the Republican struggle was now stronger than it had been for many years, all thanks to the stubbornness of Thatcher, the bravery of Sands and his comrades and stupidity and weakness of Haughey and Fitzgerald.

In Cobh, the H–Block Committee took a conscious decision to remove the H–sign from in front of the Lusitania monument in the weeks after the ending of the hunger strike. Around that time, a two-foot high thick plated steel H had been fabricated at a local shipyard and had the names of the ten H-block martyrs painted on to it. After the Cobh Urban Council had already refused permission to allow a monument to be erected in the town to the memory of the hunger strikers, some members of the committee now wanted the steel H to be put in place permanently at the Lusitania monument. A majority of the committee were opposed however, feeling the purpose of the H–sign had already been served and the memory of the hunger strikers would not be justly served by antagonising others.

In the years immediately after the hunger strike, the Republican Movement in Cobh was left in a stronger position than it had been before it. Sinn Féin and the Irish Republican Socialist Party had each attracted new members, though the latter remained stagnant and didn't appear to move beyond the aspirational. After a time of being a member of the IRSP and deliberating on its policies and comparing them to Sinn Féin's, I took the long-term view and decision to leave and join Sinn Féin. I had some time before taken the unusual step of joining the Volunteers first. Republicans in Cobh were working hard in a number of areas around this time, some publicly, some not. By the time of the 1984 European election campaign, Republicans from Cobh undertook a lot of the legwork in postering and canvassing the East-Cork area for the Sinn Féin candidate, Richard Behal.

In the closing months of 1983 and early 1984 a number of armed robberies occurred in different parts of the country. Cobh was once again brought into the headlines by a spate of armed robberies in the Carrigtwohill/East Cork area. This began with the taking over of a security van containing a large amount of cash at Slatty's Bridge outside Cobh (the money was destined for the Labour Exchange in Cobh). On 14 April 1983 the security van was held up near Cobh Cross and some £135,000 was taken in the daring raid. A house at Slatty Bridge, belonging to the Greene family, had been invaded earlier by the raiders, and the family, was held hostage for six hours while the men waited for the van. That patience pays off was clearly illustrated on this occasion when after lying in wait for some six hours, the Greene home was finally used as a base from where the security van and Garda escort were attacked when they passed on the Cobh road. The raiders intercepted the Garda car following behind the van by blocking it with Mr Green's car. The three Gardaí were then ordered to lie down on the ground and to stay quiet, while shots were fired at the tyres to immobilise the squad car. The money was seized, the raiders absconded in a get-away car, drove to a switch point situated at a farm near Knockraha.

The media at the time attributed the robbery to INLA leader Dominic McGlinchey, and following the robbery six Cobhmen were arrested in early morning raids and taken to the Bridewell Garda station in Cork for questioning. They were later released without being charged. I happened to be one of the six Cobhmen taken into to custody and was only released when I was able to prove that I had been delivering coal in the Belmont area of Cobh at the time of the raid. It also became clear to me then that the Special Branch were desperate and clutching at straws in their search for suspects as out of the other five men arrested with me, only one had any political involvement and he had concealed it very carefully. The other four men were nothing more than people who happened to support the hunger strikers during the H-Block campaign of two and a half years earlier. In the months which followed, a cat and mouse game ensued between the INLA gang led by McGlinchey and the Gardaí. McGlinchey was at this time regarded by the public as a sort of a Robin Hood figure, and to live up to that reputation, the latter day Robin Hood carried out another raid in East Cork on 14 October, exactly six months later of the other raid. The October raid showed remarkable similarities with the previous one in March, only this time the raiders got away with a mere £60,000. The six intruders took over the Twomey farm, held all three occupants at gunpoint for six hours, and then launched an attack on a post-office van and Garda escort from the building. Four of the raiders used Mr Twomey's car to immobilise the Garda car by ramming it from behind, while two other gunmen waited in hiding until the driver of the van had delivered two of the mail bags into Carrigtwohill post-office. He was then about to collect more bags when he was accosted and told to get back to the van. The captured Gardaí and post-office personnel were then tied up in the post office, and the driver of the van was ordered to drive to a switch point at Carrigane Road, where the vehicle was ransacked and several of the mail bags were taken away.

On 2 December Gardaí made a call to a bungalow in Carrigtwohill, only several hundred yards from the scene of the October post-office raid, in connection to the robbery. The Gardaí were invited in by the elderly couple who lived there, only to find two men and woman pointing a machinegun and a revolver at them. The policemen wisely decided not to offer any resistance, and they were tied up. After some two hours in the highly uncomfortable position the Gardaí finally managed to untie themselves and raise the alarm. By then of course, McGlinchey and his two accomplices had long fled in a get-away car driven by a Cobhman. Roadblocks were thrown up throughout the East Cork area, without result however. The elderly couple that occupied the bungalow were later charged with falsely imprisoning the Gardaí. McGlinchey and his group of

Easter Parade descend Ticknock hill 1989.

men were eventually captured when a house in Co. Clare was surrounded by Gardaí on St Patrick's Day 1984. It was a miracle that no casualties occurred, with the Gardaí firing indiscriminately at the house and in the knowledge that there were children inside. It later emerged that one of the arrested Volunteers was from Cobh, and a grandson of an IRA training officer from the Tan War. When the Dublin government introduced service charges through its local authorities, Sinn Féin threw its weight behind people all from over the state in their resistance to the water and refuse charges.

In Cobh, Sinn Féin members went head to head with the local council for most of the 1980s in the fight against the unjust charges. They confronted and picketed local councillors who voted for the charges outside of meetings, and physically reconnected people's water supply after it had been cut off by the council. These campaigns became very high profile, resulting in Sinn Féin members being prosecuted in court. Not only I had the personal experience of spending five days in Cork Prison in 1988, for refusing to pay a fine for interfering with council property (reconnecting a family's water supply), but Cobh Urban Council was also responsible for sending a local housewife to prison in Limerick for a week after she too refused to pay her Service Charges bill. Some years earlier at the 1985 local elections, I found my name thrown into the ring when at the eleventh hour. The man who had earlier been groomed to stand as the Sinn Féin candidate, Ó Cinneide, had pulled out and left the country. O'Cinneide had earlier been charged with a trumped up IRA membership ploy on the sole basis of a poster that was found on his bedroom wall and which had the letters IRA on it. He was taken in to custody and stood to serve up to seven years on the membership charge if brought before the non-jury Special Criminal Court. As things transpired, the Special Branch didn't hold O'Cinneide and dropped the membership charge, where he not long after left the country to find work. Another Republican Don O'Leary from Cork City was also later charged with IRA membership based on a poster he had in his home with the words 'The IRA calls the shots'.

The same poster was readily available and on sale in Republican bookshops up and down the country. O'Leary was not as fortunate as O'Cinneide and when he was brought before the three judge special court in Dublin, he was sentenced to five years imprisonment. As Sinn Féin was not a registered political party at that time, the only way it could have its name placed on the ballot paper along side that of its candidates was for the candidates to change their names by deed-poll. So when I and my election agent Ger Halligan, went along to Town Hall to sign the registration papers, I had to submit legal papers which had earlier been sworn in front of a commissioner of oaths, which declared that my name had been changed to 'Sinn Féin – Kieran McCarthy'. With virtually no experience or understanding of the political system at that time, we surprised ourselves and others by receiving 125 first preference votes, which brought us close to being elected. Some who had fared less well in first preferences and were already sitting councillors, later past the post when they accumulated substantial transfers, something we in Sinn Féin were unable to muster. After the elections, the local Cumann continued to work hard on local issues relevant to ordinary people. The Cumann also began publishing a monthly political newsletter called the 'Cobh Watchdog' which was popular with most Cobh people and almost everyone who weren't politically aligned themselves. Throughout the mid to late 1980s there was virtually no difference in the local issues which the Sinn Féin party campaigned around and those that the Worker's Party through its Councillor Leo Owens also highlighted. The only visible difference between the two parties was that Sinn Féin continued to campaign vigorously on the northern issue while the Worker's Party was noticeable by the dropping of the words Sinn Féin from its name and with the ghosts of its Republican past being visibly excised.

In May 1986 Cobh Sinn Féin revived the campaign to have a local ambulance service set up in the town. In its local newsletter, it outlined a set of proposals which it intended putting to the Town Council to move the campaign forward. A month later the Council received the Sinn Féin deputation which outlined its plans. The proposals involved a request that the Council would write off a £100,000 debt owed to it by the receiver who had by then taken over the recently closed Verolme Dockyard at Rushbrooke, in lieu of a fully functional Ambulance unit that was laying idol at the yard. The Council was told that Sinn Féin had already established a long list of Volunteers from the local labour exchange who were qualified drivers, nurses and people with first aid qualifications. Sinn Féin suggested that the Council would manage the service in conjunction with the then Southern Health Board. The Chairperson of the Council, Cllr Stella Meade, complimented the Sinn Féin deputation for the effort and time they had put into the presentation. When the Council received its reply back from the Southern Health Board some weeks later however, it couldn't have been more negative. The Board insisted that it could not allow any such voluntary service to operate in the town, and further insisted that Cobh was adequately covered by its existing services in the event of emergencies.

By the time of the 1986 Sinn Féin Ard Fheis, there was only one issue which dominated proceedings and that was the matter of abstentionism and whether the party should drop its age old Civil War policy of not recognising the Leinster House parliament in Dublin. An internal debate had progressed throughout the party for months in advance of the Ard Fheis. Local Volunteer Units had earlier debated the pros and cons of the matter too, before voting on the issue. Delegates then took those views and voted accordingly at an army convention. The Ahern/Crowley Cumann from Cobh was represented at the Ard Fheis by two delegates and three visitors, with only delegates having the right to vote. The Ard Fheis was held at the Mansion House in Dublin, the meeting place of the first. From early into the debate, it became clear that those advocating change were substantially numerical and in the ascendancy. For those who were undecided and wanted to move the struggle forward, the nature of the arguments for change were also superior than those who were demanding the party stuck with the failed policy of the past. Both sides debated with passion and it was only when a spokesperson representing the Army Executive addressed the Ard Fheis on the issue that it became clear that the vote for change would be overwhelming. A small minority led by Ruairi O'Bradaigh got up and left the building before the result of the ballot was even announced.

Sinn Féin had at last abandoned its policy of abstentionism to Leinster House, it now had to decide how it was going to manage it, but before it could get to grips with this new approach, it found itself thrown straight into the deep end when a snap General Election was called for January 1987. The party would soon discover that it was operating on a totally new playing field to the one it was used to in the North.

As the party had virtually no organisation or party structures in place in East Cork at that time, those from areas outside of the Cork City had their Cumann's attached to the City Comhairle Ceantair. Sinn Féin Head Office in Dublin had earlier made it clear that it wished to contest every constituency in the twenty-six counties where it had some form of an organisation in place, so when a convention was called to nominate a candidate to contest the Cork East constituency, it was held at the party offices in Barrack Street Cork.

The convention was chaired by Don O'Leary of Cork Sinn Féin, who himself had earlier been selected as the candidate to contest the Cork North Central constituency. O'Leary opened up the meeting to the floor and asked for nominations. Ger Halligan of the Cobh Cumann nominated me and was seconded by John Kinevane. Batty O'Brien of Midleton then proposed Donal Varian and was seconded by another. The matter then went to an open vote to decide who would represent the party in the Cork East constituency. When a show of hands was called for after each candidates name was called out, there were eleven votes registered for the Cobh candidate, with four or five votes shown for the Midleton candidate.

Once the campaign got underway, it soon became very clear how much we were out of our league in terms of personnel and resources. Every party in the race with the exception of the Workers Party had a sixty-year head start on us. We had virtually no personnel at the northern end of the constituency to canvass with or put up posters, leaving us to spread what bodies we had in other areas very thin on the ground. Our overall weakness though was a national one. A decade and a half of political censorship would play a very significant role in keeping voters from offering their support to Sinn Féin. Not only were the media prevented at that time from interviewing Sinn Féin members from expressing an opinion on local issues, like service charges, pot holes or housing, but whenever the media did comment on the party, it was almost exclusively to do with the North. Therefore and understandably so, as far as many voters in the twenty-six counties were concerned, Sinn Féin was only a one issue party, with many people feeling it had little to offer them in return for their vote. Others who were undoubtedly ill-informed by a combination of the Section 31 of the Broadcasting Act (censorship) and by the British and Dublin establishment's view of the conflict in the North, probably refused to vote for Sinn Féin, believing Republicans to be responsible for the war. When the votes were counted, this reality quickly registered with the broad membership. Almost exclusively, the overall votes that candidates received were in their hundreds, with only a few exceeding the one thousand.

Easter commemoration 2004.

In Cork East, I received 534 first preference votes. It was clear that we had a long way to go to build up our votes, but first we would have to build a party organisation. Almost immediately after the election, the Garda Special Branch swung into action and began raiding houses all over Cobh. In many cases the detectives called when they knew the persons they were looking for were not home, and just wanting to intimidate their parents and families. As the 1987 election campaign was run almost exclusively by about twenty workers and supporters from the Cobh area, the Special Branch were determined to frighten away and disrupt any recruitment of new blood into the party. It probably also felt that it had the political authority to behave in such a manner since Sinn Féin registered such a poor election result. Other police forces in Eastern Europe which behaved in a similar way at that time were regularly decried by western leaders for their disregard for the democratic process. In 1980's Ireland, where Section 31 of the Broadcasting Act kept the masses ignorant and not wanting to ask awkward questions, the suppression of Republicanism and what Republicans had to say was paramount and always took precedence over the secondary matter of democracy. For those who were brave enough to pop their heads above the parapet and question the justification of Section 31 or the excesses of the Garda Special Branch, stood to be branded as Provo fellow-travellers themselves by politicians and supporters of the sys-

Easter Comemoration 2004 where SF Euro candidate David Cullinane addresses crowd.

tem of repression, and even risked the possibility of receiving a visit from the Special Branch (Securitate) themselves.

Unfortunately, the tactics of the Special Branch at that particular time did prove fruitful in that they managed to frighten away some who were considering joining the party. For one or two others, it had the reverse effect and led to strengthen their resolve to get involved and try to expose how rotten the state was and to establish a more just society on this Island.

On a different level of Republican activity, but in tandem with the work Sinn Féin was engaged with in the local community, Volunteers in Cobh and the Great Island were busy working in support of the northern war effort. Much of this work went on unbeknowst to the general public and bore no relation to what Sinn Féin was engaged in. The Volunteers worked quietly away from the public eye and did so with the assistance of individuals and families who were never seen at Republican rallies or had ever given reason to draw attention to themselves. Such was the level of discrete local networks which the Volunteers had established at that time, that a quick word in a person's ear could have provided them with the loan of a clean boat, a van, a car, a house etc, within hours of making the request. During the 1989 European elections, Sinn Féin members in

Cobh mounted a big canvass of the town with the Republican candidate Fr Paddy Ryan. That Ryan was wanted by the British and that both the Belgian and Irish authorities were refusing to extradite him into British hands, struck a chord with many voters throughout the Munster region. Fr Ryan later came close to being elected after receiving more than 30,000 votes.

By the latter part of the 1980s the IRA opened up a new front in its war against the British Army, after vowing to attack the enemy forces wherever it could locate them in Europe. This offensive began in 1988 and carried on through to 1991 in mainly Holland, Belgium and Germany. The campaign coincided with an influx of Irish migrant workers to those same countries. In May 1990, I was one of twelve people from Cobh who travelled to Antwerp in Belgium for work, after answering a notice posted in the local Social Welfare office seeking workers to travel there with an Irish construction company. When we arrived, we found that work was plentiful. Our arrival also coincided with the beginning of the Italia '90 World Cup finals, where Jack Charlton was leading out the boys in green for their first major tournament. This fed into the already big buzz that was flowing through the Irish community there that summer. While most Irish workers were glued to the TV each evening to get the football scores and see how their team was progressing, I used to tune in to see how the other Irish Volunteer teams on tour were progressing and what results they were notching up. The company we worked for, M.F. Kent's were a Clonmel based concern and had thousands employed throughout Europe of mainly Irish, from North and South, English and Scottish descent, and some locals. I was under no illusion at that time that both British and local intelligence services had probably infiltrated our work forces in a desperate attempt to locate the Volunteer Units that were wreaking havoc upon the British Army around Europe. While all of us were enjoying the summer and celebrated every time Jack Charlton took our team a step further to glory, I was also doing discretely what I was trained to do with my eyes and ears. Five months later, at the end of the summer, when the World Cup was all but a fond memory, I was among many Irish people that had decided to head back home for the winter.

Within weeks, I was back in Belgium again, only this time strictly for Republican purposes. By December however, I and two others, Gerry Roche and John Daly were captured in possession of a quantity of arms in an Antwerp apartment. The British, who were still smarting over their earlier failure to persuade the Belgian authorities to extradite the Republican priest Paddy Ryan to Britain, were determined that charges would stick this time. There was much speculation in the media as to what our purpose was with the quantity of assorted weapons found in our possession, with the British tabloids resorting to the weird and whacky. If it was going to be possible to influence the Belgian courts, then the British press wouldn't be found wanting. One report speculated that our intended target was the Prince and Princess of Wales who were due to pay a visit to the region in the following month, while another suggested we were about to assassinate a senior British Army General who was due to attend a NATO meeting in Brussels the following week. An Irish paper quoted a Belgian source as suspecting our target to being a company payroll. When our trial came around five months later however, it became clear that all the speculation was just that, and the best the Belgians could or wanted to charge us with was a broad conspiracy charge to commit some act which endangered the Belgian people. The three-judge non jury court whose proceedings were conducted in Flemish allowed one of us to address the court through an interpreter near the end of the case when all the legal arguments were dispensed with.

Our lawyer told us beforehand that it would be an unusual step but since it was a high-profile case, it probably would be allowed. Our leader, Gerry Roche began to read from a prepared script where he started to outline the history to the present conflict and explained how we were three ordinary Irishmen who would never have found ourselves in a Belgian court were it not for the British inspired conflict in our country. As Roche began to read, I took to studying the body language of the three judges who appeared to understand English and his every word perfectly. He explained that if it were not for the injustices and brutality meted out to peaceful Civil Rights campaigners in the 1960s, he would never have got involved in revolutionary politics and would have had a totally different life to the one he has today. When he came to the period of Bloody Sunday and what had happened on that day, I could see the three Judges nodding in agreement with him, with one particular Judge appearing more emotional and receptive than the others. Roche had earlier gone to great pains to dispel the British lie that the conflict in Ireland was one of two warring religious communities and that it was but a neutral honest broker trying to keep the peace. He carefully laid out the sequence of events of the war which showed the British to be anything but neutral and showed how much they had and were investing in their war effort and to control how the International Community views the conflict. When he came to the period of the 1981 hunger strikes, Roche explained that he had been a personal friend and comrade to one of the martyrs, Patsy O'Hara and how it had affected him. The three judges were by now hung on every word that came off Roches' tongue, with the one who had earlier shown the most emotion looking like he was about to break down in tears. At that point my attentions turned to a number of reporters in the press box. I

Easter Commemoration 2005.

was hoping to identify any who might have represented the British papers so I could give them a good smile, as they must have been horrified by that point at the way Roches' speech was going down. Unfortunately I couldn't tell who was who from among the various reporters. If the facial expressions of the judges were anything to go by, things were starting to look good for us and maybe Belgium wasn't the worst place in the world to find ourselves captured. We knew that if we were arrested in similar circumstances back home, we would be looking at a fifteen to twenty-year sentence, in Britain we could expect to be facing twenty-five to thirty years, Germany – probably twenty years and in Holland we could expect a possible ten year lockup. We couldn't tell with any certainty what we were going to receive here but we were probably in the best and most sympathetic of the five countries mentioned.

When the three judges finished deliberating and returned with their verdicts, they found that we were guilty beyond doubt. They decided that Gerry Roche and I were very much part of the conspiracy but accepted that we were acting as part of an unselfish cause against the British occupiers of our country. They believed however, that our presence with weapons of war in Belgium posed a danger to the public there. They also accepted that John Daly had entered the country only the night before his arrest and therefore played a minimal part in the overall conspiracy. When handing down the sentences, the chairman of the court announced that he was giving Gerry Roche three years as he clearly led the operation. I was given a two year sentence and John Daly was given six months which meant he was to be released with immediate effect for time already served. The British Tabloid press expressed its distain for the court's decision the next day while attempting to ridicule the intelligence and integrity of the Belgian judiciary. One headline proclaimed 'Irishman released from jail to get home for daughter's holy communion', a reference to a point our lawyer had made in Court while arguing for the immediate release of John Daly. What the sentences clearly told us loud and clear was that there were still some sovereign nations in the free world that didn't buy into Britain's account or view of its war in Ireland. It also reminded us of the unfortunate level of collusion with which the twenty-six-county state was involved in, while willingly allowing itself to be part of the British propaganda effort.

An earlier experience that I had in the remand prison in Antwerp probably demonstrated how well the Belgians understood the Irish cause, or perhaps how much they disliked the British. On the morning of Friday 8 February 1991, I relayed a note to the governor of the prison requesting that he allowed me to associate with my two comrades whose cells were on the opposite wing to me. I had absolutely no contact with them since our arrest, as their wing went to the exercise yard at different times to mine. We were considered to be a high security risk so were not allowed normal exercise times for the first six weeks or so. When I was allowed to exercise during the normal times, the only contact I had with an English speaking person, was with a Belfast man who occupied the cell next to mine. Anthony Kerr was a member of the IPLO, a break away splinter group from the INLA, who was coming to the end of his sentence for shooting a policeman. Since Kerr had only a week or two of his sentence to serve, he was accorded full prison privileges which allowed him to exercise at all times with the prisoners of all wings. This allowed me and my comrades to communicate with each other through Kerr, with the basic of normal routine information. When I wrote to the Governor, I had no idea how he would respond to my request, and thought it probable that he would refuse me permission. On the day before, Thursday 7 February, I had been glued to the TV in my cell after earlier reports that morning suggested IRA Volunteers had possibly mortar attacked John Major's war cabinet meeting at Downing Street London. All the news networks CNN, Sky, and the BBC, were speculating as to who was responsible, the IRA or the Iraqis, as we were at that time in the middle of the first Gulf War. With pictures of the vehicle that had fired the improvised mortars all over my TV screen, it didn't take rocket science to figure out who was responsible.

It was later reported that the presence of a cherry-blossom tree at the rear of No. 10, prevented the mortar from making a direct hit on its target.

I had only met our prison Governor once, and that was on the morning after our arrest when I was brought before him in his office. He was a pleasant grey-haired man with a white goatee beard and who spoke good English. He put me in mind of Colonel Sanders, of Kentucky Fried Chicken fame. I had a preconceived image in my head of prison governors, what type of people they were, and what they were meant to represent. This image was based on my own short experience at Cork prison nearly three years earlier and from a good deal of reading I did around the issue of Republican prison struggle.

The governor in this remand prison in Antwerp certainly didn't fit into that image. When I passed on my application for a wing shift on the morning of Friday 8 February, I didn't expect to receive a reply until the following Monday at the earliest, giving that we were heading into a weekend. I also expected that with 500 or so other inmates in the prison, my application would be just one in a long queue of correspondence that would eventually cross the desk of the governor. So imagine my surprise when just before midday on that Friday, my cell door swung open and standing there before me was the tall grey-haired governor with a piece of paper in his hand and a beam on his face from ear to ear. I was at first a little startled and couldn't understand the reason for his smiling face. There was nothing in the note that I sent him that was funny, or at least not that I could recall. Then the big man piped up,

'Ah Mr McCartney' No one in Belgium could pronounce McCarthy — prisoners or screws alike. 'I have your application here to be reunited with your compatriot colleagues. I was wondering when you would make this request, infact I thought you would have made it long before now'.

'Well', I replied, 'we have long past the six week solitary period and I don't see any good cause to keep me isolated from my comrades, especially as I have no one else that speaks English to communicate with in this place'.[157]

The man continued to smile as he took in what I was saying. He knew well that I was exaggerating, as there was hardly a person in Belgium under the age of thirty who didn't speak good English. Then through a big roguish grin he declared,

'I'll tell you what I'll do for you so Mr McCartney, I will allow you onto the same wing as your friends on one condition'. I knew there was going to be a sting coming near the end of this. My mind started trying to guess what it was he was going to ask me for. Surely, I asked myself, he isn't going to demand that I talk to the police or something like that before he grants my request? The man knew he was rising me and continued to smile as he waited for my cautious reply

'What is it, what's the condition?' I asked with tempered exasperation.

'That you don't mortar attack my office', he roared, followed with howls of laughter.[158]

It took me about ten seconds to register what I thought I had just heard and only then did I see the funny side. Still in fits of laughter, my Head-Jailer, pointing his finger at me exclaimed, 'you people are something else, as if the British haven't enough problems with their other war.' Then, as if another personality had just kicked in, the man's face took on a more serious demeanour before declaring, 'Now you won't try to escape from here on me, will you Mr McCartney?'[159]

By October 1991, after receiving a grand tour of the country's prison facilities and having served short spells in five of them, I found myself released from custody in Belgium. My sentence was more than halved after I received remission for a combination of good behaviour and six months automatic remission for the King's birthday.

43. End Game

Almost immediately, I took up where I had left off in Sinn Féin and continued to work on all the local issues which we previously campaigned around. Since there had been no local elections held since 1985 and because they were now billed to take place in 1994 along with the European elections, we were determined not to miss out on securing a seat the next time. Cumann members were around knocking on doors well in advance of the elections, discovering from people what problems they had and highlighting them through our newsletter the *Cobh Watchdog*. This proved very successful and helped to show local voters that we were more than a single issue party.

We also at that time issued local and county councillors with a party document called 'A Scenario for Peace' in an attempt to engage them and their parties in our efforts to find a peaceful solution to the war in the North. None of the local councillors or their parties responded however, or even acknowledged receipt of the document. I had earlier allowed my name to go forward as the party European candidate for the Munster constituency. Apart from polling very poorly with only 5,171 votes, I learned an awful lot, particularly about some of the other candidates and their parties. I was amused for example to discover that anytime I found myself sharing a panel on radio or TV with Dessie O'Malley of the PDs or John Cushnahan of Fine Gael, they would refuse to sit on the same platform with me. On one such occasion while an Election Q&A session involving all the Munster candidates was held in the Distilleries in Midleton, all the candidates were seated behind a long table on the stage with the Chairman seated in the centre. Dessie O'Malley was seated over on the far right which would have made him the first speaker, if the chairman chose to work in that order. John Cushnahan, the failed Northern Alliance leader was situated about two seats left of me. O'Malley was visibly very upset about something before the show began and was puffing on cigarettes as if there was no tomorrow.

Each candidate was invited to give a small spiel about themselves and what they stood for and what they would do if elected to Europe. When it came to my turn to speak, the hall was alerted to a loud shuffle as O'Malley rose to storm out. He arrived back shortly afterwards when it was the next candidate, Dan Boyle's turn to speak. When it came to John Cushnahan's turn to address the hall, he decided to go for broke and to immediately appeal to the blue-shirt vote. He protested about my presence on the platform, saying no one that advocates violence should be allowed to sit down with democrats. The Chairman appeared to be stuck for words, or maybe agreed with Cushnahan, but he certainly didn't do or say anything to correct him or lay down the rules of how the programme was to work.

When the next question came back to me, I said it was regrettable that Cushnahan and O'Malley were behaving in such a manner but it probably said a lot more about the sort of people they were than anything I stood for. The Chairman by that point had found his voice and told me to back off and stick to the question in hand, which I then addressed. Dessie O'Malley didn't at all look well and every time I past a smile in his direction, he looked like he was about to burst a blood vessel. My instinct told me that O'Malley was motivated by a pure hatred of Republicanism and rightly or wrongly, that was what he believed in. Cushnahan on the other hand, was a totally different kettle of fish. He was the opportunist who knew he was going nowhere up North and grabbed the chance to jump into bed with a like-minded party in the South when the opportunity presented itself. My suspicions about Cushnahan were borne out when I again joined him on an RTE Q&A election show in their Limerick studios. The Fine Gael candidate again availed of the opportunity to attack me and my party in public, but later in the canteen area at the back of the studios when the show had finished, he boldly came up to me and a party colleague and asked 'How's it going men, will you have a drink?'.[160]

The media was in a bit of a frenzy at this time as there was plenty of speculation about an IRA ceasefire in the offing. There had shortly before being a relaxation of Section 31 of the Broadcasting Act, which allowed broadcasts of Sinn Féin personnel. This is what allowed me to participate in TV and Radio election programs. The experience of contesting Europe, while being totally out of our league against the big parties, didn't do us any harm locally, and when the votes were counted for the council elections, I came in with the third highest first preferences and comfortably secured the first Sinn Féin seat in Cobh in seventy years.

By the end of August, the much speculated about IRA ceasefire was declared, and despite it being spoken and written about for months before it actually happened, there were some self declared experts who refused to believe it was genuine. Some, who made careers from writing weekly and daily anti-Republican columns in the national papers, predicted it wouldn't last. One writer, Conor Cruise O'Brien the former Minister for Posts and Telegraphs who had introduced Section 31 of the Broadcasting Act nearly twenty years before, forbidding Sinn Féin from having access to the airways, predicted Civil War and claimed the IRA ceasefire was a carefully crafted plot to force a North–South bloodbath. Not only was O'Brien's ridiculous predictions the stuff of Hollywood script material, but in a short period of time, people began to see also the craziness of what Section 31 had been all about, and how if anything it may have prolonged the war. While there was clearly a lot of goodwill among many of the players involved in the peace process, there were also others who were totally knocked off balance by the IRA initiative. Northern Unionism was in disarray in the short term and after spending so many decades saying no, couldn't bring itself to say anything positive about the IRA's ceasefire.

In Cobh people were obviously happy about the way things were moving towards the prospect of lasting peace. When I however, attempted to address the Town Council in September on the matter and to praise those involved in the process, including the men and women of the IRA who happened to contribute to the process in no small way, I was greeting to a chorus of discontent and eyes up to heaven in the chamber. It seemed that all the members of the different political parties in the south wanted peace, but didn't want to give credit to anyone unless their own parties had a role in it or could capitalise from other people's efforts. British Prime Minister, John Major and his cabinet welcomed the ceasefire but were not ready or prepared to move things on beyond that. Major, who three and a half years before had a close escape when IRA Volunteers dropped a mortar bomb outside of his war cabinet meeting at Downing Street, was in no hurry to get into talks with Irish Republicans, especially as he relied more and more on Unionists support in the House of Commons to stay in office.

For the next eighteen months, John Major's government continued to pander to Unionism while he hung on by the skin of his teeth to keep power. He did so however at the expense of the fragile peace in Ireland, and as he was to discover to his own detriment on 10 February 1996, to the peace in Britain too. Just after 5pm on that evening after a ninety minute coded warning had been delivered, a massive half-tonne bomb detonated at the Docklands area of London. The bodies of two young men were later dragged from the rouble, after a policeman had earlier mistakenly directed them towards the bomb. With the bombing, the IRA announced the end of its ceasefire, blaming the British Government's lack of goodwill in refusing to grasp the opportunity for peace which it had been offered over the previous eighteen months. Sinn Féin President Gerry Adams spoke about the need to continue the Peace Process and urged others to follow his call. Other Nationalist leaders echoed Adams' appeal and in doing so, found it hard to contain their anger with John Major and his government for allowing the situation to deteriorate to such a level.

Nine days later another bomb exploded in the heart of London's West End. The bomb exploded prematurely on the New Cross to King's Cross bus while it was being ferried by Volunteer Edward O'Brien of Wexford. O'Brien was one of three people killed in the explosion. Then on 24 April, 32lb of semtex, the biggest bomb of its kind ever planted in Britain, failed to explode on Hammersmith Bridge in west London. On 15 June, another massive explosion rocked the centre of Manchester. Although there was an eighty minute warning given by the IRA, the explosion resulted in hundreds of injuries but no fatalities. Despite the best efforts of Republicans, Dublin and Washington to get the London government to re-engage in the Peace Process, John Major and his cabinet were reluctant to do anything meaningful that would lose him Unionist support in parliament. Republicans and nationalists were also very concerned about John Bruton's leadership in Government, particularly his handling of the Peace Process and his reluctance to meaningfully engage and manage it. Those concerns were added to when it became public that Bruton had allegedly remarked when asked for an interview by a female reporter, 'Don't talk to me about that fucking Peace Process.'[161]

At 4.30a.m. on morning of 23 September, a specialist armed police unit, the SO19, raided a small hotel at Glenthorne Road, Hammersmith, London. When the police smashed their way into the apartment, they found three unarmed IRA Volunteers attempting to surrender to arrest. One of the Volunteers Diarmuid O'Neill was shot six times and even though he was severely injured, he was dragged down the steps of the hotel outside of the building where he was denied vital medical care for twenty-five minutes, despite there being an ambulance on site. Twenty-seven-year-old O'Neill died later in hospital. The results of the post mortem examination carried out on the body of O'Neill showed a patterned bruise on his scalp which in the opinion of the pathologist for the British Home Office may have resulted from 'an individual treading on his head.'[162] The police never recovered the explosives and weapons they insisted were in the hotel apartment before they smashed their way into it.

Although born and raised in London to Irish parents and educated at the London Oratory School in Fulham, the same private school where the future Prime Minister Tony Blair's children would attend, Volunteer Diarmuid O'Neill took a big interest in Irish culture and nationalism. He was later laid to rest at St Mologas Cemetery, in Timoleague, County Cork. On 5 April 1997, the IRA, armed only with a phone and a coded bomb message, forced the Aintree Grand National to be called off. Without there being the slightest chance of harm coming to anyone, the IRA's coded message probably did more to focus British minds on their Government's failings around the Peace Process, than had all the exploded bombs to date. Then after 6 June, Bertie Ahern and his party returned to government with the Progressive Democrats. There was much anticipated speculation as to whether Ahern would be able to re-ignite the Peace Process and demonstrate the same level of interest and commitment towards the north that his party predecessor Albert Reynolds had shown. Many surmised that were he to remain in bed for half of every day, he still would be able to give the Peace Process more attention than had the previous Taoiseach John Bruton. There was also an air of optimism that both Ahern and Republicans would be able to move things along in the right direction with the arrival of the new British Prime Minister Tony Blair. Blair and his New Labour Party had swept to power at the beginning of May after winning 43.1% of the popular vote. Now that there was a British Government that wasn't reliant on Unionist support to keep its hands on the levers of power, it was generally expected and hoped that things would move forward swiftly in the Peace Process.

Earlier in the process, after the IRA had made the first gesture by announcing its ceasefire, the then Prime Minister John Major made the unbelievable and provocative statement that the Republican Movement would have to go through a period of decontamination before the government would enter into talks with it. While the statement was meant to buy time for the government and was probably really meant for Unionist ears, it also smacked of the sort of arrogance one would expect to hear from an old imperialist leader, forcing Republicans to issue a stern response. Sinn Féin's Chief Negotiator Martin McGuinness then issued a statement which carefully outlined a series of meetings he had shared with representatives of Mr Major's government. What was of further embarrassment to the Prime Minister was the content of those negotiations being put into the public domain.

While many people might have been disappointed by John Major's unhelpful remarks, few would really have been shocked by a Tory Prime

Minister making such a declaration about an Irish political party. But such political condescension towards Sinn Féin was not the preserve of the British Tories or even Irish Unionists however. An incident which took place in Cobh around that time, demonstrated that there were some in Fianna Fáil who also believed Sinn Féin and those who voted for the party to be entitled to a different standard of treatment than everyone else in our political system. In the run up to the election of a new Town Council Chairman (Mayor) in June 1995, I received a phone call asking if I was prepared to enter into discussions regarding the formation of a new alternative voting arrangement to secure the position of Council Chairman. The existing arrangement or 'pact' in place involved three Independent and two Fine Gael councillors. One of the Fine Gael members who was due to assume the position of Chairman in June, had been extremely vocal in his opposition to everything my party stood for and was particularly unkind when asked to recognise the part Republicans had played in the Peace Process. When it was therefore brought to my attention that a crack was discovered in the existing pact, I agreed to attend a meeting to discuss the possibility of forming an alternative arrangement. I can't exactly recall whether I received that initial phone call from John Mulvihill of Labour or from Joe Dowling of Fianna Fáil but I do remember vividly the meeting taking place at John Mulvihill's home on the Tay Road. I also remembered when entering the room, seeing a bottle of Irish whiskey on the table, presumably intended to seal whatever deal would later be made.

Present in the room with John Mulvihill and me were Joe Dowling and Kevin Foster of Fianna Fáil. I was under no illusions that there was obviously a lot of wheeling and dealing after taking place before anyone decided to contact me. I was told that a certain Independent councillor was reluctant to support the previously agreed Fine Gael candidate for the position of Chairman at the upcoming AGM. This told me that at least some of the people in the room with me had already had earlier meetings and that my support was only considered late into the game.

I asked John Mulvihill what the story was and whether he was asking for my support? He said yes, but they must first work out in what order the Chair and Vice Chair would rotate for the remaining four years. Then out of the blue, he asked me if I was interested in the position of Vice Chair. The office of Chairman (Mayor) or Vice Chairman has never appealed to me personally. I believe a good hardworking Councillor doesn't need such trappings to represent the people who voted for them. I also know however, and was very conscious in those early days of the Peace Process, that to be granted such a position, would have greatly benefited my party's image and standing in the community. But before I could answer John Mulvihill's question, Kevin Foster, the longest serving member on the council, interjected to say, 'Ah I'm not quite sure people are ready for Kieran's party to hold such a position. I think I would like to see things develop a bit further in the Peace Process first.'[163]

In fairness to John Mulvihill, I think he was just as surprised as me to hear those words uttered. I liked Kevin Foster as a person but felt it was an incredible position which he had adopted towards me and my party, especially as I had earlier received more first preference votes than he or his party colleague in the election. He also appeared to have a poor handle on his own party's history, where it came from and how it was once described by one if leaders as being a slightly constitutional party. Did he believe that the people who voted for me were less entitled to see their choice of candidate assume the office of Chairman or Vice Chairman, than Fianna Fáil or any other party? Needless to say, that was the end to that short alliance, and if my memory serves me correctly, the Independent councillor who had earlier expressed dissent in the Fine Gael pact, relented in favour of a reconfigured arrangement. I have no idea if Kevin Foster was just expressing a personal view or if he was proclaiming his party's policy at that time, but twelve years on and as developments in the run up to the 2007 general election had demonstrated, Fianna Fáil still seems to have a problem accepting Sinn Féin's democratic mandate.

As a party, Fianna Fáil has never had a problem accepting, even seeking Sinn Féin's support when it was needed, it just refuses to accept the party's democratic mandate as equal to that of everyone else. Despite the irony being lost on Fianna Fáil for investing so much time and effort in getting all the northern parties to recognise each others electoral mandates so they would share power with one and other, it also seemed lost on them as a party that had more than a few serving and former government ministers including a former and serving Taoiseach brought before Tribunals for land rezoning scandals and corrupt payments, that Sinn Féin has not nor is it ever likely to have an elected member brought before such a forum.

With the two new Government leaders of Blair and Ahern throwing their full weight behind the Peace Process in 1997, a new air of hope started gathering pace throughout the country, leading many to believe something new and big was possible. A year later, the prize for everyone's tireless efforts eventually presented itself in the form of the Good Friday Agreement. The agreement had the potential to transform the political landscape on the island of Ireland and the relationship between the Irish people and those of the neighbouring island.

Few people doubted Tony Blair's sincerity, and that he was different to any British Prime Minister that went before him. Republicans however, were still concerned about elements of that other secret British government (secret services) which seemed determined to undermine the agreement and prevent any hope of establishing a future power-sharing government in the north with a new dynamic for creating a United Ireland. Republicans in Cobh, while having some concerns about anti-agreement forces at work in the North, embraced the agreement, and agreed in the main with the Republican leadership's long-term strategy. One local Sinn Féin member and former Cumann Chairman dissented however, feeling the Republican Movement was heading in the wrong direction. Dick Donovan, the son of former Volunteer and Republican Internee Simon Donovan, left the party soon afterwards and stood as an Independent Republican candidate in the 1999 local council elections, but failed to be elected. In the 2004 local council elections, Dick offered his support to the Republican Sinn Féin candidate, Donal Varian who although missed being elected, polled well on his first outing. That had been an interesting election campaign in terms of confusion and who people believed they were voting for. At one stage during the election count, which took place at the Cobh GAA Hall, one particular Fianna Fáil candidate approached me to congratulate our party as it looked to him like Sinn Féin was about to gain a second council seat through the election of Donal Varian. Then in the weeks which followed the election, it was learned from other people, that they had also voted for Varian, believing him to be a second Sinn Féin candidate.

One morning in 2001, two Garda detectives called to my home to inform me they had leaned from the police in the North that my name and personal details had been discovered on a computer in a house in north County Down. The detectives, while remaining in my hallway as they spoke, also advised that I'd take measures to cover my personal security. I asked them was it a Loyalist house where the file had been found but they either couldn't or wouldn't reveal anymore than they already had. I invited the two policemen into my apartment sitting-room but they declined. Over the many, many years that I had dealings with Garda detectives, I could never get them out of my home fast enough after they would arrive on one of their many unwanted visits, but now when I had invited them into my home, they were the ones who wanted to get away fast from answering my questions. They did surmise however, that my details were probably picked up and passed onto Loyalists while I was in Belgium eleven years before. In the days which followed that visit by the detectives to my home, there were widespread media reports that the names of many other Republicans from around the Munster region had been found on the County Down death list. I never had any doubts but that British Intelligence had played a part in the arrest of me and my comrades in Belgium in 1990. Now it was becoming increasingly clear that the same forces were hard at work again, and not only was it very likely that they had fed Unionist murder gangs with our personal details, but they were more than likely releasing this information to the Gardaí at this particular time for a well thought out political reason. My reading of the situation at the time, was that those pulling the strings wanted to paint a positive image of the new police force in the North, (the force which allegedly had located these files), so that Republicans would buy into the new policing arrangements, and that those in the Dublin Government who were watching these developments unfold, would also apply pressure on Republican leaders to press on.

After a number of false starts and disruptions inspired by dirty tricks operations from anti agreement forces, including the encouraged departure of the Unionist leader David Trimble and the revelation of a pseudo spy-ring at Stormont, power sharing finally took place between Ian Paisleys DUP and Sinn Féin on 8 May 2007. Before that happened however, the IRA, had announced the formal ending of its military campaign on 28 July 2005, while instructing all its units to dump arms. Two months later on 26 September the Republican Army announced, along with the International Decommissioning Body that it had put all of its weapons beyond use.

While some Republican Volunteers may have opted for a quiet retirement after the formal closure of the war, it would seem the vast majority had joined with their brothers and sisters in Sinn Féin in continuing to establish Irish unity through exclusive political activity. While it was always expected there would be some who would refuse to embrace the new dispensation and remain tied to the politics of rejectionism, it is never the less clear that the situation has moved far beyond what ever limited obstacles that dissident Republican or Loyalists micro groups could throw at it. On 18 April 2008, the North's First Minister Ian Paisley visited Cobh after being invited to speak at the fiftieth anniversary dinner of the Cobh and Harbour Chamber of Commerce. A protest against the Paisley visit was organised by 'Republican Sinn Féin' (RSF) with leaflets having been distributed throughout the town before-hand calling on people to join the protest. Many Cobh people who had followed Paisley's colourful career expressed annoyance that he should be invited to their town, with some telling local Sinn Féin members they were considering joining the protest. However, when it came closer to the date of Paisley's arrival, it had become apparent to many of those who were organising the protest. Protesting against Paisley the former preacher of sectarian war was one thing, but to get caught up and allow oneself to be used in an anti power-sharing exercise was a totally different matter.

Had R.S.F. spokesman Donal Varian come straight out on his flyers and said his party was behind the protest and that they were opposed to all forms of power-sharing, people may have had some respect for what they were about. Claiming as he did during a radio interview that we in the south are competing with the people of the North for jobs, may have also exposed the poorly thought out and warped form of partitionist Republicanism by which he and his party operates. On the evening of the protest, it was reported that less than fifty people turned up, many as mere spectators and less than a dozen from Cobh.

Paisley the old dinosaur of 'No' politics is truly yesterday's man and it may also be accurately said that those behind the Cobh protest are another breed of dinosaurs, trapped in the past and with little positive to offer the future.

What was also noted in contrast, thanks to the brave efforts of the Irish Republican Volunteers who had spent much time debating, deliberating and mapping out the Republican road for the future, is that they had made it possible for a First Minister of the North to visit Cobh. Now at last, it is possible for us all to get down to the real business of creating a new historic post of First Minister for the entire island of Ireland.

Less than a month after Ian Paisley's historic visit to Cobh, a move was made to right another historic wrong which was done in the town's name. On 12 February this year, which happened to fall on the 92nd anniversary of the execution of James Connolly, I had the honour of moving a motion at Cobh Town Council, which called for a posthumous apology to be made to the Republican Socialist leader for the manner in which he was ran out of the town in March 1911 by a violent mob in the company of the Town Chairman. The motion was unanimously supported and at the time of writing, will allow for a future awarding of an official apology to be presented to a member of the Connolly family.

Conclusion

Any student of Irish history that examines the existence of the Irish Volunteers, from their beginning in 1913 right through to contemporary times, will be struck by the number of times it had in its relatively short evolving history repeatedly diverged and tactically changed its policies as the times and situations it often found itself dictated. As there were always those in the Volunteer Movement who resolutely refused to go along with those changes and new tactics, the Movement often found itself split and divided, some times bitterly. Some of those splits would lead to bloody feuds, others would be bloodless and relatively peaceful, while one would actually lead to a bitter all-out Civil War.

The reasons for these splits have been diverse and varied. The first split faced by the then fledgling Volunteer movement was over a decision whether it should fight a World War on Britain's behalf in 1914, or to fight a war against Britain and cede from its empire. The next split was one which was forced upon the Volunteers by outside forces, namely its enemy Britain, leading to Civil War. Next the Volunteers split over a decision to enter Leinster House and recognise the southern State, and this was repeated a number of times since over different periods. Others split from the Volunteers because of decisions taken to end armed struggle, believing there was no other way to achieve a United Ireland. The one common thing which every faction would later claim, regardless of which side of the debate it came down on, was that it remained committed to the ideals of the Irish Republic as declared at Easter 1916 and endorsed by the Irish people through their franchise in 1918. Regardless of how any Volunteer or former Volunteer later behaved, in the Civil War or post Civil War, in the middle of a bitter split or post-split, or through their political or military actions, they would still or at least in public anyway, insist they were still committed to a united Ireland.

More often than not, for many of those former Volunteers, there would be a caveat or carefully rehearsed reason why it cannot happen now, or in some cases why it shouldn't happen now. A united Ireland would always be for another time, though the often Volunteer come politician would endeavour to build his or her career on the premise that they were actively working to achieve a united Ireland. In some cases, former Volunteers would often find themselves making public contradictory pronouncements. This would especially happen when they were found to spend more time publicly attacking their former comrades whom they had split from, than actively working to achieve a United Ireland. When asked, they would often publicly defend there own military pasts, while carefully disassociating themselves from the campaign which their former colleagues were now engaged with.

In his witness statement to the Bureau of Military History, Mick Burke pointed a critical finger at the old Fenian Movement in Cobh for refusing his generation of Volunteers assistance and support before, during or after the Tan War. His daughter Eimer, later told me that her father had often spoken about this, and was very put out by the lack of identification which the old Fenians had shown towards his struggle. The people, to which Mick Burke referred, were John O'Leary of East Hill, Dr Fitzgerald, Captain R. O'Sullivan, Batt Dennehy, Bob Driscoll and Messrs Savage, Kenefick, MacDonnell and others. It would appear from Burke's assertion that unlike other veteran Fenian's and IRB members like Tom Clarke who plotted and participated in the 1916 Rising, the old Fenians, in Cobh at least, had no time for a struggle which they must have regarded as being less honourable and worthwhile than the one they previously had been associated with. I often wondered if this was in part due to the level of popularity and success of Burke's generation of freedom fighters (something that was always out of reach of the old Fenian Movement). After Cobh Fenian John O'Leary passed away in 1929, a subsequent obituary published in a local newspaper, said that one of the last appearances made by him in public before his passing, was to cast his vote, not for Sinn Féin or even Fianna Fáil but for the non-Republican Labour Party.

During the course of a conversation with another Republican in the 1950s, Mick Leahy was said to have referred to the Volunteers who were then grabbing the national headlines through the launch of their Border Campaign as 'a gang of Blackguards.'[164] The former Brigade commander must also have felt his fight was a cleaner and more honourable one than that of those who were now attacking RUC barracks along the border, despite Leahy himself, being renowned for leading the capture of the first RIC Barracks in Ireland (Carrigtwohill 3 January 1920). It is also probable that Mick Leahy may have been personally disappointed, if not angry that the party to which he had earlier given allegiance, had abandoned the struggle to unite the country, thus forcing other young men to take up the gun. Leahy's earlier 'Blackguard' comment was later contradicted by his more noble action, for shortly after the conflict blew up onto the streets of the North in 1969/70 and the full horrors of life for Nationalists living in the sectarian state appeared on people's television screens, the former

Brigade O.C. produced an old Lewis machine gun which had lain buried in Dungourney for more than fifty years and had it shipped off across the border to those looking to defend themselves.

Another example of such double-speak and confused thinking around the issue of armed struggle, meaning different things to different generations came from former Republican Volunteer and Workers/Labour Party TD Joe Sherlock when he was interviewed on RTE radio in the 1980s. I happened to listen as Joe was eager to point out to the interviewer, who incidentally gave him a free run to push his party line on the matter, that there was no resemblance whatsoever between the struggle then being waged by the IRA in the North and that of his generation. His war was a clean stand-up one against the crown forces we were told, and wasn't sectarian. It didn't seem to occur to Joe that the RUC stations that he and his comrades had blown up and attacked around the border in the 1950s and 1960s were manned by a police force which happened to be mainly Protestant, a fact to which his party would later use to describe the IRA's campaign as sectarian. Despite trotting out the party line however, Joe would have been well aware that the latter's campaign was not sectarian. He knew that the IRA didn't ask British soldiers to declare their religion before deciding whether to shoot them or not, that Catholics who made up a tiny percentage of RUC membership were also regarded as legitimate targets, and although there may have been some incidents in the early 1970s where Protestant civilians were targeted in revenge attacks, as well as the isolated incident of the Remembrance Day attack at Enniskillen in 1987, following which, the unit responsible was stood down by the leadership, the IRA's twenty-five-year northern campaign was by and large anything but sectarian. Just like in the previous cases mentioned, Joe and his party leaders probably viewed their campaign as being cleaner and more honourable than the later one, but they would also have never forgiven the leadership of the Provisional Movement for exposing their total failure to defend nationalist communities during one of their most vulnerable periods in the history of the sectarian state.

Such insistent claims or questions of legitimacy between different generations of freedom fighters are about as pointless and incredible as the recent demand by some Unionists which recently called upon the British government to say it never had been at war with the IRA. The Six County Statelet was for nearly thirty years, the most militarised part of Europe since the Second World War, with military helicopter bases and fortifications dotted throughout the region, with tens of thousands of troops, an army of full-time reserve troops, a machine gun carrying police-force driving around in armoured vehicles, where special SAS units were in place, special police and military interrogation centres in place, where a huge super holding prison and Internment Camp, the Maze, was built to hold thousands and its political enemies. Where billions was spent annually to operate an intelligence war, including the purchase and distribution of weapons to Loyalist Paramilitaries for its counter insurgency campaign. Despite the British army having on a number of occasions throughout the conflict entered into agreed ceasefire with the IRA, while negotiations were taking place between both sides. With all of this and much more in place, and with the British State and its Republican enemies determined to do all that they could to defeat one and other, I think it's safe to say that 'yes', a war had been fought. It's also safe to say that there was no outright military winner to that war, and despite the overwhelming odds and resources reigned against it, the IRA actually fought the British to a stand still. It is therefore quite odd that some Unionists in the North as well as some in the Fine Gael party in the South should insist, with not a little irony that the war was not a war, especially since they had spent years themselves, calling on the IRA to say its war was over.

So while relationships on this island and between ourselves and our neighbouring island have been transformed in recent times through the subsequent peace process, no one can say with any certainty what the future may hold. While most of us will look to the future with confidence that that which was previously sought through military actions, will in future be realised through common agreement, there may always be some who will insist on striving for change through the old ways. It would be both wrong and hypocritical of me as someone who participated in the war mentioned above, to now sit in judgement of others following behind, who might in all conscience believe themselves to be right. I do not accept that my war was less honourable or just than Mick Leahy's, Mick Burke's or Joe Sherlock's, and neither will I be so arrogant as to claim that it was more clean or just than that which may or may not follow. I would however, like the rest of the Irish nation, condemn anyone who would engage in any armed action which has the publicly stated purpose of trying to bring British troops back on to Irish streets.

Personally, I believe the war is over and no future military campaign can succeed because it will lack the popular support if its own community. That support is clearly with the Peace Process and with the decisions taken by the IRA and Sinn Féin, and is not likely to change in the foreseeable future. It is with Sinn Féin because through its actions, it has effectively smashed the one-party sectarian State of the past. Nationalists for the first time in their history, now hold power in equal measure to that of Unionists. Now the next stage of the Republican programme is to demonstrate and persuade Unionists that their future interests lie in a united, peaceful and prosperous Ireland, and to persuade the sceptic political parties in the South that it's no longer good enough for them to be mere spectators in this process. I also happen to believe that those politicians in the South, who have consistently scoffed at Sinn Féin and tried to ridicule the notion of a United Ireland, have a major responsibility to face up to reality. I speak of the anti-nationalist elements in Fine Gael and the Labour Party, particularly the former Workers Party/Democratic Left elements which are now in the ascendancy of that party. They had already deserted the people of the north in the past and have demonstrated through public comments in more recent times, their unwillingness to countenance, let alone accommodate or assist in a United Ireland coming about. It could very well be against the background of their words and actions, particularly if they should ever take power in the southern state, that a new generation of young men and women will decide again that armed struggle is the only alternative. I can remember a time when my generation of Republicans were drip-fed the line by our so-called betters, day in and day and out of 'Give up the gun and give politics a chance.' Well the Fine Gaels, the Labours and the Fianna Fáil now have their chance to show that politics works, by at least not trying to hinder those who are working to bring about national unity. Will they blow it?

One of the most remarkable things I had discovered while researching and writing this book, was how Cobh or Queenstown as is was then called, was probably one of the last places on earth that one would have expected to discover a Revolutionary Republican Army. Not only that, but one certainly wouldn't have expected the inspiration and driving force for organising other Volunteer areas in East Cork to also come from Cobh. Cobh in 1913-21 was a bastion of British military and naval activity. The Admiralty Headquarters for the western approaches covering the south of Ireland was situated in the heart of the town where a Company of Royal Marines was also stationed. A battalion of infantry troops was stationed further east at Belmont hutments and was situated close to a military hospital overlooking the harbour. Another regiment of British Coastal Artillery Gunners were stationed a mile away on Spike Island, as were others at two other occupied installations, at Forts-Carlisle and Camden further out near the harbour mouth. Also close by in front of the town was the British naval base and dockyard at Haulbowline. Many of the families which then made up the population of Cobh had in some way or other, someone employed at these installations. The RIC barracks at Westview also had many personnel who had families in the town. In other words, the British rulers should have had every good reason to expect their subjects in Cobh to be loyal and law abiding ones.

Many of the founding Volunteers in Cobh were employed at the Haulbowline dockyard, and this was not a problem initially as the British were not aware that at least one of those was a member of the IRB. Because for now at least, the only issue on the agenda for the Volunteers was that of Home-Rule, the British Authorities didn't seem too concerned about the Volunteers, or that some of its own ex-naval personnel were engaged in training them, or that some of the Volunteers themselves were in its employment. It would appear that many people didn't take the Volunteers very seriously at first. Many of their fathers, who had previously been servicemen themselves, didn't feel a conflict of interests existed between them and their sons. It was not until after the 1916 Rising that people, including the authorities, decided to wake up to what the Volunteers were really about. Mick Burke gave us a good flavour of the public opinion in Cobh at the time, when re-told of when news of the Dublin Rising reached the town, he said those of his age who were gathered outside of the Railway Station with him when a policeman broke the news, were so outraged, that they were eager to assist the British cause, yet within a short time they had become Republican Volunteers too. Despite this, they and other Volunteers were allowed employment and when ever possible, to engage in military training at the Haulbowline dockyard. Furthermore, when Mick Leahy and Seamus Fitzgerald were released from Frangoch Interment Camp in late 1916, their jobs were waiting for them back at Haulbowline, despite a recommendation from the police that they should no longer be employed there. It is interesting to note the Vice Admirals reason for keeping their apprenticeships open for them, was based on the simple fact that they had not been convicted of any offence, despite both men being the commander and vice-commander of the local Volunteer Company and being clearly observed by the police marching out to link up with MacCurtain and McSwiney on Easter Saturday.

It is interesting to note also how the Irish authorities have dealt with its perceived threats to security in more recent times and to compare it against the manner in which the British dealt with security around the early Cobh Volunteers employed at Haulbowline.

The local RIC kept comprehensive files on Leahy, Fitzgerald and many others in the local Volunteer Movement. From some of these files, we can see that an Inspector at the Westview Barracks regularly appraised both Dublin Castle and the Admiralty in Cobh of such Intelligence matters. There is little doubt but that the RIC had the goods on the Volunteers immediately after 1916. It is less clear however, why the Admiralty continued to be so lenient towards them, as they were clearly a threat to security and in many cases openly flaunted it.

If one compares that to the actions of the Irish naval authorities in more recent times, when exercising a policy which denied its own members promotions because of family members who happened to belong to the Republican Movement, they may well conclude that the former had been asleep on the job, or that the latter was at best paranoid, or at worst downright vindictive. These latter decisions were taken despite the naval members involved having long and impeccable service records, and with absolutely nothing to indicate they would ever pose a security risk to the Irish State. One can only conclude that such decisions were taken not to safeguard against some perceived threat to security, but as a punishment for being guilty by association of birth. Most of all, it would seem to be a policy of warning to others of what to expect if a relative should choose to express Republican beliefs. It was also by extension, a denial of the fundamental right to political expression by civilian family members. Such security policy procedures were and are not confined to the Irish Navy alone. The Army, Gardaí, Civil and Public services are also subject to strict scrutiny, but probably under an atmosphere of far less paranoia.

But it isn't just a question of whether the southern defence forces really believed or imagined a threat to its security existed by virtue of some of its members being blood related to Republicans. The consequences of this paranoid policy seemed to stretch a lot further.

In August 2001, a case involving two Sinn Féin members, employed on contract work, at the Haulbowline Naval Base exposed how ridiculous the security policy at the base was. One of the men, Jonathan O'Brien was a well respected Cork City Councillor; the other John O'Callaghan was a member of the party at the time. Both had joined the party post-ceasefire. When the men had started working at the base a week and a half earlier, they were told like all other workers on site that they would have to get security clearance. Then one morning, they were informed that they had failed to receive security clearance, and would have to leave the island at once. The men's union (The Operative Plasterers and Allied Trades Society of Ireland) as well as the main contractors, immediately made contact with the Department of Justice but were told they would not discuss the case with them, only to say the men were a threat to national security and could not be allowed entry to any Government sites. While one could well understand why the naval authorities would have previously oper- ated such a policy at the height of the war in the North, it is quite another thing to make sense of or justify such a policy three years after the Good Friday Agreement was accepted by the Irish people and their government, and five years after the IRA Ceasefire. It exposed the fact that the State was incapable of making a distinction between the IRA and Sinn Féin. One man, who took up the men's case at the time, was Martin Ferris TD.

Ferris, who no doubt was one time on top of the list of people forbid- den from entering Government sites, was now a representative of one of its most important sites: Leinster House. 'I find it difficult to believe in

2001 that the naval authorities would behave in such a reprehensible way, depriving two good workers of employment on Haulbowline because they are members of Sinn Féin,' said Ferris. He continued:

> There was no problem with their work. The only thing they have in common is their membership of Sinn Féin. Jonathan O'Brien is a very able Cork Corporation Councillor, active on five important committees, yet the navy does not consider him suitable to work on their base. This is a clear example of political discrimination. Sinn Féin will be using every remedy possible to have these men reinstated and an apology made to them. Sinn Féin has been in the forefront of the fight against discrimination in the Six Counties and we will not allow our own members to be discriminated against in Cork [163]

But the two men were not reinstated, nor did they ever receive an apology. In June 2007, Jonathan O'Brien came close to being elected to Leinster House for the constituency of Cork North Central. One wonders what the navy's policy would have been if he had been elected and decided to pay a visit to those from his constituency who voted for him at the Naval Base.

It is no accident that the formation of the Irish Naval Service in 1946 happened to coincide with the period when the Republican Movement started to decline in Cobh. Around the same time as the last prisoner Seanie Walsh was being released from the Curragh Internment Camp, the Irish Government was in the process of purchasing three old naval Corvettes from the British Ministry of Defence to start its own navy at Haulbowline. Recruits soon started arriving from all over the State to join the fledgling Naval Service. Within a few short years, many of those sailors started to settle and marry young women from the locality and within a further generation, some of their sons joined the force too.

Today, there is hardly a family living in Cobh who doesn't have someone who is either directly a member of the naval service or who is employed at the naval dockyard or some other ancillary service on Haulbowline. While the Republican movement has undoubtedly suffered locally in terms of numbers because of the inherent deterrents placed upon the families of service personnel, records have also shown that Republicans have fared a lot better when it comes to receiving the support of naval personnel through the ballot box (postal votes) at election times. This might be seen as offering some evidence that in spite of whatever strict indoctrination the authorities try to impose on its members in the defence forces, it cannot prevent or strangle the basic desire in most Irish people to see their country re-united. It is no coincidence also that Sinn Féin in Cobh today has no less than three former Naval Service members in its Cumann. Even though the struggle to bring about a United Ireland has now entered into what many would regard as its final unarmed phase, it's through these latter undeniable facts that the spirit of the Irish Volunteers can be seen to still live on in Cobh.

Leabharlanna Poibli Chathair Bhaile Átha Cliath
Dublin City Public Libraries

Bibliography

Published works

Sheehan, W., *British Voices* (Collins Press: Cork, 2005).

Borgonovo, J., & O'Donoghue, F. & J., *War of Independence* (Irish Academic Press: Dublin, 2006).

Knockraha, *History of No. 1 Brigade (E) Company* (Knockraha Macra Na Firme, 1977).

Costello, F.J., *Enduring the most, The life and death of Terence McSwiney* (Brandon Press: Kerry, 1995).

O'Neill. T., *The Battle of Clonmult* (Nonsuch Publishing, Dublin: 2006).

The Irish Volunteers 1913-1915, Edited by F.X. Martin O.S.A., (Duffy and Co. 1963).

Sands, B., *One day in my life*, (Mercier Press Ltd: Cork, 1983).

Ambrose J., *Dan Breen & the IRA* (Mercier Press Ltd: Cork, 2006).

Ryan, M., *The Real Chief – Liam Lynch*, (Mercier Press Ltd: Cork, 1986 & 2005).

Wills, C., *That Neutral Ireland* (Faber & Faber: London, 2007).

MacCurtain F., *Remember it's for Ireland – a family memoir of Tomás MacCurtain* (Mercier Press Ltd: Cork, 2006).

Ryan, M. *Tom Barry – IRA Freedom fighter*, (Mercier Press: Cork, 2003 & 2005).

White, G., & O'Shea, B. *The Burning of Cork* (Mercier Press: Cork, 2006)

Coogan, T. P., & Morrison, G., *The Irish Civil War* (Weidenfeld & Nicolson: London, 1998 & 2005).

Morrison. D., ed. *The Hunger Strike* (Brandon Press: Kerry, 2006).

Girvin K., *Seán O'Hegarty, O.C. First Cork Brigade* (Aubane Historical Society: Cork, 2007).

White, G., & O'Shea, B, *Baptised in Blood, The formation of the Brigade of Irish Volunteers 1913-1916*, (Mercier Press: Cork, 2005).

Coogan, T.P., *Michael Collins* (Arrow Books: 1991).

Hart, P., *The IRA and its enemies, Cork 1916-1923* (Clarendon Press: Oxford, 1999).

Adams, G., *Hope and History* (Brandon Press: Kerry, 2003).

Hartnett, N. ed., Foreword by Oscar Traynor, *Prison Escapes*, (Pillar Publisher Ltd: Dublin, 1945).

Lynch O'Donoghue, *The IRB and the 1946 Insurrection* (Mercier Press: Cork, 1957).

Barry, T., *The Guerrilla Days in Ireland* (Anvil Books: Dublin, 1949 & 1999).

McInerney, M., & O'Donnell, P., *Irish Social Rebel* (O'Brien Press: Dublin, 1974).

Wolfe Tone Annual, *Salute to the Soldiers of 1916* (Brain Higgins. 1960)

Murphy, B.P., *Patrick Pearse and the lost Republican Ideal* (James Duffy & Company: Dublin, 1981).

Adams, G., *An Irish Eye* (Brandon Press: Kerry, 2007.).

Hobson, B, *Ireland Yesterday and Tomorrow* (Anvil Books: Dublin 1968).

McCarthy, K., & Christensen B., *Cobh Contribution to the fight of Irish Freedom* (Oileánn Mór Publications: 1992).

Nevin, D., *James Connolly* (Gill and Macmillan: Dublin, 2005).

O'Hearn, D., *Bobby Sands* (Pluto Press: 2006).

MacEoin, U., *Survivors* (Argenta Publications: Dublin, 1980).

Cork Jail Souvenir (Lee Press: Cork, 1948).

Media (Newspapers, Magazines/Pamphlets)

Cork Examiner

Cork Constitution

Irish Press

The Irish Times

Evening Echo

An Phoblacht

IRIS Republican Magazine

'The Irish Republican Congress' by George Gilmore, Cork Worker's Club 1974.

'The Good Old IRA' Tan War Operations – Sinn Féin Publicity Department –1985.

'Ireland Free State or Nation?' by Diarmaid O'Suilleabhain, ELO Press Dublin, 1977.

'Prison Poems' Bobby Sands, Sinn Féin Publicity Department 1981.

'Seamus Costello' ELO Press, Dublin 1980.

Unpublished Oral Interviews

Séan Walsh

Joe O'Neill

Emer Burke & Ina Ahern

Simon Donovan

Geraldine Norris
Nuala Davis
Kevin Damery
Christy Griffin
John Dorrity
Jim O'Donovan
Anne Donnachie
Pat Guilfoyle
Timmy Leahy
Nuala Healy-Killcullen
Mary Crowley
Former Provisional IRA Volunteer
Former Official IRA Volunteer (A)
Former Official IRA Volunteer (B)
Former Naval Officer
Jim Halligan
Tom Collins
Séan óg Walsh
John Kidney
Liam O'Callaghan
Tom Kelleher
Ted Noonan
Gerry Murphy
Tom Conway
Mary Moynihan
George O'Mahony
Mick Fitzgerald
Eddie Collins
Michael McCarthy
George Ireland
Paddy Butler
Paddy Kindey Snr

Unpublished Sources/Witness Statements

Captain Michael Leahy 1913-1921, WS 94, File No S548, Bureau of Military History, Cathal Brugha Barracks.

Captain Micheal Leahy, Vice O.C. Cork 1 Brigade, WS555, File No S548, Bureau of Military History, Cathal Brugha Barracks.

Vice O.C. Commander Michael Leahy 1915-1921, W1421, FileNoS548, Bureau of Military History, Cathal Brugha Barracks.

Michael Leahy papers – Cork City and County Museum, Fitzgerald Park Cork.

Seamus Fitzgerald, TD, 1st Dáil Éireann, WS 1737, File No 3039, Bureau of Military History, Cathal Brugha Barracks.

Captain Michael, J. Burke 1917-1922, WS 1424, No File S2746, Bureau of Military History, Cathal Brugha Barracks.

Lieut Jack O'Connell 1916-1921, WS 1444, File No S2757, Bureau of Military History, Cathal Brugha Barracks.

Commander Paddy Whelan 1916-1921, WS 1449, File No S2755, Bureau of Military History, Cathal Brugha Barracks.
Seamus Fitzgerald Papers (PR/6) City & County Archives, Blackpool Cork.

Footnotes

1. *James Connolly*, Donal Nevin, (Gill & Macmillan, Dublin) p. 389.
2. 15 December 1913, *Cork Examiner*, Cork City Library archives.
3. Witness statements of Paddy Whelan WS-1449, Bureau of Military History, Cathal Brugha Barracks.
4. Letter to Seamus Fitzgerald by former Volunteer, PR-6 Fitzgerald papers, County and City archives.
5. Witness statement, Paddy Whelan Ws-1449, Bureau of Military History, Cathal Brugha Barracks.
6. *Baptised in Blood: Formation of the Cork Brigade of the Irish Volunteers 1913-1916*, Gerry White and Brenda O'Shea, 2005 p. 66.
7. Quote from Lesley Pearce, son of British Garrison Adjutant to Jasper Wilson.
8. Witness Statement Michael Leahy, WS 94, File S548, Bureau of Military History.
9. Letter to Seamus Fitzgerald in prison from his cousin in England WS 1737, File No 3039.
10. Letter to Seamus Fitzgerald from Ann Hannon from Cobh, WS 1737, File No 3039
11. *Cork Examiner,* 1916, Cork City Library Archives.
12. Witness Statement Michael Burke, WS555, File S548, Bureau of Military History.
13. Lesley Pearce, son of British Garrison Adjutant to Jasper Wilson.
14. Witness Statement of Paddy Whelan, WS1449, File No 2755, Bureau of Military History.
15. Interview with Geraldine Norris.
16. Witness Statement of Seamus Fitzgerald, Ws1737, File No 3039, Bureau of Military History.
17. *Cork Examiner*, 1918, Cork City Library Archives.
18. Cobh UDC Recorded Minutes, Cork & County Archives.
19. *Cork Examiner*, 28 February 1920, Cork City Library Archives.
20. *Cork Examiner*, April 1920, Cork City Archives.
21. Witness Statement Paddy Whelan, Ws1449, File No S2755, Bureau of Military History.
22. *ibid.*
23. *Cork Examiner*, Cork and City Library.
24. *British Voices 1918-1921*, William Sheehan, Collins Press, Major General Douglas Wimberley.
25. Witness account reported in *Cork Examiner* 29 August 1920, Cork & City Library Archives.
26. *British Voices 1918-1921*, William Sheehan, Collins Press, Major General Douglas Wimberley.
27. *ibid.*
28. *British Voices 1918-1921*, William Sheehan, Collins Press, Chapter 11, Major General Douglas Wimberley.
29. *Enduring the most*, FJ Costello, Brandon Press, *Life and Death of Terrance MacSwiney*.
30. *ibid.*
31. Witness Statement Michael Leahy, WS 1421, File No S548, Bureau of Military History.
32. Witness Statement Seamus Fitzgerald, WS1737, File No 3039, Bureau of Military History.
33. Witness Statement Paddy Whelan Ws 1449; File No S2755, Bureau of Military History.
34. *ibid.*
35. Witness Statement Michael Leahy, WS 1421, File No S548, Bureau of Military History.

36. Cobh UDC Recorded Minutes, City and County Archives.

37. Witness Statement Seamus Fitzgerald, WS 1737, File No 30039, Bureau of Military History.

38. *ibid.*

39. *Cork Examiner*, Friday 21 May 1921, Cork City Library Archives.

40. Witness Statement Seamus Fitzgerald, WS 1737, File No 30039.

41. Examiner Archives, Cork City Library.

42. *ibid.*

43. From interview with internee from Irish Press 1938.

44. Account given by William Quirke, Prison Escapes, Noël Hartnett, forwarded by 45. Oscar Traynor (Pillar Publish Ltd: Dublin, 1945) p. 33 (1921).

46. *Cork Examiner* 1921, Cork City Library Archives.

47. Killing of Sergeant Major Mackintosh, Knockraha, History of No1 Cork Brigade E. Company.

48. *ibid.*

49. *ibid.*

50. *ibid.*

51. *ibid.*

52. Cobh UDC Recorded Minutes, City and County Archives.

53. Dáil Records, Cobh Contributions to the Irish Freedom 1992, Oileánn Mór Publications pg 108.

54. Cobh Contributions to the Irish Freedom 1992, Oileánn Mór Publications p. 108.

55. Cobh Contributions to the Irish Freedom 1992, Oileánn Mór Publications p. 109.

56. Dan Breen and the IRA, Joe Ambrose, Mercier Press, Cork 2006, p. 129.

57. Witness Statement Michael Burke WS 1424, File No S2746, Bureau of Military History.

58. Cobh UDC Recorded minutes, Cork City & County Archives, p. 122.

59. Cobh Contributions to the Irish Freedom 1992, Oileánn Mór Publications, p. 117.

60. Cobh UDC Recorded Minutes, Cork City & County Archives.

61. Cobh Contributions to the Irish Freedom 1992, Oileánn Mór Publications, p. 119.

62. Fitzgerald Papers PR6, City and County Archives.

63. *ibid.*

64. Cobh Contributions to the Irish Freedom 1992, Oileánn Mór Publications p. 121.

65. *ibid.*

66. Fitzgerald Papers PR6, City and County Archives.

67. *Cork Examiner* Archives, City & County Library Archives, 9th August 1922.

68. *Cork Examiner* Archives, City& County Library Archives ,14th August 1922.

69. Letter to Seamus Fitzgerald, Fitzgerald Papers PR6, City and County Archives.

70. *ibid.*

71. Cobh Contributions to the Irish Freedom 1992, Oileánn Mór Publications, p. 126.

72. Interview with Emer Burke, 2001.

73. *Cork Examiner* Archives, City & County Library Achieves, November 1922.

74. Letter to Seamus Fitzgerald, Fitzgerald Papers PR6, City and County Archives.

75. Cobh UDC Recorded Minutes, City and County Archives.

76. *ibid.*

77. Nita Murphy Telegram, Cobh Contributions to the Irish Freedom 1992, Oileánn Mór Publications, p. 133.

78. Mary MacSwiney Statement, Fitzgerald Papers PR6, City and County Archives.

79. Moylan Letter to Mick Leahy, Leahy Papers, City & County Museum, Fitzgerald Park, Cork.

80. Declaration, Leahy Papers, City & County Museum, Fitzgerald Park, Cork.

81. Letter to Mick Leahy, Leahy Papers, City & County Museum, Fitzgerald Park, Cork.

82. *Cork Examiner* Archives, City & County Library Achieves

83. *Cork Examiner* Archives, City & County Library Archives.

84. Statement by Nita Murphy to Board for Military Pension, courtesy of Mick Fitzgerald.

85. *ibid.*

86. Letter from Seamus Fitzgerald, Fitzgerald Papers PR6, City and County Archives.

87. *ibid.*

88. Seamus Fitzgerald address at Foundry, F.F meeting in Cork, Fitzgerald Papers PR6, City and County Archives.

89. Seamus Fitzgerald letter to *Cork Examiner*, Fitzgerald Papers PR6, City and County Archives.

90. Letter from Seamus Fitzgerald, Fitzgerald Papers PR6, City and County Archives.

91. *ibid.*

92. Copy of newspaper report in Mick Burke Papers, Witness Statement Michael Burke, WS555, File S548, Bureau of Military History.

93. *ibid.*

94. *ibid.*

95. *ibid.*

96. Fitzgerald Papers PR6, City and County Archives.

97. *ibid.*

98. *ibid.*

99. *ibid.*

100. *ibid.*

101. *ibid.*

102. *ibid.*

103. *ibid.*

104. *ibid.*

105. *ibid.*

106. *ibid.*

107. Interview with Simon Donovan, 1988.

108. Cobh Contributions to the Irish Freedom 1992, Oileánn Mór Publications, pg 157.

109. *ibid.*

110. *Cork Examiner* Archives, City and County Library Archives, April 1936.

111. *ibid.*

112. *ibid.*

113. *Cork Examiner* Archives, City and County Library Archives, 27 April 1936

114. *Cork Examiner* Archives, City and County Library Archives, April 1936.

115. Interview with Seanie Walsh and *Cork Examiner* Archives, City and County Library Achieves, April 1936.

116. Author's Notes.

117. Fitzgerald Papers PR6, City and County Archives.

118. *ibid.*

119. *Cork Examiner* and Cobh UDC Council Records, City and County Archives.

120. *Cork Examiner* Archives, City and County Library Achieves, July 1938.

121. Fitzgerald Papers PR6, City and County Archives.

122. Ryle Dwyer, *Examiner,* 2006.

123. Letter, Fitzgerald Papers PR6, City and County Archives.

124. Fitzgerald Papers PR6, City and County Archives.

125. *Cork Examiner* Archives, City and County Library Achieves, 12 May 1940.

126. Interview with Simon Donovan 1989.

127. Fitzgerald Papers PR6, City and County Archives.

128. Cobh UDC Recorded Minutes, City and County Archives.

129. Fitzgerald Papers PR6, City and County Archives.

130. Interview with Seanie Walsh, 1988.

131. *ibid.*
132. *ibid.*
133. Fitzgerald Papers PR.6, City and County Archives.
134. Brookeborough DVD, Print Factory 2007.
135. *ibid.*
136. Interview with former officer IRA Volunteer 2007.
137. Sean O'Hegarty, by Kevin Girvin, Aubane, Historical Society 2007, pg 158.
138. *Cork Examiner* Archives, City and County Library Archives, 23 November 2007.
139. Interview with Eddie Collins, 2008.
140. *Cork Examiner* Archives, City and County Library Archives, 20th August 1971.
141. *Cork Examiner* Archives, City and County Library Archives.
142. *ibid.*
143. *ibid.*
145. *ibid.*
147. *ibid.*
148. Interview with former Provisional Volunteer, 2008.
149. *Irish Times* Archives 1971, online archives.
150. *Cork Examiner* Archives, City and County Library Archives, 1972.
151. Interview with Eddie Collins, 2008.
152. *ibid.*
153. Joe Cahill interview, An Phoblacht.
154. Joe Cahill − *Irish Times* Archives, May 1973, online archives.
155. IRA Statement − *Irish Times* Archives May 1973, online archives.
156. From personal recollections from Army Recruit training.
157. Statement by Army Training Officer.
158. From personal recollections of the author.
159. From personal recollections of the author.
160. *ibid.*
167. *ibid.*
168. *ibid.*
169. From personal recollections of the author.
170. *Cork Examiner* Archives, City and County Library Archives.
171. *An Phoblacht* Archives.
172. From personal recollections.
173. From a conversation with a fellow worker and Republican during 1950s Border Campaign.
174. *Evening Echo* Archives, August 2001.

List of Cobh Republican Dependents: 1924

Joseph Collins	Tay Road
John Duhig	The Mall
Joseph Kiely	Seaview
John Scott	Cobh
John O'Connor	Old Street
Thos. O'Shea	Ringmeen
John Higgins	Carrignafoy
Jer Grayley	Smalls Well
William Glavin	French's Ave
Richard McAuliffe	Rushbrooke
John Kiely	King Street
Der Kilty	King Street
Tom Foley	Orelia Tce
John Moore	Ticknock
R. Verling	Newtown
W. Palmer	Barrymore Ave
T. Lehane	Tay Road
D. Duggan	Tay Road
D. O'Brien	Roches Row
E. Fowler	Ballymore
W. Hannon	Carrignafoy
P. Rafferty	Barrymore Avenue
P. Twomey	Cloyne Tce
M. Twomey	Cloyne Tce
W. Walsh	Queens Street
P. Ahern	Ballymore
Leo Buckley	Middleton
M. Burke	Donelan Tce
P. O'Shea	King Street
M. Fitzgerald	East Hill
B. Dynan	Roche's Row
E. Butler	Belvelly
J. Halloran	Cottrell's Row
M. Keohane	Thomas Street
M. Griffin	Haulbowline.
D. Dennis	Rossleague.
G. Albert	French's Ave
J. Keneavy	Middleton Street
W. McCarthy	Carrignafoy.
G. O'Reilly	East Hill
Jas. Corcoran	Barrymore Avenue
John Glanville	East Hill
P. O'Neill	Ticknock
G. Geasley	Ballymore
C. Reed	Harbour Row
A. Butterley	Plunkett Terrace
John Stack	Newtown
Joseph Stack	Newtown
B. McGinn	Harbour View
W. Leahy	Carrignafoy

P. Leahy	Carrignafoy
P. Galvin	The Mall
P. Hurley	Bishop Street
F. Oakley	Bishop Street
P. O'Keeffe	Bishop Street
M. Murphy	Orelia Tce.
J. Stockdale	Orelia Terrace
John Collins	Thomas Street
Denis Sheehan	Ballydulea

Forgotten

Jim Fitzgerald
Count Murphy
Spud Murphy
J. Ahern
P. Daly
B. Cavanagh
Jerry O'Keeffe
J. Daly

Dolphin's Barn Library
Tel. 4540681